REVOLUTIONS FROM GRUB STREET

Revolutions from Grub Street

A History of Magazine Publishing in Britain

HOWARD COX AND
SIMON MOWATT

OXFORD
UNIVERSITY PRESS

OXFORD
UNIVERSITY PRESS

Great Clarendon Street, Oxford, OX2 6DP,
United Kingdom

Oxford University Press is a department of the University of Oxford.
It furthers the University's objective of excellence in research, scholarship,
and education by publishing worldwide. Oxford is a registered trade mark of
Oxford University Press in the UK and in certain other countries

First Edition published in 2014

Impression: 1

Published in the United States of America by Oxford University Press
198 Madison Avenue, New York, NY 10016, United States of America

British Library Cataloguing in Publication Data
Data available

Library of Congress Control Number: 2013954063

ISBN 978-0-19-960163-9

Printed and bound in Great Britain by
CPI Group (UK) Ltd, Croydon, CR0 4YY

Preface

Magazines are a perennial feature of British life. Indeed, our appreciation of times past are informed not only by the stories and images provided by contemporary magazines, but also by the magazines themselves, which evoke the look and feel of the era that created them. When looking to our history, magazines afford us with a view of people's concerns and interests, and provide a window on to what people thought, bought, and looked like. Magazines also tell us about the history of business, with display advertisements showcasing consumer goods and services, themselves becoming reflections on the state of the industries that they report on. It would be difficult, for example, to examine the development of the fashion industry without referring to *Vogue* or *Harper's Bazaar*. And while trade journals report directly on business, consumer magazines give a different insight, offering a view of how people perceived, defined, and interacted with markets and firms. As magazines have been shaped by social, political, and market forces, these have left their own imprint in the pages and form of the magazines themselves. Different business models adopted by magazine publishers have also changed the physical look and feel of the product, from hefty glossy photogravure-printed pages of titles seeking to differentiate themselves on quality, to the thin paper of the postal subscription-based magazine.

Today, people still rely on magazines to inform and entertain as they have since the eighteenth century, making their continued presence something that we can often take for granted. Although the magazines have a forefront position in our lives the fact that they represent a business in themselves is also often overlooked, something which is surprising given both the historical and contemporary importance of the publishing sector to the British economy. Outside of the industry, the names of the firms behind even the biggest titles are not widely known, and many loyal readers of a magazine title would struggle to name its publishing house. And yet at the end of 2010 the UK magazine industry was worth an estimated £4.88 billion—over three times the size of the UK recorded music market (£1.4 billion) and over a £1 billion more than the UK film industry (£3.71 billion)—with consumer magazines contributing around £2.97 billion of that total, and the industry directly employing over 114,000 people.[1] Despite the importance of the industry as an economic sector, surprisingly there has not been a comprehensive history of the British magazine publishing industry comparable to, for example, those on the American industry.[2] Our book aims to remedy this omission by providing a history of the business of British magazine publishing from its beginnings in Grub Street at the time of the Glorious Revolution to the digital age and the launch of the

Apple iPad. In this undertaking we have chosen to focus on the consumer magazine industry and the publishing companies themselves, analysing the changing forces that shaped competition within the industry.

A study of this industry is instructive, as from its original Grub Street inception the industry has been shaped by constant revolution. The first of these revolutions concerns the shift from the industry being physically located in Grub Street, London, to becoming a national and then a multinational industry. As the enterprises of Grub Street evolved ino modern publishing firms so the reach of the industry grew, the distribution of magazines expanded internationally, with the simple export of the finished products giving way ultimately to the publication of locally adapted titles coordinated by complex business and licensing networks. Although the industry now has a global reach, it has found a way to embed itself firmly back into very specific locations, be it a national territory or global niche market, and in many ways the global magazine is a more local product than ever.

The organization of firms and the technology that they employ have also undergone a series of revolutions which themselves reflect the changing nature of Britain's economic development. The industry has cycled through periods of being driven by small independent firms, to monopoly and back again. Management and organization have developed from owner-manager models to large vertically integrated hierarchies, and disintegrated back to small entrepreneurial teams employing a network of external contractors. The process and labour relations of printing have at times formed a key part of company strategy, as the changing technologies of printing—from the letterpress through to computer-to-plate web-offset photolithography—provided a key dynamic for the sector. Driving these revolutions has been the changing dynamics of company organization in response to new technology. Consumer magazines have also reflected revolutions in social change. Firms that have been able to adapt to changing conditions have reinvented themselves, finding new consumer groups and markets, and experimenting with new formats. This long-run examination of the industry highlights therefore how firms have responded to new competitive challenges, from hot metal to broadband Internet, from mass-production through to the digital age, from the creation of a mass market to the most specific of niches, and changes to the industry structure from domestic to global competition.

In writing this account of Britain's magazine industry we have had to employ a large variety of sources and approaches in order to present a complete picture of the industry to date. The sources we have used to examine this period have included the traditional approaches of the historian. Where business records exist in archives—sadly few and incomplete in the field of magazine publishing—we have made an effort to consult them. The records prior to the Second World War of Condé Nast in the UK, for example, were pulped along with now-priceless original photographs as part of a wartime publicity stunt to recycle paper, alongside a jaunty photograph with the photographer Cecil Beaton sitting on top of the pile awaiting destruction. Fortunately in this case copies of much of the correspondence were saved in Condé Nast's New York head offices, one of the few companies to have its own archive, although its records only cover the period until Condé Nast's death in 1942. Many of Britain's magazine firms became incorporated into the International Publishing Corporation (IPC) in 1963 and were lost. On moving to King's Reach Tower in 1976 IPC found that its records, stored in the basement of the *Country Life* building in Covent Garden, had been used for nests by rats encroaching from the flower market next door. Many of the remaining records were thrown out as staff making the move were encouraged to clear out rubbish by giving them a £1 bonus for every filing cabinet returned empty.[3]

In addition to primary sources we examined secondary sources on the newspaper and publishing industry, including company reports, company newsletters, industry trade journals, books, and the academic literature. We also conducted a longitudinal study into the consumer sector from 2002 to 2008, for which we conducted a large-scale series of interviews with magazine company executives, mostly publishers (who in the USA are known as general managers), although there was much overlap between those who were editors, publishers, proprietors, and senior managers, and of course many of those in this position had formerly had experience in other roles in the industry. We also interviewed managers in the related wholesale, retail, and distribution industries. To some extent we have also examined the magazines themselves, although they have not been our primary focus.

In order to examine the changes that companies were making in response to new digital technologies, we conducted a Leverhulme Trust-funded census survey of the industry focused on technology and organisational change from 2000 to 2002, with the support of the then Periodical Publishers Association (now the Professional Publishers Association, PPA). In addition we conducted research into the international operations of Condé Nast in the inter-war period as a separate project during 2008–10 which has informed our understanding of the inter-war years.[4] We have attempted to triangulate our information as much as possible, and in presenting this study to make full use of our selected sources.

Our study would not have been possible without the assistance of a host of people, from archivists to publishers and funders, who provided advice, information, and encouragement and to whom we extend our thanks. We would like to extend formally our thanks to the Leverhulme Trust for providing a grant which supported part of this study, and The Business and Labour History Group, AUT University, for supporting this research from 2009. The University of Worcester provided a period of study leave to one of the authors. Our research has benefited from the support of the PPA from the start, and their assistance in developing our survey was invaluable. We have especially appreciated the support given by chief executive Barry McIlheney, former chief executive Ian Locks, and communications manager Tom Hawkins.

Our archival research would not have been possible without the help of business archives and the archivists, and our appreciation goes to the following: Paul Phillips, internal communications manager at IPC Media for arranging access to *IPC News* and for allowing the use of our cover image of *The Strand Magazine*; Nigel Roche and the staff at the St Bride Print Library, London, who were always an excellent and patient source of information and assistance in our research since we first began in 2000; Shawn Waldron of the Condé Nast Archives, New York, whose excellent archives helped reveal new insights into the strategy of the industry in the inter-war years, and also to Brett Croft at the London Condé Nast Archive for his assistance; Chloe Veale, Curator at the History of Advertising Trust, Raveningham, Norwich, was extremely helpful, especially in relation to the PPA archives. Our thanks also go to Dr Lesley Whitworth at the Brighton Design Archives, which holds the Alison Settle Archive. We also thank the staff of the reading rooms at the British Library and the Colindale Newspaper library of the British Library, and the Women's Library, London Metropolitan University, as well as the librarians at London South Bank University, Auckland University of Technology, and The University of Worcester, who helped with endless inter-library loan requests. Simon would like to thank the Centre for International Business History, Henley Business School, for a Visiting Fellowship in 2012. Thanks are due to James Walker and Peter Scott for arranging the visit, and to Lucy Newton for the loan of her office. A vote of thanks also goes to the friendly retired hot-metal print workers who demonstrated their Linotype machines for us at the Museum of Transport and Technology, Auckland, New Zealand, and allowed us to get our hands dirty.

A mention should also be made of Magforum, an eclectic online resource on the history of British magazines developed by Tony Quinn, a former group editor at BBC Magazines/Redwood Publishing, with an academic interest in the industry. The website always provides something of interest, has many interesting images of magazines past, and is a great resource for the enthusiast looking to find information about specific titles.[5]

Naturally we must thank all the magazine publishers, editors, and managers from the printing, distribution, and publishing industry who gave us their time during our Leverhulme funded study 2000–2, and in follow-up interviews over the next eight years. We cannot list all the names of those who generously gave us their time and the benefit of their experience in the industry, but we thank you for your enthusiasm in supporting our project, and for your patience in awaiting the publication of this book. Finally, our heartfelt thanks go to David Musson and Emma Booth at OUP for their care and patience (and mince pies) as we struggled to bring this project to its ultimate conclusion. The usual disclaimers apply.

Preface

A note of personal thanks also has to go to those who supported the ᵥ and helped us arrive at this juncture.

Simon: I would like to thank my parents for putting me up and putting with me on my visits to London for research. Love to Una for your suppor I promise to stop bothering you for your opinion on women's magazines now.

Howard: Love and thanks to Jill.

Howard Cox and Simon Mowatt
July 2013

Contents

1

Creating the Market for Popular Magazines

GRUB STREET ORIGINS

In Britain the origins of published periodicals aimed at a popular audience—the forerunners of today's consumer magazines—can be traced back to the closing years of the seventeenth century. As elsewhere in Europe, the historical trajectory of the published word in early-modern England was significantly influenced and constrained by the decisions of government. When the first widely printed newsbooks, dating from the 1620s, evolved into the flurry of pamphleteering that was a key feature of the English Civil War, the problem of seditious publications was made manifest. Following the restoration of the monarchy, legislation was passed in 1662 by means of the Printing Acts which limited all printing to the master printers of the Stationers' Company of London and the presses of Oxford and Cambridge Universities. Publishing of official news from this date was the responsibility of a Surveyor of the Press, under whose auspices was published in 1665 an official government news-letter entitled the *London Gazette*.[1] For the next two decades the free development of the printed word in Britain was effectively suspended. It was not until the lapsing of the Printing Acts, following the Glorious Revolution of 1688, that Britain's periodical publishing activities resumed significant forward momentum. Publication of the *Athenian Gazette* in March 1691 by John Dunton has been viewed by one authority as the first practical demonstration that 'there was a market for publications which contained a wide range of miscellaneous information'.[2] The *Athenian Gazette* was issued at various intervals between weekly and four times weekly, surviving until 1697. In January 1692 another miscellany, the *Gentleman's Journal*, published its first issue. Printed by R. Baldwin and styled as a 'Letter to a Gentleman in the Country' this could perhaps be considered Britain's first example of a genuine monthly magazine seeking a commercial audience.[3]

The opening decade of the eighteenth century witnessed a flourishing of publishing activity. The first daily newspaper, the *Daily Courant*, was issued in 1702 and the presses of its publisher Samuel Buckley were later used to print the first copies of *The Spectator* magazine in 1711.[4] The following year, however, the first tranche of the 'taxes on knowledge' were introduced; these took the form of a newspaper stamp of ½*d*. or 1*d*. (depending on the size of the sheet)[5] along with a duty of one shilling on advertisements. As a result, several of the dozen or so newspapers that had been circulating in London at this time were put out of business. The decision to control the growth of publishing by fiscal means rather than simple censorship meant that, as Black has pointed out, the character of the news-based press in Britain became commercially oriented.[6] From the 1720s, meanwhile, the demand for entertaining reading matter on behalf of an increasingly literate population began to be satisfied by the creation of the first lending libraries. By the 1730s the opportunity existed for enterprising publishers to create a market for book-related periodicals and this decade witnessed the establishment of Britain's first long-standing literary magazines aimed at an affluent audience.

The publication of the *Athenian Gazette* in 1691 had been among the earliest stirrings of an emerging industrial district of printing and publishing activities clustered around Grub Street near the Fleet River in London. John Dunton, its originator, had lived close by Grub Street, while the main centre for book publishing developed around the area of Little Britain, barely half a mile away. During the eighteenth century Grub Street emerged as a metaphor for the group of hack journalists who tended to hang around the area, seeking work. From within the confines of this unruly neighbourhood in the 1730s emerged the publishing business of Edward Cave, a hack who had saved enough of the guinea a week he earned through his freelance journalism to purchase a printing press and set up a small publishing operation in St John's Gate, in the vicinity of Grub Street. Having tested the market with a number of pamphlets, including one colourfully entitled *The Benefits of Farting*, in 1731 Cave launched a monthly journal which he called the *Gentleman's Magazine*, using the term 'magazine' for the first time in a publishing connection.[7] The initiative was a conspicuous success and the *Gentleman's Magazine* came to hold the distinction of being Britain's longest running literary periodical, appearing monthly for over 175 years and providing the template for many of the nineteenth century's one shilling monthlies. Ownership of the magazine changed hands several times, with the book publisher Chatto and Windus eventually acquiring the title in 1877, around which time it had a respectable circulation of 100,000. Thereafter it lost a clear sense of purpose and ultimately folded in 1907.[8]

The commercial success of the *Gentleman's Magazine* spawned a number of imitators. Some of these, most notably the *London Magazine* (1732–85), were extremely similar in form and purpose: monthly periodicals providing excerpts from other published works as well as shorter materials such as poems and airs. The originators of the *London Magazine* were a consortium of booksellers, and the book trade as a whole played a significant role in the development of the early magazine industry. A variety of serial publications, covering both part-books and magazines, gave book publishers in the mid-eighteenth century a source of regular income which they could use to provide the capital required to publish for the much riskier market in new books.[9] This trend of using magazines to subsidize new book publishing activities continued into the nineteenth century; the acquisition of the fledgling *Punch* magazine in 1842 by the Grub Street jobbing printing firm of Bradbury and Evans, for example, provided this organization with the revenues it needed to emerge as a serious rival book publisher to the likes of Chapman and Hall, Longman, and Macmillan for a period in the mid-1800s.[10]

The latter half of the eighteenth century saw a trend towards magazines that were more geared towards a specialist audience. Clarke gives examples of the *Spiritual Magazine* (1761–84) and the *Sporting Magazine* (1792–1870), and notes that to retain market share the *Gentleman's Magazine* also began to specialize in antiquarian subjects.[11] This period also marks the beginning of professional attempts to develop a title aimed exclusively at female readers with the launch of the *Lady's Magazine* in 1770. A sixpenny monthly, the magazine ran successfully under the management of an editor/proprietor until the 1830s, by which time a number of rival titles had also developed.[12] In general, the 1780s and 1790s saw increasing competition among publishers of periodicals for the custom of an affluent and expanding group of middle-class consumers. However, the outbreak in 1789 of the French Revolution, and the wars with France that followed, also saw the rise of a more radicalized press in Britain. Between 1780 and 1815 the stamp duty on newspapers rose in stages from 1½*d.* to 4*d.* and the advertising tax increased from 2*s.* 6*d.* to 3*s.* 6*d.* Almost inevitably, the rise in taxes encouraged the revival of an unstamped press whose message was uncompromisingly radical. A series of political tracts followed the lead provided by William Cobbett's *Political Register* which had been launched in 1802. In a climate of political instability, which included the massacre at Peterloo, the Blasphemous and Seditious Libels Act and the Publications Act were passed through Parliament in 1819. The latter Act significantly widened the scope of the newspaper stamp, to cover all publications that either reported or commented on news as subject to the levy. In tandem with higher duties that had been levied on paper in 1802, the legislation of 1819 led to an increase in prices and a reduction in the number of periodicals in circulation.[13] At the same time, they created certain opportunities for publishing entrepreneurs.

TOWARDS THE *PENNY MAGAZINE*

The development of a radical press, whose suppression had been the focus of the Stamp Act legislation of 1815 and 1819, helped to create a publishing underworld within the area of London embracing the Strand and Fleet Street. A variety of technically skilled printers and engravers mixed cheek by jowl with a creative throng of writers and editors. Enterprising publishing businesses were therefore in a position to exploit this rich mix of talents to promote commercially oriented new titles. One such innovative publisher to emerge during this period was John Limbird, who had set up the first of his stationery-cum-publishing businesses just off the Strand in the autumn of 1818. Over the next few years he developed his activities in close association with the more established Thomas Dolby, a publisher of radical tracts who had experience of, and a reputation in, the market for twopenny publications. After an unsuccessful attempt to establish a cheaper rival to Henry Colburn's *Literary Gazette*,[14] Limbird set up his first twopenny weekly paper called the *Londoner*. The *Londoner* was designed as an essay-based periodical, similar in nature to the *Spectator*, but it failed to take off and was abandoned after five issues. In 1822 Limberg launched a literary-based weekly called the *Mirror of Literature, Amusement and Instruction* featuring snippets of established literature and other miscellaneous items. Utilizing Dolby's experience in managing a publishing enterprise of this kind, Limbird brought on board an 'archetypal Grub Street hack' in Thomas Byerley, as editor, and a contact of Byerley's, Matthew Sears, as illustrator.[15] The latter decision was particularly fruitful, since the one or two woodcuts with which Sears embellished each issue of the sixteen-page paper proved to be an appealing innovation of the *Mirror*, and made its 2*d.* retail price unusually good value when compared with the otherwise dull alternative fare on offer at the time.

With manager, editor, and engraver successfully engaged, the *Mirror* quickly developed into a popular weekly miscellany, the first issue of which is credited with ultimately selling 150,000 copies.[16] Limbird was able to produce this huge output, despite the fact that his newly installed printing capacity did not feature the relatively recent innovation of steam-driven presses.[17] Rather, it was his adoption of the technique of stereotyping that provided economy and flexibility in his printing processes.[18] At this time stereotyping involved the use of plaster moulds to create a permanent plate that could be used again and again, allowing back issues to be reprinted without the need for resetting the type. At the same time it avoided the need to hold unsold editions of the magazine and the consequent costs of carrying stocks of expensive paper. The low price of the *Mirror* made it highly unpopular with the established bookselling and wholesale trade, whose profits depended on the addition of a fixed margin to the selling price, and Limbird was therefore obliged to publicize and distribute his weekly paper using improvised methods that included bill-posting and employing provincial agents. The *Mirror*'s popularity with the public, however, meant that the venture was successful in overcoming these obstacles, spawning a multitude of imitators and enduring until 1849. From this beginning, Limbird was able to establish a significant enterprise in the area of cheap publishing, undercutting the price of other publishers of works of fiction.[19]

By the time of Limbird's death in 1883 both the man himself, and his legacy as 'the father of our periodical literature', had been largely forgotten in the public mind.[20] The same fate was not to befall other men who, during the 1830s and 40s, exploited the demand for low-priced reading matter from those customers possessing slender means. Beginning in 1832, Charles Knight and the brothers William and Robert Chambers brought into the public sphere successful weekly periodicals priced, respectively, at one penny and three halfpence. Both Knight's *Penny Magazine* and Chambers' *Edinburgh Journal* brought an enhanced level of quality to the cheap periodical marketplace by commissioning their main articles from professional writers. Knight's *Penny Magazine* was particularly innovative in terms of its extensive use of illustrative woodcuts; a feature which even allowed the semi-literate to derive substantial enjoyment from its pages.[21] By contrast early editions of *Chambers's Journal* contained no pictures but featured a broader mix of editorial, notably a weekly short story.[22]

The core mission of both of these low-priced weekly papers was to provide the new urban industrial workers of Britain with secular reading matter that would be educational, enlightening, and thus improving. Knight had been involved in publishing since 1812 as editor and joint proprietor with his father of the *Windsor and Eton Express*, a post he continued to hold until 1827. By this time he had gained substantial experience in publishing but had fallen into financial difficulties. Subsisting by means of hack journalism, Knight found employment through the recently established Society for the Diffusion of Useful Knowledge (SDUK) with whose founder, the Whig MP Henry Brougham, the struggling publisher had become acquainted in 1826.[23] Knight was employed by the Society to act as its superintendent—principally performing the role of editor-in-chief—in July 1827 after the SDUK had issued its first publication (the Library of Useful Knowledge) the previous winter.[24] In 1828 Knight oversaw the publication of the *British Almanac*, setting in train the start of a publishing collaboration with the SDUK which endured for the best part of the next two decades. Seeking the widest possible dissemination for its utilitarian reading matter, between 1828 and 1832 Knight initiated a series of publications on behalf of the Society including the Library of Entertaining Knowledge, the *Working Man's Companion*, and the *Quarterly Journal of Education*, the latter being aimed at the emerging teaching profession.

In Scotland, meanwhile, the Edinburgh-based bookseller and small-scale publisher William Chambers also developed the idea for a weekly publication which would provide affordable entertaining reading material for the 'humbler orders'. Working in partnership with his more literary-oriented brother Robert, the pair launched their eponymous *Edinburgh Journal* in February 1832. The 1½*d.* magazine quickly reached a circulation figure of 30,000 copies per week, with a second edition being printed in London by W. S. Orr by the thirteenth issue.[25] Chambers' idea for a cheap weekly paper had pre-empted that of Knight by a matter of weeks, for in March 1932 the SDUK launched its own version of a Saturday magazine aimed at precisely the same audience. The *Penny Magazine of the Society for the Diffusion of Useful Knowledge* constituted a publishing phenomenon, with the early issues selling up to and beyond 200,000 copies.[26]

Working in collaboration with the leading London printing firm of William Clowes, the *Penny Magazine* made use of innovations in the paper and printing industries in the early nineteenth century that had facilitated a major increase in productivity. The introduction into England's paper manufacturing during the early nineteenth century of the Fourdrinier process allowed reels of paper to be manufactured which substantially reduced the unit costs of the key raw material of magazines.[27] These rolls of paper were used in conjunction with steam-driven impression cylinders that enabled printers to increase the speed of printing and more effectively integrate text and illustrations. Knight also made effective use of stereotypes, and the Clowes print works included a foundry that manufactured its own typefaces.[28] By 1850 Clowes was one of four large-scale London-based printing firms that dominated the letterpress industry of the time. Employing around 400 men, it had played a significant role in the modernization of printing in the two decades after 1830, a period in which the printing of books and periodicals emerged as the industry's leading area of growth.[29]

In creating Britain's first truly mass-produced popular weekly magazine, Knight was confronted by two distinct management challenges. One of these was the creation of a system of distribution and selling that could provide consumers with much larger quantities of printed material; effectively an industry-wide question of vertical management. The other was the need to generate sufficient revenues in order to cover the high costs of producing a relatively high quality, low-priced magazine. This latter challenge had implications for the financing of the publishing enterprises of the SDUK and was thus, in effect, a matter linking business and corporate strategy. Although the SDUK was a non profit-making organization it was nevertheless necessary for its publications to operate on a commercially viable basis. One of Knight's earliest tasks, in 1828, had been to tour industrial towns in the North and Midlands in an effort to create local committees that could support the development of subscriptions to the Society. However, as early as 1830 the income from memberships and subscriptions was falling and Knight, together with the SDUK's other main publisher Baldwin and Craddock, became increasingly self-reliant for the provision of working capital. In 1835 Knight and the Society became embroiled in a financial dispute, and from that time the publisher effectively operated on terms that were financially independent of the SDUK.[30]

The publication of the *Penny Magazine* involved substantial weekly expenditure. Using archive data, Bennett has calculated the break-even point for an issue of the *Penny Magazine* in 1833 and compared it with other contemporary periodicals, including *Chambers's Journal*. Bennett shows that the *Penny Magazine* had a break-even point of 112,000 while the *Journal* required sales of only 23,000 to cover its costs. In terms of profitability, for a level of sales 15 per cent above break-even, the *Journal* generated a return on capital of 6 per cent, while the *Penny Magazine* returned only 2 per cent. Sales figures suggest that the *Penny Magazine* was selling fewer than 112,000 copies by 1835; thus whatever economies Knight had been able to introduce into the production of his weekly paper were clearly sorely required by this point in order to maintain its viability. When, by 1845, circulation of the magazine had dropped to a mere 40,000 Knight was facing insolvency. In a final attempt to secure economies he took the decision to substantially reduce the number of illustrations, but this only served to ensure that the decline in readership became terminal and the *Penny Magazine* ceased publication in 1846.[31] In general terms, this analysis of costs and revenues demonstrates that a small circulation title with a secure readership can remain financially solvent while titles aimed at a mass readership, and which thus necessarily incur high fixed costs of production, are extremely vulnerable to declines in sales revenue.

Difficulties faced by Knight in managing the publication of Britain's first low-priced, mass circulation magazine were only partly the outcome of the structure of costs and revenues. Distribution also constituted a key barrier to success. When Knight made his visit to the industrial Midlands and North in 1828, part of his mission was to put in place a distribution mechanism that would see the Society's publications distributed to subscribers through a network of local committees. However, it was quickly understood that, in all but the smallest towns, such a strategy would generate fierce opposition from the traditional wholesale and retail book trade. Thus the strategy of the SDUK was to distribute its publications through the established mechanism, but in doing so it faced hostility from the leading London booksellers who complained that the low profit margins attached to the trade in cheap weekly magazines would damage their viability, not least by undermining sales of their key trade in books. Longman in particular took a strong stance against the *Penny Magazine*, but were ultimately confounded in their opposition to the new trend by the sheer importance of the trade. For periodical publishing in mid-nineteenth-century Britain, as Bennett concludes, 'A new power was making itself felt in the trade, the power of massive numbers of readers.'[32]

MAKING THE PENNY DREADFUL

By the 1840s, the impact of the *Penny Magazine* had been seen in the development of a range of successful rival weekly titles. While a reduction in the stamp duty on newspapers from 4*d.* to 1*d.* in 1836 actually did little to increase opportunities for small publishers of daily newspapers,[33] a variety of weekly periodicals did emerge in the 1840s as the demand for low-priced reading matter continued to expand. Three broad categories of publication can be discerned: cheap fiction-based weekly periodicals; weekly (for the most part Sunday) newspapers; and the sensationalist, bloodthirsty 'penny dreadful' genre. Spearheaded by Herbert Ingram's *Illustrated London News* in 1842,[34] the emergence of a number of new weekly newspapers was a particularly important feature of periodical development in the 1840s, leading to a strong commercialization of the working-class audience thereafter. Two individuals who were instrumental in this development were George Reynolds and Edward Lloyd.

Both Reynolds and Lloyd were responsible for bringing to market a popular Sunday newspaper, but they did so through rather different routes. In Reynolds' case, a career in the world of publishing developed on the strength of his abilities as an editor and novelist, in which latter capacity he was nothing short of prolific.[35] After undertaking a variety of journalistic and editorial roles, in 1845 Reynolds was appointed as the inaugural editor of the *London Journal*, owned by a former engraver of the *Illustrated London News*, George Stiff, and published by the small-time printer and bookseller George Vickers.[36] The *London Journal* had set out to imitate the fiction-based penny weekly formula that had been most successfully pioneered from 1842 by the *Family Herald*. With an obvious attempt to lure readers of the *Penny Magazine*, who were seeking a higher quota of entertainment over instruction, the *Family Herald or Useful Information and Amusement for the Million* had been launched by the publisher George Biggs, and was the first journal in which the process of typesetting, printing, and binding had been fully mechanized. Having begun unsteadily, due to severe labour disputes resulting from the exclusive employment of female workers,[37] the *Family Herald* was successfully relaunched in May 1843 and by 1855 was credited with a circulation of 300,000.[38]

Establishing periodicals aimed at the mass market on a paying basis was fraught with difficulty, and it is not surprising to find that the publisher of the *Family Herald* sought to keep down the costs of labour. King has estimated that in the case of the *London Journal*, for example, with a circulation of 20,000 copies for the first issue, the enterprise will have made a loss of as much as £30. As circulation rose, however, and particularly with the reduction in the cost of paper following the scrapping of the duties, by 1861 the *London Journal* was selling an average of 313,000 copies per issue and making a clear annual profit of £4,500.[39]

Reynolds' term of office as editor of the *London Journal* lasted only for about a year, and he experienced significant financial difficulties for the period of time thereafter. Quitting the *London Journal* in 1846, he launched his own weekly periodical, *Reynolds's Magazine*. However, it was his decision to form a working arrangement with the publisher John Dicks in 1847 that initiated his most successful epoch.[40] That year he renamed his magazine *Reynolds's Miscellany*, and together with the *Family Herald* and the *London Journal*, these three titles provided the mainstay of the cheap fiction-based weekly press even if, as Altick has observed, 'The popularity of such journals did not give conspicuous comfort to those who, a few years earlier, had felt that the welcome given the *Penny Magazine* and *Chambers's Journal* was a sure sign that the reading tastes of the masses were improving.'[41] Reynolds and Dick formed an effective partnership and in 1850 they revamped another of Reynolds' publishing initiatives, *Reynolds's Political Instructor*, to create *Reynolds's Weekly Newspaper* (from 1851 *Reynolds's Newspaper*) as one of Britain's most popular Sunday newspapers in the second half of the nineteenth century, although falling well behind *Lloyd's Weekly* in terms of circulation after the mid-1860s.[42] Reynolds and Dicks entered into a formal partnership in 1863 and following Reynolds' death in 1879 Dicks purchased the copyrights to his erstwhile colleague's popular works. In 1862 Dicks launched his most conspicuously successful penny weekly, *Bow Bells*, into which he merged *Reynolds's Miscellany* in 1869. Thereafter Dicks' firm proved a mainstay of the early magazine publishing industry, continuing to operate until 1929.[43]

Unlike Reynolds, Edward Lloyd had few pretensions as a man of letters. His career as a purveyor of cheap, frequently sensationalist literature had begun in earnest when in 1835, at barely 20 years of age, he published *The Calendar of Horrors*. This was succeeded by a series of reproductions of Charles Dickens' part-novels which, flaunting the inadequate laws on copyright, featured bogus titles such as *Nikelas Nickelbery*. Lloyd muscled into the expanding market for popular weekly magazines in 1842 when he launched *Lloyd's Penny Weekly Miscellany* and, the following year, *Lloyd's Penny Atlas and Weekly Register of Novel Entertainment*. These titles met with limited success—the *Atlas* ceased publication in 1845—but they were merely part of his wider attack on the British reading public of limited means. Lloyd also engaged in two other publishing initiatives between 1842 and 1843. Displaying his business acumen, if little by way of integrity, he rapidly followed Ingram's successful launch of the *Illustrated London News* by issuing an unstamped alternative version called *Lloyd's Illustrated London Newspaper*, which briefly sold for the bargain price of one penny before being brought to heel by the tax authorities. The following year he set up offices in 12 Salisbury Square, near Fleet Street, in which he developed an operation devoted to the production of his notorious 'penny blood' offerings, a publishing genre subsequently referred to by the derogatory epithet 'Salisbury Square journalism'.[44]

Notwithstanding the dubious qualities of much of Lloyd's published output, his role as a Victorian business entrepreneur and his industrious temperament mark him out as a major figure in the development of Britain's periodical publishing industry. In January 1843 he merged his weekly newspaper with the *Illustrated Sunday Herald*, dropped the illustrations, and relaunched the title as *Lloyd's Weekly Newspaper*. Under the editorship of popular writer Douglas Jerrold from 1852, *Lloyd's Weekly* began to make substantial progress, allowing Lloyd to abandon his penny dreadful publishing activities and focus on the newspaper business as he sought a veneer of respectability. His flair as an innovative entrepreneur, which included the introduction of a system of sale or return that badly upset elements of the trade, also took in publicity stunts like stamping coins paid to its workers with the firm's name—which again attracted official opprobrium—and embryonic attempts at market research through a policy of seeking views from individual members of the public on the worthiness of his published output.[45] On the production side, he seized the opportunity for expanding sales provided by the abolition of newspaper duties in 1855[46] by becoming, in 1856, the first British publisher to install the high speed rotary press manufactured by the New York firm of Richard Hoe. In 1873 he also introduced the web perfecting press, which printed both sides of paper simultaneously.[47]

By the early 1850s Lloyd had effectively focused his publishing activities on the newspaper side of his business and ceased his involvement with magazines. He did, however, go on to become a major player within the paper manufacturing industry. In 1861, following the abolition of duties on paper, Lloyd set up a paper mill on the River Lea at Bow in order to secure the supplies he needed for the expanding circulation of his Sunday newspaper, now set on a growth path that would see it become the first British newspaper to reach sales of one million copies in 1897. When, in 1874, his firm purchased the *Daily Chronicle* he satisfied the additional requirements for paper by setting up a second paper mill in Sittingbourne, Kent, in 1877. As the raw material used to produce paper shifted from expensive rags to cheaper esparto grass, Lloyd's business expanded further through the leasing of land (or by obtaining grass cutting rights) in Algeria and Southern Spain. Shortly before his death in 1890 he converted his company into a limited liability concern and, as the basis for paper production shifted again from grass to wood pulp, Edward Lloyd Ltd bought a site in Honefos, Norway, to construct pulp mills. By the turn of the century, Edward Lloyd Ltd constituted the first British enterprise to have a stake in every stage of papermaking, printing, and publishing, providing the paper requirements of some of Britain's leading magazine and newspaper publishers; in the twentieth century it became increasingly focused on the paper business.[48] Lloyd's move from cheap magazines to large-scale, mechanized newspaper production and then into papermaking foreshadowed the late nineteenth-century publishing entrepreneurs Newnes, Pearson, and Harmsworth.

DEVELOPING A MAGAZINE BUSINESS: BEETON AND CASSELL

Around the middle of the nineteenth century the business of printing and publishing was firmly centred on London. A study of the letterpress industry that comprised book, periodical/magazine, government, and jobbing forms of printing, has estimated that of the 26,000 printers working in Britain at this time 10,000 worked in London and together these firms accounted for over half of the entire output in value terms.[49] At this point, the London printing industry was dominated by a small group of large firms whose businesses had been favoured by government printing contracts.[50] In the second half of the century the situation began to change as the importance of government printing declined relative to the strictly commercial branches such as periodical publishing. Medium-sized printing firms were able to exploit the growing demand for reading matter and take advantage of the increases in productivity that were being created by technological progress. These gains in productivity were spread across the whole range of the printing industry; even hand presses that were capable of producing only 250 sheets per hour in 1850 were anything up to eight times more productive by the end of the century.[51] With the gradual introduction of steam-driven presses, the printing capacity of the London-based press-work industry expanded significantly after mid-century,[52] assisted considerably by the abolition of paper duties in 1861.

The growth in the number and range of printing establishments in the second half of the nineteenth century facilitated the development of publishing firms who were specialists in the management of periodicals rather than direct producers of the finished printed article. These publishing enterprises were precarious in nature and were often forced by the vagaries of finance to sell their valuable copyrights to their more financially secure printers. A good example of this is provided by the career of Samuel Beeton, whose launch of *Queen* magazine in 1861 was part of a successful portfolio of periodicals that his firm created in mid-nineteenth-century London. After making a start in book publishing, in 1852 Beeton joined forces with Frederick Greenwood who had been writing copy for leading magazines including the *Illustrated London News*. In May the two launched a cheap monthly magazine entitled *The Englishwoman's Domestic Magazine (EDM)*, selling at twopence and aimed at women who managed and attended the needs of households.[53] Hughes has pointed out that the *EDM* contained many features of the modern women's weekly and mid-market monthly magazines: 'There is a problem page, tips on fashion and beauty, instructions on how to make your own clothes, an essay competition, advice on gardening and pets, and a system of loyalty rewards: save up your tokens from twelve consecutive issues and you get the chance to enter a draw and win anything from a gift voucher to a piano.'[54] Compared with earlier magazines aimed at a female audience, Beeton's new magazine is generally credited with extending the reach of women's magazines into the homes of middle-class Britain.[55]

Buoyed by the successful growth of the *EDM*, Samuel Beeton's career in magazine publishing reached its zenith during the early 1860s. Beeton's wife Isabella, known to succeeding generations merely as 'Mrs Beeton', emerged as a strong creative force in support of Samuel's publishing initiatives. From the perspective of fashion, Isabella's major contribution occurred in 1860 when Beeton's company decided to reissue the *EDM*, now apparently selling 60,000 copies per issue, as a luxury product.[56] In order to revamp the *EDM* Beeton established a collaborative arrangement with Adolphe Goubaud, owner of the Parisian-based fashion monthly *Le Moniteur de la Mode*, a journal which carried as inserts high quality colour plates illustrating the current fashions, and the accompanying dress patterns. English language copies of *Le Moniteur* were exported to London where they sold for the exorbitant price of 3s. 6d. However, with a recently agreed reduction in the excise duties on trade between Britain and France now in force, Beeton recognized that an opportunity existed to purchase these patterns and plates for insertion in the *EDM*. Thus in May 1860 Samuel and Isabella, the latter now ensconced as 'editress', undertook an excursion to Paris to secure a deal with Goubaud. Shortly afterwards, a higher quality version of the *EDM* was launched, selling for 6d., that included a plate from *Le Moniteur* showing 'two or three anatomically impossible young women dressed in the latest fashions', while a second version of the magazine was offered for one shilling which included paper dressmaking patterns. Fashion notes, provided by Isabella Beeton, were written under guidance from the wife of the owner of *Le Moniteur*.[57]

By this time Beeton had begun to establish a stable of publications. These included the popular *Boy's Own Magazine*,[58] launched in 1855 and now selling in the region of 40,000 copies a month, as well as a variety of part-works including Mrs Beeton's *Book of Household Management*, for whose creation Isabella was to become posthumously revered.[59] Samuel Beeton recognized that the female audience provided a potentially lucrative readership, and one year after the revamp of *EDM* he had launched *Queen*, targeted at the more conventional ladies' society market. As Beetham points out, this was essentially an illustrated newspaper that took as its model the *Illustrated London News*.[60] Public and social interests lay at the heart of *Queen*'s constituency: society news and cultural gossip featured heavily, as well as an emerging concern for social issues and women's expanding employment and education opportunities.

With the launch of *Queen*, Beeton's firm now published two of the most fashionable women's periodicals in mid-nineteenth-century Britain. By the time of Isabella's tragically early death in 1865, however, Samuel Beeton's business affairs were collapsing into disarray. As early as 1861, barely six months after its successful launch, Beeton had been forced to sell his ownership of *Queen* to the publishing business of Cox and Wyman, to whose presses he had contracted the printing of his new periodical.[61] Beeton had taken a significant financial risk in pushing ahead with the expansion of his business in 1860, anticipating the reduction in costs that would accrue from an expected repeal of the tax on paper. Although the duties on paper were indeed abolished in 1861, Beeton's business was unable to finance its short-term losses and as a result one of the most talismanic titles in British magazine history fell out of his possession. Worse was to follow Isabella's death. Faced with a constant battle for investment capital, Beeton had turned to the finance house of Overend Gurney to support his now struggling business; when this firm collapsed with debts of over £5 million in May 1866 Beeton's business was ruined.[62] Forced into liquidation, Beeton sold his valuable copyrights to the rival publisher Ward, Lock and Tyler. Although he continued to work on the *EDM*, the title lost impetus and eventually gained a degree of notoriety in Victorian society for publishing salacious correspondence relating to, among other things, the merits of ladies' corsets.[63] The career of Samuel Beeton provides a telling demonstration of how the creation of a successful magazine title was not, of itself, a guarantee of business success.

Around the time Beeton was launching the *EDM*, another entrepreneur was also beginning to establish a publishing enterprise which would bear his name and endure well into the twentieth century. John Cassell & Co. had already initiated a thriving business in coffee and tea trading when, in the 1840s, its proprietor began publishing periodicals as a sideline. His trade in beverages was allied to a concern with alcohol abuse, and in 1846 he published the monthly *Teetotal Times* in association with his work for the National Temperance Society. Perhaps aware of a potential readership that had been deprived of the *Penny Magazine* two years earlier, in 1848 Cassell launched the *Standard of Freedom*, a magazine that was driven by an alignment with the same radical programme of working-class improvement that had motivated Charles Knight. Although neither of these magazines appears to have made a profit, by the beginning of the 1850s the somewhat pompous Cassell had clearly begun to relish the status and influence that the publication of such periodicals could bring.[64] In January 1850 he launched a further two: *The Working Man's Friend, and Family Instructor*, a penny weekly magazine, and *The Freeholder*, a threepenny monthly. *The Working Man's Friend* was designed to provide instruction and rational entertainment for the family circle of artisan workers. Cassell claimed a weekly circulation for this magazine of 100,000 after twelve months.[65]

With a portfolio of publications under his belt, Cassell now extended his reach into the business of printing by buying out the printer of the *Standard* newspaper, William Cathrall, and employing for the first time the famous imprint 'Printed and published by John Cassell, of 335 Strand'. The decision to undertake the printing of some of his periodicals raised the capital requirements of Cassell's publishing business and he began to draw substantial credit for his paper requirements from Thomas Crompton, owner of the *Morning Post* and the Farnworth paper mills at Bolton. Expansion of Cassell's business continued apace in the early 1850s. Realizing that, as printer of his own magazines, an increase in the output of periodicals would require physical expansion, in 1851 Cassell moved his business into larger premises at Belle

Sauvage near the foot of Ludgate Hill. From here he used his additional capacity to expand further into the popular idiom of illustrated papers. These began in 1851 with the *Illustrated Exhibitor*, a catalogue that reproduced the wood engravings of the Great Exhibition and which was later transformed into the *Illustrated Magazine of Art*. Most successful and enduing, however, was the launch in December 1853 of *Cassell's Illustrated Family Paper*, a penny weekly title that was soon second only in circulation among popular illustrated magazines to the *London Journal*, whose style and readership it clearly was designed to rival.[66] *Cassell's Illustrated Family Paper* ran continuously, in different forms and under different titles, until 1932 when the monthly *Cassell's Magazine of Fiction* died under another ownership.[67]

Cassell's unbridled success in magazine publishing during the early 1850s was thrown into abrupt reversal in 1855. During the 1840s Cassell had begun to display a strong hostility towards the newspaper stamp and paper duties that he felt were constraints on freedom of expression and a fetter against business. In 1851 he gave testimony to the Select Committee on Newspaper Stamps in which he castigated the so-called taxes on knowledge. In doing so, however, Cassell placed himself in conflict with his chief source of finance, Thomas Crompton, the proprietor of the *Morning Post*. Existing newspaper businesses such as Crompton's were concerned that the abolition of the newspaper stamp duty would bring a flood of competitors and hence damage their financial viability. In late 1854 Crompton suddenly demanded from Cassell full payment of the credit he had extended on stocks of paper. Unable to meet his liabilities, the publisher was forced to take a number of drastic steps, including the closing of some of his magazine titles, before ultimately being forced to sell his business and copyright in the *Family Paper* to the printing firm of Petter and Galpin. Under their tutelage the business at Belle Sauvage continued to expand and the trademark of John Cassell became firmly established during the late Victorian era as producer of high quality publications aimed at a popular audience. Cassell continued his active involvement in the business, although his influence waned in later years.[68]

W.H. SMITH AND RAILWAY DISTRIBUTION

The development of periodical publishing businesses such as Cassell's during the 1840s was supported significantly by the development of the railway system. Beginning with the development of the London North-Western line that linked together the capital with the industrial centres of Birmingham and Manchester, railways provided the publishers of mass-audience magazines a potential national market for their products from the beginning of the Victorian era. By 1851, Cassell's *Working Man's Friend* magazine was selling

1,800 copies through the business of Abel Heywood, one of Manchester's leading periodical wholesalers, while leading papers such as the *Family Herald*
and the *London Journal* were finding around 14,000 buyers in Manchester
each week.[69] The railways were not merely responsible for the conveyance of
magazines and newspapers; they also provided a network of retail outlets for
the travelling public via a chain of station bookstalls. During the 1850s this
business was captured as an effective monopoly by the London firm of W.H.
Smith & Son.

In 1821 the ambitious newsagent William Henry Smith, together with his
elder brother Henry Edward,[70] had set up a reading room at their premises
located at 192 Strand, based in the heart of London's publishing and printing
trades. As the coffee houses had done in earlier times, such public reading
rooms, which charged a subscription fee of between one and one and a half
guineas a year, played a vitally important role in allowing a wider circle of
readers access to the growing but relatively expensive range of newspapers
and literary periodicals in the 1820s and 1830s.[71] By the late 1820s Smith's firm
had also begun to exploit a postal trade to help satisfy the public's demand for
periodicals. They promoted this service through adverts in popular journals
such as *Bell's Life in London and Sporting Chronicle* which, from its launch in
1822, was the first paper to feature sport as a major component of its editorial
content. Published on a Saturday, *Bell's Life* was available by post in any part of
the country within a hundred mile radius of London the following morning.[72]
At this point newspapers were dispatched on the mail coach service of the Post
Office, which left London at 8 o'clock in the evening. Thus the provinces were
permanently a day behind in receiving their news from London. Realizing
that an opportunity existed to make use of a growing and increasingly extensive service of private stage coaches, in the 1830s William Smith developed a
national plan of distribution that could deliver newspapers to their ultimate
destinations on the day they were published, far earlier than the conventional
mail services. It was, according to Wilson, largely due to the tenacity of the
firm's owner that the venture was a success, and it allowed W.H. Smith to issue
the famous claim to be 'First with the News'.[73]

In 1846 William Smith formed a partnership with his son, also named
William Henry Smith, bringing into existence the firm of W.H. Smith & Son.
Two years later the younger W.H. Smith rented a bookstall at the London and
North-Western (LNW) Railway's London terminus at Euston station, which
he then negotiated to extend in 1851 to a monopoly of the entire LNW network of bookstalls.[74] The 1850s represented the crucial period of development
in the history of the firm, increasing its scope both as a retailer of periodicals
and as a wholesale distributor. By 1862 Smith's firm, by virtue of its ability to
generate a reliable source of rental income on behalf of the railway operators,
had secured exclusive bookstall rights on all the important English railway
systems, raising the number of its outlets from 35 in 1851 to 290 in 1870.[75] In

addition, it had set up a number of wholesale operations, most significantly in Birmingham (1857), Manchester (1859), and Liverpool (1867). By the 1870s, therefore, the firm of W.H. Smith & Son had emerged as one of the most successful businesses in the field of periodicals by taking advantage of the inherent monopoly rents that accrued from the operation of an efficient, integrated distribution network.[76]

NED HULTON'S GAMBLE

W.H. Smith's rapid expansion from the start of the 1850s was materially assisted by the abolition of the three taxes on knowledge that had served to hold back the growth of periodical publishing in the first half of the nineteenth century. The 3s. 6d. duty on advertising was the first to be abolished, in 1853. Advertising had proved particularly significant in supporting the growth in the number of provincial newspapers,[77] which were given a further substantial boost by the withdrawal of the stamp duty in 1855. In Manchester a total of fifty-nine new periodicals can be identified for the decade of the 1850s, twice the number compared with the 1820s.[78] However, access to sources of news for the provincial newspapers only became comparable with that of the London press following the nationalization of telegraphy between 1868 and 1870, meaning that London-based daily papers still continued to lead the field throughout the 1860s.[79]

An area of news coverage in which the provincial press did have an inherent advantage over the London-based papers, however, was in the sphere of sporting intelligence. The localized nature of sports events and club affiliations meant that a far greater value was placed on news from the immediate vicinity of the readers. One type of intelligence that was particularly valued was horse-racing tips; particularly those that predicted the outcome with a good record of success. A substantial publishing enterprise that developed from this field was the Manchester-based business of Edward (Ned) Hulton. Although London publishers had produced a number of sporting themed periodicals, including *Bell's Life* and later penny titles such as *Sporting Life* (1859) and the *Sportsman* (1865), the demand remained for much more specific racing intelligence. Hulton, who was employed by the leading Manchester daily newspaper, the *Manchester Guardian*, supplemented his income during the 1860s by providing horse-racing tips under the pseudonym of 'Kettledrum' for the *Daily Sporting Bell*. As his reputation as a reliable tipster gained credence among the local racing punters, Hulton switched his allegiance to a rival publication called the *Prophetic Bell* which he was able to take control of with the financial support of a Manchester cotton merchant. In 1871 Ned Hulton and his business partner, Edward Bleakley, launched the *Manchester Sporting Chronicle and Prophetic Bell.* The timing of this move was perfect. The main daily newspapers in Manchester had agreed as a group to acquiesce to demands from the anti-gambling lobby and had suspended coverage of race meetings. At the same time, the cost of telegraphic charges to press organizations transmitting news had fallen dramatically following the decision to vest monopoly control in the Post Office. Hence transmitting intelligence from the racecourse to the newspaper office could be undertaken with minimal costs.[80]

Having exploited horse-racing to establish his first successful publication, Hulton turned to other sports for his next publishing initiative. In 1875 he launched the *Athletic News* as a weekly paper covering rugby, association football, cricket, and cycling, as well as athletics. The previous year he had set up a modern printing works at Withy Grove, providing the base from which to further expand and to share costs across an increasing range of publications.[81] The cost and first-mover advantages that such an investment provided enabled Hulton to face down a number of rival sporting papers in the years that followed. In 1883 the Hulton enterprise was able to use its extensive network of journalists and horse-racing experts to win the lucrative Press Association contract to supply the national news agency with a racing service that was distributed to morning and evening papers across the country.[82] By the time that he relinquished control of the business during the 1890s to his son, also named Edward, Hulton had launched the *Sunday Chronicle* and provided the basis of a substantial publishing empire which would continue into the opening decades of the twentieth century.[83]

2

Pioneers of the New Journalism Revolution

FEEDING THE POPULAR DEMAND

By the end of the 1870s *Mitchell's Newspaper Press Directory* estimated that the total number of magazines titles circulating in Britain (including Quarterly Reviews) was in the region of 930, of which around 30 per cent were of a religious character. At the time of the abolition of the paper duties in 1861 the number had been barely more than half of this total—about 480—with around 43 per cent of these being periodicals that focused on religion. Thus a substantial growth in the volume of secular reading material on offer to the British public had taken place during these two decades. What can be said of the firms that made this growth possible? Clearly many of them were extremely small operations that printed and sold their offerings to a limited audience. Although circulation data are extremely sketchy, Altick's figures indicate that the estimated 450,000 weekly sales of the *London Journal* during 1855 provide a high-water mark for popular journals before the 1880s.[1] Among the more established firms, magazine publishing had tended to make up only one element of a business portfolio which was normally focused on books. Chapman & Hall and Macmillan are both examples of firms who, like Cassell, laid a variety of publications before the public. Indeed, provision of low-cost books was a feature of the third quarter of the nineteenth century and had, to some extent, undercut the sales of popular literary magazines by 1880.[2] Other early exponents of magazines, such as George Reynolds and Edward Lloyd, had also shifted their main business activities towards the publication of newspapers and, in the latter case, paper manufacture.

The Sunday newspapers published by Reynolds and Lloyd were the most important source of growth in reading matter for those on a modest income during the 1860s and 1870s. The leading Sunday newspaper, *Lloyd's Weekly*, increased its sales from 350,000 in 1863 to 750,000 in 1886, as that firm became a substantial vertically integrated business enterprise.[3] Penny daily newspapers, on the other hand, continued to serve the upper and middle classes, and whilst they earned a comfortable profit for their owners their operations were not seen primarily as a commercial enterprise.⁴ The growing demand for low-priced works of fiction, meanwhile, was being met increasingly through the publication of cheap books. By the early 1860s the rapidly expanding business of W.H. Smith, in collaboration with the publishing firm of Chapman and Hall, had set up its *Select Library of Fiction* which sold popular titles at a low price.⁵ Growth in the number of magazine titles published during this period came about as the result of a process of increased specialization in both the subject matter and target audience. Many of these new magazines tended to stress the home and family and, reflecting this focus on domesticity, titles aimed exclusively at female readers grew in significance during the 1870s.⁶

GROWING A PUBLISHING PORTFOLIO

A brief account of two of Britain's leading publishing firms, Cassell & Co. and Ward Lock, whose growth during the third quarter of the nineteenth century was due in good measure to their output of popular journals, provides a perspective on the prevailing state of Britain's magazine publishing industry. The early history of these two firms finds a common thread through the printing business set up by George Petter and Dixon Galpin in 1852. The partnership of Ward and Lock had begun in 1854 when Dixon Galpin had introduced his cousin George Lock to Ebenezer Ward, while the latter man was working for the publishing firm of Herbert Ingram and Company.⁷ In 1856 the firm of Ward Lock assumed control of the financially stricken business of Ingram, bringing with it the right to publish *Webster's English Dictionary*. Utilizing the Petter & Galpin firm as its printer, Ward Lock become established as a significant publishing concern, moving into expanded premises in Paternoster Row in 1861. By this time, however, their relationship with Petter & Galpin had been fractured when the printing firm had themselves entered the realm of publishing. In 1859 Petter & Galpin acquired control of the bankrupt business of John Cassell, including the right to publish that firm's highly popular magazine *Cassell's Illustrated Family Paper*. Thus by 1860 Ward Lock and Petter & Galpin had become publishing rivals.⁸

As magazine publishers, Ward Lock's business made a major step forward in 1866 when it acquired the bulk of the periodicals that had been successfully developed by Samuel Beeton. Beeton's empire had begun to crumble in 1860 when adverse financial circumstances forced him to sell the copyright of his newly launched *Queen* magazine to the printing firm of Cox and Wyman. Soon after this Beeton's business partner, Frederick Greenwood, left to join rival publisher George Smith, whose flagship title was *Cornhill Magazine*. Together they successfully launched the London daily evening newspaper, the *Pall Mall*

Gazette, in 1865. When Beeton's business was finally thrown into liquidation the following year by the collapse of the finance house Overend Gurney, it was Ward Lock (and their newly acquired partner Charles Tyler) who picked up the baton.[9] Now finding themselves as publishers of such popular titles as *Boy's Own Magazine* and the *Englishwoman's Domestic Magazine*, Ward, Lock and Tyler began to build a substantial business in the field of popular publishing. In 1870, however, aware of the increasing market potential offered by book sales, they acquired the important literary publishing firm of E. Moxon, Son and Company and from this point seem to have turned their attention towards the growing demand for books. Increased competition in the market for magazines, where entry barriers to new firms were relatively low, seems to have been a factor in this decision to diversify towards book publishing. During the 1860s a number of rival titles had emerged to challenge the pre-eminence of Beeton's original *Boy's Own Magazine*, typified by the 'penny-dreadful' publications of Edwin J. Brett, and in 1874 Ward Lock withdrew the title from circulation.[10] By this time the currency of the *Englishwoman's Domestic Magazine* had also begun to wane. The introduction of a clutch of rivals from the mid-1870s, particularly *Myra's Journal of Dress and Fashion* and *Weldon's Ladies Journal*, both founded by Beeton's erstwhile colleague Charles Weldon, precipitated the termination by Ward Lock of its remaining legacy from the Beeton enterprise in 1879.[11]

The move into books was consolidated in 1885 when Ward Lock purchased W.H. Smith's *Select Library of Fiction*, at which time the firm moved also into bookbinding and printing via the acquisition of the Botolph Printing Works. Not until 1893, when James Bowden was appointed as managing director and the firm was converted into a limited company under the title of Ward Lock and Bowden Ltd., do magazines seem to have resumed their importance as an element of the firm's expansion.[12] Around this time the firm became increasingly active in the United States through its office in New York. For a number of years the company exploited this link with the United States by publishing English editions of the American magazines *Lippincott's* and *Atlantic Monthly*. In 1895 the company made a significant effort to re-establish a presence in the British market for popular monthly magazines through the launch of the *Windsor Magazine*, which used the firm's office in New York to obtain some of its copy from American publications. Following the retirement of Bowden in 1897, however, this surge in new initiatives at Ward Lock seems to have largely dissipated.[13]

While Ward Lock deviated towards the publication of books, Petter & Galpin made significant strides in the periodical field during the 1870s and 80s through their ownership of Cassell's publishing business. Maintaining their printing business as a distinct entity, Petter & Galpin operated the publishing side of their activities as an effectively independent operation and thus, despite the change in ownership, the House of Cassell remained an enduring feature of the British publishing scene. Furthermore its founder, John Cassell, continued to work for the organization that bore his name until his death in 1865, bringing to the market an evangelical weekly entitled the *Quiver* in 1861 which lasted until 1926. Under the managerial direction of Dixon Galpin, Cassell's portfolio of magazines grew steadily. The firm had already put out the pioneering weekly *Photographic News* in 1858 and now, as well as revamping *Cassell's Illustrated Family Paper* in 1867, a number of other successful magazine titles were introduced into the firm's portfolio: *The Echo* (1868); *Little Folks* (1871); *The Magazine of Art* (1878); *Bo-Peep* (1882); *The Boy's Newspaper* (1883); and *Cassell's Saturday Journal* (1883) all found a willing audience.[14] By the beginning of the 1880s, although its range of publishing activities extended beyond that of periodicals alone, the House of Cassell can be fairly credited with the position of Britain's leading magazine publisher.[15]

Progress on the printing side of the enterprise had been more faltering during these years. In 1859 the manager of Petter & Galpin's printing department designed an innovative one- and two-colour printing machine that the firm took out patent protection against. The machine held pre-eminence in its class for thirty to forty years, but Petter & Galpin disposed of this side of their business in 1863. Likewise in the realm of paper manufacturing, the firm purchased the patent rights for an improved method of pulp manufacturing in 1871 on the strength of which they developed the Turn Lee mills at Glossop, but once again this venture faltered and the mills were sold off after just three years.[16]

By the mid-1880s, the firm's failure to successfully extend its operations on the printing side was being matched by setbacks in its launch of new publications. In 1886 Cassell put out a new monthly journal in an effort to capitalize on the growing demand for magazines aimed at a female audience. *Lady's World*, subtitled *A Magazine of Fashion and Society*, began its life as a relatively conventional offering and made little impression in the marketplace. In an effort to invigorate the title Cassell's proprietors decided to place more emphasis on providing the magazine with literary appeal, and in 1887 the firm's management appointed a new editor in the shape of Oscar Wilde. Wilde insisted that the title of the magazine should be altered to that of *Woman's World*, a change of nomenclature which set in train an irreversible fashion within the industry. Predictably though, after an initial period of mutual enthusiasm, Wilde's unconventional working practices began to clash with the more puritanical attitudes of Cassell's owners; Wilde stood down as editor in 1889 and the title was abandoned in 1890.[17]

In 1888 Petter & Galpin's ageing proprietors had placed the management of its periodicals under the literary direction of the deeply conservative Sir T. Wemyss Reid. For Cassell's the years between this appointment and Reid's death in 1905 were blighted by the emergence of new sources of competition; a process that heralded the transition of Britain's magazine publishing industry from one dominated by family-owned concerns, such as Cassell's and Ward Lock,[18] to one in which the leading actors were modern industrial corporations capitalized at up to £1 million. Perhaps a surprising coincidence is that two of the key agents in promoting this process of revolutionary change in Britain's periodical publishing industry were both sons of congregational ministers: the campaigning editor and journalist William Thomas Stead and the upstart commercial publisher George Newnes.

GEORGE NEWNES LAUNCHES *TIT-BITS*

Stead's impact on the direction of journalism in Britain began in 1871 when he replaced his mentor John Copleston as editor of the Darlington-based *Northern Echo*. Stead's first act had been to seek out the advice of Wemyss Reid (later director of Cassell's) who at this point was editor of the *Leeds Mercury*.[19] Under Stead's guiding hand the *Northern Echo* developed into a campaigning journal, advocating Gladstone's radical Liberal agenda of constitutional reform and strongly supporting the Christian-based social aims of the Salvation Army. Having established his reputation as a pioneer of a new style of campaigning and investigative journalism, Stead joined the *Pall Mall Gazette* as assistant editor to John Morley in 1880. The *Gazette* had recently altered its ownership and become converted to a mouthpiece for the Gladstone interests,[20] giving Stead free rein as editor from 1883 to introduce his radical editorial style to a wider and more influential audience.[21] As well as introducing a new style of campaigning journalism, his editorial approach included innovations in the presentation of news, such as the use of bold headlines, themed leading articles, and special interviews, all of which marked Stead out as a key pioneer of an emerging 'new journalism' in Britain.[22] Stead's work for the *Pall Mall Gazette* during the 1880s brought a number of significant legislative changes in their wake, most notably in relation to the issue of child prostitution and the raising of the age of consent for girls from 13 to 16 years.[23] The campaigns were frequently controversial, dividing opinion and generating hostility from within the established London press, particularly as the *Gazette's* circulation began to rise sharply in the mid-1880s. By 1889, however, Stead and the owner of the *Gazette* had fallen into an irreconcilable dispute, and in January 1890 the editor left to pursue his idea for a new monthly review-style magazine. He had already outlined his thoughts to Wemyss Reid, now based at Cassell's, with a view to gaining financial support for its publication through the Petter & Galpin firm, but had received no encouragement from that quarter.[24] The next person to whom he turned was George Newnes.

Unlike Stead, who had been his contemporary at Silcoates School in Yorkshire, Newnes had no background in publishing whatsoever when he launched his weekly magazine *Tit-Bits* in October 1881. Having failed to interest any of his Manchester business contacts in financing the idea, Newnes scraped together sufficient capital to pay for the printing of the early issues by opening a vegetarian restaurant and banking the profits.[25] His aim had been to create a periodical that brought together a selection of snippets of information—tit-bits—that might appeal to the popular reader, but which would represent a more wholesome diet than the prevailing cheap weekly press with its emphasis on gambling, crime, and sensationalism. Newnes had gained enough business sense in his earlier career as a sales representative of a London haberdashery and fancy goods firm to be able to negotiate effectively with printers in order to keep down costs; within a matter of months he had switched the printing of *Tit-Bits* across four different firms, largely it seems as a result of financial disputes.[26] He had also clearly gained the knack of motivating the growing strata of urban workers to part with their modest wages. When he launched his new magazine, Newnes arranged for the 100-strong band of the local Boy's Brigade to promote the event by marching up Market Street in central Manchester with the *Tit-Bits* legend emblazoned on their caps; within two hours he had sold 5,000 copies of his penny magazine.[27]

As a budding publisher, Newnes' most important innovations were in the areas of marketing and distribution. Forty dozen copies of the first print run of *Tit-Bits* were consigned to a leading London firm of newspaper distributors, almost certainly W.H. Smith, on a sale or return basis. When these bundles were returned unopened, Newnes hastened to the capital and demanded a meeting with the firm's managing director in order to effect a change of policy.[28] For Newnes, gaining support from the likes of W.H. Smith and Son was extremely significant. As he evolved his marketing strategy for *Tit-Bits*, Newnes clearly recognized that the growing band of urban commuters could provide a vital source of readers. Thus an inspired move in the early promotion of his new magazine was the provision of financial assistance to the relatives of any person involved in a fatal accident while travelling on the railway, as long as the deceased could be shown to have been in possession of a copy of *Tit-Bits* at the time of his or her demise. It has been estimated that this free insurance scheme cost Newnes no more than 20 to 30 sums of £100 in his lifetime, while providing an incentive to consumers that helped to rapidly take the circulation of *Tit-Bits* beyond 500,000.[29]

Although *Tit-Bits'* editorial formula of collating together snippets of information was by no means a novel one, Newnes did take significant steps towards defining the nature of modern magazines. Jackson has suggested that his most important innovation in this respect was the introduction of an editorial voice, and his use of this device to encourage the ongoing involvement of its loyal customers; establishing what was in effect a 'reading community'.[30] *Tit-Bits* promoted various forms of interactive engagement,[31] particularly by giving readers the opportunity to submit items for publication in the magazine, as well as by means of myriad competitions featuring such forms of engagement as puzzles and treasure-hunts; in one particularly celebrated contest the magazine offered a newly built house in Dulwich as a prize—the so-called *Tit-Bits Villa*—which Newnes had purchased for £400.[32]

The success of *Tit-Bits* soon required an expansion of the publishing business. In 1885, the same year as he was elected to parliament as Liberal MP for Newmarket in Cambridgeshire, Newnes moved his offices from Manchester to London. For the next decade he was obliged to juggle his political and business activities. In 1886 he moved the business from a small office in Farringdon Street into substantial premises in Burleigh Street, where the printing process could be carried out in-house. As the size of its readership grew, the magazine also became a potential medium for progressive businesses who wished to bring their products and services to the attention of the public. To begin with Newnes had eschewed the inclusion of advertising in his magazine, but in 1889 he was persuaded by the advertising agency T.B. Browne to include a four-page wrapper to *Tit-Bits* that brought in £200 per week[33] and this income was more than doubled when Newnes' firm later set up its own advertising department. By 1890 the *Tit-Bits* title was generating his business annual revenue of just under £30,000.[34]

Despite the huge success of his magazine, almost ten years elapsed before Newnes was prepared to launch a second title; an initiative that stemmed from the approach by William T. Stead in 1890. Stead's idea was for a monthly review-style magazine and this proposal was put into effect by Newnes' publishing house in January of that year. The ensuing sixpenny *Review of Reviews* was an immediate success, but the business relationship between Newnes and Stead was not a happy one. Within six months Newnes withdrew from his role as publisher of the journal, unhappy with Stead's proclivity to court controversy, and Stead was forced to turn to his friends in the Salvation Army to provide financial support for the publication.[35] Under these new financial arrangements the magazine progressed quickly, and very soon Stead had created foreign editions of the *Review of Reviews* in both Melbourne and New York as his desire to promote the cause of world peace led him to become increasingly cosmopolitan in his outlook.[36]

For Newnes, the decision to withdraw from publishing the *Review of Reviews* left him with a good deal of spare printing capacity. In January 1891, motivated seemingly by the desire to avoid creating redundancies within his organization, Newnes collaborated with H. Greenhough Smith, a member of his editorial team, to launch his own high quality sixpenny monthly magazine, centred on fiction. The new publication was named the *Strand Magazine*, drawing its title from the main London thoroughfare that led to his publishing offices in Burleigh Street.[37] Influenced by the high-quality American literary journals such as *Harper's* that were now finding a market in London, the *Strand* soon developed a devoted audience for English short-stories both in Britain and across the Atlantic, adding a substantial number of American readers to its initial circulation of 300,000 in Britain.[38]

With two successful magazines in harness, Newnes took the decision to reconstruct his publishing business as a limited company. In November 1891 400,000 £1 shares in George Newnes Ltd. were created, with slightly over three-quarters of the total being owned directly by the proprietor himself.[39] A succession of new titles now flowed from the Burleigh Street presses: *The Million* (1892); *Picture Politics* (1894); *Navy and Army Illustrated* (1895); *Woman's Life* (1895); and, jointly produced with the Southwark-based printers Hudson and Kearns, the enduring *Country Life* (1897).[40] This period also saw Newnes launch his only successful daily newspaper, the highly influential but perennially unprofitable *Westminster Gazette*, in 1893.[41] Whilst the range of new magazine titles that Newnes brought to market in the 1890s varied considerably in their degree of commercial success,[42] the business overall continued to gather strength and in August 1897 Newnes was able to wind up the original George Newnes Ltd. and float a public company on the London stock exchange capitalized at £1 million. The additional capital allowed Newnes to acquire still larger, purpose-built premises in Southampton Street, also off The Strand, and generated profits to the tune of £60,000 per year.[43] In 1898 Newnes expanded his publishing activities still further by taking control of the portfolio of women's titles put out by the publishing house of Charles Weldon, forming Weldons Ltd. in the process.[44]

TECHNOLOGICAL BREAKTHROUGHS

The expansion of George Newnes' magazine publishing enterprise between 1881 and 1900 took place in an industry that was undergoing a technological revolution, the impact of which was to significantly reduce the average cost of producing large volumes of a single magazine issue. The breakthroughs from 1880 included more efficient methods of producing paper, rapid increases in the speed of letterpress printing, the mechanization and automation of the process of typesetting, and methods to reduce the cost of reproducing illustrative material by making the technology of photography compatible with the letterpress.

A prerequisite for the development of mass production within the printing and publishing industry was the availability of low-cost sources of paper. Although the abolition of the duty on paper reduced the cost of the basic material needed to produce magazines, the scale of paper manufacturing remained severely limited by shortages in the traditional raw material of rags. The main alternative raw material to rags was esparto grass, grown largely in Spain and North Africa, and imports of esparto into Britain rose spectacularly from

under 1,000 tons annually in 1860 to over 200,000 tons per annum by the closing years of the 1870s.[45] However, it was only with a further shift in raw material from esparto to wood-pulp that a substantial reduction in the unit cost
of paper became possible. From the 1880s, mechanically ground wood-pulp
established itself as the core ingredient of newsprint, while for the better class
of magazines and periodicals chemical wood-pulp, made using the sulphite
process, yielded a finer quality form of paper.[46] As had been the case with
esparto, the new raw material was available in the quantities required only
outside of Britain, mainly in Scandinavia and Canada, and between 1887 and
1900 the volume of imported wood-pulp increased sixfold.[47] By this time the
leading manufacturer of newsprint in Britain was Edward Lloyd Ltd., which
had been transformed into a public company by Lloyd shortly before his death
in 1890. During the 1890s Lloyd's sons, who had assumed control of the business, made significant investments in new paper mills in Norway.[48]

The production of wood-pulp-based paper at rates between 100 and 200
feet per minute, using the well-established Fourdrinier process,[49] enabled the
paper industry to provide the required raw material for the web-fed rotary
presses that were being developed in the United States principally by Richard
Hoe and Company of New York. In the 1860s William Bullock had developed a web-fed rotary perfecting press that could print both sides of the paper
simultaneously, but from the 1870s it had been Hoe's innovations that had
taken the rotary technology forward, such that by the late 1890s this firm's
three-roll machine was capable of turning out 12,000 magazines of 16 to 24
pages per hour. By this time, too, the use of steam to drive the printers was
increasingly being replaced by the more economical power source provided
by electricity.[50]

Firms in the United States also led the mechanization and automation of
the process of typesetting. Significant strides were made in this area during the
1880s thanks to the introduction of the hot-metal process developed through
the use of Ottmar Mergenthaler's Linotype machine. Compared with the output of even the most experienced hand compositors, the operators of Linotype
machines were able to increase levels of productivity between four and five
times.[51] The hot-metal Linotype process employed a keyboard operator whose
machine created 'slugs' of type out of molten lead and set them directly in a
forme. As such, the Linotype machines avoided the need to continually reas-
semble type, reducing labour-time and saving the need to maintain a vast
stock of type in-house. By the late 1890s the changes in typesetting wrought
by the hot-metal process allowed periodicals to increase the number of pages
produced without a comparable need to increase either the number of compositors or the amount of floor-space dedicated to typesetting.

Further technological developments were pioneered in terms of pictures.
Given the importance of illustrations for widening the demand for popular
magazines, another significant innovation was the development between 1878

and 1886 of half-tones, particularly through the work of Frederick E. Ives at Cornell University.[52] By the 1880s half-tone blocs were being used by magazines such as the *Illustrated London News* to reproduce photographs in a way that made their incorporation compatible with the basic technology of the letterpress.[53] The commercialization of half-tone technology, allowing its widespread use in magazines, was the result of developments by Levy Brothers in Philadelphia, who began to manufacture the necessary screens on an industrial scale around 1890.[54] Thereafter magazines such as the *Review of Reviews* and the *Strand* began to make extensive use of half-tones, which had the effect of dramatically cutting the cost of reproducing illustrative material.[55] This graphical breakthrough was also of great significance in the development of display advertising during the early years of the twentieth century, and for the development of a pictorial daily news press. Taken together, these changes in printing and typesetting technologies during the closing decades of the nineteenth century were instrumental in allowing firms engaged in printing and publishing to emerge as key actors in the second industrial revolution.[56]

DEVELOPMENTS IN AMERICA

The successful development of half-tones, and thus the use of photo-engraving as a means of producing low cost illustrations, was a significant factor in the revolution in magazine publishing that occurred in the United States during the 1890s. In the previous decade the leading illustrated American magazines such as *Century* and *Harper's Monthly* were selling for 35 cents and were beyond the reach of those potential readers with modest levels of incomes. These latter consumers were catered for by the daily or weekly news press, whose weekend supplements increasingly offered a miscellany of items that could provide an effective substitute good to conventional popular magazines. Moreover, these news periodicals were easily available via street vendors. Rather than purchasing magazines from news-stands, as they did in Britain, in the United States most readers of weekly and monthly periodicals obtained their journals by means of postal subscriptions, and thus the decision of the US Congress to reduce the rate of second-class postage on monthly magazines from three cents to one cent in 1885 was instrumental in helping to boost the industry in America.[57]

One of the first publishing firms to take advantage of the lower postal rates to expand the circulation of their newly devised 5 cent monthly for women was the Curtis Publishing Company of Philadelphia. The magazine, called the *Ladies' Home Journal*, was launched in December 1883 and sought to provide reading matter for housewives at the cost of a 50 cent annual subscription.[58] Over the course of the next five years, making extensive use of advertising to promote the magazine, Curtis had successfully increased the *Journal*'s circulation to something above 500,000. As a result, he was able to successfully exploit his publication to provide an advertising platform for America's rapidly expanding manufacturing firms. In 1889 Curtis hired as editor of the *Journal* Edward Bok, an employee of the established magazine publisher Charles Scribner and Sons, and at the same time raised the cover price to 10 cents and the annual subscription rate to a dollar. Although in the short term this reduced the circulation of the *Journal* it served to place it on a more secure financial footing, and Bok then began to utilize similar devices to those Newnes had employed to promote *Tit-Bits* in Britain. These included the use of an editorial voice to directly engage readers, as well as offering a series of prizes for items of feedback on the magazine and for introducing new subscribers.[59] During the 1890s, Bok raised the status along with the circulation of the *Ladies' Home Journal*, bringing it into competition with the traditional monthly illustrated magazines. In the 1890s the magazine featured 48 profusely illustrated glossy pages, showcasing the work of leading writers, and at the turn of the century was claiming a circulation of 850,000.[60]

By this time the established American monthly magazines had found themselves assailed by a range of lower-priced rivals from Britain. Among the earliest of these was Newnes' own *Strand Magazine*. Newnes had originally been inspired to create the *Strand* as a rival to the American monthlies which had made significant inroads into the British market during the 1880s.[61] By pricing the *Strand Magazine* at sixpence Newnes had undercut *Harper's* in England by 50 per cent, and soon after its launch in Britain the *Strand*, along with the *Review of Reviews*, was selling an American edition priced at a highly competitive 20 cents.[62] These examples of low-priced monthly publications introduced by Curtis and Newnes offered other American publishing firms a potential strategy for gaining a share of the market for popular magazines. The first of these to direct a challenge to the established publishers was Frank A. Munsey who relaunched his eponymous weekly magazine as a 25 cent illustrated monthly in 1891. Munsey's long-term vision was the establishment of a publishing empire featuring the large-scale production of a string of newspapers and magazines, many acquired through the use of mergers and takeovers, along the same lines as James Duke's recently founded tobacco trust, an aspiration that he ultimately shared with William Randolph Hearst.[63]

By 1893, the cost-cutting impact of the new half-tone technology began to allow further incursions into the market for popular illustrated magazines. In June of that year Samuel Sydney McClure launched the first issue of his monthly *McClure's Magazine* with a capital of just $7,300, of which $5,000 was reputedly committed to pay the annual salary of an advertising manager.[64] *McClure's* sold at 15 cents a copy or a dollar and a half per year (i.e. 12½ cents per issue for annual subscribers). The next month John Briben Walker trumped McClure's initiative by cutting the cover price of his *Cosmopolitan* magazine to 12½ cents. In September 1893, however, Munsey reacted by making the critical strategic move of slashing the price of his monthly from 25 to 10 cents, or a dollar a year on subscription, initiating the era of the 10 cent popular magazine.[65] Munsey faced severe opposition to his 10 cent strategy from the American News Company, holders of monopoly control over the news-stand distribution system in the United States, who offered him only 4½ cents a copy for his magazine. However, in an echo of the ploy adopted in Britain back in the 1820s by John Limbird, Munsey was able to use the huge demand that the 10 cent cover price generated as a lever to force it through to consumers, initially using the services of an independent group of distributors. The magazine's circulation growth was quite phenomenal: 40,000 copies in October 1893; 60,000 in November; 200,000 in February 1894; 275,000 at the end of 1894; and 500,000 by April 1895.[66] Both Munsey and Curtis developed their publishing businesses into industry leaders during the early years of the twentieth century. Munsey used a programme of extensive corporate acquisitions to move mainly into newspaper production; Curtis used the revenues generated by the *Ladies' Home Journal* to develop the *Saturday Evening Post* and quickly came to dominate the market as the leading provider of national magazine advertising space.[67] Both *McClure's Magazine*, and *Cosmopolitan*, by contrast, fell under the control of others. McClure was forced to sell out his interests to a syndicate led by his son-in-law, Cameron Mackenzie, in 1911.[68] In 1905 Walker sold *Cosmopolitan* to W. R. Hearst, whose newspaper publishing business had launched its first magazine, the *Motor*, two years earlier.[69]

ALFRED HARMSWORTH'S 'SCHEMO MAGNIFICO'

The expansion of Curtis and Munsey in the United States during the 1890s was paralleled in Britain by the rise of two substantial publishing concerns to rival the one created by George Newnes: C. Arthur Pearson Ltd. and Harmsworth Brothers Ltd. Arthur Pearson's precocious talent had made itself apparent to George Newnes in 1884 when, as an 18-year-old, he had successfully responded to a competition in *Tit-Bits* which offered the winner employment as a clerk in the magazine's offices with a salary of £100 per year.[70] One year later Pearson was appointed as manager of *Tit-Bits* and by the time Newnes agreed to publish the *Review of Reviews* with W. T. Stead in 1889 his salary had advanced to £350. Anxious to harness his energy and evident flair for management, Newnes appointed Pearson as business manager of the *Review* but, unwilling to further increase his salary, there followed a parting of the ways in 1890.[71] By this time Pearson had developed his own ideas for a weekly publication to rival the appeal of *Tit-Bits*, and had been able to secure sufficient funds to set up on his own.[72]

Three weeks after resigning from Newnes' firm in June 1890 Pearson, together with two colleagues who had followed him, laid before the public *Pearson's Weekly*, 'a bigger pennyworth [than *Tit-Bits*] that offered larger and more attractive prizes in its competitions'.[73] After a faltering start, the introduction of a 'Missing Word' competition in December 1891 led to an upsurge in sales that Pearson exploited to the full.[74] The circulation of *Pearson's Weekly* reached its peak of 1.25 million in 1897, by which time the firm's proprietor was the 51 per cent owner of C. Arthur Pearson Ltd., a business valued at some £360,000.[75]

The advent of *Pearson's Weekly* came as numerous would-be emulators of the Newnes formula sought to muscle in on the market for penny weeklies. One of the many who had tried their luck at launching a new magazine in 1888 was the impetuous but charming Alfred Harmsworth.[76] Having been brought from Ireland to London as an infant, Harmsworth began his formal involvement with publishing[77] when at the age of 19 he was appointed as the editor of *Youth*, a short-lived magazine published by William Ingram.[78] In April 1886, at age 20, he moved from London to Coventry, the centre of Britain's bicycle manufacturing industry, where William Iliffe had set up a specialist magazine publishing house as an arm of his father's stationery, printing, and wallpaper business.[79] Iliffe invited Alfred to edit the firm's ailing *Bicycling News* title. As an enthusiast of this new form of exercise and transport, Harmsworth had already made contributions to the Iliffe's *Cyclist* magazine[80] and enjoyed a brief but successful stint as the editor of the *Bicycling News* where he strongly encouraged female participation, both in the activity of cycling itself (the idea of which was widely lampooned) and as contributors to the magazine.[81]

In 1887 Harmsworth parted company with Iliffe and returned to London.[82] He had for some time contributed articles to *Tit-Bits*, among other freelance writing assignments, and is reported to have confided in his friend and fellow journalist Max Pemberton his view that Newnes' magazine would transform popular journalism in Britain and that they 'could start one of these papers for a couple of thousand pounds' as he set about finding a source of funding.[83] In 1888 he formed a partnership with W. F. Dargaville Carr, and under the identity of Carr & Co. they produced a number of booklets and published a magazine for the owners of private schools.[84] Carr was reluctant to indulge Alfred's idea for a rival to *Tit-Bits*, but Harmsworth used his other contacts to raise further capital from a Captain Beaumont and his wife, and in June of that year Carr & Co. launched the inaugural edition (No. 3) of *Answers to Correspondents*.[85] The paper was printed in Coventry on credit allowed by the Iliffe firm, but it was quite an amateurish product and, despite having handed out the bulk of the first print run for free, *Answers* at first made slow progress.[86] William Iliffe's patience, as well as his bank account, was soon tested beyond endurance, and Alfred transferred the printing of *Answers* to the London firm of Allen & Scott located in Bouverie Street, half a mile from Carr & Co.'s office at 26 Paternoster Square. Some financial relief was provided for the magazine's owners by the sale of advertising space, assisted by the T. B. Browne agency. In June 1889, Alfred's younger brother Harold joined the publishing business from his post as a civil servant at the Board of Trade. Harold's involvement was crucial in providing book-keeping skills and a level of attention to financial detail that his older brother lacked.

As with *Pearson's Weekly*, the breakthrough for *Answers* came via an attention-grabbing competition. Unable to finance prizes that could effectively match the extravagance of Newnes' *Tit-Bits Villa*, in October 1889 a competition in *Answers* offered the opportunity to win a pound a week for the rest of their life to the reader who could guess most accurately the value of the gold reserves held by the Bank of England at the close of business on 4 December 1889. With the help of Alfred's booming, the idea of the prize captured the popular imagination and entries are claimed to have numbered over 700,000. Moreover, since each entry needed to be 'witnessed' by five people, who were neither relatives nor living at the same address, the competition succeeded in bringing Alfred's magazine to the attention of millions of potential readers. The Christmas 1889 issue of *Answers*, in which the results of the competition were reviewed, sold over 200,000 copies.[87] Harold had already set up the Answers Company Ltd. and the management of his magazine was now transferred from Carr & Co. to this new entity, for which Harold initially acted as company secretary.[88]

Following a move to new premises at 108 Fleet Street, the two Harmsworth bothers now initiated a process of rapid corporate expansion, which over the space of the next six years enabled them to create a publishing company with a capital value of £1 million. Alongside Answers Company Ltd., in 1890 the brothers set up the Pandora Publishing Company Ltd., which they launched with £500 capital and used to bring to market a humorous halfpenny magazine called *Comic Cuts*. This was followed quickly by *Illustrated Chips* featuring the comic-strip character Chips. By introducing the British public to the undemanding and inherently amusing comic-strip form of presentation, the Harmsworth concern was able to wrest control of a substantial readership among juvenile and adolescent males who had previously been adherents to the 'penny dreadful' genre of low-cost magazine publishing. *Comic Cuts* soon amassed a circulation of 300,000 and became dubbed by critics 'the halfpenny dreadfuller'.[89] Despite opposition from within the distribution trade, who were concerned at the slim margins generated by such cheap publications, the halfpenny papers made significant progress. Further efforts to exploit this market segment followed during the early 1890s, including *Marvel*, *Wonder*, *Union Jack*, and the *Boy's Friend*. However, it was through a widening of the market for women's magazines that the future press lord sensed the most lucrative returns to investment lay. From his time as editor of *Bicycling News* Alfred had understood the potential value in directing publications towards the female reader. His next move, therefore, was to set up another small business called the

Periodical Publishing Co. whose first offering was *Forget-Me-Not*, an illustrated penny weekly aimed at young females, particularly the growing number of shopgirls. As the 1890s wore on, Harmsworth's publishing operations increasingly targeted women with modest levels of disposable income. In March 1895, placing the emphasis on good value as he attempted to undercut his main rivals, Harmsworth launched the highly successful women's magazine *Home Chat* as a penny weekly competitor to Arthur Pearson's sixpenny monthly *Home Notes*.[90]

In 1884 the logic of relentless expansion was applied to the religious segment of the periodical market, where a vast array of low circulation magazines featuring a diet of unalloyed dullness, such as Cassell's *Quiver*, abounded. The popular tone struck by the firm's first offering, the *Sunday Companion*, generated a frenzy of opposition which included the public incineration of the magazine. Unfazed, the firm persevered and two years later the Harmsworths' business extended their offerings within this segment by adding a story paper entitled *Sunday Stories*. Later that year, in a move foreshadowing the future pattern of corporate expansion in Britain's magazine industry, the Harmsworths acquired an established publishing business, W. B. Horner & Sons Ltd., whose leading *Penny Stories* magazine was added to the firm's armoury.[91] It appears that from his earliest days as an aspiring publisher Alfred Harmsworth, rather like Frank Munsey in the United States, had set the objective of developing a portfolio of large circulation magazines that would serve to overwhelm competitors. Harmsworth had written down his ideas in a business manifesto that he kept locked in a safe and which he referred to as his 'Schemo Magnifico'.[92] While Alfred provided the main source of creative inspiration for the business, Harold's ability to keep down costs of production was equally important to the successful prosecution of the 'Schemo'. Although the brothers argued about the level of fees that should be paid to contributors, Harold was given free rein to apply his ruthless cost-cutting in the sphere of inanimate raw materials, and the use of very cheap forms of paper for its penny and halfpenny journals allowed the firm's profits to develop handsomely in the early 1890s.[93]

The two Harmsworths clearly appreciated the economic realities of modern publishing as the industry developed in the late nineteenth century. At a basic level, Harold well understood that value was added to a stock of paper through the application of ink via printing presses. The margin of added value, and thus the rate of profit, depended upon the ratio of the cost of inputs to the revenues generated by the cover price and sale of advertising space. Keeping down variable costs, particularly the cost of paper (i.e. newsprint), directly benefitted the bottom line of the business. On the other hand, the overall volume of profit depended on the speed of turnover of this process of value-adding. For a given level of fixed costs, the higher the circulations and the greater the range of titles that could be sold in a fixed period of time, the more profits could be generated. This, it would be fair to assume, was the key insight that attached to Alfred's 'Schemo Magnifico'. In addition, there was a question of the distribution of the total profits generated through the value-adding system of the periodical production process as a whole. Publishing was a high-risk business, with great fluctuations in the level of profits it returned; bankruptcy was a constant feature of publishing life. However, with a substantial portfolio of periodicals this financial risk could be effectively spread, and those titles that were failing to deliver could, in Harold's brutal phraseology, be 'knifed'. Compared with publishing, the business of printing was far more stable, as long as a steady stream of throughput could be guaranteed to keep the increasingly expensive presses at work. With this in mind, as soon as the profits derived from its publishing activities were sufficient, the Harmsworths engaged in a process of backward vertical integration in order to generate value from directly undertaking the printing of their expanding range of periodicals. They began this process of backward vertical integration through the creation of yet another business enterprise: the Geraldine Press Ltd.[94]

In June 1893 the Harmsworths reconstructed their main company as Answers Ltd., with a capital of £275,000. Better provisioned financially, they now acquired a property in Whitefriars Street, off Fleet Street, where they installed eight rotary presses together with modern typesetting machines. The Geraldine Press was little more than a stop-gap, given the company's expanding printing requirements, and within four years the Harmsworths had begun work on a purpose-built site south of the River Thames, in Lavington Street, Southwark. These premises were completed in 1899, but almost immediately a new printing plant was commissioned in Gravesend, Kent. The integration of publishing and printing on such a scale transformed the capital value of the Harmsworths business. In October 1896 the four constituent enterprises that the Harmsworths had established to date were consolidated into Harmsworth Brothers Ltd., with a headquarters at 24 Tudor Street, London. Harmsworth Brothers Ltd. had a nominal capital of £1 million, divided equally between £1 ordinary shares and £1 preference shares. The issued capital was largely used to purchase the Harmsworths' four existing businesses: Answers Publications Ltd., £511,680; the Periodical Publishing Corporation Ltd., £202,800; the Pandora Publishing Co. Ltd., £151,320; and the Geraldine Press Ltd., £89,200.[95] A further £50,000 preference shares were issued in 1898 to fund the firm's first corporate acquisition; the aforementioned purchase of 75 per cent of the shares of W. B. Horner & Sons Ltd.[96]

MAGAZINES AS BIG BUSINESS

At the time of its formation in 1896 Harmsworth Brothers Ltd. was very much a family concern. As well as Alfred and Harold, the initial list of directors was completed by three more Harmsworth brothers, namely Cecil, Leicester, and

Hildebrand. Cecil briefly took on the editor's column of *Comic Cuts* and for a spell was nominally in charge of *Answers*, but seems to have lacked the aptitude required for a career in journalism. Leicester became the first editor of *Forget-me-Not*, having been responsible for devising the magazine's title, but both he and Cecil soon ceased their active involvement with the firm in order to enter politics as Liberal MPs.[97] A more central figure in the development of the Harmsworths' periodical business was George Augustus Sutton, who as Alfred Harmsworth's personal secretary had been able to gain his trust and favour.[98] In 1901 the directors of Harmsworth Brothers Ltd. applied to the Board of Trade to change the name of the company to Amalgamated Press Ltd., and this was duly sanctioned by the Board in February 1902.[99] At this point Sutton was appointed a director of the firm, together with another Harmsworth brother, St John, and a further non-family member S. J. Summers. This change of name, and the accession of George Sutton to the board of directors, can be seen as marking the start of Alfred's increasing detachment from the periodicals side of his publishing empire.

A few months before consolidating the periodical publishing side of his business into Harmsworth Brothers Ltd., Alfred had made the most momentous decision of his career by launching the *Daily Mail* in May 1896; effectively ushering in the era of popular daily newspapers in Britain. The move into newspapers had begun in 1894 when Alfred and Harold had been persuaded to purchase the *Evening News* by its new co-owner, the journalist Kennedy Jones, for £25,000. Together Jones and the Harmsworths refashioned the paper—placing much more emphasis on the provision of entertainment—improved its distribution, reduced its costs of production, increased its circulation, and brought it into profit. Now Jones, who had already conceived the vision of a halfpenny daily morning newspaper that could be produced in London and then sent by telegraph to provincial cities for local printing, was given the overall responsibility for developing the style and content of the *Daily Mail*.[100] An unprecedented degree of preparation was put into the development of the newspaper, with over 60 dummy versions being produced at an estimated cost of £40,000. When it finally arrived, the *Mail* was less unconventional in its appearance than many had anticipated, retaining the tradition of the *Times* in devoting its front page to advertisements. The approach to presentation fitted with the newspaper's two enticing strap lines: 'A Penny Newspaper for One Halfpenny' and 'The Busy Man's Daily Journal'. In content, however, the *Daily Mail* reflected Alfred's and Kennedy Jones' empathy with the mass consumer's desire for readability. Booming its impending arrival, advertisements for the new paper had emphasized its fresh approach: 'Four leading articles, a page of Parliament, and columns of speeches will NOT be found in the *Daily Mail* on 4 May, a halfpenny'. Rather, the emphasis was on gaining and maintaining the reader's interest. In 1896, and for the first time, the British reading public were to be tickled by a daily morning newspaper.[101]

George Newnes made an effort to steal the Harmsworth's thunder by launching his own halfpenny newspaper, the *Daily Courier*, as a rival to the *Mail*. The failure of this initiative along with that of the expensively produced magazine *The Million*, which utilized colour printing, was a harbinger of more difficult times ahead for Newnes whose firm around this time diversified into the production of books.[102] In 1897 he floated his company on the stock exchange, with a nominal share capital of £1 million, but with *Tit-Bits'* circulation now eclipsed by both *Pearson's Weekly* and *Answers*, Newnes' main bulwark remained his highly popular sixpenny monthly *Strand Magazine*.[103] The success of this had naturally generated a range of imitators. In January 1895 Ward, Lock & Co. had launched the *Windsor Magazine* but this made limited progress.[104] Cassell had expanded its house magazine in an unsuccessful attempt to be a more effective competitor to the *Strand* and Arthur Pearson's company, now capitalized at £400,000, had launched *Pearson's Magazine* in 1896 whose richly illustrated contents brought it some significant success, in both Britain and the United States. During 1898 the Harmsworth Brothers firm utilized their substantial printing capacity to launch its own title in the sixpenny monthly market. In May of that year Harmsworth's Magazines Ltd., was registered with a capital of £20,000 and in July the *Harmsworth Monthly Pictorial Magazine* was brought to market as a direct competitor to the *Strand*, but priced at just threepence. The initial print run of 500,000 was fully subscribed, but the enthusiasm of the public was not mirrored by retailers. W.H. Smith boycotted the magazine and the Harmsworths for once found themselves on the back foot. The second issue of the magazine featured a price of 3½*d*. and the trade press carried rumours that the Harmsworths had reached an agreement with Smith's on the latter's terms.[105] A double Christmas issue was priced at sixpence to test the market, and eventually the firm was forced to conform to the existing sixpenny level.[106] Thus, in Britain, the phenomenal success of mass-produced penny weeklies could not be successfully emulated in the monthly segment through the medium of a threepenny title.

In the space of less than a decade during the 1890s, therefore, the British magazine publishing industry was transformed from a relatively stable area of business enterprise, under the control and management of self-funded family-owned firms, to a modern, capital-intensive industry dominated by increasingly vertically integrated, publicly listed corporations paying substantial dividends to their shareholders. For the leading firms, a strategy of growth in both the number and range of titles they produced became critical to the maintenance of commercial success and, as a consequence, the use of corporate acquisitions took on more and more significance as the industry developed an explicitly oligopolistic character in the early twentieth century. The market for magazines also became clearly segmented, with penny weeklies, halfpenny comics, and sixpenny monthlies becoming the competitive battlegrounds on which, and through which, the leading firms addressed and shaped the reading desires of the British public. At the same time, the companies which had pioneered this publishing revolution diversified their activities into other areas of the printed word. While book publishing had traditionally been a complementary activity to that of periodicals, in the twentieth century the development of the magazine industry became increasingly subjugated to that of newspaper publishing. For the first two-thirds of the new century, the fate of magazines was determined, in large measure, by the decisions made by a new element in Britain's traditional ruling aristocracy: the Fleet Street press lords.

3

From Mass Periodicals to Mass Production

LETTERPRESS GIANTS

During the Edwardian era, both the economic and political influence of the press in Britain increased significantly. George Newnes, Arthur Pearson, and, especially, Alfred and Harold Harmsworth, all expanded their range of business activities from magazines into national daily newspapers with growing circulations. Of these three great publishing houses, however, only that of the Harmsworths was successful in achieving pre-eminence in the field of newspaper proprietorship. Newnes' direct attempt to compete with the Harmsworths' *Daily Mail*, through the launch of his *Daily Courier*, foundered inside four months,[1] while Pearson's *Daily Express* never truly thrived in his lifetime. The power of the *Daily Mail* was underpinned by the Harmsworths' success in building a substantial, vertically integrated organization that made them not simply Britain's leading press barons but also captains of industry. By 1919, the aggregate value of the Harmsworths' publishing-related businesses placed them within the top twenty industrial enterprises across the entire British national economy. This growth was an outcome of a deliberate strategy that Alfred Harmsworth had set out during the earliest days of his career, coupled with Harold Harmsworth's desire for security over key resources. It meant that newspaper and periodical publishing held relatively more significance in economic and business terms in Britain than was the case in the United States, Germany, or France in the early twentieth century.[2]

This modernization process which entailed increases in both the scale and scope of Britain's leading publishing firms, was married to significant developments in the sphere of industrial and employee relations. The concentration of printing into ever-larger units of production helped to make the unionization of the workforce and the implementation of restrictive practices, based on the precise demarcation of tasks, an increasingly significant feature of Britain's printing and publishing industries. Mass production of newspapers and periodicals provided a unionized workforce with growing members, and hence income, while creating a system of industrial organization whose revenue flows could be easily and effectively fractured through industrial action, both actual and threatened. Throughout much of the twentieth century, an uneasy truce existed between the organized groups of specialized print-based workers within the labour force and the publishing enterprises that relied upon their compliance. Although the consumer magazine industry was never as deeply affected by this power struggle as were newspapers, it was nevertheless by no means unaffected by it. The fact that the leading magazine publishers all utilized the dominant letterpress technology for printing their mass circulation periodicals at the beginning of the 1900s meant the writ of the various printing trade unions extended widely across the industry's product range.

BRITAIN'S PRINTING UNIONS

The evolution of the printing trade unions that came to practically dominate the periodical publishing industry for much of the twentieth century had a long gestation period. Although the full picture of trade unionism within Britain's printing industry is exceptionally complex, the principal features can be traced alongside the development of the key technologies employed for the tasks of type compositing, page layout and make-up (origination), and printing.[3] At the outset of the nineteenth century the craft of letterpress (relief) printing was already a practice that dated back 350 years.[4] The process involved foundry-cast lead-alloy moulded type being composed into lines by hand, assembled in a forme, lifted into a wooden press, inked, and transferred onto paper by means of pressure. The main breakthrough in the early years of the nineteenth century had been the replacement of wooden presses with more durable and accurate iron versions, notably the Stanhope Press,[5] but this had little impact on the actual methods of production or on the rate of output. Such hand presses were usually operated by two men, one of whom applied ink to the typeface while a colleague placed and removed the paper and operated the levers of the press itself. By 1850 around 26,000 men in Britain were making their living as compositors and printers, and the typographical societies which had developed by this time negotiated their terms and conditions with each of the individual master printers who owned and operated Britain's many printing shops. Most of these enterprises were extremely small; Alford has estimated that at mid-century around 500 printing firms operated in London alone, by far the majority of which employed three men or less.[6] Throughout the United Kingdom, however, typographical societies were formed in cities and towns to support the interests of this highly fragmented group of print workers.[7]

The origins of the printing industry trade unions can be found in these typographical societies, developed by the journeymen practitioners of the letterpress trade during the early part of the nineteenth century. Control over working practices in the printing trade by this time had shifted away from the traditional system of gild regulation—hitherto overseen by the Stationers' Company—to one in which the journeymen printers themselves began to take responsibility for their working conditions.[8] These men formed alliances to influence wage rates, working hours, and the employment of apprentices. Evidence from both London and Manchester indicates that by 1800 journeymen were engaged in a form of collective negotiation in an effort to promote consistent practices among the group of master printers who provided their employment.[9] In such cases the societies of printers were formed through an alliance of workplace-specific chapels, whose practices were administered under the authority of their most senior member; the Father of the Chapel.[10] By 1817 skilled compositors in London were earning a negotiated wage of £2 8s. per week, and a formal association of printers, the London General Trade Society of Compositors, was established in 1826. The development of these societies meant that printing workers provided a leading example of the early growth in craft-based trade unions in nineteenth-century Britain.

Before 1830 the employment conditions relating to typesetting in the book-based and the newspaper trades were negotiated separately. Following the successful launch of the *Penny Magazine* and its many would-be rivals, however, a sharp rise occurred in the number of London-based compositors working on periodicals. Since these were neither classified as books nor as newspapers, a different arrangement was required to set the wages of this group of workers.[11] To begin with it was simply agreed that the rates of pay of these compositors would relate to the prevailing conditions for either the book or news trade, depending upon whether the content of the publication in question was primarily concerned with news or other matters. However, demarcation difficulties of this kind were resolved in 1834 when the London Union of Compositors was formed and given authority to act on behalf of all interests engaged in the trade of typesetting. Meanwhile, the growing use of steam-driven presses around this time led to the employment, in the leading centres of the industry such as London, of a significant group of non-apprenticed, printing labourers. These workers were not offered membership of the compositors' union and so, in 1839, the London Printing Machine Managers' Trade Society was established and became the first body to support the interests of non-craft-based print employees. This move set in train a long tradition within the British printing industry of union-determined segregation of labour based on the nature of the task performed.[12]

The London Union of Compositors represented a parallel development to that which had been introduced in the north of England following the initiative of the Manchester Typographical Society in 1830 to create a Northern

Union. The new union formalized the chapel-based structure of the earlier societies and took forward a range of objectives. These were designed to regulate hours and wages,[13] control the number of apprentices and their conditions of work, and provide relief against loss of members' income due to strikes or temporary unemployment. Frequent episodes of unemployment were a particular problem among itinerant printers, and during the 1830s this led to the practice of tramping by unemployed journeymen as they sought work outside of their original apprenticeship location. The existence of 'tramps with tickets', which required individual societies to provide relief to newly arrived 'foreigners', was a major factor in encouraging an alliance between individual societies. In the early 1840s a sharp deterioration in economic conditions brought about a sudden rise in unemployment among printers and, as the problem of tramp relief grew acute, a National Typographical Association (NTA) was formed in 1844 with five districts covering the whole of Great Britain and Ireland. A key objective of the new association was to abolish tramp relief and replace it with weekly allowances to the unemployed provided by their own districts, but after a short period of growth the NTA quickly found itself struggling to cope with the financial demands placed on it. The problem of supporting unemployed printers was often exacerbated in situations where workers affiliated to the NTA used strikes as a negotiating tactic, since this frequently led employers to take on additional apprentices and non-affiliated labour. The disintegration of the NTA began in 1848 when the London section of its South East Division seceded and reformed as the London Society of Compositors (LSC), effectively recreating the earlier London-based body. After this the NTA quickly broke apart, and the old Northern Union effectively reconstituted itself as the Provincial Typographical Association (PTA), pledging to fix strict limits on the number of new apprentices each firm could employ.[14] For over one hundred years following this breakdown of the NTA, the LSC (from 1954 the London Typographical Society) and the Manchester-based PTA (from 1877 renamed as the Typographical Association) retained a separate existence until they jointly formed the National Graphical Association (NGA) in 1963.[15]

The skilled function of composition also underwent a further technological transformation during the 1890s with the introduction of Ottmar Mergenthaler's Linotype machine into the composition room of the *New York Tribune* in 1886.[16] This mechanical keyboard-based composition machine set type automatically by filling a mould with molten lead—the 'hot metal' process—and could operate at speeds more than four times those achieved by hand-composition.[17] Typesetting was still the essential task of composition, and the existing craft-based Typographical Association (TA) remained the dominant union in this field. Faced with the introduction of Linotype, the union's strategy was not to oppose the implementation of the new technology, but to secure effective control over these machines.[18] Various developments enabled the mechanization of typesetting to be increased, but the Linotype technology could not automatically surmount the technical difficulty of break-ing print lines and hyphenating words. These decisions had to be made by the machine's operator, thus preventing complete automation and preserving, at least in name, the craft origins of the task.[19]

LINES OF DEMARCATION

The late nineteenth century saw the trade union composition of the printing industry become increasingly complex. This was partly a result of the need for unskilled workers to operate the industrial-scale rotary presses, and partly due to the alternative technologies to that of the letterpress which provided poten-tial solutions to the problem of printing illustrations. In this latter respect, while the replication of black and white text was the great strength of letter-press, the integration of illustrations posed considerable difficulties. The devel-opment of half-tones did provide a method of graphical reproduction directly related to the letterpress technique. In this system, photographic images could be reproduced through the method of relief printing by means of different sized black dots printed on a white background. However, such images could only be printed from negative plates that had to be laboriously prepared from the original.[20] The importance of developing techniques for the printing of illustrations in magazines necessitated even more pronounced labour speciali-zation, and also brought those employed in typesetting alongside those essen-tially concerned with the reproduction of images, thereby creating an issue of union demarcation between letterpress and graphics that was to endure in newspaper and magazine printing into the mid-1980s.[21]

With increasing complexity and specialization emerging as a feature of printing, the late nineteenth century witnessed a number of other printing trade unions evolving in parallel with those of the letterpress typesetters. The earliest of these stemmed from the two alternative techniques for print-ing illustrations that were to become increasingly significant for magazines during the twentieth century, namely, gravure and lithography. Gravure was the technique of engraving (an intaglio printing process) which was used for early forms of magazine illustrations such as woodcuts and became of great importance as the technology of photography matured. During the 1890s the technique of photogravure, in which photographic images were converted into etched printing surfaces, was developed by the Bohemian émigré Karl Klic for the Lancaster-based Rembrandt Intaglio Printing Company. This allowed the commercial reproduction of photographic illustrations, initially in mono-chrome but by 1906 in colour, that were highly suitable for integrating into magazine printing processes that used rotary plates.[22] Lithography, a chemical process of reproduction utilizing a perfectly flat stone-based surface to replace the raised (relief) or etched (intaglio) forms of printing, became much more important for publishing following the development of the offset process in the early years of the twentieth century.[23] Lithography ultimately proved its worth by allowing publishers to flexibly integrate textual matter with illustrations, but for many years the method was unable to match the efficiency of the letterpress for large-scale print runs.[24]

During the 1880s, practitioners of the two techniques developed craft-based trade unions separately to those of the letterpress workers. The first involved lithographic printers, whose work at this point tended to focus on the production of labels, posters, packaging, and such like, rather than published reading matter. This group formed the Amalgamated Society of Lithographic Printers and Auxiliaries of Great Britain and Ireland in 1880. It soon numbered ten branches and after three years had a membership of just over one thousand men.[25] Five years later, a grouping comprised of artists who specialized both in lithographic and intaglio-based forms of illustration set up the Society of Lithographic Artists, Designers and Writers, Copperplate and Wood Engravers. Despite a number of proposals to amalgamate these two closely allied groups of workers, they remained independent for the ensuing one hundred years before they, too, became incorporated into the NGA.[26] With the emergence of lithographic and gravure printing techniques, magazines had at their disposal a variety of reproductive media. More significantly still, as the twentieth century wore on it also began to gradually differentiate the printing technologies employed in magazine printing from those of the newspaper industry, where resistance to technological change proved to be severe.

To these craft-based printing unions, and that of the machine managers, was added in 1889 a new society comprised purely of unskilled industrial printing workers. During this year of widespread trade union advances in Britain,[27] a dispute involving the rate of wages for machine labourers in London led directly to the formation of a trade union to serve the interests of the remaining unorganized workers within the printing industry. In August a strike had been initiated at the house of Spottiswoode, a printing firm with origins that could be traced back to its founding in 1739 by a freeman of the Stationers' Company.[28] The workers who took the action were employed to feed paper into the machines, a task considered sufficiently unskilled to deny them membership of the London Printing Machine Managers' Trade Society. The Spottiswoode employees were soon joined in their demand for a weekly wage of 20 shillings by workers similarly engaged at fourteen other London printing establishments. Under the initiative of the strike committee leader, George Evans, the momentum generated by the strike was used to form a society under the banner of the Printers' Labourers' Union (PLU).[29] Emulating the earlier craft unions' use of a system of workplace-based chapels, over the course of the next two months the membership grew in number to 500 workers and, at those houses where solidarity was achieved, no man was allowed to work as a printer's labourer without belonging to the union, taking forward the closed-shop tradition within the industry.[30] The PLU increased its influence during the 1890s as the rotary press became established as the core printing technology in both newspaper and magazine publishing activities. Individual chapels were set up at both *Tit-Bits* and the *Strand Magazine*, as well as at the printing facilities of the Amalgamated Press and other large magazine publishing houses.[31]

In response to these developments both the employers and the creative journalists began to establish associations to pursue their own interests. For the employers, the Provincial Newspaper Society had been in operation as a pressure group for much of the nineteenth century, but this organization displayed a marked reluctance to engage in negotiations with the trade societies. An important development in this respect was the formation of an employers' Linotype Users' Association, which in 1896 concluded the first national agreement on behalf of Britain's printing firms.[32] In 1906 the Newspaper Proprietors' Association (NPA) was constituted, and the following year the NPA negotiated a wage agreement with the successor to the PLU, the National Society of Operative Printers' Assistants (NATSOPA).[33] In 1907 the National Union of Journalists (NUJ) was formed following the groundwork of a Manchester-based journalist, W. N. Watts, adding a further layer to the group of printing employees' trade unions.[34] Over time the various printing trade unions affiliated themselves into a coordinating body for printing industry employees, the Printing and Kindred Trades Federation (PKTF) which after 1901 took the lead in developing nationally agreed working conditions in the industry.[35] By the end of the first decade of the twentieth century, therefore, a pattern of industrial relations based upon collective bargaining between employers' groups and trade unions, featuring closed shops and strictly defined distinctions between the varying printing tasks, had become an established feature of Britain's newspaper and magazine publishing industry. After the First World War the various regional associations of master printers were formed into a national federation. This facilitated the creation in 1919 of the Printing Trades' Joint Industrial Council, comprised of 64 members, 32 representatives of the master printers, and 32 from the trade unions.[36]

NEWSPRINT EMPIRES

During the first half of the twentieth century, the development of a common set of industrial relations practices across the newspaper and magazine industries was most pronounced where technological convergence supported large-scale methods of machine-based production, utilizing the newly electric-powered web-fed printing presses. The development of high-speed printing technology was led by the American firm of Richard Hoe, and during the 1890s this company established production facilities in London to build its presses in the heart of Britain's booming publishing industry. In 1898 Harmsworth Brothers had installed two of Hoe's 'Century' magazine and book web presses, which printed sixteen-page folded sections of a magazine at a time, in order to undertake the printing of their new eponymous monthly.[37] These machines allowed substantial increases in productivity by enabling levels of output to be achieved on individual presses that would previously have required anywhere between six and twelve rotary or flat-bed machines, along with ten separate folders. Thus output per square foot of floor space could be increased up to eightfold, and substantial savings achieved in unit labour costs. By the end of the nineteenth century, the 600,000 copies of *Tit-Bits* printed each week at Newnes' plant were being produced on a single Hoe machine, cut and stitched into a complete magazine with the cover included, at the rate of 48,000 per hour.[38]

Alfred Harmsworth had invested heavily in the new printing technology as he drove the *Daily Mail*'s circulation figures beyond the half million mark.[39] In his footsteps at the start of the twentieth century followed one of his chief rivals in the market for popular magazines, Arthur Pearson. Within the space of a few years in the 1890s, the phenomenal success of *Pearson's Weekly* magazine had enabled him to create a substantial business enterprise. Like Harmsworth, Pearson had extended backwards from publishing into printing, and this allowed the company to earn additional revenue from producing magazines on behalf of other firms. Thus as well as publishing his own successful sixpenny monthly, Pearson took on a substantial contract for the production of the *Royal Magazine*, printing one million copies of the first issue.[40] By this point, however, Pearson's own focus of attention had begun to move away from magazines. In 1899 he briefly teamed up with Newnes on the board of the British Mutoscope and Biograph Company, the leading British film company of the period, but its idea of providing illustrated journalism through motion picture devices for the home failed to provide a remunerative form of investment.[41] Returning to the printed medium, Pearson now followed Harmsworth into the world of newspaper publishing.

Pearson's original stimulus to publish his own daily morning newspaper seems to have been inspired by the possibility of featuring a good deal of news drawn from America, using the firm's contacts in the United States, but his initial explorations quickly established that the cost of this would be prohibitive.[42] Instead, when his halfpenny *Daily Express* was launched on 24 April 1900 it became the first British national daily newspaper to follow the American tradition of putting news on the front page. This was a decision that cost Pearson dearly, since the *Daily Mail*'s front page adverts brought in massive revenues.[43] Partly as a consequence of this, the *Daily Express* struggled to be a paying concern for much of its early existence.[44] Following the launch of his morning newspaper, Pearson adopted a highly acquisitive approach to the development of his publishing business. The same month that the *Express* was laid before the public Pearson bought the *Morning Herald*, which five months later he merged with his new daily. In 1903 the *St James's Gazette*, an evening paper, was acquired and the following year he purchased both the *Standard* and *Evening Standard* from James Johnstone, quickly merging his two evening titles and floating shares in both of the *Standard*s in 1908.[45] The purchase of the *Standard* was undertaken on behalf of a political syndicate centred on Joseph Chamberlain and was designed to provide a platform for the Tariff Reform League's campaign of Empire-led protection, a cause then taken up by the *Daily Express* as well. This latter decision had the effect of undermining the political neutrality Pearson had claimed for the *Express* at the time of its launch.[46]

In addition to this group of national daily papers, Pearson also built a provincial publishing empire that included newspapers in Birmingham, Newcastle, and Leicester. In Newcastle the Morning Mail Company was bought in 1901 and another newspaper, the *North Mail*, was founded there the same year. By 1905 he had also acquired the Midland Express Company (which published the *Midland Express*), the *Birmingham Daily Gazette*, and the *Leicester Evening News*.[47] However, this attempt to develop a network of provincial daily newspapers eventually foundered on the persistent unprofitability of many of the titles.[48] Moreover, in pursuing these activities and devoting much of his time between 1903 and 1905 to the cause of tariff reform, Pearson's attention became diverted away from the *Daily Express*. By 1904 he had delegated the management of his principal news publication to others, placing its editorial direction into the hands of American-born Ralph D. Blumenfeld.[49] Pearson's own position within the newspaper industry began to be seriously undermined in 1908 when his bid to take control of the *Times* was thwarted by Alfred Harmsworth's clever piece of subterfuge,[50] and from this point his publishing empire rapidly began to disintegrate. In 1910, aware that he was gradually losing his eyesight, Pearson sold the morning *Standard* and *Evening Standard* to Tory MP Davison Dalziel and Sir Alexander Henderson,[51] and in 1911 he turned the *Daily Express* into a public company, with Blumenfeld as general manager as well as editor.[52] The *Express* limped on under Blumenfeld, but was ultimately provided with the finance required to continue successfully through its acquisition by Max Aitken in 1916.[53] The *Standard* perished the same year that the *Express* was saved, but its evening counterpart was taken over at this time by the Manchester-based firm of Edward Hulton.[54]

Pearson also sold off his provincial newspapers after 1910 but for a period after this he maintained control of the magazine business, continuing in his role as chairman of C. Arthur Pearson Ltd. By 1913, however, Pearson had lost his sight completely and from now until his death in 1921 he channelled the bulk of his energies into charitable work for the assistance of other blind people. At this point he offered the ownership of his magazines to George Riddell, best known as the proprietor of the populist Sunday newspaper, the *News of the World*.[55] As Pearson's star faded, that of George Riddell moved into the ascendancy. Riddell had developed his interests in the press when acting in his capacity as solicitor on behalf of the *Western Mail*, a Cardiff-based newspaper owned by Lascelles Carr. In 1891, with Riddell handling the legal aspects of the transaction, Carr bought control of the *News of the World*, and installed his cousin Emsley Carr as editor.[56] Over the course of the next ten years Riddell built up his shareholding in Carr's business, and by 1903 had assumed the role of managing director of the *News of the World*.[57] The extension of Riddell's activities into magazine publishing began in 1910 when he acquired control of George Newnes' company, following the death of its founder earlier that year. Newnes' business career had faltered badly in the twentieth century. A book publishing department set up in 1895 had embarked on a number of loss-making projects, a venture into Sunday newspapers via the acquisition of the *Weekly Dispatch* had been a financial disaster, and Newnes' other investments, outside of publishing, had also served to diminish his fortune. In addition, he had developed a reliance on alcohol. His son Frank had joined the board of George Newnes Ltd. in 1897 but, following his father's death, he had only been able to continue as a director of his family concern by virtue of a personal loan guaranteed by Leicester Harmsworth.[58]

George Riddell, despite having no formal background in the world of publishing, proved to be a far more astute businessman than either Newnes or Pearson, as well as a highly industrious one.[59] He made a great success of the *News of the World*,[60] and having acquired control of George Newnes' business in 1910 he clearly appreciated the potential benefits to be gained through consolidation. He rapidly brought other titles under his control, including the literary *John O'London's Weekly* magazine and the firm of Country Life Ltd., whose *Country Life* magazine title had been spun off as joint venture by Newnes and its original proprietor Edward Hudson in 1905.[61] Soon after gaining control of Pearson's enterprise Riddell sought to coordinate this firm's activities with those of Newnes'. At the 1915 AGM of C. Arthur Pearson Ltd., still in fact presided over by Pearson himself but now effectively under Riddell's control, the chairman alluded to 'the friendly business relations which had been established with the great publishing house of George Newnes, Ltd.' These friendly relations were used by Riddell to arrange the joint acquisition by the two firms of the old established publishing business of Messrs. Leach in 1914.[62] This firm published a wide range of children's and ladies' fashion papers and helped to provide the emergent Newnes-Pearson Group with a portfolio of magazine titles that made it the leading rival to Harmsworth's Amalgamated Press by the time of the First World War.[63]

AMALGAMATED PRESS

Around the turn of the twentieth century the magazine publishing interests of the Harmsworths had grown rapidly. Two years after the incorporation of Harmsworth's Brothers Ltd. in 1896, the various publishing activities
undertaken by the firm were brought together in a purpose-built edifice in
Carmelite Street on the Thames Embankment. Housed in the sumptuous luxury of Carmelite House's 'Room One', and with a bust of Napoleon reputedly
displayed above one of the room's two mahogany-framed fireplaces, Alfred
Harmsworth presided over this new bastion in Britain's publishing industry.
To his staff, their leader's form of address now shifted from 'Mr Alfred' to the
Hearst-inspired 'Chief'.[64] Ensconced nearby were his private secretary, George
Sutton, and Alfred's ever-watchful sibling Harold. The dress code for the entire
enterprise was formal and Alfred was now the model of a twentieth-century
newspaper proprietor. Within seven years of the firm's move into Carmelite
House, in April 1905, the Harmsworths created a new public company called
Associated Newspapers with a fully paid up capital of £1.6 million, designed
purely as a newspaper operation. Its creation can be taken to mark, as Ferris
has observed, the formal beginning of the modern British newspaper industry.[65] Harmsworth's existing newspapers, the *Daily Mail* and *Evening News*, by
now had been joined by the *Weekly Dispatch*, bought from a declining George
Newnes in 1903, and the *Daily Mirror*. The *Mirror*, launched in 1903 and
designed by Alfred as a newspaper to be produced by women for an audience of well-bred ladies, had flopped and its circulation had dropped to 24,000
within the first three months. It was saved by its reinvention as an illustrated
newspaper, filled with half-tone photographs printed by high-speed rotary
presses under the guiding hand of technician Arkas Sapt.[66] Developed independently of the Associated Newspapers group, the *Daily Mirror* was soon a
valuable property in its own right, its success acting to undermine the popularity of traditional Victorian illustrated magazines, promoting instead the
development of more gossipy upper-class alternatives such as the *Sketch*, the
Tatler, and the *Bystander*.[67] And while a daily newspaper aimed at women
had failed to prove its worth, weekly magazines aimed at that audience would
prove far more successful.

Following the creation of Associated Newspapers, the periodical publishing side of the Harmsworth's business was developed as an independent entity under the auspices of the Amalgamated Press. Their focus on the
female market had already been evident in the 1890s through the successful
publication of magazines such as *Forget-Me-Not* and *Home Chat*. The wom-
en's penny weekly formula was further developed in 1903 with the launch
of *Woman's World*. This essentially fiction-based publication also featured
domestic matters such as cookery, housework, and handiwork, along with
a problem page and another devoted to religion. Despite its unchallenging

editorial matter and its staid appearance, with poor quality paper allowing very limited opportunities for illustrations, the new publication was a tremendous success in terms of circulation figures, and by the outbreak of the First World War it had become the top-selling women's paper in Britain.[68] Meanwhile, *Home Chat* had made progress since its launch in 1895, thanks largely to the policy of supplying its readers with free dress-making patterns. In 1908 the management of Amalgamated Press deployed one of its leading editors, Leslie Clark, to further develop this aspect of women's interest.[69] Clark began by reviving a languishing title, *Fashions For All*, and from this he created a group of similar but targeted publications which included *Home Fashions*, *Children's Dress*, *Mabs Fashions*, and the *'Best Way'* series.[70] These types of publication, which offered practical support as well as a measure of easy reading to an emerging audience of working women, drew no small measure of caustic reaction among other elements of the press for pandering to a readership of 'waitresses, typists and shop-girls', but they undoubtedly provided a welcome source of diversion to the weekly routine for this growing segment of the British workforce.[71] As the firm experimented further with this audience, so it began to develop a sense of what appealed to a more general readership of women, and in particular the attraction of cost-conscious fashion items. In November 1911 Amalgamated Press brought onto the market its most enduring women's journal: *Woman's Weekly*. At the outset this magazine targeted the female interest in clothing, stating boldly that the magazine's fashions, 'ignoring the extremes of taste, consisted of the ordinary garments which will be worn by the average woman, supplemented by a complete wardrobe of patterns for home dressmaking which readers could collect over several months'.[72] With the established *Woman's World* now complemented by the successful launch of *Woman's Weekly*, Amalgamated Press entered the second decade of the twentieth century well positioned to capture a mass female readership that would provide the mainstay of Britain's popular magazine market for decades to come.

Whilst the Harmsworths' newspaper operations dominated the scene in Carmelite House, the Amalgamated Press had developed its magazine and other periodicals in a piecemeal way, with various branches of the firm located in outlying offices. Some publications, for example, had shared their accommodation with the *Daily Mirror*, whose operations were conducted in Bouverie Street. In 1912 a new headquarters was constructed for the firm's magazine business in London's Farringdon Street. The Fleetway House, a purpose-built and attractive building, provided a homely setting for the 800 staff engaged in the production of the firm's magazines and part-works.[73] Among the numerous editorial teams was Arthur Mee, previously employed by Newnes on *Tit-Bits*, who had been invited to join the staff of the *Daily Mail* by Alfred Harmsworth in 1898. Mee, together with his long-time collaborator John Hammerton, proved to be a stalwart of the Amalgamated Press, developing a collection of weekly and fortnightly part-works aimed mainly at children, beginning with the 48-part *Self Educator* in 1906.[74] Along with the mainly weekly magazines, these sixpenny (later sevenpenny) part-works were an important early source of income for Amalgamated Press, who by the outbreak of the First World War had issued a total of twenty different series.[75] These included a variety of self-educators and encyclopaedia—the latter constituting a major fad in the early twentieth century—as well as the hugely successful and lavishly illustrated account of the Boer War, *With the Flag to Pretoria*. Although the demand for these serials inevitably fell away during their publishing life-cycle, a rolling programme of different topics could be guaranteed to keep the firm's presses sufficiently busy to make the exercise pay a handsome dividend. Reflecting on the development of this market segment, John Hammerton later observed that, 'Few of the book publishers in London had then, or have now [1932], any notion of the immense circulations obtained by the Harmsworth organization for fortnightly part publications, issued in pre-war days at 7*d*. apiece. The sales, by comparison with any to which they were accustomed, were almost incredible.'[76]

Alfred Harmsworth's preoccupation with his newspapers, meanwhile, meant that the Amalgamated Press began to assume an increasing degree of independence in its decision-making. By 1909 George Sutton clearly felt able to oppose some of his Chief's more extreme instructions, such as the extraordinary demand to reduce the vulgarity of *Comic Cuts* which Alfred had directed at one of his managing editors, George Cantle, via Sutton's office.[77] Nevertheless, it seems reasonable to infer that Alfred maintained ultimate strategic control and that it was his hand which was responsible for the decision in 1912 to dismiss one of the firm's most senior managing editors from his post as controller of a group of 38 of Amalgamated Press periodicals. The firm's corporate records show that the severance cost to the company of this decision comprised a £52,500 cash payment along with 15,000 shares, which certainly made the action a significant one in financial terms.[78] Elsewhere, Harold's restraining influence continued to impact. Ferris notes that when anyone at the Amalgamated Press wanted to spend more on a magazine Harold would resist, arguing in his own idiosyncratic way that it was 'time they returned to the "fried fish and stewed eels" of the business'.[79]

Harold also appears to have been the main influence behind the decision in 1905 to secure the firm's own pulp and paper mills in Newfoundland; a decision based, according to his nephew Cecil King, on 'an irrational fear that that the supply of wood pulp for newsprint would run out'.[80] The Newfoundland investment was undertaken specifically with the need for newsprint supplies in mind, since the paper requirements for the magazines published by Amalgamated Press were much more varied in nature. These latter needs were provided for directly in 1909 by the formation of the Imperial Paper Mills Ltd., based in Gravesend, Kent, where the firm had earlier located its main periodical printing facility. Again the initiative to build the Gravesend plant stemmed from the cautious Harold, but the control of the enterprise was transferred to Arthur E. Linforth, an expert in the field of paper manufacturing who was thereby elevated to the position of director. After the First World War it was Linforth, in his role as chairman of Imperial Paper Mills, who oversaw on behalf of Amalgamated Press the acquisition of two-thirds of the Gulf Pulp and Paper Company of Clark City in Canada. This organization provided the firm not with paper, as the Newfoundland plant had done, but with mechanical pulp which could be manufactured at Gravesend into the different types and grades of paper that an increasingly sophisticated range of magazines demanded.[81] Given that the firm had also been manufacturing its own ink since 1899, by the early 1920s Amalgamated Press had assumed the form of a fully vertically integrated business, deriving profits from the entire process of the value chain from wood pulp to published journal. When the company was reconstructed, shortly before Alfred Harmsworth's death in 1922, its nominal share capital was valued at £3.8 million.

HARMSWORTH'S RIVALS

The Harmsworth's business strategy of building a rolling portfolio of mass circulation magazines, which seems to have provided the basis of Alfred's 'Schemo Magnifico', came with certain inherent limitations in terms of the nature of the periodicals that the firm produced. The approach certainly sat more easily in terms of weekly penny magazines than with the higher quality monthly offerings, as did Harold's obsession with the use of low-cost paper as much as possible. Whilst Alfred's strategy required the regular launch of new titles, its practical execution does seem to have significantly stifled the development of truly novel ideas and editorial adventure. As one of the leading editors of Amalgamated Press, John Hammerton, noted, the firm offered financial incentives to its editorial staff based on the formula of an extra shilling per week on their basic pay for every additional 1,000 copies of a penny magazine sold. Hammerton's point gave substance to his argument that the emphasis at Amalgamated Press was placed firmly on building large circulations.[82] Evidence that the desire to achieve high circulations was promoted by the introduction of hierarchical management at Amalgamated Press can be gathered from the testimony of Newman Flower, another Harmsworth employee, who found the degree of centralized control at the firm oppressive: 'The Harmsworth periodicals were so organized that some five chief editors controlled the papers and left little room for initiative or individual development among the junior members of the staff'.[83] Flower found more opportunities to express his creativity when, in 1905, he moved to the publishing house of Cassell & Co.,[84] but the Harmsworth's business strategy did not disappoint the shareholders of the Amalgamated Press.[85]

At the time Flower joined Cassell's that firm had experienced a period of stagnation, with poor financial returns and little progress in terms of successful new products. Flower's appointment was a sign of a revival of fortune for the long-established publishing house. Despite working with a minuscule budget, Flower was able revamp the firm's *Penny Magazine* along lines that had been successfully developed by the Harmsworths, switching the production process to the more cost-efficient newsprint and thereby allowing for an increase in the number of pages from 40 to 64. In 1907 he successfully launched a new magazine, the *Story-Teller*, on a total budget of £1,600 at a time when the Amalgamated Press was launching new magazines with an expenditure on each of £20,000 for publicity alone. Flower's efforts were supported by a new general manager, Arthur Spurgeon, who in 1905 had taken over the managerial reins from the hidebound Wemyss Reid. Under Spurgeon's direction Cassell's underwent a period of rapid modernization. He appointed a new advertising manager, Thomas Young, who remodelled the company's advertising department, and he also oversaw significant investments in the firm's printing capacity, which included the introduction of electrical power to replace the now obsolete steam-driven machinery. The revival of Cassell's magazine portfolio under Flower's creative leadership was further consolidated by the launch of the *New Magazine* in 1909. In turn, these developments in periodicals allowed Cassell's to restore its fortunes as a book publisher. The same year as the *New Magazine* was taken to market the organization established a subsidiary concern, the Waverley Book Company, under the management of Andrew Bain Irvine. This new enterprise provided a subscription book service and offered its customers an innovative inspection copy service which proved to be highly successful.[86] Thus Cassell's entered the second decade of the twentieth century as a revived competitor to Newnes/Pearson and Harmsworth.

Outside of London, the early twentieth century brought two significant competitors to the new industry leaders. These were the firms of D. C. Thomson in Dundee and the Manchester publisher Hulton Press. In both cases, these companies combined substantial newspaper publishing activities with a successful magazine title. The origins of the Dundee-based enterprise had been the firm of W. and D. C. Thomson which had been set up in 1886 by David Couper Thomson's father, William, to manage a group of Dundee newspapers that he had acquired as a sideline to his core shipping business.[87] Thomson's firm first published its *My Weekly* magazine in 1910, and by aiming the journal primarily at the working women of the Dundee jute mills Thomson effectively created a Scottish equivalent to Harmsworth's *Woman's World*. A second newspaper business in Dundee, that of John Leng & Co., had begun publishing a magazine entitled the *People's Journal* in 1858 and had launched a popular counterpart to this in 1859 called the *People's Friend*.[88] The *Friend* had established a tradition of Scottish working-class reading matter which Thomson's female-oriented *My Weekly* further developed.[89] Leng's business built its own paper mill in Aberdeenshire as it consolidated on the success of its various publications, but it was Thomson's firm that most effectively used its weekly magazine to widen its market into England by opening an office in Manchester in 1913.[90] The two firms merged in 1926 under the Thomson banner, but retained a strong degree of operational independence until well beyond the Second World War.[91]

The Manchester-based publishing empire that Edward (Ned) Hulton developed during the final quarter of the nineteenth century was founded on the growing demand among the working class for sports news, beginning with the *Manchester Sporting Chronicle* in the early 1870s. By 1900 Hulton's *Athletic News* had become England's leading periodical for reporting stories relating to the increasingly popular spectator sport of professional association football.[92] To support the growth of his business, Hulton developed his operations in Manchester via the creation of a huge printing facility located at Withy Grove. For many years this investment was claimed to be the largest newspaper plant in the world and by 1901 it was reported to be employing a staff of no fewer than 600 hands.[93] During the 1890s control of the business passed into the hands of Ned Hulton's son, Edward Hulton.[94] Under his direction a number of significant new initiatives were pursued, most notably the *Manchester Evening Chronicle* (1897) and the *Daily Dispatch* (1900). Rivalry with the Harmsworths was made manifest, however, by Hulton's decision to start a national illustrated newspaper in competition with the *Daily Mirror*. The profusely illustrated *Daily Sketch* was launched in 1909 from the firm's presses in Manchester, but was quickly moved to London when Hulton realized that he could not compete on an equal footing without a base in Fleet Street. Once a substantial printing operation had been established, just off Fleet Street in Shoe Lane, it was a logical extension to supplement the *Sketch* with an illustrated Sunday newspaper. In 1915 Hulton brought to market the *Illustrated Sunday Herald*, but when word of its impending publication came to the attention of Harold Harmsworth he pre-empted the Manchester man by launching at very short notice the *Sunday Pictorial*. The decision badly undermined Hulton's initiative, causing him to hold a bitter resentment towards Harold Harmsworth for the rest of his life.[95]

LORD NORTHCLIFFE'S LEGACY

By the end of the First World War, the principal characteristics of the consumer magazine industry as it would operate in Britain over the course of the next fifty years or so had effectively been set. A handful of large firms who were led, and in some respects typified by the Amalgamated Press, produced the bulk of the magazines that were read by the British population at large. These firms used high volume, extremely efficient methods of printing to build high circulations and maintain prices at a level low enough to act as an effective barrier to most potential new entrants. Numerous, well-publicized new titles were launched by these firms and, despite the rise in firm concentration, the total number of magazine titles in circulation continued to rise until after the outbreak of the First World War.[96] Weekly magazines dominated the market and advertising, although growing in significance, remained less important than cover price revenues in determining the leading firms' business strategy at this time.[97] In overall terms, the material quality of the leading magazines could be said to have compared unfavourably with many of those produced in the nineteenth century, for the key areas of increased productivity in letter-press technology had been in raising the speed and overall quantity of magazine printing rather than enhancing the appearance of the finished product. In editorial content, too, it can be argued that these mass-produced weekly periodicals exhibited a mechanical monotony. The Americans denigrated such popular British magazines with the pejorative term 'pulps'.

The most significant, and enduring, feature of the industry was that the publishing firms who dominated magazine production were also, for the most part, those which produced Britain's leading popular national newspapers. The prime implication of this overlap was that the working practices which ruled within the newspaper industry, and particularly in Fleet Street, also held sway across large areas of magazine production. After the end of the First World War, a strong degree of rapprochement developed between the trade union organized workforces and the leading newspaper proprietors. The General Strike certainly tested this relationship, but only in far-away Dundee, where D. C. Thomson banned its workforce from trade union membership after 1926, did the state of harmonious affairs seriously experience a prolonged fracture.[98] When Alfred Harmsworth died in 1922, sick and virtually insane, he was lauded by George Isaacs, the general secretary of NATSOPA and a future Labour MP, for his sympathetic attention to the working conditions of those in his employ.[99] Accommodating trade unions was clearly a strategy that made sense, when even brief stoppages could seriously damage a firm's earnings. Trade union influence continued to grow apace in the years before and after the Second World War.

Promoting a contented labour force allowed the press owners to concentrate on building their political profile, raising their national status accordingly. Alfred Harmsworth had been made a baronet in 1905, assuming the title of Lord Northcliffe, and his brother Harold, subsequently honoured in equal measure, acquired the title of Lord Rothermere in 1914. The politically active Max Aitken rose to become Lord Beaverbrook shortly after acquiring the *Daily Express* in 1916. After the war, such ennoblements became a common feature of the industry. George Riddell, saviour of the businesses of both Newnes and Pearson, became Lord Riddell in 1918 and Julius Elias, who between the wars built a publishing empire on behalf of Odhams Press, gained the title Lord Southwood in 1937. Between these two dates the Berry brothers, William and Gomer, moved into Fleet Street, purchased among other properties the Amalgamated Press, and emerged as Lords Camrose and Kemsley respectively. Ownership of the printed word provided its controllers with power and influence, and by 1919 the Harmsworths' various publishing and ancillary activities constituted Britain's fifteenth largest publicly owned manufacturing enterprise.[100]

4

The Dominant Female

A characteristic feature of the first half of the twentieth century was the emergence of the media in Britain as big business. A process of growth and concentration in Britain's periodical publishing industry between the wars is well illustrated by the pattern of change that occurred in the most dynamic sector of the trade: daily newspapers. Of the national morning dailies, in 1920 only two titles were selling more than one million copies; by 1930 there were five; and by 1939 two at or above two million (*Daily Express* and *Daily Herald*) and three at over one million. Set against this growth in sales volume was a process of concentration that witnessed a decline in the number of national morning titles from twelve in 1921 to nine in 1947. Even more pronounced was a shift from local to national newspapers, with the number of provincial morning papers falling from 41 in 1921 to 28 in 1937.[1]

To a significant extent, the expansion of Fleet Street's popular daily newspaper industry between the wars overshadowed developments in the magazine business. Northcliffe's failure to sustain a newspaper for women suggested that the popular daily newspapers, although widely read by both sexes, held slightly more appeal to men who were attracted by the entertaining blend of easily digested news and sports coverage.[2] There is a dearth of newspaper circulation data before the 1930s, but surveys undertaken for the period 1933–6 by the London Press Exchange and the Incorporated Society of British Advertisers indicated that the readership of the popular newspapers tended to be weighted towards men in the proportion of 11:9. The London evening newspapers were reported to have a predominantly masculine readership and it was also noted that men were more in the habit of reading a second newspaper than women.[3]

The inter-war years in Britain were thus characterized by a boom in the sales of illustrated daily newspapers and, as a counterpart in many respects, of a large variety of women's weekly and monthly magazines. By the 1930s the leading examples of these latter periodicals were being produced using the high-speed photogravure process, providing a product that was clearly distinct from its conventional, staid letterpress rivals. The firm that most effectively exploited the growing popularity of national daily (and Sunday) newspapers, together with the advances in the technology of printing of illustrations for low-prices weekly magazines was the Long Acre-based firm Odhams Press. Although Odhams had been established as a printing firm since the mid-1800s, its flowering as a major competitor to the likes of Amalgamed Press and Newnes came much later, and owed a great deal to the success of one of Britain's most notorious magazines: *John Bull*.

THE EMERGENCE OF ODHAMS PRESS

Like *Tit-Bits* and *Answers*, the popular newspapers of the early twentieth century were products of the new journalism school, which both informed and entertained their readers, but they did not exhibit the same trend towards muckraking as the so-called 'Yellow Press' in the United States.[4] This form of sensationalist and combative journalism, which in America was directed particularly against large monopolizing corporations such as Standard Oil, was only briefly emulated by the *Daily Mail* in their unsuccessful campaign against the 'Soap Trust' (i.e. Lever Brothers) in 1906.[5] The muckraking trend in America had been particularly pronounced among the mass circulation magazines such as *McClure's* and *Collier's*.[6] In Britain, during the period before 1914, only one periodical among the best selling magazines stood out as being comparable to the American-style muckrakers: this was the highly successful weekly *John Bull*.

John Bull was edited by, and served as a mouthpiece for, its proprietor Horatio Bottomley. Elected to Parliament as a 'nominal Liberal' MP in 1906, Bottomley created *John Bull* as a weekly magazine from the remnants of his failed evening newspaper, the *Sun*. Bottomley had purchased the ailing *Sun* in 1902 and had attempted to revive its fortunes by embracing a sensationalist editorial approach, more akin to the style of the popular Sunday newspapers. Although the circulation of the *Sun* rose as a result of its new orientation, it never became a profitable concern and was sold off in 1904. However, various features of the *Sun* were revived by Bottomley when *John Bull* was launched in May 1906. The most notable of these was the editor's muckraking weekly column which had carried the title 'The World, the Flesh and the Devil'. While Bottomley himself was addicted to that most exclusive of products, French champagne, he nevertheless purported to use *John Bull* to support the interests of the small man against big business. In truth, Bottomley more often than not exploited their gullibility in matters financial.[7] His career featured numerous swindles, for one of which he was eventually sentenced to seven years in jail, but in the early 1900s he used his publications to cultivate a successful public profile and this, together with the notorious contents of *John Bull*, ensured the magazine's widespread popularity. By the outbreak of the First World War he was extravagantly claiming that his journal sold in excess of a million copies weekly.[8]

For the magazine's publisher, the printing concern headed by W. B. J. Odhams, Bottomley's magazine was a distinctly mixed blessing. The Odhams firm had been founded in 1847 as a partnership between William Odhams and William Biggar, both of whom had begun their careers in publishing during the 1830s as compositors on the London daily newspaper the *Morning Post*. William Odhams had founded his printing business on the strength of a contract he had obtained to produce a sixpenny ecclesiastical paper called the *Guardian* which by the 1860s was selling around 4,000 copies per week. The business made slow but steady progress and in 1892 it passed from father to son, by which time the company was printing a further three titles. On taking up the reins William J. B. Odhams set himself the goal of printing 'more and more newspapers till we should become the largest business of the kind, either in London or elsewhere'.[9]

Odhams' first step in achieving his espoused objective was to engineer an expansion of the firm's printing capacity. From the original base in Burleigh Street, the firm acquired its second premises in Floral Street, Covent Garden, and in June 1894 this new facility was incorporated as Odhams Brothers Ltd., an independent business with an authorized capital value of £7,000.[10] Shortly after establishing this enterprise, the new company took on a 21-year-old clerk named Julius Elias, with whom W. B. J. Odhams quickly formed a close and productive working relationship. Within a year Elias was appointed as manager of the new business and he immediately began to develop further printing opportunities for the firm, serving the growing number of magazine publishers. Prior to Elias' appointment, Odhams had focused solely on the business of printing, but one of the new man's first acts had been to persuade the nearby Hotel Cecil to launch a house paper called *Table Talk* which Odhams would publish on its behalf. According to W. B. J. Odhams' own account of the company's early history, this provided the firm with an opportunity to learn 'something about artistic lay-out and good half-tone printing' the mastery of which were critical for engaging in magazine publishing.[11] The impact of Elias on the firm's fortunes was dramatic, and in 1898 the two enterprises were consolidated into the newly incorporated Odhams Ltd., boasting a share value of £50,000. The dynamic young manager was by now one of the new firm's directors.[12]

Around the time of the launch of Odhams Ltd., the firm struck up a working relationship with the rival printing house of Southwood, Smith & Co. Although the two firms remained largely independent operations in terms of the clients they served, Elias took over the general management of both. As Odhams continued to receive more printing orders, informal collaborative arrangements were made with other printing firms around the area of Covent

Garden. The continuing growth of Odhams' workload made further expansion of the company's premises a pressing issue. In 1905 the company was able to secure a substantial building in Long Acre, and from this base it developed into a leading enterprise in the world of periodical publishing.[13] An adjacent site was acquired a short while after, into which the printing assets of the Fleet Street publishing firm of E. J. Brett were transferred. Brett's 'penny dreadful' style of publishing had become outdated and was marginalized during the 1890s by Harmsworth's new halfpenny comic strips. It seems that Alfred Harmsworth had offered to purchase Brett's business on generous terms, but his advances had been rebuffed by the company's board of directors. This left the way open for Odhams to become a major creditor of the business when it was reconstructed in 1907, before its ultimate collapse and liquidation in 1909 placed its assets in Odhams' hands.[14] With the Brett enterprise absorbed into the firm's operations, the planned expansion of Odhams' production capacity was now well in train.

Soon after the move into Long Acre, Elias agreed to assume the task of printing *John Bull*. This was undertaken initially on a commission basis but, once Bottomley's marked reluctance to settle his printing bills became apparent, Odhams took over as both the magazine's publishers and its advertising managers, effectively assuming control of the business side of the operation. In many respects the decision to publish *John Bull* provided Odhams with the platform for its ultimate commercial success, but it was a role that remained fraught with difficulties owing to the magazine's contentious, and frequently libellous, editorial content. Providing his own legal counsel, Bottomley thwarted efforts to bring the magazine down through court actions, and during the early years of the First World War he was able to use his position as MP and magazine proprietor to exert a significant influence in the public sphere. This was done partly to promote the interests of the Lloyd George camp, but more pointedly to secure Bottomley's own financial gain. *John Bull* promoted its editor's various money-making ploys; most notoriously the post-war Victory Bond Club scheme which was ultimately to bring about Bottomley's financial ruin.[15]

By 1919, despite the magazine's circulation pushing towards two million copies, Bottomley's spendthrift tendencies had placed him in financial difficulty and he agreed with Odhams' management a scheme of restructuring. In 1920 Odhams Press Ltd. was formed with an authorized capital of £1.5 million and this company absorbed both the existing Odhams Ltd. and Bottomley's property John Bull Ltd.[16] Bottomley's responsibilities for *John Bull* were now limited to those of a salaried editor. The following year, as his reputation became still more sullied through the exposure in court of his financial swindles, the Odhams' board took the decision to sack their controversial editor. By ejecting Bottomley from his own magazine, the company placed its own position in jeopardy and by the time, twelve months later, he was convicted of fraud and his reputation ruined, the impact on the sales of *John Bull* had been catastrophic. By 1922, the magazine's circulation figure had plummeted from its post-war high point of 1.7 million to 300,000.[17] Sensing that Odhams' reputation was inextricably linked to that of its leading magazine, Elias put all available resources into reviving *John Bull*'s fortunes. Within two years, while Bottomley languished in jail, the magazine's sales had been restored by Elias to an acceptable level of one million.[18]

At the time of Bottomley's ejection as editor of *John Bull*, Odhams was still dangerously reliant on this single title for its core business. Nonetheless, Elias had made sure that the firm moved ahead on a variety of other publishing projects, On the eve of the First World War, as the success of *John Bull* began to generate increasing revenues, Elias sought out opportunities to emulate the Harmsworth's strategy of developing a portfolio of fully owned publications to feed the firm's growing production capacity at Long Acre. To do this, the strategy was adopted of acquiring existing titles that could be further developed in terms of their editorial strength, circulation performance, and capacity for generating advertising revenue. Initially Elias targeted publications that served an embryonic market arising from the growth of movie theatres. Although in 1913 such cinemas were scarcely more than a collection of disused shops, used to exhibit rudimentary films featuring short dramas and news items, Elias correctly recognized the potential these venues offered as future theatres of mass entertainment. By 1914, therefore, Odhams had acquired ownership of two titles that served Britain's fledgling film industry: *Kinematograph Weekly* and *The Picturegoer*. *Kinematograph Weekly* was more technical in its style, being aimed at film exhibitors and distributors, whilst *The Picturegoer*, which was already printed by Odhams' partner firm, Southwood, Smith & Co., was devoted to a readership drawn from the audiences that watched this new form of entertainment.[19]

During the war *The Picturegoer* began to build a respectable circulation among Britain's entertainment-seekers, and in 1915 Elias looked to capitalize further on this type of reader by launching Odhams' first internally conceived and developed magazine title the *Passing Show*. A new editor, Comyns Beaumont, was hired and given the brief of producing a popular magazine designed to provide humorous light relief for readers confronted elsewhere with the daily horrors and deprivations of war. Equally important, Odhams' circulation and advertising departments were immediately set to work on the new title. Although the sales were unable to rival those of *John Bull*, the company found that, given the new magazine's editorial style and content, advertisers could more readily be attracted to its pages. Far less controversial than Bottomley's creation, the *Passing Show* was soon generating levels of advertising revenue for Odhams' advertising manager, Philip Emanuel, significantly beyond those achieved through *John Bull*. As the First World War drew to a close, therefore, Odhams was well on the way to establishing a core group of its own periodicals to provide a bulwark against its dependence on the sales of *John Bull*.[20]

ARRIVAL OF THE BERRY BROTHERS

Given the prevailing advantages of scale economies that accrued to the industry's leading firms, making a substantial impression in the market for popular magazines in Britain at the end of the First World War must have seemed a virtually impossible goal, even to the highly energetic Julius Elias. The position achieved in the market for weekly titles by the Newnes/Pearson group and Harmsworth's Amalgamated Press was already so dominant by 1914 that the success of *John Bull* appeared to be virtually an anachronism from the Victorian Age. Once the war had ended, the Amalgamated Press undertook a further substantial investment in its periodical-based production capacity, placing that firm's pre-eminence in the market beyond any doubt. In 1922 the production activities of the Amalgamated Press were transferred to a purpose-built, six-storey plant in Sumner Street, Southwark, which employed 30,000 hands. This facility housed eighty rotary presses and seventy other presses, with one entire floor of the building given over to mechanical typesetting. In all, 12,000 bales of printed journals (7,500 miles of paper) were dispatched from this magazine factory each week.[21] However, the untimely death of Alfred Harmsworth in August of that year helped to give rise to a remarkable transformation of Britain's magazine publishing industry between the wars. The process of consolidation, evident since the turn of the century, continued apace, but by the mid-1920s there had occurred a significant change in the ownership and management of Britain's leading magazine business.

The organization that was to about assume the position of Britain's largest periodical publishing business was created by two brothers from South Wales, William and Gomer Berry. William Berry had made the first steps on a career in journalism at the *Merthyr Times* in 1894, before a move to London found him employed briefly on the *Investor's Guardian* and the *Country Gentleman* magazine. A falling-out with the proprietor of these publications led to a period of unemployment and reflection, followed by the crucial decision to begin a periodical of his own: *Advertising World*. Having met with some initial success, William summoned his more business-oriented brother Gomer from Merthyr to join him on the enterprise. Displaying the same complementary mix of capabilities as the Harmsworth brothers before them, the Berrys gradually pieced together a group of successful periodicals under the umbrella of their publishing company Ewart, Seymour & Co. A key breakthrough was the successful launch of *Boxing* magazine in 1909, which by the outbreak of the war was selling 250,000 copies. By this time the decision had been taken to dispose of the successful *Advertising World*, bringing in a significant capital sum. Further small journals were purchased, including the *Penny Illustrated Paper* and *Health and Strength*. It nonetheless constituted a significant gamble on behalf of the Berrys in 1915 to raise the substantial loan required to purchase the ailing *Sunday Times* for around £80,000.[22] William Berry devoted his flair for journalism to reviving the fortunes of the paper, which had steadily lost ground to its main rival *The Observer* and seen its circulation decline to a mere 30,000 copies per week. In 1918 a bid for the newspaper of around £200,000 by the proprietor of the *Daily Express*, Lord Beaverbrook, indicated that the resources invested in the *Sunday Times* were certainly creating value. Beaverbrook's approach—linked to the interests of the Lloyd George group—was rejected owing to the Berry's political affiliations within the Liberal Party, but it does seem to have served to encourage the brothers to develop and execute a strategy of financial expansion thereafter.[23]

During the 1920s, the Berrys created a British media conglomerate to rival that of the Harmsworths. A significant up-scaling of their publishing interests began in 1919 when two financial newspapers were purchased, including the *Financial Times*, along with the substantial printing plant of the St Clement's Press. The firm's range of magazine titles was greatly expanded in 1920 when the Berrys put up a bid of 22*s*. 6*d*. per share for the capital of Cassell & Co.'s book and periodical publishing enterprise. These £1 shares had been trading at 75 per cent of their face value and the Berrys' generous offer was accepted with alacrity by the shareholders of Cassell.[24] This move brought a range of established magazine titles under the Welsh brothers' control, including the popular *Story-Teller* and *Cassell's Magazine*. In the short run relatively little effort was made to integrate the Cassell operations into the rest of the Berrys' organization, which by this time had also expanded by acquiring ownership of the Graphic Publication Company's *Daily Graphic* newspaper as well as their *Graphic* and *Bystander* magazine titles. In 1922 the business of *Kelly's Directories* was purchased from Sir Edward Illife, a move that saw the Berrys develop a long-term association with the owner's Coventry-based publishing house.[25] Hence within the space of a few years William and Gomer Berry had emerged as major players in Britain's periodical publishing industry.

Another landmark acquisition, undertaken together with Edward Illife, led to the formation of the Berrys' flagship Allied Newspapers concern. This came as a result of the ailing Edward Hulton's decision to sell his London- and Manchester-based newspaper and periodicals chain of publications. During the spring and summer of 1923 Hulton engaged in negotiations with the Berrys over the sale of these properties, and the terms of a deal had been struck and set for completion on 1 October. However, this proposed transaction never came to pass. During the course of the negotiations Harold Harmsworth (now Lord Rothermere) had made an abortive attempt to acquire the Hulton papers for his own Associated Newspaper group, but since the Manchester man retained a long-standing grudge against Harold, dating back to Rothermere's decision to launch the *Sunday Pictorial* in competition with his *Illustrated Sunday Herald*, his approach was rebuffed. Undeterred, Harold enlisted the support of Lord Beaverbrook, fortuitously a close neighbour of Hulton's, who succeeded in visiting the seriously ill, bedridden newspaper proprietor and persuading him to agree a price for the papers there and then. Although Beaverbrook did not possess sufficient capital of his own to finance the transaction, he was able to exploit his connection with Reginald McKenna, chairman of the Midland Bank, who agreed on the telephone to guarantee an immediate down-payment of £1 million and to further underwrite the full purchase price of £5 million. With the deal for the Hulton newspaper chain secured, Beaverbrook then sold the papers to Rothermere at par, but retained a 51 per cent controlling interest in the London *Evening Standard* as his commission.[26] Although it now appeared that the Berrys had been thwarted in their bid to acquire ownership of Hulton's newspaper empire, in fact this turned out not to be the case. Recognizing an opportunity to profit financially himself from the deal, in 1924 Rothermere sold to the Berrys the provincial newspapers segment of the Hulton portfolio, and later the national *Daily Sketch* too, pocketing a reported profit of £1.8 million.[27] Although the acquisition of these papers reputedly cost them £5.5 million, this sum was comfortably recouped when the Berrys floated their public company, Allied Newspapers Ltd., in 1924 for £7.9 million.[28] Control of Hulton's newspapers and periodicals thus completed their transition to the position as a major force in Britain's inter-war newspaper and periodical publishing industry.

The mantel of being Britain's leading magazine publishing house was achieved in 1926 when the Berrys struck a further deal with the Harmsworth group, bringing into their stable the entire business of the Amalgamated Press. Following the death of Northcliffe, a long drawn-out series of negotiations had begun with the British tax revenue authorities in relation to the amount of death duties to be paid on his estate. The task of acting as Northcliffe's executor had been given to his trusted long-time private secretary, and now chairman of the reconstituted Amalgamated Press (1922) Ltd., George Sutton. Needing to raise substantial finance to pay off the tax authorities, Sutton contracted to sell the Amalgamated Press to the Berrys' subsidiary Graphic Publications Ltd., for £8 million.[29] To effect the transaction, a new Amalgamated Press company was floated by the Berrys with a capital value of slightly over £10 million. This new entity also incorporated the various assets of Cassell & Co., meaning that this organization now became formally subsumed into the Amalgamated Press. Cassell's twelve magazine titles[30] were turned over to the management of the parent company, and the printing facilities which had been previously used to produce them were disposed of; a decision made partly as a consequence of the strong union support among Cassell's printing workforce at the time of the General Strike. The book publishing arm of the company was then sold off, being purchased by Cassell's long-standing literary director Newman Flower using outside finance.[31] George Sutton, meanwhile, declined the Berrys' invitation to remain at the helm of Amalgamated Press following the transfer of ownership.[32] He continued in the role of director of the new company until February 1928, a few weeks after his erstwhile deputy chairman at the old Amalgamated Press, Arthur Linforth, had resigned his post. The death, later that year, of Leslie Clark at the age of 37 removed another stalwart of the original firm from the list of Amalgamated Press' directors.[33]

Sutton's resignation was formally recorded at the first Annual General Meeting of the new Amalgamated Press on 28 June 1928. As well as paying tribute to Sutton, Linforth, and Clark, William Berry's first speech as chairman also underscored the growing importance of magazines aimed at the female reader. The titles *Home Chat, Women's Pictorial, Woman's World,* and *Woman's Weekly* were all saluted for the abiding prosperity which they had contributed and, more importantly, continued to provide to the firm. The recently launched sixpenny monthly *Woman and Home* was commended for reaching a sales figure of 350,000 copies per issue. In addition, the new one shilling *Woman's Journal* was heavily promoted to the captive audience as a magazine of the highest class of which they, as shareholders, could be justly proud.[34] In the years that followed, up until the outbreak of the Second World War, Berry's statement at each Annual General Meeting gave further credence to the dominant role played by women's magazines in the future development of Amalgamated Press. Referring to this firm in his review of the British magazine industry, Reed points out that after Alfred Harmsworth's death 'his magazine empire never again launched one magazine that was outstandingly successful'. The record of the firm's publishing initiatives nevertheless shows that a number of new titles were put up for public consideration during these years. *Woman's Companion, Wife and Home, Woman and Beauty, Home Making, Mabs Weekly,* and the first 3*d.* all-photogravure weekly *Home Journal* were all launched with little obvious purpose or impact other than to crowd out would-be competitors in the increasingly advertising-rich women's segment.[35] Speaking in 1935, William Berry noted that 'we have nearly a hundred monthly and weekly periodicals and the pages of more than half of these are open to the advertiser. They afford him (especially if his main interest is in selling goods to women) a unique coverage of this market.'[36]

It is certainly the case that *Woman's Weekly,* launched in 1911, remained the best performing periodical of the company, with a circulation figure in excess of 500,000 claimed for the journal in 1936.[37] By this time, however, the financial performance of Amalgamated Press was in serious decline. Reported profits had dropped each year from 1930 and, apart from a small rise in 1936, continued to fall until the outbreak of the war. Most of the problems arose from the company's paper-manufacturing subsidiary acquired as part of the Amalgamated Press enterprise, Imperial Paper Mills, which had contracted to sell newsprint at prices that were uneconomic given the prevailing costs of the raw wood-pulp. Rising costs at the company's printing plants also caused concern, and in 1938 Berry castigated the exorbitant wage rate agreements reached between the British Federation of Master Printers and the Printing and Kindred Trades Federation, as he informed the assembled shareholders of a cut in the level of dividend to be paid on their ordinary shares.[38] The organization also had been obliged to make an investment in the *Kelly's Directory* business, inherited from Iliffe, which for most of the 1930s was an extremely lame duck. In many respects, the outbreak of the war, when it came in 1939, acted as a blessed relief to the Amalgamated Press.

The performance of the Amalgamated Press was unlikely to have been helped by the distractions provided by the Berry brothers' other publishing interests. In December 1927 they had acquired control of the *Daily Telegraph* from Lord Burnham for the sum of £1.2 million which thereafter assumed the position of their flagship publication.[39] In 1937 the Berrys and Iliffe formally divided their publishing interests into three separate groups. William Berry (Lord Camrose) continued to control the Amalgamated Press, the *Daily Telegraph* (which was amalgamated with the *Morning Post* in October 1937), and the *Financial Times*. Gomer Berry (Lord Kemsley) took control of Allied Newspapers Ltd. (including the *Sunday Times*), the provincial Allied Northern Newspapers Ltd., and the *Daily Sketch*, while Lord Iliffe held the controlling interest in *Kelly's Directories* and Associated Iliffe Press, a press empire that also included a string of periodicals including *Autocar* and *Wireless World*.[40]

CONSOLIDATING NEWNES AND PEARSON

In contrast to the broad-based publishing interests within which the Amalgamated Press operated through the Berry/Iliffe group until 1937, its main rival between the wars, the Newnes-Pearson group, focused its efforts entirely on periodicals. By 1918 the controlling interest in the two companies had been assumed by George Riddell,[41] who brought their activities together under the umbrella of a joint operating committee which met weekly under his chairmanship. The links between the two companies were consolidated in 1920 through the formation of the Newnes and Pearson Printing Co. Ltd.[42] The decision to form this company had come about when the George Newnes firm, chaired by his son Frank Newnes but with Riddell as his guiding vice chairman, had decided to build a new printing facility in London. A site had been acquired at Stamford Street in 1919, but soon after this site had been secured the business of the London Colour Printing Co. in Exmoor Street, west London, had become available. As a more substantial investment, it was decided to purchase this facility jointly on behalf of both the Newnes and

Pearson publishing firms in order to act as their consolidated printing arm. With the deepening of collaboration that this entailed, from 1921 the two publishing firms agreed to adopt a joint board of control, chaired by Riddell, and to pool and divide their profits in fixed proportion.[43] Nonetheless, throughout the 1920s the Newnes and Pearson publishing businesses continued to operate independently, with each holding its own Annual General Meeting for shareholders.

The Newnes organization was placed under the general management of Walter Grierson with an advertising department directed by Alfred Johnson. The company held shares in various other publishing firms, including a controlling interest in R. S. Cartwright Ltd., which owned the stable of Leach-branded women's publications, and Country Life Ltd. The publications of this latter firm, notably *Country Life* and *Homes & Gardens*, were great successes during the 1920s and held a distinctive place in the market under the guiding hand of their founder Edward Hudson. Another great money-spinner for Newnes in the 1920s was the contract with the recently established British Broadcasting Corporation (BBC) to publish on its behalf the *Radio Times*. The first issue of this listings magazine was put out in September 1923 under the terms of a deal that reputedly saw Newnes receive two-thirds of the profits up to a certain point and one-half thereafter, with a guaranteed income to the BBC of £1,000 per year. With the magazine's circulation reaching 750,000 by December 1924, the BBC quickly assumed greater editorial control over the *Radio Times*, and in 1926 renegotiated the terms of its contract with Newnes under which the publisher received a commission on the net receipts of sales and advertising revenues. Despite ceding editorial control, the *Radio Times* remained a major source of profits for the Newnes business. By 1927 the magazine's circulation had moved beyond a million, an occasion marked by a celebratory lunch hosted by Riddell.[44]

The Pearson side of the organization was supervised by Riddell, with Arthur Pearson's son Neville acting as his vice chairman and Percy Everett as business manager. During the 1920s this firm invested significantly in the women's weekly segment, launching *Peg's Paper*, *Peg's Companion*, and the *Woman's Friend*. The first two were centred on fiction and directed at a working-class readership, while the last represented one of a growing number of service-style magazines aimed at middle-class housewives.[45] In a situation of increasing oligopolistic rivalry in the women's segment, the *Woman's Friend* was a direct response to the launch by Amalgamated Press of the *Woman's Pictorial*.[46] As the 1920s wore on the scope for further expansion within the consumer magazine market seems to have been limited, and the reported profits of the two parts of the Newnes-Pearson Group stagnated. In 1929, a scheme of consolidation was put forward in which the ordinary shares of C. Arthur Pearson Ltd., and Country Life Ltd., were acquired by George Newnes Ltd., and the nominal capital of the Newnes business was increased to £1.25 million, with

Neville Pearson joining the board of Newnes for the first time. The move allowed for some consolidation through the amalgamation of overlapping titles. Nevertheless, the reported profit of £155,000 in 1930 remained the new company's high water mark until the outbreak of the war, despite the further economies that were derived from bringing together the editorial, publishing, and administrative staff of Newnes, Pearson, and Country Life under one roof in 1934. Thus when Riddell passed away at the age of 69 in December 1934, the Newnes and Pearson staff had been effectively consolidated into a single enterprise of George Newnes Ltd.[47]

HEARST'S NATIONAL MAGAZINE COMPANY

One of the editors employed by Newnes during the early years of the twentieth century was the highly talented young Alice Head. She had originally been assigned to the staff of *Country Life* magazine as a qualified shorthand typist before being transferred to one of Newnes' literary titles, *The Academy*, as a secretary at a salary of £1 per week. On this magazine, as well as providing secretarial support, she also began to write some small items of copy, clearly creating a favourable impression on Newnes' new proprietor, George Riddell. Soon after her assignment to *The Academy* the title was purchased by Sir Edward Tennant and became independent of Newnes' management. Head retained her position with the magazine and was appointed as secretary to the new editor, Lord Alfred Douglas. Following the change in ownership, the printing of *The Academy* was contracted out while the business side of the operation was handled entirely by W.H. Smith's. Thus Alice Head and Sir Alfred, together with an office-boy, were the only people working directly on the production of the magazine, with Head effectively acting as the managing editor. Before long, however, Head's working conditions were adversely affected by the incorporation into the magazine's editorial office of the abrasive T. W. H. Crosland, whose demeanour upset the young editor to the point where she resigned.[48] Riddell offered the now unemployed Head the consolation of a position in his solicitor's office as a temporary measure, while seeking an opportunity for her to return to magazine work. In 1909, he purchased on behalf of Newnes a half share in a magazine called *Woman at Home* which had been published since 1893 by the firm of Hodder and Stoughton. The founding editor of the journal, Annie S. Swann, had decided to stand down, and Riddell considered that Head, at the tender age of 22 years, would be a good choice to succeed to the editor's chair.[49] From these beginnings, Head prospered to become reputedly the highest paid woman in Britain by the outbreak of the Second World War, albeit not as an employee of the Newnes organization.[50]

Woman at Home continued to be a moderate success under Head's direction, but the outbreak of the First World War brought about a decline in its sales and growing shortages of paper led to a diminution in its editorial content. In 1917, Head was offered a position on another literary magazine: *Nash's*. Seeking Riddell's advice, Head was informed by her employer that *Nash's* was similar in stature to Newnes' own highly popular *Strand Magazine*, and Head's subsequent decision to shift to a new company thus seems to have been made with Riddell's blessing.[51] The firm to which Head transferred was the National Magazine Co., an organization that had been set up by the press magnate William R. Hearst in 1910 as the British arm of his American media empire. Hearst had been engaged in publishing since taking control of the *San Francisco Examiner* in 1887,[52] but had not moved into magazines until 1903 when he was inspired to create his first title, *Motor*, by a journal he had come across during a visit to England called *The Car*.[53] A far more significant development for Hearst's American magazine business was his purchase in 1905 of *Cosmopolitan*, which at this point was a literary rather than a women's title.[54] By 1914 the circulation of *Cosmopolitan* had grown from 400,000 to over 750,000, and Hearst had also acquired further US magazine titles including the *World Today* (which he renamed *Hearst's Magazine* and later *Hearst International*), *Harper's Bazaar*, and *Good Housekeeping*.[55] The original *Good Housekeeping* had been launched in 1885 and was edited by George W. Bryan who claimed that it was directed towards 'the interests of higher life in the household'.[56] The publication made good progress, but changed hands a number of times after Bryan's death in 1898. Early in the twentieth century, while under the management of the Phelps Publishing Company, it launched the Good Housekeeping Experiment Station. From this grew the Good Housekeeping Bureau and the Good Housekeeping Institute, which set up laboratories and kitchens in order to test the quality of the products advertised within the magazine. Advertising from manufacturers was rejected if their products were found to be substandard.[57]

Hearst had first begun publishing in Britain when he purchased *Nash's* from the original owner Eveleigh Nash in 1909.[58] It was the decision to launch a UK version of *Good Housekeeping*, however, that ultimately brought the National Magazine Co. to prominence in the British market and which provided Alice Head with a stage upon which her talent was able to flourish. Her initial assignment for the Hearst organization had been as assistant editor to J. Y. McPeake under whose editorship *Nash's* circulation had reached in excess of 200,000. Towards the end of 1920, McPeake had suggested to Head that an opportunity existed to use the profits generated by *Nash's* to launch a British version of *Good Housekeeping*. Thus in 1921 the offices of the National Magazine Co. were relocated from Fleet Street into larger premises near St Paul's Cathedral and Fred Bigelow, editor of *Good Housekeeping* in the United States, was seconded to London in order to provide advice to McPeake and Head in preparation for the British launch of *Good Housekeeping*. The new magazine was eventually laid before the public in March 1922, funded with a relatively modest capital sum of £13,500. As with *Nash's*, McPeake paid top rates to leading authors for their contributions to the fledgling title, but it was the practical aspects of the new magazine which provided its distinctive flavour. A home management section, under the direction of Mrs Cottington-Taylor, provided consumer advice across a range of new household products that were becoming available in Britain for the first time during the 1920s. In September 1924, a UK version of the Good Housekeeping Institute was set up at 49 Wellington Street, Strand, thus providing British consumers with their first effective source of consumer advice and protection.[59] According to Head's own account, *Good Housekeeping* gained such a strong reputation in the field of consumer support and household advice that it was able to thwart the various attempts on behalf of competitors to usurp its leading position in the field, providing the magazine with a strong platform from which it was able to generate 'a very large circulation and enormous advertising revenues'.[60]

For Alice Head, working as an employee of the Hearst organization was a world away from the parochial experience she had been familiar with during her time at Newnes. Moreover, her responsibilities at the National Magazine Co. quickly grew following the launch of *Good Housekeeping*. McPeake's health had been failing since 1921 and Head had been required to stand in for him on numerous occasions up until his death in 1924. At this point Hearst dispatched Joseph Moore, general manager of the Hearst Magazine Company in America, to appoint McPeake's successor. Impressed by her technical knowledge as well as her editorial skills, Moore was quickly persuaded that Head was well qualified to take overall control of the National Magazine Co.'s affairs, although he also brought in Ivor Nicholson from Cassell's as general manager to provide support. Head now entered the charmed circle of Hearst's top employees, and visits to the United States soon left her agog with wonder. In April 1925 she was invited to New York to meet the editors of Hearst's other magazine titles, culminating with two interviews with the Chief himself, at the end of which Head confessed to feeling as if she were walking on air. A visit to Hearst's castle at San Simeon the following year seems to have created a similar impression, as did the Chief's instruction for her to purchase St Donat's castle in Wales which he had earlier glimpsed in a copy of *Country Life* magazine. For various reasons she thought it wise to buy the castle in the name of the National Magazine Co., whose funds she was expending; Hearst, it seems, fully concurred with this idea.[61] Three years were to pass before Hearst was able to find the time to visit his new Welsh stately home.[62]

Throughout the 1920s the Hearst organization continued to develop and exploit its presence in Europe. The benefits of operating parallel titles in different markets came strongly into play for example when the editor of the American *Cosmopolitan*, Ray Long, secured serial rights for material that covered both the US and British markets. International expansion beyond the English-speaking countries was also on Hearst's agenda. In 1928 Dick Berlin, who was to emerge as a key figure in the Hearst organization during the 1930s, was appointed to the position of general manager of the Hearst Magazine Co. The following year he and Head travelled to Berlin in order to explore the possibility of a German edition of *Cosmopolitan*. Exploratory interviews with the heads of some of Germany's leading business houses, however, quickly established that the potential for generating the required level of advertising revenue from that quarter was far too limited.[63] Nevertheless, further magazines were launched by the National Magazine Co. in the UK, most notably the American-originated *Harper's Bazaar* in 1929. Indeed, the UK side of the Hearst publishing empire fared well during the early 1930s[64] but the depression in America badly affected the company's financial performance as a whole during this decade. By the mid-1930s a Conservation Committee had been created at the US headquarters to manage the organization's overwhelming financial liabilities, in the activities of which Dick Berlin played an increasingly important role.[65]

ATTRACTING THE MODERN WOMAN

The significance of American involvement in Britain's magazine industry between the wars is strikingly pointed up in a review published by the trade journal *Newspaper World* in 1930. It noted two interdependent areas of significant change that had transformed the appearance of British magazines—in particular the shilling monthlies—namely a growth in the use of illustrations employing clever design layouts, and the increased importance of display advertising. Women's monthly magazines were identified as the most progressive force within the industry in this respect. Among the service-style magazines it highlighted '*Good Housekeeping* [as] an admirable pioneer of this type [which] has the benefit of a unique organisation in its domestic Institute, run solely for the benefit of readers', while in the area of fashion the new style of monthly was 'typified by *Vogue* and *Harper's Bazaar*, featuring luxury undreamed of before the war'.[66] In comparison with the workaday fare provided by the cheap weeklies, these American-inspired monthly glossies represented a shaft of bright illumination for Britain's magazine-reading public between the wars.

National Magazine's launch of a UK version of its fashion-bible *Harper's Bazaar* in 1929 had been a response to the success achieved in Britain by *Vogue*, and it represented a continuation of the rivalry between the two titles that had been ongoing in the United States for well over a decade. The *Vogue* title had originated as a New York society magazine with no specific predisposition towards either gender or fashion per se. It had not been until 1898, six years after the title's launch by its proprietor Arthur Turnure, that the magazine's emphasis shifted towards providing the women of New York's social elite with advice on how to dress appropriately, anticipating that those living outside of the urban centre would wish to follow these trends within the pages of the journal.[67] One of the early innovations of the magazine during its transition to a fashion-based journal was to facilitate the use of display advertising, selling blocks rather than line-specific allocations of space, thus enabling the introduction of more attractive forms of advertising that featured illustrations.[68] This change in style had been noted with approval by Condé Nast, who as business manager of *Collier's Weekly* from 1897 had been responsible for generating a sharp increase in that popular magazine's advertising revenues.[69] In 1905 Nast made an unsuccessful offer to purchase *Vogue*, which he saw as providing the ideal medium for exploiting his theory of the 'class' publication.

Influenced by Munsey's strategy of using advertising, rather than cover price, as the main engine for generating a magazine's revenue streams, Nast had figured that a title such as *Vogue*, carrying a strong appeal to a well-defined and highly affluent audience, could be used to provide advertisers of a certain class of products (in this case the manufacturers and retailers of luxury goods) with a dedicated platform from which to promote their wares. Nast finally succeeded in acquiring *Vogue* in 1909, at which point it had a falling circulation of 14,000 but annual advertising revenues of $100,000 and a readership that included some of the richest members of New York society.[70] Within six months the new owner had implemented a number of changes to the magazine, including a reduction in the frequency of publication from weekly to fortnightly and a rise in the price from ten to fifteen cents. Coverage of fashion was stepped up, colour covers were introduced, and the number of pages grew from 30 to 100 per issue as Nast pitched successfully for more advertising clients. Despite the fact that *Vogue* charged advertisers $10 per thousand readers compared with the $2 or $3 rates required by the mass-circulation periodicals, Condé Nast's idea of providing advertisers with a clearly defined readership meant that his targeted advertising space was priced at a realistic level. In setting out his theory of class publications in 1913, Nast stated that 'the publisher...must...get all their readers from the one particular class to which the magazine is dedicated, but rigorously exclude all others'.[71] This was the *Vogue* formula for success.

The American-published *Vogue* magazine made its earliest appearance in the UK shortly before the outbreak of the First World War, by which time it was selling 3,000 to 4,000 imported copies per issue. Dislocations in shipping consequent upon the escalating military conflict initially acted to boost the sales of *Vogue* in Britain as they cut off the flow of alternative fashion magazines from the Continent. By 1916, sales of *Vogue* in Britain had quadrupled and it became feasible for Condé Nast to contemplate taking on the extra costs of printing the journal directly in the UK. Thus, as the Atlantic trade began to run into serious disruptions Nast took the decision to publish a UK edition of his flagship fashion magazine. A business manager was appointed in the shape of William Wood, who up to this point had handled the company's import trade, and George W. Kettle, London manager of the Dorland Advertising Agency, took charge of advertising affairs for the magazine. By the time of the first issue of British *Vogue* (known to Condé Nast insiders as *Brogue*) in September 1916, Kettle had recruited a sufficient number of clients to provide the new magazine with twelve full-page, two half-page, and 58 box advertisements. When the war ended, Condé Nast sought to develop very close links with the leading haute couture fashion houses in Paris in order to establish a strong degree of authenticity for the magazine based on an ability to gain inside knowledge, as well as to influence trends directly. Editor of the US *Vogue*, Edna Woolman Chase, was particularly successful in promoting the interests of *Vogue* within the European fashion industry. In 1921 Condé Nast issued from Paris a French *Vogue* (aka *Frog*) which, although never a profitable enterprise due to the limited amount of advertising it was able to generate, gave the company's personnel further access to and influence over the current trends emanating from the inter-war fashion capital of the world.[72]

Between the wars, the periodical press in Britain began to emulate the American strategy of seeking an increasing share of advertising to cover the costs of production. Advertising agencies had developed from embryonic buyers of space to full-range providers of services, and magazines in general were among the principal recipients of their outputs. Figures cited for the inter-war period by Nevitt show that advertising in the press was completely dominant throughout this period, accounting for between 87 and 91 per cent of total advertising expenditure, with the remainder made up almost entirely of poster and transport advertising.[73] A breakdown of the press-based expenditures for the year 1935 by Kaldor and Silverman, however, indicates that only 17.7 per cent of all display advertising was accounted for by some 600 surveyed general interest magazines.[74] Trade and technical journals and special interest magazines[75] accounted for 21.8 per cent, and newspapers for the remaining 61.5 per cent. In terms of the significance of advertising as a source of revenue, by 1935 income from all forms of advertising accounted for 45.6 per cent of revenues for general interest magazines, compared with almost 60 per cent of revenues for newspapers taken as a whole.[76] Predictably, monthly titles achieved a higher ratio of advertising revenue as a percentage of the total revenues, with an estimated 48.4 per cent compared with the weeklies' 45.0 per cent.[77] Without doubt, the rapid growth in newspaper sales between the wars drew away revenues from the weekly and monthly mass circulation titles, leaving the narrow-segment, class-based strategy of Condé Nast greater scope for competitive advantage. Targeting a well-defined audience on behalf

of advertisers became the key to producing a financially successful magazine
title; and by far the most important targets were female readers.

THE GLAMOUR OF GRAVURE

In the first issue of British *Vogue* one of the advertisements, from the retail
department store Selfridges, had commented on how the magazine was beau-
tifully printed.[78] The high quality of printing was one of the ways in which the
American magazines sought to satisfy demands of their advertisers. To begin
with, as British *Vogue*'s editorial direction oscillated between highbrow fiction
and exclusive fashion, it was Hearst's *Good Housekeeping* under the direction
of Alice Head that made the most impressive progress on the targeted advertising front. This magazine not only provided a high quality product for its
advertisers, but also sought to guarantee to its readers the quality of the products which the magazine's advertisers promoted.[79] In the case of British *Vogue*,
it was only with the transfer from New York of Harry Yoxall to act as its business manager in 1924, and the appointment of a new editor in Alison Settle, to
replace the literary-inclined Dorothy Todd in 1926, that the magazine found
its true direction.[80] In the meantime an attempt by Nast to launch a British
version of *House & Garden* in 1920 quickly ran into the rocks.[81] Once in post,
Yoxall sought to adopt the prevailing trend among American magazine producers, led particularly by the Curtis Publishing Company, to interact with
and discover more about the nature of their consumers.[82] This involved not
simply market research into the readership of *Vogue*, but also the formation
of close links with the advertisers themselves. For example, during the 1920s
Yoxall persuaded a group of its key advertisers, the leading British clothing
retailers, to purchase copies of *Vogue* and post them as promotional devices to
their customers. Yoxall wrote to Nast at the time informing him of the strategy, and noted that 'I can safely say that no mailing of this character, on such a
scale, has ever been done before in England.'[83]

   Improvements in printing were especially important for the high quality
magazines, and both Hearst and Nast made every effort to avail themselves
of state of the art presses. The printing technique that came of age between
the wars was photogravure. Compared with the letterpress, photogravure
was far more efficient in the reproduction of illustrations. According to one
leading practitioner, David Greenhill, it had been the *Illustrated London
News* that in 1912 set up the first complete photogravure installation used to
print a weekly periodical in Britain.[84] Before the First World War, Greenhill
had been the manager of a printing company called André Sleigh Ltd., a
subsidiary of Cassell's, where he was responsible for developing the company's gravure printing facilities. In August 1914, André Sleigh Ltd. was

purchased by the Anglo Engraving Co. and Greenhill was made managing director of the expanded company. At the end of the war in 1918, André Sleigh & Anglo Ltd. absorbed the Menpes Press, taking control of the substantial letterpress printing and photoengraving production facility which that firm had built at Whippendell Road in Watford in 1906. By now it had become a substantial business employing close to 1,000 staff, and in 1919 the firm was renamed the Sun Engraving Co. Between the wars, Sun Engraving emerged as the main printer of popular magazines in Britain thanks to its pioneering development of a colour, high-speed rotary gravure press in the mid-1920s.[85]

When the business of Cassell was acquired by the Berrys, the printing contracts which Sun Engraving had retained with Cassell now linked it to the owners of Amalgamated Press, the leading magazine producer in Britain. In addition, when Newnes purchased one of Sun Engraving's trade press clients, the printing firm also began to develop links with Riddell's magazine publishing empire. One of Sun Engraving's most exacting customers from a quality point of view was Condé Nast. Harry Yoxall had initially negotiated for Sun to print the *Vogue Pattern Book* (actually the UK firm's main profit generator) in 1929. The terms had been set out by him in a letter to the Sun's directors and it seems that this gentleman's agreement was taken as a binding contract by both parties. In cases of dispute, the letter stated that 'any difference of opinion concerning the quality...shall be submitted to an independent printer agreed on by both parties, whose decision shall be final'. In the USA Nast had earlier purchased the Arbor Press in 1921 in order to have direct control over quality: Condé Nast consciously set high quality standards and these came to be known at Sun as '*Vogue* quality'.[86] The Sun took over the printing of *Vogue* magazine in 1937 when the W.H. Smith's Arden Press was closed. Nast had obliged Yoxall to accept the tender from Sun Engraving to print *Vogue* at this time, even though it had been more expensive than those put up by rival printers William Clowes and the St Clement's Press.[87]

A major breakthrough for Sun Engraving occurred in 1930 when it won a seven-year contract to print a number of Odham's leading magazines, including *The Passing Show*. Obtaining this contract helped push up the proportion of Britain's magazines printed by Sun Engraving towards the 70 per cent mark.[88] So significant had the plant become that, shortly before the contract to print their magazines expired, Odhams bid to purchase the entire Sun Engraving plant at Watford. Finding the owners of Sun unreceptive, Elias dispatched his printing works manager, W. H. Parrack, to New York to study the methods of the Alco-Gravure Co., the leading gravure printer in the USA.[89] On his return, Parrack was able to provide Odhams with the sole rights in Britain to the Goss gravure printing presses that had been developed by the New York firm. With this in hand, Odhams began to build a huge printing plant of their own in Watford, to provide a direct competitor to Sun Engraving. By offering better rates of pay than Sun, Odhams (Watford) was able to attract a number of its rival's employees on to its own payroll when it opened its doors in 1937.[90]

To begin with, Elias had stated to his fellow directors at Odhams that the new plant would take over the printing of *John Bull*'s weekly output of 1.5 million copies. However, in the event it was with an entirely new title that the Odhams print works commenced large-scale production. A twopenny women's weekly, entitled simply *Woman*, became a new offering in the now crowded women's weekly segment.[91] Slow to take off, the appointment of Mary Grieve as the editor revived its fortunes and its circulation quickly rose, and in the post-war era Odhams' new weekly gained an enormous following. The impact of the new competitor on Sun Engraving was partly dissipated by the need for Newnes to upgrade its *Woman's Own* magazine to compete with Odhams' new innovation.[92] It was at this point, too, that Sun acquired the contract to print *Vogue* magazine. One further stroke of fortune lay in the decision in 1938 by Edward G. W. Hulton, whose father had sold out to Beaverbrook a decade and a half earlier, to launch an illustrated magazine in competition with Odham's *Weekly Illustrated*. The magazine was called the *Picture Post*, and Sun Engraving gained the contract to print it.[93]

5

Monopoly, Power, and Politics

PUBLISHING ON A WAR FOOTING

The outbreak of the war in 1939 brought many difficulties and disruptions for Britain's periodical publishing industry. Loss of manpower, shortages of materials, and the requisitioning of plant for war-related production, as well as the physical damage caused by enemy bombardment, all took their inevitable toll on the production and distribution of magazines. As a key channel of popular communication, however, consumer magazines, particularly those aimed at women readers, provided a potentially valuable asset in the realm of propaganda. According to Mary Grieve, editor of *Woman* magazine, officials at the Ministry of Information were slow to develop the obvious potential that these magazines offered. Not until the middle of 1941, amid much prompting from the industry, were the editors of women's weeklies seriously solicited to offer views and provide advice in support of women's role in the war effort.[1] In the magazines themselves, items designed to encourage the recruitment of women to industry, together with morale-boosting stories that featured women overcoming adversity, were mixed with practical advice aimed at dealing with the shortages and deprivation of wartime living. Constance Holt, the editor of Newnes' *Woman's Own* during the war, recalls having been kept closely informed of losses suffered by Atlantic shipping convoys, so that the magazine's recipes could be adjusted to take account of the consequent changes in rationing restrictions.[2] The influential role that these weekly women's magazines ultimately played in providing assistance to households throughout the duration of the hostilities was instrumental in helping to underpin their huge post-war popularity.[3]

More general magazines, notably *Picture Post*, also exploited the dislocations suffered by the population of wartime Britain; in this case to develop a new consciousness designed to promote the role of economic and social planning in the post-war era. The origins of *Picture Post* had come about as a result of Edward G. W. Hulton's desire to reprise his father and grandfather's role as a publishing proprietor. Abandoning a career in the law, which he had pursued following two unsuccessful attempts to gain a seat in Parliament as a

Conservative unionist, Hulton launched his media career after gaining control of his late father's fortune at the age of 30. On the strength of a single acquired title, *Farmer's Weekly*, he set up the Hulton Press in 1937 and the following year he took on the publication of a small monthly magazine entitled *Lilliput*. The creator of *Lilliput* was Stefan Lorent, a Hungarian refugee with a flair for photojournalism who had previously worked for Odhams to develop its own picture magazine, *Weekly Illustrated*.[4] In October 1938, with Lorent on board, Hulton put up £1 million of his newly acquired fortune as the basis for financing the launch of the *Picture Post*. To work alongside Lorent, Hulton recruited Tom Hopkinson, a talented editor and inspired caption-writer who held strongly socialist views and who had worked with Lorent for Odhams on their *Weekly Illustrated* title. The first issue of the *Picture Post* sold out its entire print run of 750,000 copies,[5] and by the outbreak of the war was selling more than one million copies per week. Under the general management of Maxwell Raison, Lorant and Hopkinson together created an iconic publication that was hugely successful in attracting both readers and advertising.[6] In July 1940 Lorent left Britain, fearing a German invasion, and Hopkinson became the sole editor of *Picture Post*. Far more political in his outlook than Lorent, as early as January 1941 Hopkinson had begun to exploit the magazine's wide circulation in order to promote the idea of a post-war 'Plan for Britain'.[7]

In the face of many shortages, centralized economic coordination and rationing—rather than planning per se—became a defining feature of life in Britain throughout the 1940s. For the publishers of magazines, the impact of the war on the supply of paper was immediate. At their Annual General Meeting in June 1940 the directors of Amalgamated Press informed the company's shareholders that the paper trade had become subject to stringent government controls and that, effective from 28 October 1939, all users had been rationed and fresh supplies of paper could only be produced under licence.[8] Decisions relating to import quotas for pulp and paper and concerning the permitted level of operation of home newsprint mills were made by relevant administrators based at the Ministry of Supply, the Board of Trade, and the Treasury. In practice the mechanisms of supply were quickly taken over and operated by the Newsprint Supply Company Ltd., an organization formed by the newspaper proprietors and their trade associations to carry on the routine business of newsprint rationing and distribution.[9] Supply quotas were introduced and their impact of the availability of paper was drastic. For example the Imperial Paper Mills, the main paper-making facility of Amalgamated Press, was operating at 20 per cent of its capacity by the middle of 1940 and imports of both paper and pulp were halved from their pre-war level; by 1942 they had halved again. Naturally, the number and size of magazines published by Amalgamated Press were cut back. Nonetheless, the firm's pre-tax profits increased throughout the war, due in part to the elimination of unsold copies and the cost of handling any returns. By 1942, every copy of every publication was being printed to a definite order.[10] A no-returns policy was implemented by the Periodical Publishers Association who also introduced a complete ban on new titles in 1944 that continued to operate beyond the war.[11] With the allocation of paper supplies based on quotas relating directly to the pre-war level of sales, titles that had accumulated substantial readerships now saw their dominant market position reinforced.[12] Thus the rationing of paper was implemented in ways that effectively froze the pattern of sales and thereby curtailed competition amongst the leading magazine publishers.[13]

FEARS OF A PRESS MONOPOLY

The resulting tendency towards market concentration, brought about by the system of paper rationing, was exacerbated by industry-level consolidation in the form of mergers. Shortly before the outbreak of the war, Amalgamated Press had purchased the controlling share of *Kelly's Directories* from Lord Iliffe, giving them also ownership of Associated Iliffe Press which published a portfolio of around 30 periodicals.[14] During the war the firm had also acquired Weldons Ltd., publishers of a range of fashion titles, and by the end of the war this organization had been fully absorbed into the operations of Amalgamated Press.[15] Odhams, too, extended its publishing activities by means of acquisition. Shortly after the war the company expanded its interests in the field of trade magazines through its purchase of a range of weekly and monthly titles which became incorporated under the mantel of the Tothill Press.[16] The development of Odhams more generally after the war, however, was disrupted by the death of Julius Elias (latterly Lord Southwood) in April 1946. His role as chairman was assumed by Arthur G. Cousins, who had been a director of the company for the previous 23 years and whose expertise lay primarily in the area of financial management. Cousins appears to have steered a cautious line, constrained as he was by continuing shortages of paper and machinery, until his own death and succession by A. C. (Pat) Duncan in 1950.

The trend towards increased concentration of ownership within the periodical press in Britain generally, and the consequent concerns that this raised, particularly in relation to the presentation of news, led to the appointment of a Royal Commission of the Press in 1947. The impetus for the investigation came from within the National Union of Journalists. Two members of the NUJ with seats in the House of Commons put forward a motion calling for a Royal Commission in order to address 'the increasing public concern at the growth of monopolistic tendencies in the control of the Press and with the object of furthering the free expression of opinion through the Press and the greatest practicable accuracy in the presentation of the news'.[17] Before the Commission was able to publish its own report in 1949, William Berry (Lord Camrose), the owner of the publishing group which controlled the Amalgamated Press together with the *Daily Telegraph* and *Financial Times*, published his own review entitled *The British Press and its Controllers*. Towards the end of this review, he noted that '[s]omewhat surprisingly' the Commission's terms of reference had been extended to include periodicals other than newspapers. Pointing to the substantial number of titles encompassed within this category, Camrose proposed that only periodicals of a political nature would be relevant to the terms of the enquiry. These he listed and summarized as being the *Economist*, *New Statesman*, *Spectator*, *Time and Tide*, *Tribune*, and *Truth*, none of which happened to be properties of the Amalgamated Press.[18]

In the event, the Royal Commission's report paid little attention to the situation with regard to popular weekly and monthly periodicals. The Commission concluded that, 'It has not been suggested to us that the number of periodicals is too small, or their ownership is too concentrated; and in our limited study of this part of the press we have found no reason to think that the control, management or ownership of periodicals militates against the free expression of opinion or the accurate presentation of news.'[19] In terms of consumer magazines, the report's finding that prevailing ownership patterns were not 'too concentrated' was certainly open to dispute. Only four significant British publishers of such periodicals were identified (outside of Scotland), of which Amalgamated Press with over 70 periodicals, including those relating to the trade and technical press, had by far the largest number of titles. Odhams was credited with the publication of around 20 periodicals, with George Newnes owning 26 and Hulton Press just six, but included among them the *Picture Post* magazine with a circulation level that was 'comparable with that of a national newspaper'.[20] The economic implications of the cross-ownership of newspapers and other periodicals, which was a feature of all the leading magazine publishers save for Newnes, were not given detailed scrutiny by the Commission. Certainly the report raised no concerns in relation to Lord Camrose's co-ownership of the Amalgamated Press and the *Daily Telegraph*, despite the fact that the sales of his Conservative Party-supporting newspaper had expanded beyond the one million mark in May 1947.[21] Not until the events of the 1950s had unfolded did the economic issues of market concentration and cross-media ownership emerge as matters for concern in Britain's popular magazine publishing industry, stimulating the demand for a second Royal Commission in 1961.

MAGAZINES IN AUSTERITY BRITAIN

The most pressing concern posed to the magazine publishing houses by the shortage of paper, particularly after the war had ended, was the physical limit it placed on the amount of display advertising that magazines could carry, a source of revenue that the industry had developed strongly between the wars.[22] To manage this, the leading publishers of magazines developed a system of rationing the available advertising space as fairly as possible, and in turn they received a good deal of collaboration from the expanding group of advertising agencies acting on behalf of their clients. Once the controls on paper finally began to be lifted—they were raised from 35 per cent to 70 per cent of pre-war levels in 1949 and removed completely in March 1950—publishers began to nervously anticipate a return to more normal, competitive conditions. With the price of paper still high, any decision to increase the size and quality of their magazines would certainly bring about a rise in the costs of production. Thus their continued profitability was contingent upon a corresponding increase in revenue streams, both from additional sales of advertising space and from cover price revenues. Competitive pressures arising from greater access to paper thus threatened to undermine the secure position in which the leading magazine publishers had found themselves. To their immense relief, the latent unsatisfied consumer demand for their products was substantial, most particularly among women readers. Reporting to Amalgamated Press' shareholders shortly after the controls on paper were rescinded in 1950, Lord Camrose was scarcely able to disguise his astonishment at the magnitude of the uplift in sales across the entire range of the company's women's magazines. Even the firm's dreary *Woman's Weekly*, featuring as it did neither large page size nor colour printing, was now selling an average of 1.6 million copies compared with 500,000 before the war. The ancient *Home Chat* had doubled its pre-war circulation, to register weekly sales in excess of 300,000, while *Woman's Illustrated* had moved beyond 500,000. The firm's monthly women's magazines also made substantial gains in circulation, with the cheap 9*d. Woman and Home* briefly threatening to breach the one million mark, a sales target undreamed of before 1940.[23] Newnes was able to report similar figures among its women's journals. Its superior competitor to *Woman's Weekly*, the partly colour-printed *Woman's Own*, first matched and then rapidly outpaced its close rival's sales figures, en route to a circulation of 2.5 million in the mid-1950s.[24] Meanwhile Odhams' *Woman* emerged from among the company's 'Big 3' one million-selling weeklies—*John Bull* and *Illustrated* being the other two[25]—to become first, in 1950, a two million- and then, in 1954, a three million-selling publishing phenomenon. With such an expanding circulation and readership the three leading magazine publishing firms saw their advertising revenue grow exponentially,[26] and by 1953 Camrose was gleefully appraising his shareholders of the unmatched proficiency with which their magazines were able to prise open the handbags of Britain's austerity-plagued housewives.[27]

Camrose's address to shareholders at the 1953 AGM proved to be the last before his death in June 1954. In his resumé of the prevailing business conditions he pointed to the changing cost patterns that were emerging in the industry, with sharp declines in the price of paper after 1952 being offset by higher costs in the areas of publicity, editorial, carriage, and the wages of printing labour. During the mid-1950s his son and successor as chairman, Michael Berry (later Lord Hartwell), grappled with these forces as they began to reverse the post-war trend of rising profits across the industry. Labour troubles in the printing side of the business, stemming from demarcation disputes and changing wage differentials between different unions, were becoming an acute problem for magazine publishers and the newspaper trade.[28] In March 1956, following the expiration of a five-year agreement between the British Federation of Master Printers and various print unions, a breakdown in negotiations led to a severe disruption of magazine printing in London for a period of some weeks. Amalgamated Press was particularly badly hit, with 23 of its 29 weekly publications suspended at one stage, causing a severe dent in its revenues and profits.[29] During the dispute Amalgamated's trade publishing arm, the Associated Iliffe Press, sought alternative printing in Europe and Canada, and were able to avoid disruption to all but one of their titles, although in the long run such a move did not prove to be economical.[30]

Associated Iliffe were not the only British-based publishing enterprise that looked to Canada for assistance during the 1950s. When the *Scotsman* newspaper fell into financial difficulties during 1953 the firm's directors in Edinburgh responded to an invitation made three years earlier by the acquisitive Canadian entrepreneur Roy Thomson to sell their long-standing but loss-making title to his expanding group of media businesses. The Canadian magnate created Thomson Scottish Associates Ltd., to take control of the group of publications that included the *Edinburgh Evening Dispatch* and a number of weekly titles as well as the *Scotsman*.[31] The move provided Thomson with a base in the United Kingdom and in 1957 his majority-owned Scottish Television Ltd. acquired the licence for Scottish commercial television from the Independent Television Authority.[32] The Scottish television venture proved to be highly lucrative, and within the space of two years had provided Thomson with the financial capacity to purchase the publishing interests of Lord Kemsley, including the *Sunday Times*.[33] For Kemsley's nephew Michael Berry, news that the sale of the *Sunday Times* had taken place without his knowledge was greeted with astonishment. Berry's subsequent counter-bid for the newspaper title that his father Lord Camrose had purchased back in 1915 was unceremoniously rebuffed.[34] The acquisition of the *Sunday Times* brought Thomson a base in Fleet Street as well as a chain of provincial newspapers in Aberdeen, Cardiff, and across the north of England. The Canadian entrepreneur quickly set about modernizing Kemsley's newspaper businesses. He sold the *Empire News* to the News of the World Group, closed the *Sunday Graphic*, and gave much greater editorial freedom to the management of the *Sunday Times*.[35] By the end of the 1950s, therefore, Roy Thomson had emerged as a significant player in the British media scene. In 1961 his operations were consolidated under the identity of the Thomson Organisation Ltd., at which point he extended his activities for the first time into Britain's magazine field by acquiring a controlling interest in the Illustrated Newspapers group from Sir John Ellerman. He thereby obtained the nucleus of a magazine business that included the turn-of-century *Tatler* and *Sphere* titles as well as the long-standing *Illustrated London News*.[36]

Thomson's entry into Fleet Street brought on to the scene a significant new competitor, a rare event for an industry in which few other newcomers emerged during these years. For more than a decade after the end of the war the firm composition of the British magazine industry remained almost stagnant. Naturally, as from the early the days of Grub Street, many small-scale single-title organizations such as *The Lady* continued to eke out a living around the environs of Fleet Street and the Strand, and a few successful small businesses were launched.[37] Over the border, the Scottish outfit of D. C. Thomson did likewise in Dundee, publishing downmarket women's magazines such as *My Weekly* and children's comics including the *Beano* and *Dandy*.[38] Higher up in the market, the American-owned National Magazine Company successfully launched *Vanity Fair* in 1949 to supplement their *Harper's Bazaar* offering, and in 1955 found a winning formula in the popular women's market with *She*.[39] In the East Midlands the first stirrings of a future magazine giant were felt in 1953 when the four-firm amalgamation of provincial newspaper publishers and printers known as the East Midland Allied Press (EMAP) began to exploit its spare printing capacity to launch *Angling Times*. This provided a formula for similar titles in the 1950s such as *Trout and Salmon*, *Motor Cycle News* (a magazine purchased for £100), and *Garden News*. Gradually a business model based on specialist publications took shape, but EMAP did not make serious inroads in the magazine market until the 1970s.[40] For the most part during the 1950s, the competitive battles within the consumer magazine industry were fought by the same group of incumbent firms that had existed at the outbreak of the war.

The progress of Newnes and Amalgamated Press during these years had been marked almost as much by the closing or consolidation of titles as by the introduction of new ones. The counterpart to the rapid expansion in the weekly women's magazine segment had been the ever-rising costs of publicity to maintain market share within the tight three-firm oligopoly. Successful mass production of consumer magazines required expensive investments in colour printing equipment and, for a vertically integrated producer such as the huge Amalgamated Press, modern paper-making machinery. The system of high volume production also provided the printing unions with considerable bargaining power based on an ability to shut off revenues by closing down the presses. At Amalgamated Press, Michael Berry described 1956/7 as an exceptionally difficult year, with over £4 million invested in plant and machinery, a print workers' stoppage which was only resolved by a pledge to raise wages by approximately 11 per cent, the closure of four of its long-standing titles due to rising costs, falling advertising revenues for the first time in 15 years, and the extreme competitive pressures in the market for women's weekly magazines keeping up the costs of promotion and publicity. As for the introduction of fresh titles, he bemoaned the fact that, 'Quite apart from the considerable financial outlay needed, the paper and printing bills alone are so high that they are usually too prohibitive to be practicable when considering the starting of new publications.' In the year ahead, he concluded, 'hard facts and maybe hard remedies will have to be faced'.[41]

TAKEOVERS AND CORPORATE CONSOLIDATION

The remedies to the rising costs and declining profits of Britain's leading magazine publishers began to take shape in earnest during 1958. Two events provided the catalysts for the process of industry realignment which began in that year—the birth of one new magazine and the death of another. In May 1957, Edward Hulton took the decision to consign his firm's leading magazine title to oblivion. The circulation of the *Picture Post* had been in decline since the early 1950s[42] after the Conservative Party-supporting proprietor had persuaded his compliant board to dispense with the services of its socialist editor Tom Hopkinson. Tension had been growing between the two men since the end of the war, as Hulton's political outlook veered sharply away from the earlier socialist ideals of the magazine and instead became increasingly centred on the emerging American hostility towards the Soviet Union. The flashpoint between the two erstwhile colleagues arose over an item for *Picture Post* that detailed mistreatment of North Korean prisoners of war, as the American anti-Communist stance hardened into military conflict.[43] Shorn of Hopkinson's dynamic leadership, the *Picture Post* lost both editorial direction and readers. A cursory study of the cover features of the *Picture Post* from the mid-1950s, now featuring full-colour photographs, displays the magazine's changing emphasis from its wartime reputation in hard journalism towards celebrity and attractive females. The change in formula alienated the magazine's existing readership and failed to recruit a new generation, an unsuccessful transition that was not helped by a (rapidly reversed) decision in the mid-1950s to raise the cover price by 50 per cent from 4*d.* to 6*d.*[44] Looking back on his decision to close the title, Hulton cited changing readership patterns rather than his earlier explanation which had laid the blame squarely on the growing influence of television.[45] More plausibly, it was Hulton's attempt to recast the *Picture Post* in line with his perception of the British public's evolving tastes, and the frequent changes of editor and market strategy which accompanied this policy, that ultimately brought the magazine down.[46] Without its primary revenue-driver, and with no obvious successor to the *Picture Post* other than the photographic legacy of its picture library, the Hulton Press enterprise drifted rapidly towards the rocks.[47]

The demise of the *Picture Post* brought into sharp relief the declining demand for general-interest consumer magazines more broadly in Britain, as the growth in television presented consumers with a competing medium of entertainment which monopolized their attention in a way that radio programmes had not done.[48] This downward trend in sales of general-interest magazines also adversely affected Odhams, whose *Illustrated* and *John Bull* titles were similarly suffering a decline in sales.[49] As a result, Odhams' dependence on advertising revenues from magazines aimed at women was further increased. With sales of their flagship *Woman* moving beyond three million per week, the point was reached at which the company's gravure printing capacity in Watford began to experience diseconomies of scale for a single weekly title.[50] Given that demand among advertisers for space in the women's weekly segment was showing no sign of exhaustion, Odhams took the decision to launch a second periodical aimed at the more price competitive segment of the women's weekly market.[51] Under the editorship of Joyce Ward, Odhams' *Woman's Realm* immediately began to make inroads into the sales of its closest competitor, Amalgamated Press' *Woman's Weekly*. Following Odhams' move, and Newnes' launch of *Woman's Day* into the same segment shortly before,[52] an exasperated Michael Berry was moved to exclaim that, 'Each publishing house seems to act on the assumption that the appetite for women's magazines is still unsatisfied', and neglecting the fact that maintaining sales of these titles required ever-greater sums in terms of publicity. The intensification of competition in the one segment of the magazine industry that was continuing to prosper came as a severe blow to Amalgamated Press, whose own leading general magazine, *Everybody's*, was also losing sales.[53] Seen retrospectively, the successful launch of *Woman's Realm* represented a watershed moment for the UK magazine industry; in one way or another, consolidation had now become a financial imperative.

According to one biographer, Michael Berry had reached the conclusion that the leading magazine titles of Amalgamated Press were set to lose £1 million during the financial year 1958/9.[54] Under these circumstances it is hardly surprising that he and his fellow family members, who as a group effectively controlled the company via their 33 per cent ordinary share ownership, were seeking to sell their magazine publishing and printing businesses. The first offer to buy came in November 1958 from Cecil Harmsworth King, the chairman of Daily Mirror Newspapers Ltd. and a nephew of the founders of Amalgamated Press, Alfred and Harold Harmsworth. King had assumed control of Mirror Newspapers in 1951 from Guy Bartholomew,[55] with whom he had pioneered a tabloid revolution in the British popular press.[56] In the immediate post-war period the circulation of the *Daily Mirror* had risen from two million to over

4.5 million copies, and by 1950 it had overtaken the *Daily Express* as Britain's largest selling national newspaper. However, this growth subsequently stalled, particularly during the latter part of the 1950s, and King sought opportunities to expand the Mirror's sphere of media activities via a strategy of horizontal integration.[57] Recognizing the potential of commercial television to provide good long-term returns, King had begun the expansion of the Mirror organization when he purchased a minority interest in Associated Television. His subsequent move into magazines, via the Berry acquisition, was complicated by the fact that the capital value of Amalgamated Press exceeded that of Mirror Newspapers, and any deal needed to be financed primarily through the issue of new equity. Under the initial arrangement, by which two Mirror Newspaper shares would be exchanged for each share in Amalgamated Press, the net effect would have been to transfer ownership of the Mirror to the shareholders of Amalgamated Press.[58] It had therefore been agreed that the Berry family's shareholding in the expanded Mirror organization would be immediately sold on to Sunday Pictorial Newspapers, a partner company of the Mirror that owned 15.5 per cent of its ordinary shares. This arrangement allowed the Berrys to effectively sell their shareholding in Amalgamated Press for cash. At the conclusion of the deal, a proportion of this cash would subsequently be recouped by the Mirror as a result of the Amalgamated Press' own interests in commercial television. In 1957 the Berrys had bought a minority stake in Southern Television and under the terms of the ownership of such broadcasting rights, the Independent Television Authority prohibited the shares in more than one commercial television company being held by any given organization. Thus the Mirror's holding in Associated Television meant that the Amalgamated Press' Southern Television interest would need to be sold on completion of the merger, thereby generating a stock of cash.

Before the Mirror's proposed acquisition was completed, rumours of a counter-bid forced King to raise his offer to the shareholders of Amalgamated Press by a further £2 million in December 1958.[59] In the final analysis, the Mirror paid the public shareholders a total of £15 million in shares and cash, and the Berry family interests received somewhere in excess of £3 million.[60] Despite the very large sum required to purchase the business, King later boasted that the value of the two subsidiaries of Amalgamated Press, the Imperial Paper Mills and the Kelly-Iliffe group of titles, was greater than the price that the Mirror had paid for the whole enterprise, and thus that the consumer magazine part of the business had effectively cost nothing. All the same, the need for a complete revamping of the management of the consumer magazine business was readily acknowledged both by King and insiders amongst the Berry employees.[61] Another consequence of Berry's decision to sell off its magazines was the restoration of American ownership to *Vogue* magazine. Michael Berry's father, Lord Camrose, had rescued the business of Condé Nast from bankruptcy during the early years of the depression and had later disposed of his controlling interest in the company to his Amalgamated Press firm. An option to repatriate the shares allowed *Vogue* to be rescued from the clutches of Cecil King by Sam Newhouse, whose New York-based publishing and media business purchased Condé Nast and then expanded its American operations via the acquisition of the important US periodical proprietor Street & Smith.[62]

The rumoured counter-bid for Amalgamated Press which surfaced towards the end of the Mirror negotiations had emanated from the management of Odhams Press.[63] While this firm had been relatively successful in terms of its magazines, its trade journals, book publishing, and billboard advertising activities—and published the very successful Sunday newspaper *The People*—by the late 1950s its co-ownership with the Trades Union Congress (TUC) of the *Daily Herald* was causing concern for the firm's future profitability. The *Herald*'s sales had fallen below two million in 1951, soon after the quota system of paper rationing had been abolished. Thereafter it rapidly lost readers, particularly to the tabloid *Daily Mirror*, and its share of the lucrative market for consumer advertising was consequently also in decline.[64] Early in 1957 the management of another newspaper with a flagging circulation, the middle-class *News Chronicle*, approached Odhams to propose a merger of the two titles, but the offer (which had the qualified backing of Labour leader Hugh Gaitskell) was rebuffed.[65] All the same, in each of the three years to 1958, Odhams' chairman A. C. Duncan had reported rising costs and falling profits to his shareholders, and the management must have viewed with a degree of foreboding the likely impact on competition in the magazine market that would arise from the change in ownership of Amalgamated Press. King certainly wasted no time in starting the process of rationalizing the magazine portfolio of the Mirror's new acquisition. Within three months of taking control, the company had followed Hulton's lead by killing off its own general consumer weekly publication, *Everybody's*, along with *TV Mirror*, a relatively recent venture in the TV segment which had been unable to overcome the listing monopolies of the *Radio Times* and *TV Times*,[66] and a stalwart from the halcyon days of Alfred Harmsworth, *Home Chat*, which had been founded in 1895.[67] Clearly, sentiment was now playing second fiddle to profitability in Britain's magazine industry as King promised shareholders further modernization of the consumer magazines business.[68]

By the late 1950s the vagaries of time were beginning to take their toll on the management of Odhams. In 1958 chairman A. C. Duncan had reported the passing of one of the firm's joint managing directors, W. H. Parrack, who had served for 42 years. Duncan himself was shortly to retire from his role at the head of the company, and there is a strongly held impression that his leadership during his period in charge had tended to look back to the legacy of Julius Elias rather than forward to the newly emerging popular consumer culture of the late 1950s and early 1960s.[69] In recognition of the need for new blood, early in 1959 the Odhams board appointed Sir Christopher Chancellor, general manager of the Reuters news agency from whom the *Daily Herald* had drawn much of its overseas copy, as vice chairman.[70] Following hard on the heels of Chancellor's appointment, Odhams' board put forward a bid of £1.8 million for the Hulton Press business. With no concern for overlap between the two firms' general interest publications, given the recent closure of *Illustrated* magazine's main rival title, *Picture Post*, the move provided Odhams with access to a range of new outlets, including children's publications and a number of sporting titles.[71] With 59 per cent of its ordinary shares controlled by the Hulton family, agreement to go ahead with the takeover was unproblematic given Edward Hulton's willingness to sell.

Across Britain's magazine industry, the takeover juggernaut now gathered significant momentum. Within a month of the acquisition of Hulton Press (re-titled by Odhams as Longacre Press), a bid just short of £10 million was lodged for the business of Newnes on behalf of the owners of the *News of the World*.[72] Had this move been successful, each of the three leading magazine enterprises in Britain would have been allied with one or more popular newspapers, providing advertising clients with a mixed portfolio of press advertising options. The creation of such a potentially stable three-legged firm structure within the magazine industry, however, was thwarted by the new management at Odhams. Despite the fact that the *News of the World* bid was subsequently raised to over £11 million, it quickly became apparent that Odhams were prepared to trump the newspaper group's offer. Using a combination of cash and equity, Odhams mounted a counter-bid of £12.3 million which they placed before the Newnes shareholders. The offer was immediately accepted by the Newnes board, under its chairman Charles Morris, and the company's ordinary shareholders duly voted in support.[73] The merging together of Odhams, Newnes, and Hulton within the course of a matter of months of 1959 meant that the British-owned segment of the consumer magazine industry, outside of D. C. Thomson in Scotland, now lay almost exclusively in the hands of just two firms.

FROM DUOPOLY TO MONOPOLY

Throughout the whole of 1960, the magazine and newspaper publishing industry in Fleet Street was in a state of ferment. The emergence of Roy Thomson as the new owner of the *Sunday Times*, the sale of Amalgamated Press to King's Mirror interests, and the swallowing of both Hulton and Newnes by Odhams Press were followed in October 1959 by the decision of the Cadbury family to close their *News Chronicle* and *Star* titles. These papers were sold overnight to Esmond Rothermere's Associated Newspapers and subsumed into that firm's competing *Daily Mail* and *Evening News* titles respectively.[74] The demise of the *News Chronicle* was a particularly traumatic event in the history of British national daily newspapers as it represented the remaining mouthpiece of the Liberal Party.[75] However, its dwindling sales and substantial losses meant that the paper's commercial viability was compromised. Its closure inevitably raised fresh concerns over the future position of Odhams' *Daily Herald* title, with which the *News Chronicle* had pursued an abortive merger three years earlier. By virtue of its new acquisitions, Odhams had grown spectacularly over the course of the year which preceded the closure of the *News Chronicle*. At his final Annual General Meeting of the company as chairman, A. C. Duncan had informed Odhams' shareholders that the asset value of their company had virtually doubled over the course of 12 months, and was now estimated to be £40 million.[76] He also noted that the sales of the *Daily Herald* stood at 1.4 million, but omitted to mention the fall of 50,000 copies that had occurred since the previous year's AGM.[77]

The first task of Christopher Chancellor, Duncan's successor as Odhams' chairman, was to revamp the *Daily Herald*, ending its long-standing relationship with the unions under which the TUC held ultimate editorial control.[78] To effect this process of disengagement, in August 1960 Chancellor appointed as editor of the *Herald* a Labour right-winger from the *Manchester Evening News*, John Beavan, whose brief was 'to embrace the new meritocracy and move the paper upmarket, with features and reviews likely to attract a widening middle-class'.[79] At the Mirror, meanwhile, Cecil King was concerned to improve the profitability of his newly acquired magazine portfolio by reducing the total number of women's weekly magazines competing for the same readers. According to his own account, King proposed to Chancellor late in 1960 that Odhams and the Mirror (now operating the Amalgamated Press business under the new mantle of Fleetway Publications) form a joint venture, majority owned by Odhams, which would handle the women's weekly magazines.[80] Alternative accounts given by Odhams' directors suggested that King had proposed to sell them a number of Fleetway's magazines and plant for a sum of £10 million.[81] Chancellor viewed King's overtures as a veiled takeover threat and sought protection from a white knight in the shape of Roy Thomson, who was seeking to add a national daily newspaper to his expanding British press empire.

The future shape of Britain's consumer magazine publishing industry now became inextricably linked with the fate of the *Daily Herald*. Once again, Hugh Gaitskell played an active role in the events that unfolded, this time by encouraging Chancellor to seek an arrangement with the Thomson interests in order to prevent the *Herald* from falling under the control of King and the Mirror organization.[82] A series of discussions between Odhams and Thomson eventually resulted in a joint statement on behalf of the two companies' boards in January 1961 in which they outlined plans to merge under the aegis of a holding company. The merger was to be structured as a takeover bid by Odhams for the shares of Thomson, but the conjectured holding company, Thomson Odhams Ltd., would be effectively controlled by Roy Thomson's minority share owner-ship.[83] Speaking at a joint press conference on 26 January, Odhams' prospec-tive new owners gave assurances that no publication would be closed down as a result of the merger. Thomson referred to the arrangement as a 'Marriage of Convenience'. At the same time, Chancellor stated that the TUC had not been informed of the negotiations, despite their 49 per cent shareholding in the *Herald*, 'because this was essentially a deal between Thomson Newspapers and Odhams Press'.[84]

The announcement was greeted immediately by calls to investigate the growth of monopolistic control in the newspaper and periodical publishing business. A question to prime minister Harold Macmillan was tabled on the issue for discussion in Parliament on 2 February. Before it could be posed, however, the Mirror launched a counter-bid for Odhams. A statement that accompanied this bid emphasized the substantial economies that would be gained by the closer cooperation of the two groups' respective magazine interests via the elimination of overlapping expenditure on promotion and publicity. Giving assurances that the future of the *Herald* as an independent, Labour-supporting paper would be secure, the statement added that, in the event of the Thomson–Odhams merger going ahead, it would be the inten-tion of the new owners of Odhams to use its powers to sell off the whole of the Thomson interests, including the participation in Scottish television.[85] The Mirror's bid was thus a mortal threat to the Canadian's continued participation in the British media industry on his own terms and, within days, Thomson had signalled his intention to withdraw from the arrangement with Odhams.[86]

As these events unfolded, the political response was rapidly taking shape. Initial discussions at the Home Office played down the likely impact that the Thomson–Odhams merger would have on the range and political com-plexion of newspapers available in Britain. When, a few days later, attention switched to the Mirror bid for Odhams, the effect on Britain's national news-papers was considered to be unaffected, with no closures similar to that of the *News Chronicle* likely to be forthcoming. Rather, the commercial motive of the Mirror–Odhams amalgamation was assumed to be based around the peri-odical and magazine interests of the two firms. This latter point was reiterated by Gaitskell at a meeting convened with prime minister MacMillan, Liberal leader Jo Grimond, and the home secretary on 1 February. Gaitskell argued that the magazine war lay at the root of the latest developments and the threat to the *Daily Herald* was a consequence rather than a cause of these develop-ments. Grimond, meanwhile, expressed his concern about the power of the print unions which he considered to represent the main problem facing the industry.[87] Responding to questions in the House of Commons, MacMillan drew attention to the issue of monopoly control over magazine publishing that might stem from the Mirror's takeover of Odhams. Given that the new concern would control somewhere in the region of 300 popular periodicals, MacMillan promised that any significant increases in price or reductions in choice arising pursuant to the merger taking place could trigger a reference to the Monopolies Commission.[88] MacMillan's statement was based on advice given to him by the Attorney General who had considered that a reference to the Monopolies Commission, although technically possible, was unlikely to be of any value due to the limited public interest concerns but should not be actively discounted for fear that it might encourage the merger to go ahead.[89] Nevertheless, MacMillan's statement in the House ruled out an immediate Monopolies Commission enquiry.

With Thomson no longer in the picture and no concerns regarding a Monopolies Commission investigation, the Mirror bid for Odhams moved to its conclusion. Understandably, Chancellor and the board of Odhams initially opposed King's advances. The thrust of the argument to their independent shareholders was that, whereas the Odhams–Newnes–Hulton portfolio of magazines were largely operating on a sound economic basis, the Amalgamated Press (now Fleetway Publications) stable of periodicals, were in many cases very likely to be losing money and could thus only be maintained in business by means of ruinous levels of expenditure on publicity and promotions. In a letter to Odhams' shareholders they explained their company's willingness to reach an accommodation with King in order to reduce 'the problem of competition in the women's magazine field'—the very proposal over which they had previously cavilled.[90] King's response was simply to raise the value of the Mirror's bid by another £5 million. In addition, acting on a suggestion from his deputy Hugh Cudlipp, King laid to rest any public concerns over the fate of the *Daily Herald* by pledging that the Mirror would continue to publish the paper for a minimum of seven years if the merger went through.[91] On 24 February Christopher Chancellor wrote to Odhams' shareholders advising them to accept the revised terms, which amounted to around £37 million in total, and the takeover of Odhams by the Mirror was effectively completed on 1 March.[92]

Chancellor and Thomson had thus been vanquished, but trade union opposition to the merger now became King's central cause for concern. Fearing redundancies, the general secretaries of unions affiliated to the Printing and Kindred Trades Federation sought a meeting with King to discuss future scenarios.[93] Given that the logic of the Mirror's takeover of Odhams had been based on the benefits of rationalization in the women's weekly segment there was little choice other than to make some adjustment in this field. Consequently, the Fleetway publication *Woman's Illustrated* was rolled into Odhams' *Woman*, and two Newnes publications, *Woman's Own* and *Woman's Day* were merged under the masthead of the former.[94] In sum, however, the amount of bloodletting was relatively small and King acknowledged in his memoir that both Odhams and Newnes were largely well-run businesses.[95] In terms of plant rationalization, all the existing gravure printing facilities of the old Amalgamated Press in London were closed, with the more modern presses being relocated to the Odhams facility in Watford.

While the merger negotiations were still underway, prime minister MacMillan convened a meeting to consider the issue of setting up a Royal Commission on the Press. The benefits of holding an enquiry were seen to be threefold: to allay the public anxiety about newspaper closures that arose following the demise of the *News Chronicle*; to assess the potential issues that might arise from increased industrial concentration in the periodical publishing industry for the range of views aired in the press; and to expose current weaknesses in the organization and operational efficiency of the periodical publishing and printing industry. Convened under the chairmanship of Lord Shawcross, the Commission's report, published in 1962, acknowledged the extreme degree of concentration that the Mirror–Odhams merger had brought into effect within the consumer magazine branch of the periodical publishing industry. However, the conclusions raised no concerns in terms of providing a choice to the public and the report itself pointed instead to the benefits of an individual enterprise owning multiple magazine titles, viz: 'The large magazine undertaking is better able than a concern with only one periodical to cater for changing needs and tastes among readers by stopping one publication and launching another.'[96] This ringing endorsement of big business within the magazine segment of the press did not extend to the operation of its labour force. Within the newspaper business, the huge level of inefficiency in relation to printing was the overwhelming focus of the report's recommendations for reform.

The final upshot of the corporate magazine mergers was the formation in December 1962 of the International Publishing Corporation, known subsequently as IPC. This created a corporate entity into which the interests of the Mirror Newspapers and its compatriot the *Sunday Pictorial* were subsumed. In April the following year IPC became the holding company for all the various publishing interests of the Mirror Group. Six operating divisions were created, one of which handled the publishing of newspapers, two of which published trade journals (Kelly-Iliffe Holdings and the National Trade Press which included the Hulton successor Longacre Publishing as well as numerous trade press enterprises), and three of which were primarily concerned with consumer magazine publishing (Fleetway, Odhams, and George Newnes).[97] Above it all a Harmsworth, in the shape of Cecil King, presided over a virtual monopoly of Britain's leading consumer magazines.

6

The Ministry of Magazines

THE IPC BEHEMOTH

Incorporated on 8 April 1963, with a capitalization of £50 million and a total group turnover of £112 million, the new International Publishing Corporation was the largest newspaper and periodical printing group in the world.[1] Ruling over the British publishing industry from its Fleetway House headquarters in Farringdon, the group controlled 9 UK newspapers, 11 overseas newspapers, 78 consumer magazines including comics, 126 trade and technical journals, 34 directories and yearbooks, 17 encyclopaedias, 9 exhibitions, and 25 printing plants.[2] IPC had ready access to cheap newsprint through its control of Albert E. Reed & Co.,[3] and the new vertically integrated conglomerate was to define the industry for more than the next two decades, a position acknowledged by competitors who unflatteringly dubbed it 'the Ministry of Magazines'. The Corporation's consumer magazine interests enjoyed a dominant position in the industry, secure in an almost unchallenged control of the lucrative women's weekly market.[4] Through 1961 to 1984 this segment was far and away the industry's core market, as the six women's weeklies alone comprised 33 per cent of all weekly consumer magazine sales in 1961. By 1977, IPC's 'big four' women's weekly titles accounted for 76 per cent of the segment's sales, giving IPC a 26 per cent share of all weekly magazines, and a 20 per cent share of the entire consumer market, before their other titles were even taken into account.[5]

Despite its near monopoly status, the newly formed company would find that its ability to exploit this position was to be highly constrained by a number of internal and external factors which the firm would wrestle with for decades. The consolidation of the three leading magazine producing firms by the Mirror Group under the IPC umbrella in 1963 had been the result of a politically driven corporate strategy which was as much focused on defensive moves to establish control of the newspaper industry as it was to consolidate the magazine market through cost rationalization, or attempts to leverage economies of scope across different publishing segments. Although the size and immense market power of the newly formed company would offer it protection, it also acted to mask problems and to subsidize poor productivity in the company's printing firms.[6]

Bringing the Mirror Group and Odhams together created a great duplication of resources, as well as a near-replication of magazine titles, between Newnes, Odhams Press, and Fleetway Publications, highlighting the management problems that the IPC had inherited. By the 1960s Odhams and Fleetway (previously Amalgamated Press) were suffering from long-term deficiencies which now needed serious redress. When the Mirror Group took control of Amalgamated Press in 1959 this had been the salvation of the latter, as it had been suffering from both a chronic lack of investment and attention due to Michael Berry's interest being fixed firmly on the *Daily Telegraph*.[7] The existing management at Amalgamated Press acknowledged that the company's enterprises were old fashioned compared to Odhams and Newnes,[8] and its titles dated, with even its flagship *Woman's Weekly* still being printed in black and white on uncompetitive printing presses.[9] The initial value of the acquisition to the Mirror Group was found only in the ownership of the Imperial Paper Mills and Kelly-Iliffe trade and technical publishers.[10] The acquisition of Odhams, and the crippled Hulton Press within it, had likewise brought companies together that suffered from intractable working relationships with the trade unions and ageing printing equipment. Although Odhams still operated the largest and fastest rotogravure print works in the UK, by the 1960s the presses were largely outdated in international terms, the relationship between management and union chapels was dire, and there was little integration between the printing operations and the magazine titles. In the estimation of Cecil King, Newnes alone was in a well-managed position, with a leading title in *Woman's Own*, and having already disposed of its print works.[11]

With the amalgamation of all these enterprises into a single organization there was an opportunity for the long-overdue rationalization the sector required, both in terms of the congested women's market, and across their business operations, a strategy that King himself had identified as necessary for the sector in 1960.[12] Despite this, when faced with the ownership of a strong portfolio of titles, the company lacked a clear business strategy for its magazine publishing businesses and continued to operate Newnes, Odhams Press, and Fleetway Publications as autonomous units. The main strategic innovation designed to achieve greater efficiencies was through the rationalization of support services across the trade and technical press, newspaper, printing and paper operations. This initial reluctance to take a hands-on approach to the management of the magazine interests may have been an outcome of the Mirror Group's experience following the purchase of the Amalgamated Press. In the transition to Fleetway, Mirror executives had felt that as successful newspaper publishers they could translate newspaper ideas directly into the running of magazines, but quickly discovered that the publishing requirements of the businesses were very different and were forced to rethink their approach.[13] With this expensive experience on board, a wait-and-see approach was adopted to the management of the magazine firms, leading to a long interregnum during which life for the magazine companies and their editorial teams within the new IPC largely continued much as before.[14] The stabling together of former fierce competitors, however, naturally led to some degree of internecine conflict, and the new owners were forced to step in to avoid wasteful quarrels, and a limited attempt was made in 1965 to avoid unproductive competition between titles by the creation of a management department responsible for the overall coordination of the magazine publishing firms. The conglomerate was finally given shape between 1963 and 1964 by being restructured into six separate operating Groups, the Daily Mirror Newspapers, International Printers, Fleetway Publications, George Newnes, Kelly-Iliffe (Holdings), and the National Trade Press.[15]

SOCIAL CHANGE AND THE SUNDAY SUPPLEMENTS

In this period of relatively benign neglect, new title launches were still undertaken independently by the three magazine firms. As the women's weekly sector had originated from meeting the needs of the changing role of women in society at the start of the century, the 1960s presented new opportunities as the growing economy created new women's and youth markets.[16] With the birth of IPC coinciding with the 'youthquake'[17] heralded by The Beatles' second single 'Please Please Me' reaching number one in the *New Musical Express* (*NME*) chart in February 1963, it was estimated that there were more than five million teenagers in Britain, spending £800,000 on records, clothes, and magazines.[18] Existing titles such as IPC's *NME*[19] and the *Melody Maker* capitalized on the boom, and new titles such as *Fabulous* and *Rave*[20] emerged from the IPC stable to compete with independent new entrants such as the short-lived *Hit Parade*.[21] Fleetway had been an early mover on new trends for fashion-conscious young women with the launch of *Honey* in April 1960 under editor Audrey Slaughter, often thought of as the seminal teen magazine. Newnes launched *Nova* in March 1965, a monthly designed for 'forward-thinking women', and *19* in March 1968 in the same vein as *Honey*.[22] While this illustrates that the management department's coordination of new launches remained unable to prevent some degree of overlap and in-house competition, it also shows that in its early years IPC was still capable of reacting to the changing times and finding new market opportunities. In this it was not alone, as externally IPC's market position became subject to new forms of domestic competition as the newspaper groups began to include free magazine-style supplements with their offerings, to both counter falling readerships and exploit demand

for magazines unsatisfied by IPC. The *Sunday Times* launched the first colour supplement with the *Sunday Times Magazine* on 4 February 1962,[23] which
featured cutting-edge coverage of contemporary fashion and style, capturing the changing 'permissive' and anti-authoritarian social scene of the 1960s
characterized by the new satirical journal *Private Eye*.[24] Perfectly capturing the
moment, the opening issue featured a David Bailey cover photograph of Jean
Shrimpton in a Mary Quant dress, and included a James Bond short story by
Ian Fleming.[25] The *Sunday Times Magazine* was followed by the *Observer* and
Sunday Telegraph magazines, and the circulation of the newspaper colour supplements rose from one million in 1962 to 3.4 million by 1980.[26] This development did not only serve to lure readers away from conventional consumer
magazines, but also formed a direct competitor for advertising sales, where
newspapers generally had more power relative to magazine companies.[27] Over
time the newspapers not only provided competition through the inclusion of
these supplements, but indirect competition also came from the tabloid sector
as their format and journalism gradually became more magazine-like.[28] While
the Sunday supplements market boomed, from 1961 to 1973 the magazine
market shank in terms of circulation, falling 0.3 per cent, with the women's
sector declining 2.5 per cent.[29]

For IPC, newspaper supplements presented a dilemma as they wished to
avoid cannibalizing their own magazine sales and advertising, but to also
counter the threat of potential rival supplements issued by the tabloid publishers siphoning off advertising from their weekly magazine titles, and also maintain the market-leading position of their flagship tabloid newspaper, the *Daily
Mirror*. Eventually their hand was forced by Rupert Murdoch's acquisition of
the *News of the World* in 1968, and IPC launched the *Mirror Magazine* in 1969
as a pre-emptive strike before Murdoch could establish his own offering.[30] On
the positive side, the new Sunday magazines provided IPC's printing firms
with an additional customer when Odhams (Watford) gained the contract to
print the *Sunday Telegraph* supplement.[31]

CHANGING LEADERSHIP AT IPC

Although IPC continued to develop successful new magazine titles, a raft
of problems remained: it was still overly reliant on the traditional women's
weeklies; it suffered from underinvestment in its print works; it experienced
difficult relations with the trade unions; and it had largely failed to grasp
opportunities to rationalize the group. Under King's management the magazine companies retained strong ties to their past, both through continued
managerial autonomy and by retaining Amalgamated Press and Odhams'
long-standing bonds to newspapers through the Mirror Group. These ties

were more than simply an outcome of corporate structure. Rather, they high-lighted the peripheral role in which magazine firms were placed by the indus-try's power elite, whose focus since the early days of the *Daily Mail* had been primarily on newspapers. A true heir to his uncle, Lord Northcliffe, Cecil King was also drawn to newspaper printing as a form of political engagement. King had achieved great success as a newspaper proprietor, along with his long-serving editor Hugh Cudlipp, in making the *Daily Mirror* the country's largest circulating newspaper with a clear Labour Party sympathy.[32] Given this hierarchical approach to media ownership within the newspaper-driven Mirror Group, magazines themselves were very much considered to play the role of the second cousins. Newspaper magnates, such as Northcliffe and Hearst, had long used popular journalism to advance their own political agendas, and these peculiarities of proprietorial newspaper publishing acted to conflate political and economic motivations in driving the process of busi-ness decision-making in the sector.[33]

Ultimately, political entanglements of this nature claimed the career of IPC's chairman as the man who had earned the title of 'the lion of Fleet Street'—and who had himself likened the world of Fleet Street to that of the jungle—fell prey to his own board. King had lost confidence in Harold Wilson's leader-ship of his second Labour government, which had been returned to office in 1966, and sought the prime minister's resignation both through the media and behind the scenes. His campaign came to a head on 10 May 1968 when he printed on the front page of the *Daily Mirror* a personally signed letter enti-tled 'Enough is Enough' in which he argued for Wilson's removal.[34] At this time, however, King was a member of the Court of Directors of the Bank of England, and his public criticism of the financial conduct of the government brought severe reprobation and compelled his own resignation as a director of the Bank. Moreover, just as King had once criticized Michael Berry for neglecting his magazine interests at the Amalgamated Press, so he found the same accusation levelled at him by his own board of directors at the Mirror. Meeting on 28 May 1968 to discuss the future of their chairman, the board unanimously agreed to seek King's removal on the basis that his 'increasing preoccupation and intervention in national affairs' had taken his attention away from his leadership of IPC.[35] Led by Hugh Cudlipp, his working partner of 31 years, the board offered King the option to retire immediately. On refus-ing this unpalatable offer, King was curtly informed the following day that he was no longer the chairman of IPC or director of the Reed Paper Group, and that Cudlipp had been unanimously elected to be his successor with immedi-ate effect.[36] For Britain's magazine industry this boardroom coup represented a turning point, foreclosing as it did the connection between magazines and the politicized newspaper press under whose mantle their publishing businesses had languished for years as little more than the providers of financial subsidies to their owners' true priorities.[37] From this point forward the management of the magazine interests at IPC would be undertaken as a business which would stand or fall its own merits.

THE MCKINSEY REORGANIZATION

Within the Corporation a generation of business-orientated managers had emerged who thought that King had failed to rationalize the company with sufficient speed.[38] The *Daily Telegraph* argued that IPC was now a big business, and that King's habit of upsetting plans for 'unscientific' reasons had no longer fitted in with the technically and research-minded executives who wished to govern the firm along lines of economic rationalism.[39] Within IPC itself, this drive towards a more scientific style of management had already begun before King's removal with the appointment of the outside management consultancy firm, McKinsey & Co., to examine the operation of its magazine interests following several years of steeply falling profits for the Magazine Group.[40] Following the McKinsey Report the period of quiet autonomy for the three magazines enterprises came to a traumatic end, with a shake-up that brought together the Group's magazines interests into a single arm of the company as the IPC Magazine Division.[41] This new arrangement incorporated all the Odhams, Fleetway, and Newnes titles into one of five Divisions: Women's Weeklies; Women's Monthlies; Young Magazines; General Interest; and Practicals and Juveniles—with the majority of the directors' positions going to former Newnes managers.[42] A new IPC Business Press Division was also formed by the merger of the Trade and Technical Division and Kelly-Iliffe, but initially this group did not integrate its supporting functions with the five Magazine Divisions.[43] The strategy within IPC Magazines was to create a system of unified management and administration, to improve marketing, promotion, distribution, and services for advertisers, but to retain strong editorial teams. However, there were many who thought that the benefits of fierce competition between rival editorial departments such as *Woman* and *Woman's Own*, the *NME* and *Melody Maker*, and *Ideal Home* and *Homes & Gardens* was lost at a stroke.[44] The decision to centralize magazine management through the creation of IPC Magazines had both costs and benefits, with the main advantage being that the company was able to further leverage economies of scope across its many consumer interests. The women's weeklies, which relied on advertising to generate half of their revenue, were able to use centralized support in dealing with advertising.[45] *Woman's Weekly* also benefited from access to modern printing facilities when it moved to Odhams, where for the first time it could be printed in colour,[46] and IPC was able to transfer staff from new successful titles such as *Fabulous* to the *NME* in order to bring a more modern and professional approach.[47] A widening of the role of publisher was introduced to coordinate the management of magazine titles across related areas and to take the burden of the general administration of the magazine away from the editor, although there were those who thought this change weakened the company's traditional focus on editorial.[48] In the drive towards a more modern management regime, Hugh Cudlipp had employed the advertising agency PKL for the launch of *Woman's Mirror*, and had subsequently formed a research team with advertising director Alex McKay, Bill Jackson from Fleetway, and Mac McLelland from Odhams, using the Hulton Readership surveys to develop reader profiles.[49] This centralizing impetus was actively developed, and post-McKinsey these marketing services attained responsibility for many functions that had traditionally been the remit of the editorial office. Over time the creation of such strong central administration came to be seen as a strait-jacket that took responsibility and initiative away from IPC's magazine editors.[50]

Although the overlap between the different offerings in the women's market was seen an obvious candidate for consolidation, management lacked the nerve to merge established weekly titles, and the result of centralization was that the process of launching titles became steadily more bureaucratic in order to prevent in-house sales cannibalization. Ron Phillips, director of the Practicals and Juveniles Group, for example, conceived the idea for *Shoot!*, a football title aimed at 8- to 15-year-old boys, but this brought him into conflict with IPC Business Press, which published *Goal*. All new titles now needed to be cleared at board level, which could be a lengthy and overtly political process.[51] Cultural integration between former rivals was slow. According to Phillips, 'old habits were to die hard, and for many years individual staff referred to themselves as ex-Newnes, ex-Odhams or ex-Fleetway or even ex-Amalgamated Press: anything but IPC'.[52] The former companies still maintained sports teams which competed with each other, keeping alive the old names and rivalries throughout the 1960s.[53] Although McKinsey had consolidated IPC's magazines on paper, in reality the group still operated out of more than 20 offices, with some titles moving physically together and others remaining separate from the larger group.[54]

REED INTERNATIONAL

For the companies operating from their existing offices, the burden of communication with the corporate centre now added to the lengthening bureaucracy. Gradually the consumer magazines sector began to stagnate as IPC lost impetus but new entrants to the weekly market were unable to compete with the company's low cover prices driven by its huge scale economies in printing. The Price Commission identified this lack of creativity within IPC, noting that with its focus on scale the organization spent more energy on the establishment of bureaucracy than encouraging entrepreneurship.[55] Circulations of weekly purchased consumer titles fell overall from 40 million in 1961 to 35.3 million in 1969 as magazines purchased off-the-shelf slowly lost ground to the Sunday newspaper supplements and television, which during the 1960s began the transition to colour broadcasting.[56] With its performance declining the group started to take a number of defensive measures to protect itself from potential corporate raiders, who might strip it for its portfolio of central London real estate, by selling its buildings to property funds and leasing them back.[57]

In 1970, with the IPC Group experiencing financial difficulties and using the £11 million from the sale of its properties to maintain cash-flow and pay day-to-day expenses, Cudlipp reached an agreement with Don Ryder, the chairman of the IPC-controlled paper manufacturing subsidiary Albert E. Reed & Co., for Reed to take over IPC under the banner of Reed International.[58] According to Frances Norton, 'Reed's goal for the newly formed IPC was to dominate the consumer magazine market' and this would be achieved by achieving further economies of scale in the purchasing key inputs such as paper.[59] This proposal did not find universal favour with employees, and an anonymous group started a fund to prevent the takeover by appealing to shareholders to block the deal, mounting a bitter attack on senior management in an open letter to board, but the deal was approved by a huge majority.[60]

The Magazine Division kept its existing structure under the newly created Reed International, and had a capitalization of £408 million, employed some 3,500 people, and realized a turnover of £51.5 million.[61] At this time the group had some 66 magazines, with the 24 titles in the women's groups providing two-thirds of the revenue.[62] IPC remained dominant in the women's weekly market, accounting for £15.7 million in sales in a total market worth £18.2 million. Overall the Corporation accounted for 38 per cent of total consumer magazine spending, and 53 per cent of all consumer magazine display advertising, itself 7.3 per cent of all display revenue in the UK, including television. The women's weeklies were uniquely placed to appeal to the largest advertising markets for toiletries, cosmetics, wearing apparel, and household equipment. To further the company's dominant position, the centre was strengthened with Corporate Marketing and Communications and Research and Development departments, including an enlarged Surveys Division, but there was a growing awareness that the Magazine Division needed more flexibility to remain editorially vibrant.[63] In particular although in 1971 IPC had £3.6 million of the £6.2 million young women's market and £3.5 million of the £8.1 million women's monthlies, home and feminine, and feminine interest markets, it had only £5.8 million of the growing £38.6 million general interest and specialized markets.[64]

Within Reed International the newly fledged IPC Magazines was to face a rocky initial few years as industrial disputes, such as a £3 million pay dispute with the National Union of Journalists (NUJ) and SLADE in the summer of 1971, rising costs, and weakening economic conditions all took their toll. Since formation, the group had failed to address the problem of its ageing uncompetitive print works but now, ironically, it came close to closing the modern but loss-making Southwark Offset facility, its only web-offset photocomposition press which had been established as recently as 1964 specifically for high speed colour magazine work.[65] The plant, which in its short history had already been subject to the 'Cameron' Court of Inquiry concerning inter-union squabbles over operation of the new web-offset presses, was saved from closure only at the last hour, as management gamely hoped that its modern presses could eventually be made economic with union cooperation.[66] Although an agreement was reached on changes to shift patterns and manning levels in late 1971 this only underscored the fact that new technology alone would not suffice to improve the company's performance without profound changes to working relations. Although performing better than Southwark Offset, Fleetway's Sumner Street print works was still running with annual losses of £750,000 and was finally closed when IPC's management concluded that its location and outdated equipment could not be made economically viable, even with union cooperation. Strike actions protesting against the proposed closures brought about the loss of a number of magazine issues, which damaged IPC in both the eyes of readers and advertisers, in a pattern that was to be repeated seemingly ad nauseam through to the mid-1980s.[67]

The group's reaction to these ongoing pressures in the early 1970s was driven from the centre, whose response was to decide which magazines would be selected for promotion, and to strengthen the publisher system so that groups of magazines could be sold as a unit to advertisers. New strategies were devised and implemented, such as the Retail Newsagents Profit Plan and a Shop Fitting Scheme to increase sales.[68] In an effort to standardize practices across the group, the relationship between the Magazine Group, the Business Press, and the printing firms was placed under the supervision of a new central Periodical Planning and Production Unit, adding yet more layers to decision-making.[69] Cost-cutting measures were also introduced, with the Women's Magazine Group moving out of New Fleetway House in 1972 to save rents.[70] In a more outward-looking move the Magazine Group also made a tentative initial foray into internationalization with the purchase of Sungravure Pty Ltd. in Australia, where they continued to print existing titles *Woman's Day*, *Pix*, and *People* and also launched *Dolly*, aimed at the young women's market which had been served only by imports.[71] This initiative did not receive the attention it needed from IPC's managers to become a major part of the business, however, and was not developed further.

A CHALLENGE FROM LITHOGRAPHY

The strategy of combining Odhams' large-scale printing capacity with low-cost paper inputs secured by Reed International ought to have given IPC's

magazines enhanced profitability. However, the company's management struggled to achieve the potential cost efficiencies that such a vertically integrated
structure offered due, in large part, to their inability to effectively manage
IPC's unionized workforce.[72] The most intractable industrial relations issue
centred on the problem of union-based demarcation of tasks between journalists, graphics workers, and machine operators that continued to tether much
of Britain's publishing industry to its traditional craft roots and working practices. In the post-Second World War period labour unions in the print industry
had become increasingly preoccupied with regulating the use of technology in
order to preserve existing practices and employment, and the union's right to
strike to secure their demands had been reaffirmed in the Trade Disputes Act
of 1965. Although the subsequent 'Donovan Report' to the Royal Commission
on Trade Unions and Employers' Associations 1965–8 attempted to unravel
the complexities of modern unionization, it failed to produce any meaningful
improvement in labour relations.[73] Thus, despite growing public concern of
the power of the unions, their place in Britain's industrial landscape was firmly
entrenched within the prevailing social and political consensus.[74]

By the late 1960s, however, technological change was rapidly undermining the
justification for demarcation and the system of industrial relations in the printing industry. The gradual commercialization of offset litho printing had enabled
lithography to be used for significantly larger print runs, although the replication
of text by this method still fell short of the quality achieved by the letterpress.[75]
Thus, for those publications composed mainly of text, such as newspapers, hot
metal was still a relatively efficient form of composition, and a long-standing ally
of letterpress printing methods. As late as 1972, 77 per cent of NGA members
were still engaged in typesetting for letterpress printing.[76] Nevertheless, for many
consumer magazines moving towards the integration of higher print quality and
coated paper products incorporating colour, graphics and photographs was a
desirable step. For high-end magazines, such as the long-established *Vogue* whose
strategy had always been based on high-quality reproduction, photogravure had
been the print medium of choice for images to set alongside letterpress-based
text.[77] Photogravure was also economic for large-scale colour print runs for titles
such as *Woman's Own*. However, as the process relied on engraving metal rollers,
lead-times were long and changes were slow and costly to make.

In 1965 half of IPC's output was still derived from letterpress, two-thirds
of which came from rotary letterpress, while only one title was produced by
sheet-fed litho.[78] By the 1970s the letterpress was generally held to be uneconomic for the printing of magazines, with new techniques of sheet-fed lithography found to give 45 per cent better manpower cost ratios, and 70 per cent
better when coupled with web-offset printing. The developments in the techniques of lithography heralded the potential to bring fundamental changes
to the possibilities available to magazine publishing firms. As the 1970s progressed, the need for shorter print-runs and ever greater combinations of

text and pictures demanded by advertisers created the environment where lithography became a serious alternative to the letterpress and photogravure.[79] When coupled with innovations in photo-mechanics (i.e. the use of film to provide an alternative form of layout), the technique of photolithography offered the integrated production of images and textual material without the need for expensive and complicated metal plates that were a feature of both gravure and letterpress methods of reproduction. Instead this was a non-mechanical, cold-type process using a computerized system to create a printing plate, initially on bromide paper or, as the technology advanced, film.

Clearly this process could have disastrous consequences for conventional typesetters, as well as those expressly concerned with graphical reproduction. But while photocomposition allowed for a break with the letterpress, it still required the re-typing of text into compositors which unions could continue to lay claim to as typesetting. The skilled task of composition had preserved the status of print workers and allowed NGA members in particular to charge a premium for typesetting sufficient to place its members among the highest paid of any manual craft workers in the UK during the 1960s,[80] and the introduction of photocomposition and the growing possibility of direct entry single-keystroke systems to replace hand typesetting and manual Linotype was strongly resisted by unions keen to enforce demarcation. With some understatement, the Royal Commission on the Press had noted in 1962 that this system of labour organization was 'certainly a deterrent to the introduction of new techniques and particularly to those which may cut across established spheres of influence'.[81] Through the 1960s and 1970s the NGA, SOGAT, and the NUJ were able to maintain control over the organization of the production process in much of the industry, preventing the changes in production technologies from having significant organizational impact. Looking back from 1978 on the slow adoption of photocomposition in the UK, which lagged far behind the United States and Europe, former IPC chairman Sir Edward Pickering pointed out simply that when it came to adopting new technologies, 'London...with its unique competitive situation and its own trade union problems, is not the United States'.[82] Despite advances in printing technology, Delafons considered that the unions had successfully compelled the publishing industry 'to retain the original 16th Century manual crafts...and in no other industry had the roots of ancient tradition formed so stout a barricade against any fundamental change in methods and processes'.[83]

THE IPL PRINTING CRISIS

Reed International's printing concern, the International Printers Ltd. (IPL), tied IPC to the closed-shop labour system which stipulated that union members would not work for employers who used non-union labour.[84] The basis of union power in the closed-shop system was formed by the limited number of apprenticeships, which were the exclusive route to union membership. Arranged into a dizzyingly complex 100 chapels, IPL's print workers were members of six main unions: SOGAT and the NGA with 1,750 members each; NATSOPA with 1,650; SLADE with 650; and on the maintenance side with the AUEW and EETU having 100 members each. The NGA was the major typesetting union and its members traditionally undertook the most skilled composing work.[85] Labour involved in the technical and subsidiary operations of the printing process was coordinated under the banner of the Society of Graphical and Allied Trades (SOGAT), formed in 1966 when the National Union of Printing, Bookbinding and Paper Workers (NUPBPW) and the National Society of Operative Printers' Assistants (NATSOPA) joined forces. By the time of the merger the NUPBPW had itself absorbed a startling number of allied unions under its umbrella.[86] The complexity of the relations between its constituents was apparent in the changing composition of the union as bitter intra-union conflicts raged.[87] In the print industry demarcation between these unions was a long-standing feature, and one that also gave rise to double-keying. This process would see the original text, usually created by members of the NUJ, re-typed by NGA members using a compositing machine as part of the original and make-up process, with SOGAT members involved in the processes of make-up to create printing plates. Of these unions SLADE members were the only main print union without the ability to halt production unilaterally as they supplied images which could be obtained from archives.[88]

In the absence of changes to these union-enforced traditional working practices, managers at IPL found little cost saving in switching from hot-metal to phototypesetting. For mass-market titles based on integrated text, colour, and photographs, and produced incorporating lithography such as the *Film Pictorial*, demarcation within IPL between the different printing processes was strictly enforced. Changes to working patterns and new technology were only undertaken through collective agreements.[89] In all, four types of collective agreements dictated working conditions within IPL: national agreements between federations of unions and employers' associations; national wage agreements with the individual unions; IPL's own agreements with the unions over conditions in their London printing plants; and those made by IPL with individual union chapels or branches. In order to preserve their own status and relative conditions, the print unions preferred local bargaining at the chapel level rather than national collective bargaining, as noted by the 1962 Royal Commission on the Press. Coupled with the closed-shop that this system of workplace controls created, a unique situation came into being across the printing industry in London through which the control of labour was placed securely in the hands of the unions.[90] This control was such that publishing firms also found that the regulations which were enforced by the printing unions restricted the deployment of their own employees, as union members were considered 'not employed for employers' business but one publication' which meant that they could not be transferred to work to other plants or titles.[91] Negotiations on pay increases for non-craft and lower status unions needed the tacit approval of the NGA, or as a result the NGA would seek to maintain its pay differentials by industrial action or through a pay increase, making negotiations a political minefield.[92] Management had little sanction over unions, and Sisson has argued that the asymmetric costs of printing stoppages, in terms of short-term lost wages for labour versus long-term loss of customers for the business, meant that even the ultimate threat of plant closures had little influence on attitudes and policies of the unions. The sector thus became inured to lurching from crisis to crisis.[93]

IPL had become the thorn in IPC's side, housing closed-shop printing firms responsible for ruinous ongoing losses. By far the largest part of the IPL Group was Odhams (Watford), still the country's largest high speed gravure plant employing 3,000 of IPL's 6,300 workers and accounting for £9.9 million of its of £21.1 million revenue in 1971. Whereas Odhams' plant for many years represented a key strategic asset, as Britain's largest and fastest colour press, by the mid-1970s the Price Commission found that the technologies used there were largely obsolete, highly inefficient, and the plant was locked into a union-led system of 'perverse working practices' including double-keying, and its unionized workforce was arranged into a bewildering 400 different management grades.[94] The IPL Group also was home to, in order of size, Southwark Offset, Chapel River Press, Fleetway Gravesend, Index Printers, Baynard Press, George Rose, Noakes Bros., James Cond, Contract Composing, Thompson Engravers, and Century Litho, all of which engendered varying levels of union and management distrust. As a customer IPC formed 90 per cent of IPL's business, with 57 per cent of this going to the Magazine Division. The highest operating cost was that of labour, amounting to around two-thirds.[95] For IPC to remain competitive new printing techniques would need to be embraced at IPL; however, not only did this fail to happen but management and union relations, and relations between the unions themselves, deteriorated further as technical developments in photocomposition and photolithography heightened tensions.

IPC managing director Alex Jarratt had no solution to the union problem other than to propose the sale of the print assets. After difficult negotiations with the unions, Southwark Offset, Baynard Press, Century Litho, and Contract Composing were all offered for sale in early 1973. Since opening in 1964 Southwark Offset had by the early 1970s made cumulative losses of £5 million. Despite initial interest from the Oxley Printing Group, David Brockdorff, and a failed attempt at an IPL management buyout,[96] attempts to sell the plants as going concerns were blocked by the unions who could not agree on the changes to manning levels that might make the plants economic. In 1974 the four firms were closed with a loss of 750 jobs at Southwark Offset alone. Noakes Brothers was then closed following further industrial action, and disruptions over the entire period resulted in the loss of 80 issues of major magazines which was estimated to have cost IPC in excess of £1 million.[97] More damaging in the long term, each industrial crisis saw the launch of new proposed titles as the first casualty, which were either pushed back or cancelled altogether. All this disruption, however, was but the prelude to a major crisis at Odhams, where a six-week strike in the middle of 1974 involving 2,850 workers brought a total shut-down and led IPC to incur its most disastrous losses to date. Closure of the factory was only averted at the last moment with the intervention of the employment secretary Michael Foot after the loss of 30 million magazine copies and £3 million in lost circulations and advertising revenue. Production of key slimmed-down issues of magazines began again on 29 July 1974 supported by a £50,000 advertising blitz to reassure readers that their favourite titles were back.[98] Following the Odhams dispute, IPC's remaining print interests were reorganized into IPC Printers and the firm retained its position as a printing concern for more than a further decade.[99]

INNOVATION PROBLEMS AT THE MINISTRY

Along with its internal problems IPL, and its successor IPC Printers, also faced increasing external competition, especially from European firms. It was estimated by IPC that Britain's entry to the European Common Market in 1973 would see the group's print firms thrown into the cut-throat competition of the £3.5 billion global print market. Following the 1972 Sound Broadcasting Act, IPC also faced a new challenge to its advertising markets when commercial radio stations began broadcasting in 1973. In this tightening market for advertising, there was one area where IPC's financial muscle could still provide it with a source of competitive advantage against other publishers as the cost to launch a new weekly magazine was estimated to be in excess of £1 million.[100] In 1972 IPC planned to launch *Candida*, the first entrant into the women's weekly market since *Woman's Realm* 14 years previously, in a bid to gain greater access to the growing class of three million 'aspiring and discriminating' ABC1 women in the 22 to 44 age category. In this the company was hoping to exploit its core publishing strengths to serve a market quite distinct from its other weekly titles, although there was some overlap with the now ailing Newnes monthly *Nova* which had been established to serve the emergent 60s woman over a decade earlier. The operation was entrusted to the safe business and editorial hands of Jean Twiddy, who had overseen the successful launch of *Woman's Realm*. Advertisers were confidently guaranteed an initial nine-month 300,000 weekly sale, with promises of a readership in excess of a million.[101] Launched on 28 September, with a 10p cover price, the magazine was an expensive disappointment, with initial sales of 400,000 for the first issue collapsing to 200,000 thereafter, and the title closed after only seven issues.[102] According to Gough-Yates, the attempt to understand the 'needs and motivations' of the emerging 'new woman' had been based on market research based on segmentation by attitude rather than the demographic-based approach the company was most familiar with.[103] For IPC *Candida* had also represented a move away from the high circulation mass women's market mentality it was most comfortable with. Ultimately this segment would be most successfully served by the National Magazine Company's monthly US-transplant *Cosmopolitan*, launched in the same year, and highlighting a shift in the industry towards the growing importance of monthly and specialist titles.

With continued growth in the market for teenage female and music titles, creating increased sales for *Fabulous, Mirabelle, 19*, and *Honey* along with its younger-focused spin-off *Petticoat*, the company saw another avenue to launch a new smash hit in the so-called 'weenie-bopper' market.[104] Launched with a supremely confident 435,000 print run and an ambitious 10p cover price for the pocket-money market, *HiT* also sadly failed to live up to its name as it failed to cover its high colour production costs.[105] As print mass markets declined, the Annan Committee on the Future of Broadcasting, formed in 1974, reported that English society and culture was becoming increasingly fragmented between classes, generations, sexes, and regions, an ominous portent for business models predicated on the development of blockbuster hits.[106] Clearly being able to fund large marketing campaigns to launch new titles was not in itself a guarantee of market success, and IPC had made costly errors in attempting to engage with new emergent consumer groups, such as the 'new woman', which required a closer and more sophisticated understanding of the audience.

In the face of mounting problems at the end of 1973 the retiring Hugh Cudlipp was succeeded as IPC chairman by Alex Jarratt, who had been IPC group managing director for the previous three years and would continue in that role.[107] A former civil servant with no previous editorial experience prior to IPC, the new chairman faced increasing concerns, including the Newspaper Division returning a £1.18 million loss for the year ending 1974, and falling profits for the Magazine Division.[108] Playing down the failure of recent high-profile launches, Jarratt argued that in 1973 IPC had put 12 new titles into the market, with only three failures, but despite this gloss the failures were highly significant, each having been developed as major titles in core mass-market weekly segments. Although Jarratt accepted that 'to be creative you have to take risks' he also cautioned 'what we have to be sure of is that they are highly professional, calculated risks rather than gambles taken on inadequate evidence', and the gradual shift of power away from entrepreneurial editors continued. The focus on cost reduction was reiterated, with this being seen as the key to 'beating the small publisher who can produce a small number of high quality journals in a very low cost environment'. In order to save on high central London rents, major moves were announced, with the Business Press moving from Tower House to Sutton in Surrey. The Magazine Group meanwhile, planned to move to a 270,000 sq ft development in London's South Bank complex, to be called King's Reach Tower, incorporating a 31-storey building along with a low-rise block to house the women's weeklies.[109] In a move to regain a portion of the lucrative women's advertising from competitors such as commercial television, and to build a case to international advertisers for using the women's weeklies, sales initiatives were put in place by the centre which involved high-profile conferences and generously funded overseas trips. Appeals were also made to advertisers through the ability of magazines to include regional adverts in the popular women's weeklies.[110]

As 1974 rolled on, costs continued to escalate dramatically. A worldwide paper shortage hurt the industry,[111] the price of paper doubled between January 1974 and 1978, and the industry saw general printing costs increase by 80 per cent over the period.[112] Industrial unrest in Britain was at an all-time high, and with the energy crisis forcing a three-day week the company was placed on 65 per cent power rationing. Given the national importance of printing, the government allowed three print works to run a five-day week, and distribution on the roads was less affected by outside industrial action as, unlike newspapers, magazines were mostly distributed by road as well as rail, although a lorry drivers' strike affected Scottish distribution and a post workers' strike upset the women's weeklies postal competitions promotions. In such poor conditions the company postponed planned new magazines and attempted to consolidate their position.

Following the prevailing political will of the 1974–9 Labour government's desire to combat inflation through negotiated prices and income controls, both unions and management made more effort towards rapprochement, particularly following IPC's recent industrial relations disasters. As part of this 'new deal in labour relations' an attempt was made to introduce a more inclusive open style of management, with IPC opening its books to the NUJ for the first time to show them the extent of current losses in the face of proposed pay negotiations. Progress, however, was to remain grudgingly slow, despite some headway with the unions' Joint House Committee acting to diffuse demarcation disputes to some extent.[113] Once again the unions at Odhams were to frustrate management's attempt to rationalize the print sector, by unanimously refusing to cooperate with a proposed merger with the British Printing and Communication Corporation's (BPCC)[114] Watford-based Sun Printers, seeing it as 'a threat to *their* factory'. Following £2 million losses for the year at Odhams and the promise of £600,000 in new investment the union chapels and management issued a Joint Declaration in March 1976, determined that 'a new start' would not be just 'pie in the sky' and there would be 'an immediate attempt to make Odhams a company with a progressive future'.[115]

At the end of 1974 Mirror Group Newspapers was separated from IPC. From this point onwards IPC Magazines Ltd.'s relationship with the Reed group was exclusively through the purchase of paper and printing, which still formed 29 per cent of the IPC Magazines' costs at £17 million. The Magazine Group retained their existing structure, although they were freed from the overarching level of management they had shared with IPC Business Press. Leslie Carpenter took over as chairman and managing director for IPC Magazines, Edward Pickering moved to head up the Mirror Group Newspapers, and Alex Jarratt became the chairman of Reed International as Don Ryder left to become the government's industrial adviser and head of the National Enterprise Board.[116] In an interview with *IPC News*, Magazine Group head Les Carpenter outlined his thoughts on the company now that it was less constrained within the Reed International empire. Broadly he believed that the sector had become mature, saying that 'public tastes do not change as rapidly as is sometimes believed. Habit, familiarity, constancy are factors in purchasing behaviour which are not to be ignored.' Carpenter also considered that the sector would not be subject to much further change, as the 'hard core developments [such as web-offset] affecting types of publications and their printing have already occurred'.[117] In order to counter continued falling circulations[118] IPC's strategy would clearly not embrace radical editorial or technological change, but would rely on attempting to revive its ageing stable of women's weeklies titles, such as *Woman's Realm,* and old war horses such as the flagging *Titbits,* with makeovers supported by large-scale promotional campaigns.[119] 1977 saw the company's largest ever £2.2 million promotional drive, with over half of this budgeted for the women's weeklies.[120]

INCREASING COMPETITION FROM MONTHLIES

New entrants and existing firms found that they could avoid direct competition with IPC by specializing in those markets where consumers were receptive to new leisure titles or where IPC was not contesting the market. Although the BBC had published magazines since 1923 with the *Radio Times* and later *The Listener* in 1929, they made a hesitant entry into consumer titles in 1963 with the launch of *Animals* as a separate profit-centred title managed by their Bristol-based natural history unit and printed under contract.[121] It was recognized that through their ownership of radio and television the BBC had an inbuilt marketing cost advantage over its competitors which could improve its profitability.[122] However, as long as the TV listings market remained the main province of the organization, and as its growth in other segments of the magazine market remained glacial, commercial magazine publishers were content to leave the Corporation to its own devices

In the market for weekly magazines, competitors were making slow inroads. Dundee-based D. C. Thomson successfully maintained a 'no-frills' strategy with its low-priced *My Weekly* and *The People's Friend*, and published the teen girl's title *Jackie*, despite having little ambition to expand its consumer magazine interests further. The Cornmarket Press, formed in 1957 by Clive Labovitch and Michael Heseltine, continued a move towards consumer magazines with its purchase of *Man About Town* in 1960 from John Taylor, who had started the magazine as a Saville Row-orientated companion to his influential trade publication *Taylor & Cutter*. Based around his personal interests, Taylor's *Man About Town* was a blend of fashion, style, and musings on wine and women that was further developed under Labovitch to capture the swinging sixties zeitgeist. Intrigued by the title's potential Geoffrey Crowther, chairman of the title's printers Hazell Watson & Viney, bought a 40 per cent interest in Cornmarket in 1964, blending the company names into Haymarket. Despite its influence, the publication could not compete commercially with the new Sunday supplements, and after changing its name to *About Town* and then just *Town* the loss-making title was closed in 1964. The new Haymarket however were pioneers in moving towards contacting advertisers by telephone, and in a 'no cover price' strategy of giving magazines away free to commuters.[123] This strategy slowly opened up new possibilities for distribution beyond the traditional confectioners, tobacconists, and newsagents (CTNs) which remained the dominant retail channel.

Concerned about a decline in traditional outlets, fearing a reduction from 37,000 newsagents to a predicted 28,000 in 1980, IPC had made a faltering and abortive step into retail in 1973 when it bought 14 central London newsagents.[124] W.H. Smith continued to be the major retail chain, selling magazines through its railway stalls, which declined from 755 in 1961 to 383 in 1971, and its old-fashioned urban stores, which it gradually consolidated from 393 in 1961 to 319 in 1971. W.H. Smith did start to expand the sector's retail opportunities with the opening of a series of superstores of unprecedented size and scope throughout the 1960s, although it was reluctant to upset the independent retail sector that was its major wholesale customer by expanding too fast.[125] The development of large-scale magazine superstores on the high street would cement the UK's reliance on cover sales rather than subscription. With a dense network of magazine retail stores, established distribution, and a small geographic size, Britain's consumers continued to prefer to buy their periodicals directly from the news-stand.

A degree of more serious direct competition to IPC was emerging, however, within the one sector that did experience growth through the 1960s and 1970s, that of monthly consumer magazines. Sales of monthlies rose from 12.67 million in 1961 to 18.42 million in 1977.[126] In the monthly market, Hearst's National Magazine Company, generally by this time known as NatMags, and Condé Nast, continued to play a significant role as medium-scale competitors in up-scale markets.[127] Under managing director Reverend Marcus Morris[128] NatMags began competing directly with IPC, with *She* in women's monthlies, and with *Car*, which it had acquired as *Small Car*, in automotive.[129] The company had moved to Chestergate House in Victoria, London, in 1963 and was quick to capture the sixties spirit commissioning Mary Quant to develop a new '*Harper's Bazaar* Look'. The rejuvenated *Bazaar* faced strong competition, however, not only from established titles such as *Vogue*, but also from the independent *Queen*, which had been purchased by Jocelyn Stevens in 1957. With his finger on the 'Chelsea set' pulse of swinging London, Stevens had launched the 'pirate' Radio Caroline, and with editor Beatrix Miller redeveloped the society-focused *The Queen* into a contemporary and stylish offering renamed simply *Queen*. Director Brian Braithwaite and his advertisement executive Terry Mansfield were successful in capturing a substantial share of the luxury advertising market with innovations in 'advertisement promotions'. The success of *Queen* was short-lived, however, as Braithwaite and Mansfield were lured to NatMags as part of a *Harper's Bazaar* re-launch, and Miller to edit *Vogue* in 1965. At NatMags an innovative period followed as the firm attempted to develop the postal subscriptions market with the exclusive use of the Harrods mailing list. Although this garnered new subscribers, it failed to alter the British markets' reliance on cover sales. By this time the ailing *Queen* had been purchased by its printer, Michael Lewis, owner of the Stevens Press, in 1968. Lewis then passed the title to NatMags to be merged with *Harper's Bazaar* as *Harper's & Queen* from November 1970 on the basis that he would continue to print the title.

The National Magazine Company then made a major impact with its editor Joyce Hopkirk presiding over the launch of *Cosmopolitan* in 1972, a UK version of its successful US title dating back to 1886 but reformulated for a modern audience in 1965 by *Sex and the Single Girl* author Helen Gurley Brown.[130] The promotion for the launch was handled by the fledgling advertising agency Saatchi & Saatchi and was successful beyond all estimations, with an initial print-run of 350,000 selling out instantly, and the second issue, promising the women's markets first male nude, selling out 450,000 copies in two days.[131] In contrast to IPC's experience with *Candida*, printers Hazell Watson & Viney were unable to meet demand and in 1973 printing was moved to the Hubert Burda Media Group's West German photogravure plant. With this international connection established the company moved to develop further contracts to license the title for European markets, underscoring the title's winning formula. 'Cosmo' made IPC's *Honey* seem dated, with that title's editorial team bemoaning that they were unable to compete with the newcomer as they were saddled with an outdated name from a bygone era that they feared changing.[132] Further pressure was put on IPC by NatMag's launch of *Company* in September 1978, aimed at women in their twenties. In 1977 the company also moved into third-party distribution by establishing Comag in a joint venture with Condé Nast by merging their circulation departments and becoming an early mover in the computerization of sales data.

The Thomson Group also scored a significant success in the monthly market with two magazines sold exclusively through supermarkets. *Family Circle*, launched in 1964, and its later partner *Living*, both achieved circulations in excess of 500,000, with the former established as Britain's largest selling monthly women's magazine.[133] Although supermarket distribution proved effective in this instance, these two magazines were to remain largely the only major consumer titles sold through this channel until the mid-1980s.[134]

In the face of growing competition in the monthly sector, IPC flexed its muscles, once again backing its core strength by aiming for a new blockbuster women's title in the form of *Woman's World*, originally meant to have been launched in 1974 but delayed because of the disruptions caused by a miners' strike. Once again the full force of the IPC machine was brought into action with the full-time editorial team of 18 pushing a £300,000 promotional budget and aiming for a circulation of 350,000. Although welcomed by retailers, promotions were not well integrated with distribution channels, and W.H. Smith asked IPC editors to 'come down from their ivory towers' and view competitors' products in the stores and consider how promotions might fit in with the new display possibilities of self-selecting racks.[135] Despite moderate success the title did not achieve its aspirations as the firm continued to lose touch with its markets and retailers.

One possible contributing factor to this lukewarm performance could have been the 30p cover price, representative of the steadily rising prices of the period. With the government worried about inflation, increases in cover prices were referred to the Price Commission. Although concerned about the lack of effective competitors to IPC and the worry of market power abuse by the giant firm, the Commission broadly accepted that rising costs, and the capital investment required to improve Odhams' uneconomic operation were the main motivations behind IPC's proposed price hikes.[136] IPC for its part bemoaned the loss of £1 million in revenue from having to postpone its price increases by four months.[137] In the same year the government also had appointed a final Royal Commission on the Press, and although its main findings in the 'McGregor Report' mainly concerned the relationship between the independence of the press in the guise of newspaper and advertisers relations, the commission also produced a working paper from Cynthia White on the Women's Periodical Press. Exasperated at the lack of innovation from IPC White described its organization as a 'centrally planned economy,'[138] but in a response to the Royal Commission the IPC chairman responded on the front cover of the IPC in-house journal *IPC News* to dismiss the claims, and questioned 'Ms White's' knowledge of the industry.[139] One fact was clear, however, sales of IPC's flagship titles had fallen sharply over the decade, with sales of *Woman's Own* down from just under two million in 1970 to around 1.5 million in 1980.[140]

EMAP AND OTHER NEW COMPETITORS

The prevailing lack of innovation at IPC, however, was highlighted by the entry of several small-scale publishers who were able to meet changing consumer tastes with underground and makeshift publications. While generally of low print quality and outside the purview of the traditional print companies, this emerging trend demonstrated that titles catering for consumer fads and printing 'fanzines' as low-cost magazines could create a viable entry route into the industry. Felix Dennis had some experience with the publishing world after having been promoted to co-editor of the underground cult magazine *Oz*; he had originally started out as a street distributor. Unlike the conventional IPC offerings, 'fanzine'-based publishing was quick to react to the changing cultural trends of the times,[141] although this itself could be risky, as was aptly demonstrated when *Oz*'s courting of controversial topics led to Dennis and his co-editors Jim Anderson and Richard Neville being briefly imprisoned for conspiracy before their subsequent acquittal at the Court of Appeal.[142] Despite this initial setback, Dennis was enamoured with magazines and founded Dennis Publishing in 1973, finding initial success with *Kung Fu Monthly* launched in 1974 to exploit the prevalent Bruce Lee-inspired martial arts craze. The title made £60,000 on sales by 1975 and bankrolled further forays into trend-based publishing,[143] exploiting a variety of emerging minority niches in the late 1970s with titles such as *Crossroads Monthly*, *TV Sci-Fi Monthly*, *Skateboard! Magazine*, and *Which Bike?* The maverick publisher also ventured into more conventional territory with the acquisition of *Hi-Fi Choice*. Although there had been initial profitability the firm's finances were somewhat precarious in the initial years, but the firm survived and its market-reactive approach was later to pay dividends. Small specialist firms found they could export titles successfully and expand to international markets. *Kung Fu Monthly* found a ready market in Hong Kong for example, and Northern & Shell, founded in 1974 when Richard Desmond joined Ray Hammond as co-owner of *International Musician and Recording World*, were able to offer US and German editions of the title.[144]

EMAP also continued to develop its magazine interests, but although the company was now firmly established as a magazine producer growth was

rather slow, with only nine titles successfully developed by 1972. This experience, however, had convinced the firm that there was potential for profitable
niche titles under the correct conditions, and EMAP established a corporate
planning team, led by Robin Miller and David Arculus, which orchestrated a
growth plan based around the further development of a low-cost, low-price
strategy to produce weekly periodicals such as *Gardening News.* Unlike IPC,
EMAP developed its strategy predominantly on the basis of magazine titles
that held narrow rather than mass popular appeal.[145] Developments in minority sectors, however, could lead to mainstream success, and the company's first
major circulation success came towards the end of the decade in 1978 with
youth-orientated music magazine *Smash Hits*,[146] which far exceeded expectations and built a circulation of 750,000.[147] The huge success of this title generated profits for the firm to invest in further developing its strategy, and to aim
for aggressive rapid growth which would shake up the industry in the 1980s.

   As the 1970s drew towards its close, the first portent of a new form of
competition, marrying trend-based publishing with high-end production
quality, was heralded by the architect of *Smash Hits*, Nick Logan. Logan had
served ten years at IPC's *New Musical Express* (*NME*) music title, including five as editor, where he had covered the early developments in the
punk music scene. In 1978 he had approached EMAP with the concept of a
pop-orientated title featuring lyrics and posters of pop-stars, which was the
genesis of *Smash Hits* and following this success proposed a new magazine
based on the emergent 'new romantic' movement characterized by bands
such as Duran Duran and Culture Club. Despite Logan's track record, and
the runaway success of *Smash Hits*, the firm rejected his concept. Although
IPC and EMAP both at this stage assumed the need for large-scale launch
budgets of £100,000 for even a small title,[148] the 33-year-old Logan decided
to go it alone as sole publisher and editor, founding Wagadon with a bank
loan of only £4,500. While his wife did the accounts he worked on the design,
layout, proofs, sales, and the writing himself. Unlike previous cult-based
offerings such as those from Dennis Publishing, Logan's aspirations for production quality were high: he wanted a quarto-sized magazine that rivalled
Vogue or *Tatler* for print quality, and he was able exploit the new growth in
high-end photogravure contract printing. Logan had confidence that the
new emerging trend would generate readers, and in his own mind he was
'simply putting together a magazine that I would want to read, hoping it
would survive, letting it evolve'.[149] In order to get the title into mainstream
circulation Logan also was able to take advantage of recent developments in
third-party distribution by contracting Comag to handle sales and circulations.[150] The first sales of the magazine that presented 'a totally new slant on
the modern dance' were disappointing. The first issue sold only 56,000 copies, and 'only pride stopped him canning it' as he lost £2,000 each on the first
five issues.[151] The following year the title's fortunes changed as he was joined

by Neville Brody as art director, whose fresh layouts and use of small cases and novel fonts was to give *the Face* its iconic look.[152] Logan's belief in the viability of the magazine paid off, and he won both critical acclaim and a loyal readership. With *the Face*, and later with *Arena*, an industry commentator noted that Wagadon offered 'the sort of cutting-edge titles that only an independent firm of passionate enthusiasts could really produce', leaving the competition looking stale and 'a little cheap'.[153]

The example provided by Wagadon and Dennis Publishing served to demonstrate that small-scale, independent entrants could launch new titles on a shoestring budget using contract printing and distribution, much as the Beetons had done in the 1850s, and that new trends untapped by the traditional risk-averse publishers could provide promising niche markets. EMAP had also found that it could expand based on developing smaller specialist interest consumer titles. Single-title independent firms such as *The Lady* launched in 1885 and *Gramophone* in 1923 still existed in consumer publishing, but these ran against the prevailing industrial logic of large-scale publishing, and before *the Face* there had been few successful launches of this type in the post-war period which had achieved significant circulation. Frustrated editors and publishers within IPC took note, but this entrepreneurial model was still not without high risks. Logan had extensive experience in the industry, but high production costs had almost closed Wagadon before *the Face* found its readership. With increasing possibilities for contract printing there were new opportunities for small-scale publishers, albeit still hampered by union-dictated production controls. Clearly if the barriers to originating and printing magazines could be lowered still further, then more entrants would be able to exploit social trends as a basis for new titles. At the start of the 1980s one novelty in particular would not only serve as the basis for new markets, but also be employed as the very means that would lower production costs to bring publishing within the grasp of the ordinary person. Over the course of the following decade, micro-computers would come to combine the worlds of computing and publishing, and would be exploited by entrepreneurs and firms that would provide a direct challenge to the might of the Ministry of Magazines.

7

The Competitive Landscape Transformed

A DECADE OF CHANGE

In the post-war period the British magazine industry had become increasingly concentrated, a process which reached its apogee with the formation of IPC. A report produced by the Price Commission in 1978 rationalized three reasons why magazine publishing was predisposed towards the structure of a dominant producer. The report argued that IPC benefited from mass-circulation magazine titles that enabled the ability to charge premium rates to advertisers, and thereby keep the cover price of magazines predatorily low, that IPC had scale advantages unmatched by its rivals through its ownership of the high-speed Odhams (Watford) plant, and also had an untouchable advantage in financing new magazine titles, where the launch of a new high circulation weekly magazine could cost as much as £1 million.[1] Despite these advantages, innovation at the firm had been in steady decline, and by the 1980s it seemed as though the era of the mass-market magazine could be reaching its end as sales of women's weeklies stagnated.

The 1980s were a decade characterized by several revolutions that would leave the industry transformed and overturn each one of IPC's advantages. The first of these was driven by technological developments in make-up and printing, leading to a traumatic process of vertical disintegration. Long-established working patterns were hard to change, however, but resistance from the printing unions could not eventually prevent the revolutionary breaking of the closed-shop system by the Conservative governments of Margaret Thatcher. As the power of the print unions diminished the contract print sector was able to grow, enabling new firms to enter the market, while a policy of economic liberalism allowed for a new wave of international competitors. These developments were set against the revolutionary rise of the micro-computer, which underpinned continued changes in printing, and transformed the process of magazine make-up and origination with the advent of desk-top publishing (dtp) allowing for lower cost magazine production.

Riven by internal strife at the start of the decade, Britain's dominant producer IPC struggled to embrace the new technologies and working methods being adopted by aggressive competitors, while at the same time coming under attack from the entry of large-scale European entrants. The tumultuous technological changes of the 1980s negated the strategic benefits which the Price Commission had reasoned IPC obtained from its large size and vertically integrated structure, with the Ministry for Magazines coming under attack in all of its markets, from monthly magazines to its previously impregnable women's weeklies.

THE DIVESTMENT OF IPC'S PRINTING OPERATIONS

Despite having maintained its position as the dominant magazine producer, at the start of the 1980s IPC was still wedded to its print operations in a relationship that continued to compromise the company's ability to concentrate on the business of publishing magazines. Clearly this was unsustainable and, as is evident from reports in IPC's own in-house newspaper, the company entered the long drawn-out process of addressing its seemingly intractable printing problems. A five-week NUJ pay and conditions strike had brought about a five-week stoppage,[2] during which the company lost 291 weekly issues, 25 monthly issues, and eight fortnightly issues, totalling over 35 million copies adding up to a loss of sales of £10 million and a devastating effect on consumer and advertiser confidence.[3] This action followed directly on from a series of complete print works closures instigated by the NGA typesetters union, and more pain followed with the announcement that Odhams had lost its largest outside contract, the printing of the *Sunday Telegraph* colour supplement.[4] The company also failed to gain the £126 million contract for the *TV Times*. Reviewing the loss of the *Sunday Telegraph* in an open forum with 1,500 Odhams print workers, IPC chief executive Les Carpenter expounded that 'it must be obvious that we stand at a crossroads' as comments from the floor described a 'them and us' attitude outlining the growing confrontation of views between management and the unions.[5] Despite generally falling paper prices and a strengthening pound, which further reduced the cost of imported paper, IPC's rate of profit decreased, from 10 per cent in the year ending 1978, 9.2 per cent in 1979, to 7.8 per cent in 1980. This final decline masked deeper problems because it took no account of losses arising as a consequence of the industrial actions in the printing plants which only ended in July 1980. For Odhams' management, cognizant that the firm had returned an annual loss for over a decade and accused in some quarters of buying industrial peace at the expense of high wages, this was a turning point which spurred the attempt to forge a new relationship with their print unions based on a plea to end inter- and intra-union conflict.[6] In a desperate appeal Odhams chief executive Ian Thomas said 'it's not just a question of management versus worker: we must knock down the barriers in every other area, including inter-departmental and inter-chapel'. A seventeen-point 'new industrial relations initiative' was put in place between management and the Association of Fathers-of-Chapels at the plant to discuss wages and premiums, working hours and new technology, and to link improvements in conditions to productivity gains.[7] Management was concerned that the effort exerted on union negotiations was in danger of making the company lose focus on the activity of publishing itself. However, with the general economic outlook continuing to decline through the early years of the first Conservative government of Margaret Thatcher, the com- pany's financial results made apparent the calamitous costs of the strikes, and it was clear that 'the full force of storm has started to hit the company'. Profits were down a further 37 per cent to 5 per cent, in the face of sharply rising employment costs which now jumped 20 per cent. Although circulations were still buoyant, advertising revenue was falling and IPC had closed seventeen titles and launched only ten.[8] Odhams was not alone in producing losses for IPC and a plan was also put in place with the unions to save the ailing Fleetway Press, leading to a large capital investment programme in association with a reduction in workers from 312 to 200.[9] Odhams too was to receive large-scale investment in new presses, with £5.13 million planned for 1981 out of a total group capital expenditure programme of £16 million.[10]

Initially there were tentative signs of progress: a Ferranti C.S 7 photocom- position system was installed at Odhams as a first step away from hot metal towards full filmless reproduction systems,[11] and Odhams won contracts for the printing of the *Sunday Express* colour supplement, along with a £500,000 telephone directory contract. In securing these contracts, however, the firm had been forced to bid precariously low to compete not only with Sun Printers, but also large-scale European photogravure presses which were winning an increasing share of the British print market.[12] Tellingly, the success of foreign (notably German) printing firms underscored the fact that it was not funda- mentally the quality of the output that undermined Odhams, but the working practices and labour relations that accompanied the printing technology. An Odhams management and union delegation visited a number of German gra- vure print works, including Grüner + Jahr's extremely profitable Itzehoe plant, and noted that not only were these competitors far ahead of Odhams in terms of labour productivity, but also that emerging new technologies in typesetting and printing were seen by both workers and management as being in their mutual interest.[13] Initially Fleetway showed signs of improvement, and in 1981 the firm posted its first small profit since 1974, illustrating that investment in new machinery could be profitable if it was supported by changes in working practices. Chapel River also moved into slight profit the following year after downsizing its premises and buying new machinery.[14]

The good news however could not change the underlying economic reality that Odhams was vastly overmanned, and with parent group Reed International's profits falling from £107 in 1980 to £52 million in 1981, it was only a matter of time before the group would need to make some hard decisions.[15] By October of that year Odhams was again on the brink, with expected losses for the year of £5.25 million. Management presented a 'cut or shut' deadline: lose 371 jobs and increase cost-cutting measures or the plant would close on 31 March 1982. Despite his appeal to reduce fratricidal conflict within the unions, Odhams' Ian Thomas accused many within the plant of continuing to put their parochial interests ahead of the security of the business.[16] Just as in 1974, closure was narrowly avoided at the last minute when all twelve union chapels agreed to a new productivity agreement, but this time the reprieve would be short-lived. The pressure on Reed International increased as IPC posted their lowest ever profits, and Odhams returned record losses of £16 million, including £6.5 million to cover voluntary redundancy costs. Printing subsidiary James Cond also suffered losses after failing to reach agreements with the unions to introduce new presses. Compounding the misery further, a new NUJ pay dispute in 1982 led to more editions of *Titbits*, *Honey*, and *Ideal Home* being lost.[17] In response, Reed International reorganized IPC into two main operating divisions: Reed Publishing Ltd., which took over the Business Press activities, and the Consumer Publishing Group, which specialized in popular magazines and was headed by Ron Chilton.[18] Despite being mired in industrial relations disputes, the company was aware that in addition to modernizing its printing it desperately needed to recapture some of the more innovative drive that been long been lacking, as had been noted by Cynthia White's Report for the Royal Commission on the Press some years earlier.[19] Chilton claimed that while the publisher's conventional wisdom had extolled the virtues of economies of scale, in the present world 'big is no longer beautiful for IPC. Small, separate publishing groups are now in vogue.'[20] The firm was unable, however, to concentrate on improving its magazines while it was fighting labour relations battles across all fronts. The breaking point came when the firm laid the blame for the closure of several magazines on a dispute with the NUJ in 1983, although for its own part the union accused IPC of using the action as an excuse to close unprofitable titles. Relations broke down so completely that a vote of no confidence in magazine editor by staff forced the closure of *Honey*. At the end of this long-running conflict, *Tit-Bits*, which had been losing £38,000 a week, became another casualty as it was closed along with five other titles.[21]

IPC needed to focus on one clear business—the creation of magazines—and the time for radical change had come. Les Carpenter had been appointed Reed International chief executive from the Magazine Division in 1982, and had been divesting some of the company's paper interests to focus on publishing magazines. Following Carpenter's assessment that 'national newspapers do not sit well in a large commercial organisation,'[22] on 12 July 1984 Reed International sold the Mirror Group Newspapers to Robert Maxwell for £113 million, finally separating the group's magazine and newspaper interests. As part of the deal, the huge magazine printing plant of Odhams (Watford) was sold to Maxwell's BPCC for £1.5 million.[23] IPC, which had first attempted to merge Odhams and Maxwell's Sun Printers in 1976, had now finally put an end to £30 million aggregate losses that had accumulated over the last ten years.[24] Although IPC agreed commercial terms with a £28 million contract for the BPCC to continue printing its magazine titles using Odhams' plant, this arrangement was short-lived as the following month Maxwell announced the merger of Odhams and Sun Printers, closing the Odhams (Watford) plant permanently and bringing to an end the activities of the presses that had for almost fifty years been so closely associated with the growth of Britain's weekly women's magazines.[25] IPC had long wanted to free itself of its print concerns, and between 1983 and 1984 finally broke its remaining bonds to printing by also divesting itself of Chapel River and Fleetway.[26] Following these divestments, IPC bought all its print and paper on the open market, initially using 37 contract printers across its portfolio. This was a significant volume of business; in 1983 IPC spent £48.85 million on print and £28.9 million on paper. Demand from IPC further stimulated the development of the contract print sector, which although still operating under the closed-shop system, would increasingly be able to offer services to new market entrants.[27]

ENDING THE CLOSED SHOP IN PRINTING

Maxwell had argued that his decision to close Odhams had been motivated by the need to introduce more flexibility than easily afforded by gravure printing, and had invested £10 million in the Sun Printers on web-offset presses and electronic page make-up systems.[28] Web-offset lithography offered magazine publishers a cheap and reasonably high-quality production process that could reproduce material from almost any source on cheaper uncoated papers. IPC's financial performance benefited immediately as the women's weeklies moved from gravure to web-offset. In 1981 *Woman's Realm* had been the first IPC title to show cost savings from wholly web-offset production, and now Sun Printers, who had printed *Woman's Own* since its launch, were able to utilize a hybrid printing technique combining gravure with web-offset sections in the process of translating all the titles to this technology.[29]

The ability of new entrants to engage contract printers was checked, however, by the closed-shop print union structure. Although IPC had freed itself from Odhams, the print unions still retained control over working practices in the industry. It had always been technically possible for IPC to petition the unions to use external print contractors, but this was with the proviso that other unionized establishments were engaged to take on the work.[30] Independent publishers who attempted to cut out union composition and make-up also discovered that unionized printing companies would only print work prepared by certified union members. The closed-shop system, however, was now to face a critical challenge. Although the NGA and SOGAT both recognized that they would not be able to prevent changes to working practices, or the acquisition of modern technologies, their main aim was to ensure that unionized workers shared in any benefits that the new methods would bring by maintaining tight control over production process.[31] The closures of key plants such as Odhams were setbacks for the unions in achieving this end, but they were to undergo further radical challenges from the political sphere. Since the 1870s, the printing unions had been able to effectively defend themselves by the right to strike, and other forms of direct industrial action. In the early 1980s, however, public dissatisfaction with the unions was growing[32] and they now faced a major challenge as the Conservative governments of Margaret Thatcher (1979–90) instigated a series of major changes to the structure of employment and union relations in the UK, passing a number of Employment Acts (1980, 1982, and 1984.) The Acts prohibited secondary action, such as 'sympathy strikes'. They limited picketing to six people in their own place of work (the 1980 Act), created restrictions to the closed shop and the 'blacking' of non-unionized companies, allowed employers to sue for compensation (the 1982 Act), something that had not been possible since the passing of the 1906 Trade Disputes Act, and made major changes to voting procedures, including the process of electing Trade Union officials, and the making of pre-strike ballots mandatory (the 1984 Act).[33] Following the commencement of these changes to the law, newspaper and printing companies started to mount pressure on the printing unions with a view towards union derecognition—which would remove their automatic right to collective bargaining—the creation of open shops, and most significantly, the 'right of management to manage'. The unions recognized that the real issue facing them was not only the adoption of new technologies, but the combination of these with the new government legislation.[34]

A key event in this process was triggered when the Messenger Newspaper Group, owned by Eddie Shah, sought to create new technology and working condition agreements with the NGA for a printing plant that was coming into operation for the first time at the end of 1983. Although the technology was soon agreed on, the Messenger Group considered that workers should be paid £40 less a week in the new plant (in Bury, Lancashire) as working hours were more favourable than at the company's operations in Stockport (also in Lancashire). The NGA, however, insisted on the same pay and conditions for both locations,[35] and the Messenger Group then proceeded to employ non-union workers at both these and at its main plant in Warrington, Lancashire. In protest the NGA, along with sympathetic workers in the NUJ, conducted strike actions at all the group's plants and proceeded with 'blacking' activities whereby the NGA requested that no business be conducted with Shah's operations, such as the supply of origination material from other firms or workers.[36] Following the provisions of the 1982 Act, these wider strikes which involved skirmishes between 1,200 print workers and nearly as many police officers,[37] were now classified as secondary actions which had been outlawed under the 1980 Act. The NGA felt obligated to fight its case with continued strike action, correctly surmising that at stake was its ability to dictate working conditions and practices in the future. By continuing to strike, however, the NGA found itself heavily penalized by the courts,[38] and from this point onwards the print unions found their positions much more difficult to defend as print employers increasingly used legal recourse to break their power. The response from the NGA and the NUJ was to form a joint committee to continue to seek 'new technology agreements' with employers to strengthen both unions bargaining power over the working practices that new technologies would bring.[39]

In the printing industry the position of the unions came to a head in the News International disputes which began on 24 January 1986. Once again, this bitter dispute was not primarily about the technology itself, but rather the unions' ability to dictate way the technology was used, the working methods employed, as well as wage levels across the board. At stake essentially was 'the right of management to manage' outside of the conditions which the unions wanted to bring to new technology agreements.[40] Rupert Murdoch, the proprietor of the News International Group, orchestrated a show-down with labour unions in order to quash their ability to dictate working practices, in which he was almost wholly successful. The gradual introduction of computers into the typesetting process with photocomposition had allowed technology-led unions such as the Electrical, Electronic, Telecommunications and Plumbing Union (EETPU)[41] to replace NGA and SOGAT workers at News International's new printing plant in Wapping, East London.[42] Following this dispute several other newspapers were able to launch using new printing technologies, employing open-shop agreements and low staffing levels, including Eddie Shah's *Today*, the first all-colour British newspaper, launched in March 1986, followed by the *Independent* in October.[43]

Although the Messenger and Wapping disputes formed a backdrop to radical changes in British print industrial relations, the impact of the changes within the magazine sector has largely been under-explored. Outside of IPC, the position of the individual unions such as the NGA and SOGAT was never as clear in the magazine publishing industry as in newspapers. For many small firms in the magazine industry, the importance of maintaining good personal working relationships in-house, and the precarious economic conditions under which many of them operated, resulted in a more pragmatic approach towards working conditions from local union chapters.[44] By the time that newspapers began the shift to web-offset printing, much of the magazine sector had already made the transition, driven by the need to incorporate more graphics and colour,[45] and many small magazine publishing companies had relied on contract printing and reprographics in any case. This meant that their offices were dominated by NUJ members rather than the NGA or SOGAT and thus had a different character to the large firms, with a far less rigid approach to demarcation.[46] The workplace relations that hampered IPC's adoption of new printing technologies were not representative of all magazine firms. Relations would be tested further however as changes in the typesetting and layout technologies, once securely within the remit of the printing industry, migrated into the editorial office.

Contract printing firms were quick to exploit the end of the closed-shop print industry. One innovative firm at the forefront was based in St Ives in Cornwall.[47] Formed in 1964 by Robert Gavron, St Ives plc became a major national printing firm when, after being floated in 1985, it embarked on an aggressive strategy to consolidate its position in the contract printing market. Acquiring major competitors, including Clays Ltd. and Burrups Ltd., the company established a strong base in financial printing and moved into consumer magazines with modern web-offset print works. The contract print sector attracted a growing number of competitors whose ability to service the sector would enable new firms in the 1990s to enter the market.[48]

COMPUTING INNOVATIONS IN MAGAZINE PUBLISHING

The shift away from hot-metal origination and make-up to photocomposition dominated the changes to magazine production for the larger firms, but small firms also benefited from changes in printing technology. Photocomposition machines aimed at small-scale concerns became widely available on the market in the early 1980s, notably from established firms such as Mergenthaler and new entrants such as Compugraphic. By 1982 a book entitled *The Business of Consumer Magazines* was able offer potential magazine start-ups the advice that phototypesetting machines could pay for themselves within twelve issues. They were many times more cost effective than hot type, and carried additional benefits for aspirant publishers in terms of the increased flexibility they would allow production schedules and greater control over the look of the final magazine thanks to in-house composition. The most sophisticated of these machines included disk storage for text loading, editing, and saving.[49]

The book suggested that the capital cost of these new machines could be further defrayed by using idle time to offer contract composition services to other titles, which would have the effect of further lowering barriers to entry for new entrants. Despite these advantages, the set-up costs remained significant for small firms, and photocomposition and in-house typesetting were still something of a rarity even in the late 1980s.[50]

Another emerging route to small-scale printing was provided by developments in photocopying and in-office printers. One emerging technology that would ultimately revolutionize the industry was laser-based printing. A special supplement to *Lithoweek*, the trade journal of the printing industry, on the new developments in electronic printing speculated on the coming of a day when magazines could be sent from a personal computer directly to the printer without the need to produce printing plates or the need for a reprographics function, with the prescient conclusion that 'the printing needs of the electronic office of the 1990s will probably be handled inside the office itself'.[51] Laser copiers in the UK had initially been too expensive for many smaller publishers, with the Xerox 9700 costing over £200,000 when launched in 1978, but by 1983 Robert Maxell's BPCC had established the first laser printing contract printer with four of these machines.[52] Although the quality of this technology was not good enough for consumer magazines it did lead to the creation of an 'alternative printing industry' whose impact could be discerned in the rise of free local newspaper sheets which increased from 194 in 1974 to 580 in 1983.[53] Of more significance for consumer magazines, the firm also operated the first commercial electronic page make-up system in its London Typesetting Centre after making a £1 million investment in a Hastech pagination system for the *Radio Times* printing contract for the BBC. Although the title was printed by photogravure, it demonstrated the potential flexibility of new workplace-based technology to employ a range of different print technologies suitable to the needs of the title, from composition and make-up through to printing.[54] The emerging technologies of make-up, rather than printing, now became the fulcrum for change in the industry. Within a year there were three additional electronic page make-up systems available in the UK market, and a number of further reprographics firms invested the required installation costs of around £500,000 to set up a medium-sized print shop. Initially these systems were complicated to use, and the suppliers gave no training and very little support to users in order to resolve the numerous hardware and software problems which plagued them, and thus they remained under the control of specialized print workers.[55]

Initially unsuitable for commercial magazine printing, the impact of laser printing was felt most within the magazine production office. As the office photocopier evolved from xerography to integrated non-impact laser printing, editors found that 'hard copies' could be used to produce editorial proofs and galleys. Editorial teams did not require high quality for their proofing needs, and a succession of new laser printers on the market offered lower print quality at reduced speeds but significantly cheaper prices.[56] The Xerox 8700 launched in 1983 retailed for £130,000, significantly less than its predecessor, and highlighted the steeply falling cost of quality laser printing. More dramatically still, a new low end of the market emerged in the £12,000 to £20,000 price range with machines such as the Canon LBP-10, the Mini LBP-CX, and the Xerox 2700, which were suddenly affordable to smaller concerns. These new office-scale printers began to form the basis of alternatives to compositing machines, and in 1983 IBM launched the 4250 electro-erosion printer as an alternative to a digital photosetter. This machine could produce camera-ready proofs for offset printing for an outlay of £15,000. A new generation of cheap micro-processors developed for the home such as the Commodore 64, BBC Model B, and the Sinclair QL, could now be built into limited word-processing systems for well under £1,000, and for the first time journalists working for themselves or within small businesses could abandon the typewriter to produce digital copy.[57] An emerging bubble-jet ink printing technology was then introduced to the market, of lower quality and slower than laser printers, but yet again substantially cheaper, and a good match for the office micro-computers. *Lithoweek* predicted that these new systems may 'have a more devastating effect on manning than the controversial single keystroking'.[58] These changes had the potential not only to allow small-scale new entrants to be more competitive, but also for larger firms to change their working practices as the technology allowed for new possibilities in copywriting, layout, proofing, and make-up.

These developments raised the possibility that magazines could potentially be wholly created by editorial staff and journalists in-house. Despite this, magazine make-up still fell under the remit of typesetting and graphical workers. Contract printers in many cases still required inputs created by NGA and SOGAT workers, continuing long-established working practices. As computer systems enabled the possibility of text being entered directly into a computer system, which could also be used for make-up and the creation of a printing medium, the last shreds of logic relating to the traditional lines of demarcation were blown away. Although the rough hard copies being produced by journalists and editors were initially only suitable to be used as working proofs, the writing was clearly on the wall that these systems could be operated by non-specialist workers and potentially cut out the need for further intermediary steps—something which both employers and the labour unions were acutely aware of. In 1984 the NGA, SOGAT, and the NUJ had formed the 'joint initiative on technology' to assess the threat,[59] and the NGA foresaw that, 'should the publishers be allowed to "capture the first key-stroke" in this way the implications for the NGA would be extremely serious'.[60] Tony Dubbins, the general secretary of the NGA, said that 'the issue of technological change is one of the most fundamental facing us in Britain today'.[61] By the time IPC was externalizing its print operations the process of 'single-keyboarding' was being openly discussed by magazine publishers throughout the UK, with companies such as EMAP saying that, 'we believe the majority of our staff want to begin this process of change now.'[62] Both employers and unions were keenly aware that single-keying was already long-established in the USA where unions had been unable to resist its implementation.[63]

In moving towards single-keyboarding, newspaper employers had resisted confronting unions directly and did not act together in an effective manner, opting to attempt to introduce new technology on an individual company basis. Few industry bodies acted to coordinate their introduction to new technology or dealing with the unions, although there had been a Joint Standing Committee for national newspapers, which as early as 1976 had launched an unsuccessful 'programme for action.'[64] More effectively, the long-established Newspaper Society formed a coalition of interested stakeholders in July 1982 under the banner of 'project breakthrough' to lead to the introduction of single keystroking and direct entry, moving activities out of the composing room into the realm of the editorial and advertising offices.[65]

Crucial to the adoption of direct-entry editorial systems was the cooperation of journalists. Although the NUJ represented this group, its members were far less cohesive than the print unions, because they covered a multiplicity of jobs, from reporters, sub-editors, and press officers to creative artists and teletext operators, who largely saw themselves as skilled workers with more in common with management than shop-floor workers.[66] In general, the move to single-keying and direct entry increased the power of the NUJ at the expense of the printing unions, and the concerns of the NUJ reflected less a desire to enforce demarcation than to negotiate better pay and working conditions, and to investigate the health and safety implications of the use of the new technology, such as the risk in using video display units (VDUs).[67] Although during the News International dispute the NUJ's official policy was to support the printing unions, in fact many journalists accepted the new terms and conditions, revealing a long-term resentment that some of them had felt towards the favoured status which the print unions had enjoyed.[68]

For small publishers, reliant on using unionized external typesetting, reprographics, and make-up, the possibility therefore existed to transfer many of these tasks to NUJ members. Agreement with the unions, however, was still crucial for companies wishing to change established working methods within the editorial office. The NGA was cognizant of this threat, and made a last ditch unsuccessful effort to ensure that publishers would have to bring NGA members into their firms to handle these functions, but with much of the power of the print unions broken by this time they were unable to resist the this transition, and many of their existing members in small firms were complicit in working with NUJ and non-unionized members in adopting new technology.[69] Although, outside of Odhams, industrial relations were generally better in the magazine publishing industry than in the newspaper industry,[70] the slow introduction of photocomposition and in-house typesetting was caused by many publishers' limited capital resources and the retraining that journalists needed to master the new techniques.[71] Unlike the national newspaper industry and IPC, the adoption of new working methods by small magazine publishers did not come about by a process of major industrial upheaval, but by gradual accommodations and compromises over time as the tasks undertaken by different union members blurred.

NEW COMPETITORS FROM EUROPE

Although IPC had solved its more ingrained print union problems with the sale of Odhams in 1984, it had little time to rest on its laurels before it was to face an onslaught of new competition, not only from minority players but international entrants which could use their superior scale against IPC on its own turf. Although IPC had failed to fully realize the benefits that its size conferred, it had been able to consistently maintain its dominant position through control of the women's interest market. In 1976, when IPC had moved to Kings Reach Tower near the South Bank of the Thames in London, its strategy had been very much focused on economies of scale, and it still dominated the mass market of women's weeklies. In 1984 this market was vital to the firm as the women's weeklies still comprised 70 per cent of its profits. The break with being part of a newspaper publishing empire and its printing firms represented a chance to refocus IPC, and managing director Ron Chilton emphasized that the business of IPC was now firmly on innovating magazine titles with commitment to reversing the gradual erosion of its competitive position. Chilton maintained that IPC 'always had about three ideas [for new titles] a week. The difficulty [had been] translating those ideas into commercial successes.' Despite this, Chilton's approach to dealing with new competitors still relied heavily on the thinking behind IPC's traditional scale advantages. The company's recent major launch programme had been mainly composed of plans to acquire competitor titles directly, along with responses to EMAP's recent youth-based successes *Just Seventeen* and *Smash Hit*. IPC's copycat titles were *Mizz* and *No 1*, and Chilton bluntly stated that 'if there isn't a gap in the market we'll put our head down and create a gap'.[72] Although *Mizz* enjoyed a £650,000 promotional budget and an initial 500,000 copy print-run, EMAP's *Just Seventeen* was more dynamic and already well established, and sales of *Mizz* were disappointing. In this emerging female teen market the company was not able to emulate its earlier success in the women's weekly segment, and nor was it able to find effective responses in the monthly women's sector to the now established *Cosmopolitan*. Although IPC remedied the industrial relations rigidities that had constrained their operations, vertical disintegration was not the palliative that had been expected, and the efforts to reinvigorate their portfolio of titles and editorial content were stalling. In 1985 IPC reported a £3.5 million reduction in profit as circulation revenues fell by £1.25 million, and advertising revenue dropped £3.47 million as new competitors such as Channel Four emerged. The response was to ask for 500 voluntary redundancies and to close ten titles, the cost of which was estimated to be £650,000 per title in redundancy costs and write-downs. Clearly, although it had achieved some structural reorganization, IPC needed to address the management and costs of new title development in order to arrest this continued decline.[73]

The mid-to-late 1980s, however, witnessed moves that demonstrated the emerging competitive threat of European-based firms to IPC and its British-based rivals,[74] and in particular a direct assault by foreign publishers on the jewel in IPC's crown, the women's weekly market. By the end of the 1980s, IPC's big-four titles, *Woman*, *Woman's Own*, *Woman's Weekly*, and *Woman's Realm*, were all under threat from competitors who could use even larger scale and world-class efficiency against Britain's leading magazine publisher. The initial European challenge was sounded in the monthly market by the British launch of *Elle*, positioned to compete with *Vogue* and *Harpers & Queen*, by French publisher Filipacchi Hachette in a joint venture with Murdoch Magazines in 1985.[75] Of direct concern to IPC was the launch of the monthly *Prima* by Grüner + Jahr (G + J), part of the German Bertelsmann media empire, in September 1986.[76] The Bertelsmann group had already successfully entered the French market with *Prima*, and the company held a stable of weekly titles which it could employ to attack IPC's core market directly. *Prima*'s arrival in Britain rocked the UK marketplace as it became the first monthly magazine to achieve a circulation in excess of a million copies, with weekly copy sales of 1.1 million,[77] and presented the weekly market's generally conservative readership with a monthly alternative. British women's magazines had slowly moved to appeal to a younger readership drawn towards more progressive entrants, such as *Cosmopolitan*, by providing 'a menu of younger soap opera stars, older pop stars and a sprinkling of sociology', but *Prima* reflected 'unreconstructed housewifery: with knitting patterns, sewing hints, cookery cards and money saving tips'.[78] G + J's next move was to launch *Best* in August 1987, a direct weekly competitor to IPC's big four. A few months later, fellow German publishing group H. Bauer[79] entered the women's weekly market even more aggressively, spending a record-breaking £9 million promoting the launch of *Bella*. In comparison, IPC's entire promotional budget for the year was £7 million, with £4 million across all weeklies, and £3 million on all monthlies.[80] *Bella*'s 29 pence cover price was pitched far below its competitors, but its appeal was not based purely on lower cost as British publishers were impressed by its editorial approach as well as the print and paper quality. H. Bauer could draw on the formidable resources of its Hamburg-based parent, a company that in 1988 sold 42 per cent of all magazines in the German market using a state-of-the-art press in Köln which was printing 28 million magazines per week by 1990.[81] The impact of the new European entrants was felt throughout the sector, and Natmags' group marketing director David Shields emphasized that 'the arrival of *Prima, Best* and then *Bella* and *Essentials* (the response from IPC) has had a major impact on our perception of what the women's market is all about...It has revealed that we need to look again at what we are doing.' The publisher of Natmags' *She* magazine, Cait Beaton, noted that as a response 'we are spending a lot of money on reader research. Women are becoming increasingly promiscuous in their choice of magazines and will read *She* one month, *Options* the next and *Women's Journal* the next. If you watch a woman in the newsagents you will see her take down a magazine, feel them for weight and pay particular attention to what is inside.'[82] The effect of this competition led to an overall sales decline for the women's segment of 8 per cent, once the rampant *Bella* was excluded from the figures.[83] Sales of IPC's flagship *Woman's Own* continued to tumble, falling to under a million for the first time in 1990.[84] For IPC, improving production quality was a necessary but expensive strategic response. The cost of switching to a better quality cover, comparable to those used by G + J for *Best*, was calculated as being around £1 million per annum for each magazine title.[85] The pain for IPC was further compounded in 1988 by the entry of *Hello!* magazine from the Spanish publisher ¡Hola!, which established a new women's segment in the UK market, that of the celebrity title.[86]

IPC attempted to internationalize its own titles in response to the European competition, developing international joint ventures to publish its monthly *Essentials*—a magazine it had launched in 1988 aimed at the grown-up woman—in French-speaking Canada (as *L'Essentiel*), Italy, and Spain (as *Practica*).[87] Within the next few years the company was able to add French, Brazilian, Argentine, Portuguese, Greek, and Turkish versions of the title as the competitive landscape of the 1990s became increasingly internationalized. The company's most notable international success also relied on a joint venture: the establishment of European Magazines Ltd. with French-based Groupe Marie Claire. Together the two firms launched a British version of the French company's *Marie Claire* in September 1988, a genuine and successful monthly competitor to *Cosmopolitan* under the direction of Glenda Bailey.[88]

The entry of European publishers into the UK's most lucrative markets not only shook up the competitive landscape of the industry, but by boosting sales of monthly magazines it also facilitated the structural changes that made entry into the industry easier. Moreover, it was to have a profound impact on the industry distribution system and process of supply chain management. This was the consequence of a key strategy employed by G + J in an effort to make rapid gains in market share: the re-introduction of sale-or-return (SOR). This system, whereby the publisher agreed to supply retailers but to only invoice for sales actually made, freely taking back unsold stock, greatly lowered the risk for retailers in stocking large numbers of copies.[89] One consequence of IPC's dominance had been the maintenance of a 'firm sale' distribution system, whereby retailers purchased magazines outright and thus effectively bore the cost of unsold issues. Due to the policy of G + J, by the end of the 1980s the British industry had been forced to adopt SOR completely in order to remain competitive, as retailers increasingly refused to stock titles on a firm sale basis.[90] In 1992 IPC's CEO Mike Matthews called the transition to SOR 'one of the most significant in IPC's history', as the company rapidly dropped from 90 per cent firm sales to zero and entered a more uncertain future.[91] The complexities of SOR relied on the development of sophisticated computer management systems by circulations departments, wholesalers, and distributors. The major wholesalers initially began to roll out new systems, in the process generating data about sales which they could use to develop their third-party services.[92] The move to SOR favoured aggressive new competitors, such as EMAP, who were willing to take risks in supplying magazines and investing in new inventory systems. These changes had long-term implications for magazine wholesale and distribution which greatly reduced the barriers to new magazine producers, as would become apparent in the 1990s.

EMAP'S ENTREPRENEURIAL STRATEGY

While IPC was combating the unions and European entrants, its essential concern remained protecting and consolidating the big-four women's titles. To bolster its position the Corporation acquired *Family Circle* and *Living* from the International Thomson Organisation for £28 million in April 1988.[93] During this period, however, its 'soft underbelly' of specialist magazines was being exploited by EMAP, a competitor who had consciously steered clear from direct competition in the core segments by developing niche markets which it planned to dominate. Under the joint leadership of Group chief executive Robin Miller and the chairman of its Magazines Division, David Arculus, EMAP's strategic plan was aimed around the development of strength in depth in specialist consumer markets, but the company's initial progress had been one of gradual development. With the aim of holding the leading title for each market segment in which they competed, the company continued to grow and EMAP's market capitalization reached £34 million in 1983. After the runaway success of *Smash Hits* the company was able to fund more aggressive expansion and, from having been responsible for as little as 10 per cent in 1976, by 1984 the EMAP Publishing Group was deriving over half of its revenue from magazine sales. By 1986 this figure would reach 70 per cent.[94]

The *Smash Hits* publishing team sought to consolidate their foray into the teen market with a trial of a new title designed to be 'everything a girl could ask for' as a giveaway bundled along with *Smash Hits* in October 1983. With a fresh contemporary design created by launch editor David Hepworth, *Just Seventeen* soon became the leading teen girls' title, obliging IPC to launch its ultimately unsuccessful competitor *Mizz*. EMAP continued to follow a concentric diversification strategy, which it termed 'divide and grow', developing depth in its specialist markets by continuing to launch complementary titles to its existing stable. Following its early success in motorcycling, for example, the company developed an extensive portfolio of publications within the EMAP National Magazines Publishing arm.[95] Adopting the same strategic approach, the EMAP Pursuit Publishing division had augmented the firm's original publication, *Trout & Salmon*, with a similar proliferation of angling-related titles. The success of the strategy to dominate narrow markets is perhaps best illustrated in the teen area, where by 1988 with *Smash Hits*, *Just Seventeen*, and *Looks*—which had been previewed with *Just Seventeen* in 1985—EMAP's Metro publishing division was home to the three top-selling teen girls' titles, with a circulation of 1.27 million out of a total market of 3.71 million.[96] The company had also been a first-mover in a nascent home-computing market, with *Computer & Video Games* laying claim to being the first successful consumer title in 1981. By 1984 this title was augmented by further magazines aimed firmly at the home computer user, such as *Commodore User* and *Sinclair User*. With its entrepreneurial decentralized editorial teams the firm was able to use its knowledge in specialist areas to continually spin off new magazines, the risk of which had been substantially lowered by SOR. Retailers were much more willing to trial new titles without the support of expensive marketing campaigns, which in turn would have required large print runs to spread the costs. In this system, key decisions were made at the publishing team level rather than by the corporate centre, and this facilitated an innovative expansion into related markets. From its base in teen music, the firm launched the music title *Q* aimed at a mature audience in 1987. *Q* was EMAP's first PPA Magazine of the Year winner in 1988 and firmly established the company as a serious challenger to IPC, which took three years to respond with *Vox*.[97] From the success of *Q*, the magazine's creative team launched a new title for cinema-goers, under publisher David Hepworth and launch editor Barry McIlheney, named *Empire*. The company had once again moved into a new market, and one which IPC had not contested since Odhams' *Picturegoer* closed in 1960. As significant as being able to innovate and launch new titles, the firm had established a profitable business model, with its magazine interests returning profits above 15 per cent, an extraordinary figure that rose over the following years.[98] Although the firm's titles were hits in the marketplace, they were also highly attractive to advertisers, with magazines such as *Just Seventeen* offering an industry-leading ten-day lead time that allowed advertisers to make adjustments to their material much closer to the publication date.

EMAP was not content to confine its growth to the existing portfolio of 42 consumer titles based around specialist interests alone. By 1984, together with its newspaper publishing and printing interests, the company comprised five operating divisions including Business and Computer Publications, International Exhibitions and Telemap, the latter of which handled electronic publishing. With ownership of an early digital technology, the Micronet 800 system, the company looked beyond the medium of print. With Micronet 800, effectively a telephone-accessed digital magazine available via the Post Office's Viewdata-based Prestel service (similar in look to the BBC's Ceefax service), EMAP commanded around 50 per cent of the market with 15,000 subscribers. With this incipient technology the company's long-term ambitions were outlined by Robin Miller in an address to staff in 1985: 'we are not in publishing or printing. We are in communications...our business is in creating and transmitting messages. At the moment we mostly do it by putting ink on paper and either selling it through newsagents...but that may not always be so.'[99] David Arculus masterminded the firm's growth both by internal development, based around 'decentralized entrepreneurial management teams', and through external acquisitions, such as the purchase in October 1984 of the trade publisher and exhibition company Maclaren, as EMAP sought to develop linkages between its magazine titles and event management, together with the provision of related services including contract printing. This aggressive expansion strategy led to a tripling of the company's market capitalization in 1987, from £99 million to £300 million, and a 48 per cent increase in group profits as the company spent £63 million on purchases.[100] To reflect this growth, in 1988 the company was reorganized into Consumer Magazines (including EMAP Metro, EMAP Recreational, EMAP Pursuit, Choice Publications Ltd. and Frontline), Business Magazines, Exhibitions, Newspapers, and Newspaper Printing.

Across the board EMAP strengthened its position as a consumer magazine-driven company. To support this the company reinforced its interests in wholesaling and distribution by forming a partnership between its recently formed EMAP Frontline distribution division and Haymarket Publishing in 1987, gaining a major 8 per cent stake of the market and moving distribution from rail to road.[101] With an ambition to become the leading distributor in Britain, EMAP considered offering distribution services to third parties, but instead decided to protect its competitive advantage by focusing primarily on publishing consumer magazines and growing distribution through further alliances, with the BBC joining in 1990.

In order to concentrate on the core business of publishing, and concluding that publishing did not sit well alongside the more capital-intensive activity of printing, the company began to divest its magazine print interests and then entered into a contract printing arrangement with St Ives in 1986. Unlike IPC, EMAP was built around small flexible teams which would respond quickly to adopting new editorial working practices after the externalization of printing.

This decentralized model would later form the template for the magazine publishing industry as a whole in the 1990s. At the start of the 1980s the company has been primarily a regional newspaper publisher, but by the end of the decade it had experienced enormous growth driven by its ability to use publisher-led teams to aggressively expand through differentiating titles around their core markets and had emerged as a serious competitor in the market.

INTENSIFYING DOMESTIC COMPETITION

In addition to EMAP, other established British competitors were slowly making ground, especially by exploiting links to US publications through multinational strategies. The National Magazine Company continued to develop both high-end and middle-market titles from its Broadwick Street offices, to where it had moved in 1979. In 1986 it published the aspirational *Country Living* to compete with IPC's *Country Life*, utilizing a significantly more downmarket US Hearst property as vehicle for local adaptation. *House Beautiful*, launched in 1989, was pitched as being a more practical and accessible title than *Ideal Home* and *Homes & Gardens*, and found a ready market. In addition to his Hachette joint-venture publications, Rupert Murdoch also made a short-lived attempt to establish a stronger presence in consumer magazines by attempting to translate his US-based titles, which he had acquired in 1984, into the British market. *New Woman* was the first of these attempts to enter women's monthlies, with the British version being launched in 1988, followed by another US title, *Mirabella*, in 1990 which was trialled as a giveaway with the *Sunday Times* as a marketing ploy. These titles enjoyed only moderate success, and although two British acquisitions, *Car* and *Supercar Classics*, were enjoying a good run of sales, Murdoch Magazines would not remain long in the market.[102]

Felix Dennis had continued to expand his company, at first by means of cult-based titles and movie tie-ins such as *Jaws* and *Indiana Jones*, but at times the firm's existence was precarious. Dennis claimed that 'salaries were mostly paid in cash on a Friday afternoon, providing I had remembered to go to the bank. The whole thing was a glorious shambles, held together by faith, hope, blind luck and mind-numbing workloads' but the business became firmly established after Dennis made a number of major breakthroughs in the mid-1980s with a foray into the North American market. Dennis opened offices in the USA, and in 1984 successfully launched a US version of EMAP's *Smash Hits* under licence as *Star Hits*, and then sold the British-based *Mac User* to US Ziff-Davies Publishing Company for US$23 million in 1987.[103] Felix Dennis' fortune was assured through the success of another American venture, his Mac Warehouse mail-order business. Started in 1987, the company returned US$18.4 million in 1988, and would go on to break the billion dollar sales mark in just seven years.[104] The British operations were finally set on an even keel as Dennis then modelled a British-based *Computer Shopper* on the format of an American magazine of the same name in 1988, with the insight that the falling cost of micro-computers had created an opportunity to provide home users with information about products and channels to buy them through. The business model for the British version of the *Computer Shopper* was firmly aimed at establishing a large circulation to attract mail-order advertisers, and quickly went on to become the best-selling UK computer magazine, stimulating further the burgeoning interest in home computing.

The BBC embarked on a slow transformation to becoming a serious player in the industry after its comfortable *Radio Times* duopoly with the *TV Times* faced its first challenge from a ruling by the European Commission.[105] Although the duopoly would endure until 1 April 1991, Murdoch Magazines' launch of *TV Guide* was an initial sign of a new wave of television guides that would inevitably follow the deregulation of TV listings.[106] These early moves were not unanticipated by the Corporation, and with the threat of competition on the horizon, in 1986 the BBC director-general Michael Checkland had already made the outside appointment of James Arnold-Baker, the European chief for Fisher-Price, as chief executive of BBC Enterprises, the Corporation's commercial arm. The goal for this new regime was to double BBC Enterprises' turnover within five years[107], and attention quickly turned to magazines with a move to reinvigorate the *Radio Times* by employing former *Times* features editor Nicholas Brett in 1988 to develop a more consumer-orientated focus.[108] The next move entailed the acquisition of Redwood Publishing which had emerged as the major player in a new sector of the magazine industry: customer publishing. This free-to-customer magazine publishing sector had effectively been founded in 1980 when British Airways approached Highgate Publishing with a proposal for them to produce the first edition of their in-flight customer magazine, *High Life*. Established in 1983, Redwood had initially printed an acquired home computer title, *Acorn User*, but the company found its niche with customer publishing, and was soon creating and printing titles such as *Expression* (also known as *E!*) for American Express and *InterCity* for British Rail.[109] By 1987 the company had moved into establishing new segments, such as retail customer magazines like the *M&S* title for Marks and Spencer.[110]

More significantly, as the open market in TV listings approached, BBC Enterprises made a conscious decision to enter the consumer market directly to diversify away from its reliance on the *Radio Times*, appointing a director of magazines, Dr John Thomas in 1986, who had worked both at Reed Business Press and IPC, along with experienced consumer magazines staff, in the form of Peter Phippen, in 1987.[111] Previously a publisher and marketing manager at IPC, Phippen had extensive experience in magazine launches having appointed Glenda Bailey to launch *Marie Claire*. Thomas charged Phippen, aided by Nicholas Brett, to work with staff at the newly acquired Redwood to identify which BBC television properties might best form the basis for new magazines titles. The first fruit of this collaboration was *Good Food*, published by BBC/Redwood, and an immediate sales hit in 1989.[112] Underscoring its new commitment to the sector, the Corporation joined EMAP's distribution arm Frontline in 1990 to bolster its circulation potential. Although 'Auntie Beeb' was already a magazine behemoth due to the huge sales of *Radio Times*, it had now begun a transformation that would reveal it truly to have been the sleeping giant of British consumer magazines.

THE MARKET-LED MAGAZINE

A range of start-up firms also began to enter the consumer magazine market, with some being started by industry insiders and others by entrepreneurs drawn by the lure of publishing. The success of Wagadon provided an early model for frustrated editors and entrepreneurs of how the rise of contract printing and new opportunities in distribution could be exploited to launch consumer magazines that tapped into emerging social trends. Wagadon's founder, Nick Logan, had demonstrated that there was a market for style magazines by raising the established circulation of *the Face* to well over 50,000 by 1984. He then proceeded to show that his core idea could be repeated by launching *Arena* in 1986, which appealed to a similar, but older, demographic to *the Face*. The success of *Arena* proved that men could be enticed into buying high-end fashion and general interest magazines if they were presented with the right product.[113] The title naturally also appealed to advertisers of men's fashion products: a strategy that harked back to the example set by Condé Nast with his *Vogue* fashion-led 'formula'. By the second half of the 1980s, Wagadon was managing a small stable of titles with only seven full-time staff, demonstrating that the small-scale multi-title firm model was viable.

Following Logan's lead, the men's style market was colonized by several other start-up publishers, using different small-scale market entry approaches, all of whom sold their titles using the Comag third-party system of distribution. Former *Vanity Fair* and British *Vogue* art director Terry Jones translated his initially street-distributed fanzine, *i-D* magazine, into a paid magazine with a 50p cover price by founding Level Nine publications in September 1980. Carey Labovitch founded Jigsaw Publications from her flat and offered a similar title called *Blitz*.[114] The success of these small firms underlined the potential strength of this new segment, and larger established publishers took note, with Condé Nast acquiring 40 per cent of Wagadon in 1988.[115] Editors within established firms began to see opportunities across a range of new markets, and also gained the confidence that they could prosper outside the structures provided by large firms. In 1986 for example, a group of IPC staff undertook a buy-out of twelve of the firm's magazine titles which they thought that they could manage better outside of the company's bureaucratic structures.[116]

Further opportunities were now clearly becoming available for new companies to enter the market, particularly to exploit emerging areas where existing firms had no well-established titles against which they needed to compete. Many of these new publishing initiatives made their firmest impression in the micro-computing and video-games markets. To begin with the distinction between home, office, educational, and recreational uses for micro-computers was fairly blurred, and a number of publishers from different areas of the industry were active in the market. Franco-Dutch Business publisher VNU had published *Personal Computer World* aimed at the business market as early as 1978, for example, but the first consumer computer games oriented title, *Computer & Video Games*, had been launched by EMAP in 1981. This new market proved attractive to new entrants which were often already active in the computing industry. Newsfield Publications Ltd. was founded by Roger Kean, Oliver Frey, and Franco Frey after the success of their mail-order software business in catering for the Sinclair Spectrum 48k. They set up a limited company in October 1983 to publish a magazine devoted to this market, and the resultant title, *CRASH*, had a circulation in excess of 100,000 copies by 1985. The company continued to develop titles such as *Personal Computer Games, Zzap!64*, and *AMTIX* before moving into other segments of consumer magazines such as the teen lifestyle market, horror and science fiction, and home videos, although computing remained its core area with further launches of titles such as *Prepress with the Macintosh*.[117] Based in Ludlow, Newsfield demonstrated that small publishers could establish viable publishing houses outside of London—with its dense network of journalists, typesetters, reprographics and graphic artists, and printers—if they formed a small specialist team that could collate contributions from contract writers and use the newly emergent contract firms offering layout and print services.

Chris Anderson, a former editor of two of Newsfield's first computer gaming magazines, had left the company following a decision to relocate its offices. Anderson had been responsible for some marketing innovations at *Personal Computer Games*, notably in pioneering a free flexi-disc cover-mount. His next move was to found Future Publishing with a £10,000 bank loan in June 1985. With a self-confessed obsession with the new craze of home computers, Anderson decided to capitalize on the growing interest in Amstrad machines, initially publishing *Amstrad Action* largely from his house in Somerton, Somerset, along with two former Newsfield colleagues, the former software editor Bob Wade and a freelance journalist Peter Connor.[118] After poor initial sales Anderson followed his earlier marketing innovation with a similar idea: free software on a cover-mounted cassette which then became a regular feature and ensured the success of the firm. He later employed this strategy again as Future was also the first to cover-mount computer diskettes in June

1987. Following the introduction of new products into the home computing market, such as the new Amstrad 8000 series, Anderson launched a range of leisure-oriented computer titles to cater for these users, including *8000 Plus* (later renamed *PCW Plus*), *Ace* magazine, *ST Amiga Format*, and *PC Plus*. By the autumn of 1986, Future had emerged as Britain's largest publisher of news-stand computer magazines.[119]

Moving the company to new head offices in Bath, over the next few years Anderson built Future into a major magazine publisher, principally in the video gaming market, by launch and acquisition. For example, the company acquired EMAP's original *Computer & Video Games*, now owned by Dennis who had purchased it in their drive to build a computing presence. To consolidate its position, Future also divested titles, selling *Ace* to EMAP in 1989 for £1 million, underlining its growing confidence and maturity in acting as a serious publishing house and providing capital for a period of rapid growth.[120] In 1989 Future branched out from their base in the video gaming market by establishing a Consumer Division which by 1991 had launched seven titles, such as *Needlecraft*, and had acquired *Mountain Biking UK* (*MBUK*), indicating that it could compete directly with the nation's largest established magazine producers.[121] In part it was able to do this because of its low cost structure and, in addition to leading the computing sector, the firm also led the way with the adoption of computer-based systems for the origination of magazines. The development of these software technologies served to decrease the need for regional publishers to site their operations in physical proximity to the traditional group of supporting companies, although as Driver and Gillespie have shown these ties only began to recede completely in the 1990s.[122]

ADVENT OF DESKTOP PUBLISHING

In 1987 IPC Computer Services director Steve Williams considered that 'the publishing industry in general was ten years behind the commercial world' in terms of PC adoption.[123] Typically firms were quickest to embrace the new opportunities in dealing with advertisers and classified advertising. At IPC an initial £1.5 million investment in a Computerized Advertisement Booking System (CABS) had been successfully implemented, and a £2 million system to share sales data with wholesalers W.H. Smith, John Menzies, and Surridge Dawson, named OASIS (Order, Accounting and Sales Information System), vital for dealing with SOR, was being trialled.[124] The spread of computer use for editorial and design work, however, was tempered by the suspicion among both journalists and graphical workers that this was a pretext for staff reductions and a threat to established working conditions. Contract publisher Redwood was an early mover, ditching its typewriters for a network of BBC

Acorn micro-computers in 1984, and gradually computer technology began to make its presence felt within the editorial office. To incumbent firms it was initially not clear whether centralized bespoke systems, such as the networked models adopted by Redwood and later by Condé Nast in 1986, or the provision of generic stand-alone PCs would provide the most suitable solution for editorial work.[125] At this stage IPC's offices were still dominated by manual typewriters, but in considering their replacement a major problem was evaluating new technologies as they emerged, as early systems generally represented large capital investment that would lock the purchaser into products largely incompatible with other stages of the production and printing process, such as make-up, typesetting, and printing. Reluctantly, and claiming to 'have no faith in management', the NUJ agreed an initial trial of new editorial systems for IPC's *New Scientist* title.[126] Despite this wary reception to the new working methods, IPC started a wider series of new technology trials in July 1987, under editorial systems adviser Neil Bailey, to improve the efficiency of editorial operations.

The company was anxious to avoid the industrial relations disputes which, given their fractious history, would almost certainly result from too rapid a rate of change. The firm therefore adopted a cautious approach to both new technology and working practices by using three titles as initial testing beds. For its *Woman's Journal* title the Page Planner software system was introduced to assist editors in the production of galleys. For the *New Scientist* a more ambitious attempt was made to use an S-Word text editing programme running over the central Prime Computer.[127] This generated high central re-charge costs and served to demonstrate that centralized computer systems were not a cost-effective option for magazine production. The Page Planner software was also introduced into *Woman and Home*, but a lack of hardware resulted in only one PC being available, and the software was found to be difficult to manage. A further two magazine titles were later included in the trials, *Yachting Monthly* and *Horse & Hound*, but after review only the *Woman's Journal* was able to report any savings or increased efficiency. A report on progress noted that

> the experiment has shown there are potentially significant benefits in these systems in the area of magazine operation and shorter deadlines (provided suitable management action is taken to structure the magazines to take advantage of the opportunities and enforce necessary disciplines) and that major typesetting costs can be achieved...the most tangible benefits would be from direct inputting. Industry estimates are that between 30 per cent and 70 per cent savings are possible.

To an organization of IPC's size, comprising 93 production units, even small savings could be significant. In 1987 the review recommended further investment to install dtp systems throughout the company by 1992, either with a three- or five-year implementation plan planned with hardware costs estimated between £1.83 and £2.17 million respectively. The firm assumed that 'with good management a reduction in staff...of 32...would completely offset [project] costs' and produce planned cost savings of £3 million per annum.[128] The key question, however, as to which systems to invest in, was still unclear after these trials.

Early adopters of dtp systems faced significant challenges, including problems of PC-based software and hardware incompatibilities (even when provided by the same vendor), poor ongoing product support, inconsistencies between software package upgrades, and constant training problems, to name but a few.[129] There was also the crucial issue of assuring compatibility with the systems used by reprographics houses and printers. An unpublished internal report at IPC commented ruefully that 'if [only] you were using a Macintosh...' turned out to be Linotype's catchphrase for 1988 whenever incompatibilities arose in attempting to transfer computer-based text into layout and make-up systems.[130]

Future Publishing was the first mover in employing a network of Apple Macintosh computers within the editorial office for word-processing and make-up, along with an in-house typesetter. Not surprisingly, given their intimate knowledge of the industry, publishers of magazines that focused on the micro-computing sector were the earliest to adopt the new systems. Future's adoption of the Apple Macintosh would turn out to be prophetic, as the Macintosh, better known as the 'Mac', became the new paradigm within the publishing industry. The single most important factor in the widespread adoption of dtp was the development of low-cost laser printer engines by Canon in 1985. Once the output technology was in place, other existing technologies began to exploit the capabilities of the printer within the production office. Coupled with developments in micro-processing and layout software, a new 'triple-A' standard emerged, with Adobe Systems, Apple Computers, and Aldus Software each supplying a key component. Adobe Systems developed the PostScript language, vital to enable different computer systems to be able to exploit laser printers. Apple, which had worked with Cannon and Adobe on the development of both laser printing and PostScript, integrated the system into its printers in 1985. Linotype and IBM followed suit in 1987, making PostScript the industry standard. Aldus Software had been founded by Paul Brainerd in 1984, and having previously worked for ATEX he saw the need for professional page composition systems that were not mainframe-based and were thus affordable for small businesses. Aldus' resultant PageMaker programme quickly became the industry standard when it was bundled in the Apple dtp System launched in 1985, which included a Macintosh Microcomputer and the Apple LaserWriter,[131] and was capable of making complete pages and integrating with Linotype machines.[132] For IPC, and the industry in general, this proved to be a turning point as it enabled the different stages of magazine production to share a common standard from first keystroke through to print.

As this new standard emerged, the new technology workforce at IPC recommended that Macs would be easier to introduce into the editorial and art office, citing Apple's claim to halve the training costs compared with IBM-based PCs. The group concluded that 'the Macintosh's intuitive user interface is well known. Proof of its effectiveness has been seen on the *Woman and Home* installation. The speed, and competence, with which PageMaker was adopted in the Art Department was far in excess of our most optimistic expectations.' As the costs were largely comparable to rival PC-based solutions, the new technology work-group recommended the adoption of Macs, and noted that 'the long-term advantages of installing Macintoshes... could prove decisive in the successful adoption of electronic page makeup in IPC magazines'.[133]

EMAP had reached the same conclusion and embraced direct-entry editorial systems, effectively making its transition during 1987, leaving IPC once again playing catch-up.[134] At the National Magazine Company *House Beautiful* had been put together by a small team using Macs during 1988, and the company moved to adopt this model as the standard was gradually embraced throughout the industry.[135] Following the new technology trials IPC started to change its installed technological base for magazine origination and production, with *Yachting Monthly* in 1989 becoming the first fully-direct copy title, with all inputs being made on Word Perfect before conversion into PageMaker for design and layout.[136] In 1991 QuarkExpress was adopted throughout the entire company, as this software started to supplant PageMaker throughout the industry. Despite potential of the new standard to revolutionize the way in which magazines could be produced, IPC struggled to immediately capitalize on these investments as the organization failed to make commensurate changes to the established working practices across the company, particularly in the core women's weekly titles. An internal report into the effectiveness of the new technologies questioned 'how can six people put together 124 pages of *Golf Monthly* each month but it takes fifty-six people for the 160 pages of *Women's Realm*?'[137] Not until 1990, after a series of strikes, did the company dismiss its new technology agreement with the NGA and start to shift the responsibility for the look and production of the magazine firmly back to the editorial team.

The flexibility afforded by embracing dtp systems enabled IPC to survive the initial challenges from its European rivals, as it began to reinvigorate its core women's titles. The new focus led to some notable successes although the best example, *Marie Claire*, was the outcome of its French joint-venture partnership rather than a purely in-house development. IPC's Advertisement director Gordon Brown argued that 'the Germans are finding that we are more resilient than perhaps they expected. We are fighting back and they are finding the going tougher than they thought. There was a time when people would say you could take the cover off *Women* and put it on *Woman's Own* and nobody would notice the difference. Now there are differences and the editors are concentrating their minds on appealing to specific audiences.'[138] Despite this, the pace of change was slow, and although IPC was able to start to emulate the model of the small editorial office, similar to those operated by new entrants such as Dennis Publishing and Wagadon in their specialist monthly titles, IPC's core weeklies remained locked into the bureaucratic processes of the Ministry for Magazines right through until the end of the 1980s.

TOWARDS THE DIGITAL AGE

Although the 1980s witnessed the gradual emergence of a new common standard in the field of dtp, the full potential of the changes brought about by the introduction of computer technology would remain unfilled until they were augmented with changes in telecommunications. Comprising text, pictures, and advertisements, the introduction of dtp began to open up new ways for magazine firms to gather this varied content, but to begin with the technology's impact was mitigated by data-transfer problems. IPC had been using centralized computer systems for communicating with advertisers for some time, but the ability of these systems to obtain and handle journalists' copy lagged far behind. The simplest way for a magazine title to generate editorial content was through a full-time in-house writing staff, and this was the approach that IPC used to serve its key women's weekly titles. By the mid-1980s, however, many of the more specialized magazine titles required inputs from a larger variety of contributors, especially freelancers, and most of the smaller-circulation IPC magazines were receiving much of their copy from these outside sources. Some titles were obtaining over 75 per cent of their copy in this way, while three of its best-selling titles, *Horse & Hound, À La Carte,* and *Melody Maker,* were getting more than 60 per cent of their copy from external sources at this time.[139] The compatibility between different text-editing programmes was a barrier to the transformational potential of dtp, as although the Mac quickly became ubiquitous across the industry within the editorial, reprographic, and printing stages, most freelance journalists continued to work on proprietary and assorted third-party PC-based word-processing packages. The intermediate solutions that were available to address this problem of incompatibility were unwieldy, and included using complex and expensive multi-disk readers (including portable versions known as 'milking machines'), or by telecommunications links using early modems, such as the British Telecom Gold system employed for external contributors to the *New Scientist*, but this was slow, unreliable, and costly.[140] The simplest way to capture text was by installing an optical character recognition (OCR) system, which allowed journalists to send hard copy to the magazine house to be scanned into digital format. Although expensive and time-consuming this was a workable solution. At IPC the aim was to equip offices with the ability to receive work on disk wherever possible and then scan copy with OCR software to allow for the 'full integration of systems within the IPC network...and the growing facilities offered by type-setters, Repro houses, Ad Agencies and Printers'.[141] The decade of the 1980s had witnessed a profound change in the way magazines were produced, trans-forming them from products created through the use of traditional hot metal to digital creations. However, it would take further developments in telecom-munication systems to fully reveal the profundity of these changes.

Nonetheless, it was clear by this time that working methods in the magazine publishing industry had changed beyond recognition. A well-informed con-temporary observer considered that the 'previous industrial relations restric-tions have been modified so that even unionised houses can involve their journalists in the type-setting and page-makeup of their magazines'.[142] The unions were forced to accept the reality of the converged production technolo-gies that had occurred as a result of digitization, and to reform their practices accordingly. In 1991 the NGA and SOGAT merged into the Graphical, Paper and Media Union (GPMU), and the NUJ only dropped out of the merger at the eleventh hour. For the production of magazines, dtp meant that the repro-graphics stages of production could be entirely bypassed by the internalization of these activities in the editorial office. More than collapsing the stages of the production process, this gave the editorial team control of the origination process in terms of speed, design, and quality. The ending of the closed-shop arrangements allowed contract printers to accept material from any source regardless of whether union staff had been involved in its production. The world of the craft-based print unions, and their power to control working con-ditions in the industry, would be but a distant memory for the new dtp-based entrants in the following decade.

By the end of the 1980s conditions in the industry had changed radi-cally, and the range of competitive tactics employed by firms had broad-ened considerably. The European publishers now found it possible to enter the British market by using a variety of market entry strategies, including leveraging their superior scale and efficiency to enter the long-established weekly markets directly, and employing joint-venture strategies to enter monthly markets. In response, IPC had been obliged to expand its own its international operations. Domestic competitors such as EMAP, the National Magazine Company, Future Publishing, Condé Nast, and Dennis Publishing also found they were able to create and enter new markets by launching titles to capitalize on emerging social trends and technological advances, particularly in the field of home computing. In this latter area, Newsfield had ridden the waves of successive generations of computer platforms, with constant launches of new low-cost titles, and Future had demonstrated that emerging consumer interests, such as those based around specific computer games, could form the basis of a profitable title. These publishers had to be highly engaged in their markets, and reactive to change, something also facilitated by the flexibility of the new dtp systems. Small-scale magazine publishers also attracted the attention of established firms as targets for acquisition and talent-hunting once they had established the viability of the new markets they had pioneered, but large firms could no longer simply assume a competitive advantage based on superior scale alone. With the rise of SOR, small-budget magazine launches were able to take leading positions in the market, and entrepreneurial editors who founded their own firms proved just as able to identify new niches as experienced publishers. New markets, rather than traditional ones, would now prove to be the fulcrum for further innovation in the industry, and new niche titles would exploit the radical changes made during the 1980s to printing, industry working practices, and editorial systems. In particular the developments to whole-sale, distribution, and retail in the move to SOR had also begun to unlock the innovative potential within the industry as never before, and to instigate a further lowering of market entry barriers. Far from witnessing the decline of magazine publishing in Britain, the 1980s had witnessed a series of posi-tive developments. In June 1980 BRAD had listed 1,367 consumer titles in a market that had been declining for some time. By June 1990, however, this number had increased to 2,373, and far from having reached its apex, the industry was about to enter a truly golden era—the digital age.[143]

8

Global Magazines and the Digital Age

ON THE CUSP OF A REVOLUTION

In a review of structural changes to the industry during the 1980s, Driver and Gillespie considered that the industry's natural tendency towards monopoly had reached a new phase with the entrance of the European publishers, and that from this point it would become subject to increasing global media concentration and further decline.[1] Sales in the industry had been in constant relative decline, down from a peak of nearly 2.5 billion copies sold annually in the early 1970s, to near half that in 1990.[2] At the end of the 1980s, the top 100 best-selling magazines were still created by a handful of companies. Despite its troubles IPC was still far and away Britain's largest magazine producer, with sales of £155 million (a market share of 45.6 per cent). Of the 100 top selling magazine titles nationally IPC accounted for 32, while the company still commanded nearly half of the £93.8 million sales in the key women's segment. Behind IPC, in order of the value of sales, ITP and BBC Enterprises were in second and third places with just one major selling title each: the *TV Times* and the *Radio Times*. EMAP was a distant fourth with sales of £40.2 million and 13 of the top 100 titles, and European entrant Grüner + Jahr was fifth with sales of £29.9 million, again from just two mass-circulation titles.[3]

While the consumer market still appeared to be dominated by a few firms, the changes to the printing industry and the emergence of dtp in the 1980s had profoundly changed the way in which magazines were produced. New editorial systems had greatly lowered barriers to entry, allowing new firms to enter on a low-cost basis, and also reinvigorated established editorial teams. Hence conditions were in place for growth in the sector unimaginable a few years earlier, and the industry was to experience the start of a new revolution. From its inception the industry had existed to place magazines into the hands of consumers, and although production technologies had changed radically, and the magazine evolved from black and white newsprint to a sophisticated colour product, it was still essentially a print-based article at the start of the decade. In the 1990s, however, from focusing on new methods of magazine production, the industry began to perceive that the digital revolution would also open up new possibilities for the way magazines were consumed in the future.

THE INTERNET

As communications technologies improved, the initial promise made by dtp in the 1980s began to flower. Although IPC had an internal e-mail system at the start of the 1990s, the problems of obtaining copy from outside contractors were only truly overcome by the spread of domestic e-mail systems and the Internet, with the first dial-up Internet services being offered in the UK in 1992. By 1995 all IPC staff had been connected to an internal Microsoft Windows-based network running CC mail and connected to the Internet.[4] By 1998, 78 per cent of British businesses had a computer connected to a modem, often used for access to proprietary networks, although there was rapid growth in Internet access for firms, up from 35 per cent in 1997, to 49 per cent in 1998.[5] This opened up new remote working possibilities within the sector, and in 1998 the editor of *Mountain Bike Rider*, Brant Richards, was able to edit the magazine and source copy by contracting and coordinating freelancers from his home using an Apple Macintosh and modem. Although at the end of the 1990s many consumer publishers were still receiving copy from contract journalists on disk, or even still by hard copy, by the early 2000s electronic forms of submission had become far more prevalent.[6] Likewise, the emergence of Microsoft software created a common standard where journalists and external contract writers could use their own machines with a good degree of compatibility with the magazine houses' dtp systems, allowing for the near-seamless integration of material from actors who were geographically dispersed. Editors were increasingly able to add value for consumers in the specialist magazine segments by creating networks of copy providers, including expert contributors and other industry-specific participants, which had the effect of greatly broadening out magazine journalism away from its traditional reliance on in-house professionals.[7] As patterns of provision changed, it provided new opportunities and greatly widened participation in the industry, harking back in some respects to George Newnes' *Tit-Bits* model, but it also acted to make careers in magazine journalism less stable and predictable.[8]

The contract printing sector continued to develop, with increasing competition to print magazines between companies such as Polestar (formed by the merger of the Maxwell Communications Corporation, formerly BPCC, and Watmoughs), Cooper Clegg, St Ives, Southern Print, and the Wyndham Press.[9] St Ives continued to develop as one of the major printers of consumer magazines in the UK, with a turnover of £221.3 million in 1993.[10] In 1994 the firm made a £30 million investment in a dedicated plant in Caerphilly to print 11 IPC titles,[11] and in 1997 won the contracts to print titles including *Top Gear* for the BBC, *Vogue* for Condé Nast, *Stuff for Men* for Dennis, and *Minx* for EMAP, at new high speed web-offset printing works in Plymouth and Andover. Print technology continued to lower costs and to improve quality, and a further investment undertaken to service a contract for EMAP Metro heralded a move to perfect binding, a cheaper solution than stitching.[12] A new plant in Peterborough opened in 1997, with dedicated pre-press facilities allowing quicker make-ready, and offered the facility to accept digital input straight to print, a process known as 'computer-to-plate' (CTP), with Polestar also opening a CTP-press in the same year.[13] CTP offered the promise of virtual print integration mediated through the Internet, although initially the number of magazines publishers providing digital material for direct print was disappointing.[14] In 1998, St Ives won contracts from *Condé Nast Traveller* and *House & Garden* for full CTP printing, and 2002 represented a turning point with CTP becoming adopted widely throughout the industry.[15] Although this led to major consolidation within the printing sector, for aspirant magazine publishing companies, getting to print became simpler and cheaper as the last physical links between publishers and printers were broken.[16]

TRANSFORMING DISTRIBUTION AND RETAIL

As Internet-based communications developed, publishers moved to increase control over the distribution of their titles, and to expand the possibilities for retail. Developments in third-party primary distribution had allowed the low-cost entry of independent firms through the 1980s, and changes to distribution, wholesale, and retail further accelerated the trend. Publishers also sought to improve their competitive positions by developing their circulation and distribution systems.[17] SOR required the development of a sophisticated supply-chain with integrated information systems, and acted to stimulate innovation by making magazine publishers focus on the end consumer, rather than the wholesaler or retailer, as their customer. With the aim to 'give the Germans hell', IPC created a new distribution subsidiary in 1990 named Marketforce through the merger of its in-house Circulation, Sales and Distribution department with the Independent Television Publications (ITP) sales force, and the former Reed Business Publishing Group's Quadrant Publishing Services. The aim of the strategy was to develop closer links to the customer and thereby become more responsive to changing market conditions.[18] The comparable Frontline distribution partnership between EMAP, the BBC Enterprises, and Haymarket also continued to grow, with a 50 per cent share in the formation of a new joint-venture distribution company Seymour with the French Hachette Distribution Services in 1995.[19] The Seymour partnership allowed Frontline's partners access to European, North African, and American markets, and a combined 25 per cent market share made the Frontline and Seymour partnership the largest overall distributor of magazines in the UK.[20] In 1997, Seymour formed a distribution joint venture with Dennis Publishing, and by 2002 Frontline and Seymour had increased their combined market share to 36 per cent. At this time the IPC-led Marketforce held 22 per cent and Comag 18 per cent of the market.[21] H. Bauer Publishing became Frontline's fourth partner in 2005, further enlarging the group. Comag continued to handle distribution for Condé Nast, the National Magazine Company, and for third parties. With the formalization of Marketforce as a distribution company in 1990, magazines publishers had effectively taken control of the primary distribution channels and from this point on were able to leverage greater buyer power against the wholesalers, and obtain enhanced information relating to patterns of buyer behaviour.[22]

The wholesalers themselves also became increasingly concentrated during the 1990s, as the 'big three' firms of W.H. Smith News, John Menzies, and Surridge Dawson increased their control of the trade from 52.5 per cent in 1989 to 85 per cent in 2002.[23] This concentration reflected an overall reduction in the number of wholesalers, from 502 in 1970, to 72 in 2002.[24] In 1993, a Monopolies and Mergers Commission review led to the establishment of the industry Code of Practice which granted wholesalers exclusive territories with the proviso that they supply all retail outlets that met basic criteria, including petrol stations and other new outlets which had been petitioning to stock magazines.[25] This arrangement expanded the number of retail outlets from 44,474 in 1992, to 54,621 in 2000, and was a brake on the existing trend of steady exit by small independent CTNs from the magazine trade. Although this did not ultimately restrain the growing retail power of the multiples, it did ensure that publishers could find effective channels to consumers, especially for magazines, outside of the top-selling titles listed by the supermarkets.[26] When the Office of Fair Trading (OFT) later reviewed the Code of Practice in 2005 Britain's magazine publishers, through their representative trade body the PPA, fiercely opposed any changes, arguing that their industry benefited from the expansion of the CTN sector; a position that the OFT ultimately agreed with.[27] Despite the magazine industry's support of the more broad-based distribution arrangements, many small magazine retailers were slow to adopt electronic point-of-sale (EPOS) stock-inventory management systems, as they were unable to finance and manage the necessary investment. Supermarkets, who for the most part aggressively captured, collated, and leveraged their knowledge of consumer buying patterns, found they had a blind spot in their handling of magazine sales data, and at first were generally content to let wholesalers manage their magazine stock on their behalf.[28] During the 1990s, magazine wholesalers had been in the key position to collect sales and consumption data, but through the early 2000s this control slipped as distributors increasingly invested in capturing sales data, such as through Seymour's ENIGMA system, and supermarkets upgraded their EPOS systems in a race to control and exploit consumer-generated sales data.

The issue of retailing continued to be of key importance in the British market, as consumer magazines publishers' income maintained its heavy dependence on news-stand sales, with anywhere between 60 and 90 per cent of revenue coming from the cover price for many monthly titles. In fact, changes to the structure of retail during the 1990s created conditions that were highly supportive for innovation and growth in magazine publishing. The continued growth of retail chains, such as W.H. Smith Retail and other multiple chains, led to a more sophisticated sector capable of handling a much larger quantity of magazines, both in terms of number of copies per issue and the range of stocked titles. Supermarkets in particular became more active players in magazine retail, and although ASDA had made small inroads into the retail of magazines, the turning point was the entry of Tesco in 1986 with 300 of its 6,000 supermarkets converted to selling magazines. Publishers had previously been wary of the idea of supermarket retail, with fears that supermarkets would attempt to attract sales by discounting the cover price, cream off only top-selling titles, or push for the introduction of SOR.[29] By the end of the 1980s, however, this last concern had already been realized by the entrance of the European firms, and the industry had begun to embrace the major multiples as valuable additions to their traditional outlets. By 1989, when IPC began selling titles through Tesco stores, magazine sales represented the supermarket sector's fastest non-food growth area.[30] Over the next few years other chains, such as Woolworths and convenience store chain Seven-11, also moved into magazine retail, and consumer magazines began to become categorized as a new element in the field of fast-moving consumer goods (FMCGs).[31]

Through the 1990s supermarkets greatly increased their share of consumer magazine sales, from 6 per cent in 1990, to 23 per cent in 2001. Over this period W.H. Smith Retail, the major CTNs, and other multiples' share of the market remained fairly static, while that of independents fell from 57 per cent to 35 per cent of the market.[32] As the influence of the multiples grew, many small CTNs lacked the resources to develop specialist magazine title displays or gain knowledge of new markets. Although W.H. Smith provided the widest selection of magazine titles on the high street, utilizing the risk-free SOR system, many supermarkets now readily accepted new magazine titles on a trial basis, even from new entrants.[33] For established and emerging publishers, supermarkets represented a low-cost route to a new and expanded audience of readers. With the strong participation of supermarkets, petrol station forecourts, and other new retailers, the opportunities for off-the-shelf magazine sales had grown dramatically.

THE BBC AND DTP-DRIVEN GROWTH

Through the 1990s barriers to market entry had fallen rapidly. The development of specialist low-cost, high-margin titles was made possible by the combination of dtp production coupled to the ability to work with contract journalists via electronic networks. The supporting network of contract printers and third-party SOR distribution allowed for easy access to retail, which was further facilitated by the introduction of supermarkets as outlets. In terms of staff, the large magazine publishers had always been somewhat permeable, with employees moving between titles and shifting to competitors, and although IPC had been overly bureaucratic at times in its history, it had always proved a fertile training ground for staff who went on to found new companies, including many of the most innovative. Now, in an environment of reduced costs and lower risks for those who wished to establish new enterprises, many publishers, editors, and journalists were encouraged to set up shop for themselves.

Former IPC editor-in-chief Sally O'Sullivan, for example, established Cabal Communications and entered a range of monthly markets, including those contested by her former employer with the *Loaded*-competitor *Front*. Ex-Future publishers Dianne Taverner and Richard Monteiro established Paragon Publishing in Bournemouth in 1991, adopting Future's 'narrow-but-deep' approach to launch competitor titles in the computer games market. In addition to new firms, marginal companies also found they could enter once-impregnable weekly markets. Northern & Shell, a publisher by this time better known for its adult-themed titles, moved into the mainstream women's market with *OK!*, a monthly celebrity magazine launched as an answer to *Hello!* in 1993.[34] Although the company lost a court case claiming it was outselling its Spanish-owned rival, it nevertheless established a large circulation and became a strong competitor in the weeklies market.

While the changes in technology allowed low-cost entry for small firms employing flexible production systems,[35] it also facilitated existing firms to become more innovative and consumer responsive. Magazine publishing came to be considered as a project-based form of organization, rather than a mass-production, continuous process manufacturing business. Thus the role of publisher within a large firm became more concerned with innovation, shifting its primary role to focus more on identifying and exploiting opportunities to create new offerings and spin-off magazines, and assembling new project teams for these titles comprising a mixture of internal and external contributors.[36] While this had always been a feature of the industry, the changes in working methods and lowering of coordination costs realized the potential of this system to promote rapid growth and innovation.

The BBC had been an early mover in adopting computer-based editorial systems, and when coupled with drive to exploit this technology in creating a range of new consumer magazines, found a winning recipe. With the launch of *Good Food* in 1989, the BBC demonstrated its new commitment to consumer publishing, and proved the effectiveness of Peter Phippen and Nicholas Brett's project-driven approach in translating television programme formats into magazine titles. By 1991, £97 million of BBC Enterprises' £150 million turnover came from magazines, and the BBC dominated several market segments, having 90 per cent of the food and cookery category and 43 per cent of the gardening sector by volume of circulation.[37] Buoyed along by the brand recognition and a loyal following provided by their television audiences, the Corporation was able to extend this initial success with a seemingly unending string of follow-ups, notably in the youth and teen markets. The 1989 launch of *Fast Forward* was followed by 11 more youth titles by 1999, during which year alone they published a further eight. Popular television shows also formed the continued basis for a succession of home- and leisure-based titles, notably *Gardner's World* (1991), *Top Gear* (1993), and *Good Homes* (1998).[38] Far from simply rehashing the same features of the television programmes with which they shared their brand names, the magazines were developed and written with largely new content by in-house and contract magazine writers, although they naturally incorporated columns or features by high-profile TV presenters.

The BBC's transformation from a largely dormant to a prolific and aggressive competitor did not go unnoticed by the incumbent firms, who generally felt that the Corporation had an unfair advantage in being able to promote its magazines through its broadcasting channels. A series of complaints led in part to the 'Sadler inquiry' into standards of cross-media promotion, and the outcome of this was a referral to the Monopolies and Mergers Commission in 1991. In the submissions to the investigation, IPC, EMAP, H. Bauer, G + J, the National Magazine Company, and W.H. Smith, all considered that the BBC had an unfair cost advantage in using television advertisements, termed 'trails' by the Corporation, to promote their magazines. They also argued that this lowered the risk of launching new titles, and encouraged retailers to favourably display the familiar-sounding titles—something that W.H. Smith agreed with in their testimony but, unlike the other submissions, did not actually object to. G + J was particularly strident in its criticism, alleging that the free television advertising the BBC's *Good Food* received had significantly damaged sales of its *Let's Cook!* title.[39] The resultant report found that the BBC had indeed distorted competition in the consumer magazine market, and although the broadcaster was ordered to reduce its level of magazine promotion, its titles still retained their powerful brand associations even when the BBC finally ended its television-based magazine advertising in 2004.[40] With its ownership of the *Radio Times*, the BBC had long been one of Britain's most important magazine publishing companies, but now the sleeping giant had truly awoken.

The UK's two largest consumer-based magazine publishers also continued to expand. EMAP acquired several struggling companies, including Maxwell Communications' 25 business titles in 1993.[41] Haemorrhaging money from his loss-making Sky satellite television network, Rupert Murdoch was first forced to close *Mirabella*, then to sell his remaining wholly-owned consumer magazines to EMAP in 1991 for £10 million.[42] EMAP set about improving the Murdoch Magazines portfolio of titles, as despite being the sector leader *Car* was still being printed on hot metal. EMAP now transferred the title to computer-based production as they sought to build their profile in the automotive sector. The firm had launched its own new women's monthly *Red* in 1989 aimed at those who had outgrown *Elle*, but in 1993 the company took a major step with the acquisition of Murdoch's remaining 50 per cent stake in his Hachette joint-venture titles *Elle*, *Elle Decoration*, and *Sky*, consolidating EMAP's position as the major mainstream IPC competitor.[43] To focus on magazine and media growth the company sold its newspaper division to Johnston Press for £211 million on 3 June 1996, completely breaking the ties to its newspaper-based origins.[44]

IPC entered a period of renewed vigour, in 1989 acquiring ITP's television listings titles *TVTimes* and *Chat*, and at a stroke became the market leader in this leading segment. By 1996 the company was organized around three core groups: the IPC Weeklies, IPC Southbank Publishing, and the IPC Specialist group. One problem for IPC for many years had been the constraints imposed on its activities by its ties to the Reed International group. Now, however, the company was to find itself subsumed into an even larger industrial conglomerate, Reed Elsevier plc, formed by the merger of Reed International and the Dutch giant Elsevier NV in 1993.[45] 'Independence day' finally came for IPC on 19 January 1998, when it was bought out by its management in a deal financed by the venture capital group Cinven valued at £860 million.[46] For the first time in its history IPC was now purely a consumer magazine business, and could focus on leveraging its knowledge of consumer markets unimpeded by other distractions. Although under Cinven the firm focused more in the short-term on profit maximization than new, risky investments in fresh titles, the company nevertheless acted quickly to improve communication and the spirit of entrepreneurship within the group. Links between its specialist magazines were reinforced and, in a move to strengthen editorial power, began to allow editors greater influence in decision-making—giving effect to chief executive Mike Matthews' promise to devolve 'power to the people who actually run the magazines'.[47] This trend was continued with the appointment as chairman of former arch-rival David Arculus, who had spent his time at EMAP encouraging small team-based entrepreneurship. A reorganization followed to formalize the new more autonomous ethos, and IPC Magazines was restructured around five standalone market-based businesses: TV weeklies (IPC tx), mass-market women's interests (IPC Connect), upmarket women's titles (IPC Southbank), country and leisure (IPC Country & Leisure Media), and men's interests (IPC ignite!), along with the distribution arm Marketforce.[48]

LADS' MAGS TO THE FOREFRONT

For a period from the mid-1990s, the men's interest sector emerged as the new frontier of consumer publishing and acted to drive rapid growth of both circulations and new companies. Earlier magazines had shown that there was a small but affluent demand for titles pitched at both sexes, such as *Sky*, or 'style bibles' like *the Face*. *Arena* had revived the concept of a men's fashion-based magazine, and although it did not find a large market it did encourage Condé Nast and the National Magazine Company to launch British versions of their long-standing US men's fashion titles *GQ* and *Esquire* respectively in 1989 and 1991.[49] In 1995, however, the men's interest market still represented just 2 per cent of the sales of the top 100 selling titles.[50] This situation began to change radically when Tim Southwell at IPC began exploring the potential of a new title aimed exclusively at young men as a means for capturing fresh sources of advertising revenue—ideas which eventually crystallized into *Loaded*.[51] This notion of a title aimed at young men soon came to the attention of EMAP, which in order to develop its own title, and spike IPC's guns, identified a suitable existing property in *For Him* magazine. *For Him* had been launched in 1987 by Chris Astridge's independent Tayvale firm and was initially distributed as a quarterly freebie through men's clothes shops. Later the magazine was able to find a modest news-stand circulation, together with a viable number of advertisers, much as the original US *Gentleman's Quarterly* and *Man About Town* had done previously.[52]

EMAP bought the title from Tayvale in 1994, and set about revamping the magazine's contents with the appointment of Mike Soutar from *Smash Hits* as editor, and proven publisher David Hepworth.[53] In the meantime, IPC had set about exploiting the pent-up demand in the men's market with the successful launch of *Loaded* in May 1994, and by the end of 1995 the title was registering 174,763 copy sales.[54] Offering a heady mix of outrageous alcohol-fuelled blokey behaviour, *Loaded* appeared to have responded wholeheartedly to the challenge made by Primal Scream's 1991 song of the same name to 'party' and 'have a good time'. In doing so, the publishing team of Mick Bunnage, Tim Southwell, and editor James Brown, had invented the 'lads mags' category and opened a new forum for the expression of men's street culture. In 1995 EMAP pitched their response, now simply re-titled *FHM*, initially between the excesses of *Loaded* and the refinement of *GQ* by targeting its new magazine at 'ordinary blokes'. The EMAP formula had a stronger emphasis on 'top female stars', and moved more directly into *Loaded* territory by employing innovative low-cost guerrilla marketing stunts, such as the 60-foot-high projection of a nude image of TV celebrity Gail Porter onto the Houses of Parliament to promote their '100 sexiest women poll'.[55] With a veritable army of 'ordinary blokes' now in tow *FHM* was soon out-selling *Loaded*, breaking the half-million sales mark in 1998, and reaching a circulation of three-quarters of a million in 1999,[56] with *Loaded* sales having climbed to 380,420 copies. Between 1993 and 1999 the men's interest sector achieved a tenfold increase in sales value, eventually reaching 52 per cent of that generated by the established women's monthly sector,[57] and outsell-ing many of the long-established women's monthly titles. By 2004 *FHM* was the best-selling monthly consumer magazine in the UK, and 'lads mags' became one of the defining features of the 'Britpop' and 'Cool Britanna' period that drew parallels back to the flowering of British music, fashion and art of the 'swinging 60s'.[58]

The success of the sector attracted a rash of new offerings both from existing publishing companies and new entrants, the latter of whom were able to enter the market at low cost and establish a viable circulation using contract printing and third-party distribution. Independent firms entered the sector with offer-ings such as Cabal Communications' *Front* in 1998 and Freestyle with *Boys Toys* in 1999. Dennis had already developed its own men's title with *Maxim* in 1995, but as the sector matured and the market expanded it sought in 1996 to differentiate further through the creation of *Bizarre* and *Stuff*, the latter slanted towards technology. In 2004 BRAD listed 102 men's interest magazines, with 40 titles in the men's lifestyle segment alone, and although the leading exam-ples were those created by EMAP, IPC, and Dennis, by this time there were 23 firms competing in this market.[59]

Boosted by the growth in men's interest titles, the development of the con-sumer magazines in the 1990s was remarkable. Far from experiencing the decline that had been predicted in some quarters by the concern that inter-national monopolies would constrain innovation in favour of promoting low-cost magazines, the sector's output grew dramatically. Between 1993 and 2000 the number of consumer magazine titles expanded from just over 2,000 to 3,275,[60] with an average rate of over 500 new titles being launched per year.[61] The number of consumer magazines sold annually rose year on year from 1990 to 1995 to around 1.5 billion, and after a slight dip continued to increase into the new millennium.[62] The UK had ridden a wave of new title innovation that put it into a world-leading position. According to Willings Press Guide, by 2004 the UK's tally of over 3,000 consumer titles placed it well ahead of both the leading European country, Germany with 899, and the United States with 1,127.[63] The growth of the domestic market was mirrored by the increasing internationalization of the industry, as British firms translated their innovative successes to overseas markets.

THE GLOBAL MAGAZINE

During the 1990s the leading UK magazine producers began to increasingly target foreign markets. With its *Elle* connection EMAP was already involved in the French market, and from this beachhead the company continued to expand through the acquisition of Editions Mondale for £117 million in 1994. With this purchase bringing its French portfolio to 38 titles, EMAP instantly became the third-largest magazine publisher in the fragmented French market, and derived 26 per cent of its turnover from France, and 3 per cent from Germany.[64] In 1996 it purchased three large-circulating titles from CLT France for £139 million, including *Top Santé* which had a circulation of 650,000. This brought its total of titles in France to 40, and doubled EMAP's French market share to 16 per cent. Although there was an acknowledgement that its Gallic publications were managed very differently to British firms, with a more rigid bureaucracy and a less entrepreneurial mind-set, the company pressed ahead with its international programme of expansion.[65] EMAP set its sights wider still in 1997, and acquired Mason Stewart Publishing and Bounty Services in Australia, the publisher of 22 titles across the sport, men's, teenage, music, and women's publications, including the 'surfing bible' *Tracks*. The company was renamed EMAP Australia, and handled the launch of the local version of its *FHM* title.

As the firm expanded its brands globally it had considered acquisition as suitable for the Australian market, due to the similarity of the language, but chose to enter the Pacific Rim through joint ventures. A deal was done with Panpac Media in Singapore to produce local editions for *FHM*, *Car*, and *Max Power* in 1998. EMAP hoped that using Panpac's local market knowledge it would be able to expand organically to Malaysia and Hong Kong, although its early growth was almost checked by failing to localize its *FHM* title's contents sufficiently in Singapore.[66] The biggest deal by far, however, was the purchase of Los Angeles-based magazine publisher Petersen at the end of 1999, for the staggering sum of £1 billion.[67] EMAP had embarked on the extension of its long-held plan to dominate the markets it competed in, and this led to the acquisition of the American firm's 132 title stable to complement the company's own offerings, with a particular attraction being its automotive and sports-orientated titles, and a more advanced knowledge of the growing possibilities for e-commerce.

In 1999 Future also went on the international acquisitions warpath, acquiring the leading Italian computer gaming publisher, Il Mio Castello Editore. The Italian interest was renamed Future Italy, and the firm then purchased Imagine Media in the USA, also strong in computer gaming, renaming the company Future USA. One of the key Imagine properties was *Business 2.0*, the magazine that did much to popularize the idea of the 'new economy'. International brand licences were crucial to Future's success, with the company winning the franchise to publish official console gaming titles, such as the *Official UK Playstation Magazine* in 1999, the *Official Playstation 2 Magazine* from Sony Computer Entertainment (outside of Japan), and the worldwide *Official Xbox* licence from Microsoft in 2000.[68] However, at the height of the company's first international peak in 2000, its 30 international licences were still only responsible for 7 per cent of its profits.[69]

IPC continued to develop its international licences, with titles based on properties such as *Essentials* for example. In 1991 Reed had expanded the firm's horizons with the formation of Reed Publishing Europe,[70] and by 1994 IPC had entered the German market in a joint venture with Hubert Burda Media to publish *Hair*.[71] In July 1994 the company beefed up its specialist markets, in particular buying key golfing titles, *Golf Weekly* and *Golf Industry News*, from the New York Times Co. IPC then formed a 50:50 joint venture with the Australian ACP group in a major cross-licensing deal in 1998.[72] IPC did not look to translate the domestic success it had scored with *Loaded* to other markets, and EMAP was slow to offer a US version of its phenomenal *FHM*. Spotting an opportunity, the ever alert Felix Dennis stole a march on both companies by offering a US version of the more sophisticated men's title *Maxim* in 1997. The magazine reached a peak circulation of 2.5 million copies, eclipsing all competition, including EMAP's North American version of *FHM* which it finally brought to market in 2000.

During the 1990s Britain's magazine publishers had attempted to translate their home successes into the international arena, pursuing their markets globally through a variety of market entry strategies. The coordination of these arrangements was made possible by the growth of Internet-based communications systems, which facilitated the potential of seamless international integration. As EMAP had found with its *FHM* launch in Singapore, local content had to be heavily adapted for local taste, but this was possible at low cost using dtp and computer-mediated editorial networks. As well as language and culture, however, other crucial differences between markets existed. In France, for example, magazine news-stand distribution was regulated by the Loi Bichet which guaranteed equal access to all publications regardless of their circulation level. Rules also forbade television advertising for magazine titles, acted to discourage selective display by retailers, and restrained the entry of large retailers and supermarkets before its revision in 2004.[73]

The requirements and conditions relating to advertising markets also remained largely country-specific. Although poster advertising often featured global brands, promotional campaigns using magazines were far more likely to be undertaken on country-by-country basis thus reducing the potential advantage to be gained from offering advertising clients an international portfolio of magazine brands and titles. There were also fundamental differences between some territories in terms of distribution, such as that between the European and American markets for example. This was well illustrated by the pattern of Future's international sales. In the UK the company sold 86 per cent of its magazines from the news-stand. Similarly, the figure was 84 per cent in France and 98 per cent in Italy. In the USA, on the other hand, off-the-shelf sales were a mere 25 per cent with the rest being sold through subscriptions. IPC Media found itself in the same position, with its UK operations selling primarily off-the-shelf in contrast to its US AOL Time Warner stable-mate Time Inc.[74] Physically this made the magazines in both countries look, and even feel different, as US titles were formatted primarily for postage, using especially thin papers to reduce weight, while British titles were developed for a glossy shelf-appeal. Thus although foreign investment presented Britain's magazine publishers with real growth opportunities, it also required them to spread their attention to an understanding of the differences and complexities involved in international management. Moreover, at the same time that many British firms were investing heavily in developing an international presence for their printed magazines, they were also engaged in an entirely different process of creating new electronic versions of their products in order to exploit the emerging availability of computer-based services and the growth of the World Wide Web.

ENVISIONING A MEDIA-NEUTRAL FUTURE

Future Publishing had heralded the age of the digital magazine when it originated the *Ace* title in-house using Macintosh computers in the mid-1980s. However, Future's progress in this field was disrupted when its founder Chris Anderson sold the company to Pearson plc for £52.7 million in 1994. Although Pearson expanded Future with the acquisition of the Paris-based magazine publisher Edicorp, and British-based Music Maker publications, the company did not fit well alongside Pearson's wider interests. In 1998 Pearson decided to divest itself of Future and refocus on their core activities of educational and consumer book publishing, business information, and broadcasting.[75] Fearing 'the potential horror that it would be taken over by something like an IPC, ripped apart and moved to London', and convinced that the company had much greater potential for international and online growth, Anderson bought the company back for £142 million in conjunction with Future chief executive Greg Ingham and Apax Venture Partners. In 1999 the company was floated as The Future Network plc for £577.5 million, and its value reached £632 million by the end of the first day's trading.[76] At this time the company owned 57 per cent of the British computer and video games magazines market by circulation, and in a strategy 'applauded by analysts' banked on expanding from this position to attract an audience of 'tech savvy' global consumers via the growing medium of the World Wide Web. To achieve this, Future invested

£19.7 million on 34 new titles, £10.4 million on websites, and £8 million in the acquisition of 49 per cent of the US-based Technology, Entertainment and Design Conference business in 2000. By the end of that year Future had established 13 'networks of Internet sites', and a portfolio of 30 online magazines.[77]

In moving to exploit the World Wide Web as a platform for magazines, Future was far from alone as many companies explored the alluring possibilities offered by the digital revolution. This process was widely expected to bring about a convergence between the previously discrete technologies of broadcasting, telecoms, and computing, and to provide the basis for a £20 billion business sector in Britain.[78] As Hamish Scott, manager of corporate development on 'the electronic future' at EMAP, explained at the time, ' "digitisation" means that text, pictures, video and sound can all be stored, packaged, and transferred electronically. Add to this the growth of cable and satellite transmission systems and the result is a plethora of possibilities: interactive text, data and video services shooting over cable, telephone wires or the airwaves into the television or PC; compact disks holding films, directories or multimedia, "electronic books"; TV channels serving specialist niches.'[79] Publishing firms in general realized that digital technologies potentially liberated them from the need to print and distribute a physical product, and led them to seek new business models based around online delivery, and content ownership and management. Firms were quick to create new ventures aimed at providing content in other forms of media, such as Web-based products.[80]

IPC had been developing its 'electronic future' since 1994, when the company had formed a dedicated New Media Publishing team.[81] Initially this group developed a magazine for retail on CD-ROM, *UnZip*, based on content culled from the *NME* and other IPC titles, and although this model failed after a single issue, the initiative continued to investigate electronic publishing opportunities. By 1995, IPC offered websites for three of its leading titles: the *NME*, the *New Scientist*, and *Loaded*.[82] The Corporation also entered into a short-lived multi-media partnership with British Telecom to offer an 'on demand' television service, by supplying magazine content.[83] Magazine publishing companies were increasingly able to manage their content and intellectual property as tradable assets, with IPC for example, starting the Instant Picture Network in 1996, a digital archive system for its photographs which made them available across the group.[84] By 2000 these systems had begun to be fully integrated digital asset management systems, the earliest of which in the UK is claimed to have been operated by BBC Magazines.[85] As IPC grew more confident in online publishing, it formed IPC Electric in 1999, to further develop the company's e-commerce business.[86] One outcome of this was BEME.com, whose introduction was supported by a budget equivalent in scale and cost to the company's most extravagant print title launch, and which promised to provide IPC's female audience with 'the complete online experience'.[87]

The convergence of different types of media, from print to film to broadcasting, into a common digital form brought into view the concept of media neutrality. In their effort to develop online titles and websites, Britain's magazine publishers had been keen to reduce their reliance on print by exploiting the content they generated through the rapidly expanding scope of IT systems.[88] However, this transition towards the provision of digital content had the effect of making magazine publishers of much greater value to multi-media companies who were seeking to create cross-media platforms and delivery systems. When IPC had first been formed as a publishing giant at the beginning of the 1960s, its source of competitive advantage had resided in the scale-based industrial logic of vertical integration. Now in 2000 renamed IPC Media[89] under chief executive Sly Bailey, the firm found itself the target for acquisition by one of America's giant media conglomerates. The suitor was the newly formed AOL Time Warner, which had been assembled in an attempt to leverage the perceived benefits of increased global media ownership, namely: the economic benefits accruing from digital convergence; the growth of broadband as a distribution platform; the potential of cross-selling content; and the increasing importance of international markets. In carrying through this logic, AOL Time Warner sought to expand by means of international media acquisitions.[90] At the same time Cinven was looking to realize its investment in IPC. In 2001 the venture capitalists sold their interests in Britain's leading magazine publisher to AOL Time Warner for US$1.6 billion (£1.15 billion). On completion of the transaction, Time Inc. chairman and chief executive Don Logan commented that, 'IPC will provide us with valuable synergies with other AOL Time Warner brands' including film, TV, and radio, thus creating a 'media neutral platform' company.[91] Thus rather than through the vertical integration of physical resources, it was by means of sharing intellectual property in the form of cross-media content, along with leveraging the stock of transferrable knowledge about the needs of consumers, that were considered to be the key to competitive success for the twenty-first century media conglomerate.

Elsewhere in the industry, EMAP had embarked on the most radical restructuring to exploit the potential of the digital era, aiming to reconfigure itself around markets in order to offer cross-media marketing and advertising sales as a logical extension to its growth in different forms of media ownership.[92] The company had expanded rapidly into other platforms, and had made a significant commitment to radio broadcasting with the development of its Big City Network through the acquisition of the London-based Kiss FM and Radio City for £7.5 million in 1993,[93] Trans World Communications for £50 million in 1995,[94] and six further radio stations from the Metro Radio Group for £98 million in 1996, establishing the company as number two in the UK commercial radio broadcasting market.[95] The firm also moved into digital television with a station called The Box. In order to better exploit its diverse holdings as a 'media-neutral' provider, EMAP Online, formed in 1996, became

EMAP Digital under Paul Keenan in March 2000. The company attempted to leverage its *FHM* brand into online magazine titles, websites, and spin-offs, with FHM.com recording 12 million page impressions a month from 420,000 unique users in 2000.[96] Websites were seen as viable businesses as their content, taken from the print title, was essentially cost-free,[97] but the company had wider ambitions than this alone. EMAP's brands were exploited across different media, with the *Smash Hits* print title being supported by a weekly chart show on EMAP radio, Smash Hits TV on The Box, events such as the Smash Hits Poll Winners Party, and sales of recorded music compilations. The dance music title *MixMag* was developed to become the country's largest dance music event promoter, managing 600 events per year. Ambitiously, as the year 2000 commenced, EMAP Digital made commitments for investments of around £250 million to be rolled out over three years for 40 new revenue-generating Web-based businesses.[98] Of some concern, however, EMAP Digital was losing money, with losses of £1.8 million in 1999 and £2.4 million in 2000. And although Internet access had been increasing rapidly, as late as 1998 only 16 per cent of the UK's adult population had ever used the Internet.[99]

THE DOT-COM BUST

As the firm that had truly kicked off the digital magazine, Future would also demonstrate the danger of the Internet-based strategies as the new millennium dawned. Fuelled by speculation in the potential of the Internet, between 1997 and 2000 the value of the US technology-led NASDAQ stock exchange more than doubled, and technology stocks in general had tripled. On 5 December 1996 Federal Reserve chair Alan Greenspan had sounded a warning about the 'irrational exuberance' of overvaluing technology stocks, and in 2000 the Internet bubble burst.[100] Magazine companies that had invested heavily in the growth of the 'new economy' suddenly faced a serious check, and Future, for example, found that they had not been able to form an adequate business model to monetize their Internet properties. Chris Anderson, who stood down to Colin Morrison as chief executive in 2001, acknowledged that investment across the sector in online activities had grown at a rate too fast for adequate control systems, and auditors Morgan Stanley were brought in to investigate options for the now ruinous *Business 2.0* title.[101] The magazine was sold to AOL Time Warner for £47.2 million, bringing to an end Future's dot-com-based expansion, and the company was forced to seriously re-evaluate its strategies.[102] Over the next two years Future laid off half of its staff, closed 45 poorly performing titles, and offered a rights issue to raise £33.5 million in order to survive. The company's international expansion was suspended, with a £2.3 million downgrade to its profits after Deloitte &

Touche found accounting irregularities for news-stand sales at Future France, forcing it to scale back its operations in France, Italy, and Germany to offering only its core video gaming titles, and to close its Dutch and Japanese offices permanently. Although the firm retained wholly-owned businesses in Poland, Italy, and the USA, as well as licences in 30 more countries, it had been badly damaged.[103]

With heavy investments in websites such as BEME.com, which was closed instantly the dot-com bubble burst, IPC was also forced to scale back its online commitments and to suspend non-profit-making enterprises. Online advertising, the basis of many predictions for website-based revenue generation, had been slow to materialize and evaporated once the recession began to bite. Although magazine content could be remuneratively customized for local print-based licences, it was less clear how this value could be translated into other media profitably. For the new AOL Time Warner-owned IPC, the optimistic promise of sharing intellectual properties from print through to the cinema, which had offered such great potential, now seemed wildly unrealistic. The avowed strategy of IPC operating as a core component in an integrated global media-neutral group, sharing content across global channels, was suddenly plunged into crisis.

EMAP had gone the furthest in attempting to leverage a common brand across different platforms, but had also found it hard to demonstrate how this translated successfully to the bottom line. EMAP's chief executive Kevin Hand described the dot-com bust as 'change on a scale never before known', as the company was rocked when its forecasted income and advertising spend failed to materialize. EMAP's share price plummeted from a high of £17.73 in 2000, to finally bottom out at £4.80 in 2002, bringing the group to the brink of bankruptcy.[104] With the company overextended by its heavy investment in online businesses, and its poorly performing US acquisitions, Hand resigned and the steady hand of Robin Miller was brought back as non-executive chairman, with Tom Maloney as Chief Operating Officer. Commenting on the 'salutary lessons for the media world and EMAP in particular', Miller identified the firm's American adventure and online investments as poorly conceived and executed strategies, and cautioned that EMAP needed to be 'wary of siren voices luring us into high risk ventures with no clear demand'. From this point forward, Internet-based ventures were focused on small core areas subject to 'normal business discipline'.[105] Despite this, EMAP continued to roll out new sites such FHM.com to the French market and maintained the development of its Q4music and mojo4music websites in partnership with HMV for online sales, but it was forced not only to scale back other online activities but to make major cuts to all its investments.[106] The firm took a massive £545 million write-down on the sale of its American businesses to Primedia for £366 million, although it retained ownership of the *FHM* title in the United States. EMAP had faced the first serious check in its expansion as a global media firm, and the company found it impossible to recover the furious momentum that had driven its growth through the 1990s.

SUPERMARKETS AND THE CONTROL OF DISTRIBUTION

Back in the real world, the creation and distribution of physical paper-based magazines continued to evolve. Beginning from the late 1990s large publishing firms had been able to exploit their ownership of deep-and-wide content to launch a new wave of popular magazines which reinvigorated the weekly market when coupled with widespread supermarket distribution. *Heat* magazine was the first title to benefit from this approach when it was revamped shortly after its launch by EMAP in 1999, and subsequent offerings such as *Nuts* from IPC Media and *Zoo Weekly*, also from EMAP in 2004, continued this trend by translating their 'lads mags' content into a new market for men's weeklies. The industry repeated this success by creating a new genre of women's weeklies, with the launch of *Reveal* by Natmags, which had formed a partnership with Australian ACP for developing women's weeklies, and the first weekly glossy in the form of EMAP's license of *Grazia*, from Italian publisher Mondadori, in 2006.[107] The renewed vigour of the British weekly market even attracted the entry of German group Hubert Burda Media with *Full House* in 2005.

While supermarket retail suited high-volume and rapid turnover of weekly titles, the longer-term impact of their influence on the industry was by no means entirely benign. In 2000 Tesco and W.H. Smith News proposed a joint venture to consolidate the wholesaling of magazines and newspapers. Fearing that this would lead to a reduction in the number of independent retailers,[108] the move was resisted by the publishing industry and become subject to an Office of Fair Trading review that, largely to ensure the continued widespread distribution of newspapers for consumer welfare considerations, allowed the wholesalers to preserve the regional distribution system in place.[109] Although the 'WHesco' proposal was abandoned, the impact of supermarkets' enhanced interest in magazines was being felt by publishers.[110]

As consumer magazine retail became increasingly dominated by the large supermarkets they began to wrest control of periodicals sales data from distributors and wholesalers. The multiples became more adept at maximizing margins on their retail space, now listing only the best-selling titles and moving towards a schedule of charging for preferential display, as the publishers had always feared they would.[111] On average, large supermarkets stocked around 260 titles, compared to the 870 typically stocked by W.H. Smith.[112] The supermarkets began to curtail their policies of stocking new titles on trial, and these changes acted to slow the ability of new entrants to gain access to mainstream retail channels at low cost.[113] In 2000, 43 per cent of respondents to an industry-wide survey indicated that increasing supermarket power was an impediment to new title innovation,[114] but the large retailers continued to increase their power, and by 2006 42 per cent of all weeklies were sold in supermarkets.[115] To many industry participants it seemed as though the golden age of low-cost and low-risk print-based market entry for small-scale, innovative magazine publishing enterprises had been brought to an end.[116]

RETRENCHMENT AND GLOBAL LICENSING NETWORKS

Burnt by the dot-com collapse, magazine publishers retreated to their core activity of print magazines, and found that sales of printed magazines still underpinned their profits, and circulations had in fact remained fairly buoyant throughout the crash. For the most part Britain's magazine publishers now resumed their strategic attention to innovations in the print market, with Condé Nast for example launching *Glamour* in 2001 using an A5 format, not seen in the British women's market since the 1950s. Now dubbed 'handbag' size, the innovation was widely adopted throughout the women's monthly sector over the next few years. Despite this, a sustained period of consolidation followed, with a series of acquisitions, as companies reconsidered their options. Grüner + Jahr quit the British magazine market and sold its titles to the National Magazine Company in 2000, and Highbury House acquired several other independents, notably Cabal Communications and Paragon, before selling all of its 38 consumer titles to Future at the end of 2005 for £30.5 million.[117] Dennis absorbed I Feel Good Ltd., the publishing house started by ex-*Loaded* editor James Brown, with titles such as *Jack, Viz, Bizarre*, and the *Fortean Times* for £5.1 million.[118] EMAP ended the strategic partnership it had formed with the Hachette Filipacchi Medias group to print titles such as *Elle*, as the French group acquired Attic Futura for £40 million in 2002 and appointed former EMAP chief executive Kevin Hand to head up their newly acquired British operations.[119] BBC Worldwide reviewed its magazine interests in 2004, briefly acquiring Origin Publishing, which was strong in contract as well as consumer publishing, before deciding to concentrate on its core branded titles. These were reorganized under the rubric Bristol Magazines, which later became BBC Magazines, with a stand-alone company, BBC Magazines Rights, created to handle international licensing in 2007.[120] Reflecting a renewed faith in the profitability of print-based consumer publishing, News International re-entered the consumer magazines market in 2005 through a new subsidiary,

News Magazines Ltd. The company fell short of its ambitious targets to become a major player in weekly magazines, but had some success with *Love it!*, and an interior decorating magazine called *Inside Out*.[121]

Reflecting this retrenchment back to its core activity, Future Network plc changed its name simply to Future plc in 2004. The company had stabilized since the dot-com meltdown, and from 2002 had launched 28 new titles, acquired 8, and closed or sold 14 in order to focus on publishing in a 'narrow but deep strategy' which aimed at first to return the company to a pattern of rapid international growth.[122] As part of this strategy the firm became the worldwide leader in guitar magazines by acquiring leading titles in the American market, *Guitar One* and *Guitar World*, for £11.5 million, which then were stabled with Britain's best-selling title, *Total Guitar*, and a new domestic launch in the form of *What Guitar*.[123] In 2004 however, incoming chief executive Stevie Spring abandoned the 'doubling' growth strategy to concentrate on improving UK profits, strengthening core titles with website support, and closing 22 unprofitable titles, including most of the Highbury House acquisitions.[124]

As British magazine publishers consolidated, they scaled back their international operations, and Future backed out of direct involvement in international media ownership, selling its French and Italian subsidiaries, and scrapping its planned European investments in 2007.[125] EMAP also followed a similar path, and sold its Singaporean and Malaysian businesses in 2005,[126] the poorly performing EMAP France to Mondadori for £380 million in 2006, and its Australian business to ACP Magazines Ltd. for £41 million in 2007.[127] The firm also closed the US edition of *FHM*, ceding the market to Felix Dennis' *Maxim*. Dennis then brought the short but vibrant period of British international direct investment to a close by selling the US *Maxim*, *Stuff*, and *Blender* to Quadrangle Capital Partners II in 2007.

Although British firms were moving away from the direct ownership of foreign subsidiaries and ambitions to become global media conglomerates, they increased their international engagement in a different way, through a renewed emphasis on developing their international licences. In 2004 the BBC formed Worldwide Media Co. as a 50:50 joint venture to enter the Indian market.[128] Future took direct control of its Australian licences as it concentrated on finding partners across the expanding BRIC economies, and by 2008 had licensed 168 of its titles in 35 countries.[129] EMAP grew the number of its *FHM* licences from 27 to 50 countries by 2007. From simple franchising relationships, the process of licensing had developed as companies learned better how to coordinate with their overseas publishing partners. As transnational magazine brands became more similar to fast-moving consumer goods, the dominant publishing firms increasingly took on the role of coordinating international production and managing complex systems of flexible customization to suit the needs of different audiences. Embedded within these licensing relationships was thus a complex international publishing trade in which the UK publishers traded content for local adoption and adaptation, with foreign publishers assembling their own versions of established titles using material drawn from local and global sources, thus allowing a raft of small locally based firms a place in the global magazine industry.[130] Future, for example, now saw itself as the creator of English language content that could be exploited across different platforms internationally around a core content area.[131] By the mid-2000s, a foreign edition would typically contain around 40 per cent of material supplied by the licensor, but even this would be modified substantially for local consumption. Local partners also supplied material back to the original title, which would potentially be circulated throughout the publisher's network. These arrangements differed from early forms of internationalization, which had been based much more on foreign direct investment and the creation of large-scale media conglomerates. Thus global media concentration became more diverse in form, reflecting as it did an increasing trend towards international integration of publishing firms rather than simply the creation of huge transnational media corporations.[132]

The final demise of the leading British-based media conglomerate came with the dismemberment of EMAP. Despite being Britain's second-largest consumer magazine publisher, it had been performing poorly for some years, mainly due to its various media and b2b interests. On the retirement of Tom Moloney in May 2007, EMAP's management was approached by various firms that were interested in purchasing parts of the company, triggering a strategic review.[133] As a result, the company decided to dismember itself, and EMAP's consumer magazines and radio businesses were sold to the family-owned Heinrich Bauer Verlag KG for £1.17 billion; a move which *Marketing Week* likened to a corner shop buying Selfridges.[134] EMAP's business periodicals and exhibitions operations were bought in a joint venture between private equity company Apax and Partners and the Guardian Media Group plc,[135] and 50 per cent of The Box television was sold to the UK's Channel 4.[136] The newly formed Bauer Consumer Media Ltd. immediately closed unprofitable titles to focus on core activities, which still encompassed a more limited focus on brand extensions, such as considering *FHM* and *Empire*-branded radio stations.[137] Under this new ownership, the British-based operations were to continue to operate independently within the Bauer group, maintaining their own international licensing strategies. IPC followed a similar pattern, and under CEO Sylvia Auton in 2010, remained a fairly autonomous part of a global media group operating from its new Bluefin building headquarters on the London South Bank.[138] The company remained Britain's largest magazine publisher, essentially a British publisher under American ownership, engaged in a myriad of international licences throughout the globe.[139]

VIRTUAL MAGAZINES

As the increasing power of supermarkets started to impede the growth of new print-based magazine titles, developments in broadband technology began to facilitate not only the process of international licensing, but also the development of virtual magazines, new forms of dissemination, such as blogs, and sophisticated interactive websites. The first generation of dial-up Internet services had been slow to deliver graphics and video-based content effectively, something which had hampered the utility of magazine company's online services. The gradual roll-out of broadband services made British magazine and media companies re-examine their online strategies. Following the dot-com shake-up, firms had become 'leaner and meaner', and with the reduction in staff had come a renewed focus on their central concern of magazine publishing, as the ability of cross-media promotions to generate revenue remained a matter for concern. Despite the economic turbulence at the start of the new millennium, magazine readership had remained buoyant and, according to the PPA, consumer magazines' share of total media advertising revenue remained at the same average level it had over the decade of the 1990s, at around 6 per cent.[140] Recent growth in the sector had been driven by off-the-shelf purchases, and companies were keen to deepen their relationship with readers. The renewed attempts to exploit broadband Internet-based websites and services came therefore not from stand-alone business concepts, but in the form of complementary adjuncts to support their print offering. As one senior industry figure commented in relation to Internet strategies during 2002, 'where is the revenue coming from? The Internet is important in supporting our core brand, and branded online services...rather than delivery of the magazine.'[141]

Gradually, however, the role played by the Internet began to change. The project-based form of organization and the methods adopted by publishers to generate external copy and feedback allowed much closer engagement with their readers, and also to the advertising markets that they served.[142] Online discussion boards and forums allowed editors and their staff to interact with their readers, and using feedback and online participation publishers were able to create 'content informed by data on consumer need: searchable and sharable by all communities it serves; and attractive to clients who wish to trade with those communities'.[143] From the middle of the decade broadband uptake was fairly rapid, with household penetration rising from 43.9 per cent in 2006 to 72.3 per cent in 2010,[144] and consumer publishers found for the first time that they were able to make the Internet pay, despite advertising revenues being lower in online provision than in the print-based market.

Dennis launched a wholly online 'e-zine', *Monkey*, in 2006, and by 2009 had decided to transfer its leading *Maxim* magazine to an online-only title in an effort to engage with the young male category who were thought to be migrating away from print as they increasingly sought entertainment through the World Wide Web.[145] Future renewed its online focus, spending £11.5 million on websites to support its titles in 2007, mainly under the TechRadar, MusicRadar, and BikeRadar.com banners.[146] Following a further £5 million online investment in 2008, growth in online advertising revenue grew from 7 per cent in 2006 to 23 per cent in 2009.[147] IPC Media also made a series of moves to exploit its content by strengthening its online business, starting houseto-home, goodtoknow, and shootinguk in 2007, and then acquiring a string of Web-based companies including TrustedReviews.com and Mousebreaker in 2008.[148] Despite these advances, overall online advertising represented just 1 per cent of consumer magazine revenue in 2009.[149]

As the development of 'smartphones', such as the Apple iPhone launched in 2007, facilitated mobile computing, publishers found a new mobile platform for consumers to engage with magazines. EMAP had started to offer digital clips of cinema releases and trailers to supports its *Empire* title, for example, as it considered 'migrating brands to online mobile' platforms.[150] Although the small screen sizes and embryonic mobile broadband networks acted to limit the initial potential of this strategy, publishers increasingly conceptualized their business as being based around brands, rather than platforms. The PPA considered that the industry was now based around three delivery pillars: print, online, and face-to-face, with a seamless ability to flexibly engage with consumers across multiple channels.[151] As circulations of printed titles fell, publishers attempted to boost online revenue growth. Reflecting this, *Smash Hits*, the title that launched EMAP's challenge as a serious publisher, survives as a TV and radio format and brand despite the death of the print title in 2006. Conversely, the *Top of the Pops* print magazine survived its progenitor which the BBC ceased broadcasting in 2006.

THE RESILIENCE OF CONSUMER MAGAZINES

The decade which began with a financial crisis was also to end with a financial crisis. The UK was plunged back into the longest and most severe recession since the great depression of the 1930s, as fallout from the American financial-led crisis culminating in the collapse of Lehman Brothers in September 2008 spread through international markets.[152] Challenged by recession, and the rise of the new media, print-based products faced the threat of a rapid decline in sales during the new decade. In the business-to-business press and newspaper markets, indeed, consumers increasingly found that they could obtain equally good—or in some cases identical—content online for free. As a result, these sectors entered a period of steeply declining sales, with the value of newspaper sales in Britain dropping from £8 billion to £6 billion between 2005 and 2009.[153] The business-to-business press was particularly hard hit, especially in the controlled circulation market, with a fall in advertising revenue from £1 billion in 2005 to £738 million in 2009, and an overall fall in the size of the market from £3 billion to £2.5 billion, representing a contraction of 15.4 per cent in value. B2b magazine circulations fell 12.8 per cent, with the number of titles declining from 5,113 to 4,794 between 2006 and 2010.[154]

The consumer magazine sector, however, where a mix of engagement, specific relevance, and a tactile experience, rather than timeliness, were the prime qualities valued by consumers, appeared to be more insulated from the shift away from print-based forms of provision. After the slow but sustained growth through the start of the decade, the consumer sector experienced a contraction from 2006 to 2010, as advertising revenues declined from £827 million to £633 million,[155] the value of the market declined 10.8 per cent from £3 billion to £2.7 billion, and the major publishers saw a steady decline in their turnover year-on-year from 2005.[156] The value of magazines purchased, however, declined only marginally from £1.8 billion to £1.7 billion, albeit with a sharp fall in the number of titles from 3,445 to 3,004.[157] Although the declines in circulation were lower than across other parts of the print-based media, the immediate effect of the financial crisis still hit some major publishers hard, with the majority experiencing short-term sharp declines in turnover and profits. At the end of 2009, for example, although DC Thomson's overall circulation was down only 2 per cent (despite some high-profile circulation falls for titles such as the *Beano*), its profits had halved.[158] IPC's profits fell 37 per cent as a result of the recession, triggering a review of its specialist consumer periodicals which resulted in the sale of 20 titles, including the once-iconic lads' mag, *Loaded*, which had fallen to a circulation of only 37,281.[159] Magazine publishers in general, however, were able to arrest losses by closing or divesting loss-making magazines in order to focus on both profitable titles and new launches. IPC, for example, faced a new decade as a much leaner consumer magazine publishing firm, printing 65 titles, and with signs of renewed strong profit growth.[160] Overall the consumer magazine sector slimmed down its holdings in response to the economic downturn, and concentrated on their profitability, which on the whole rebounded.[161]

From 1990 to 2010 the market for consumer magazines had witnessed a series of transformations, with the rise and fall of new segments such as men's interest and a new generation of weekly titles. Specialist monthly titles had initially driven growth, and far from disappearing the mass-market print-based magazine had also evolved. The weekly market had changed, and magazine publishers had reflected and shaped these changes. Although the traditional titles, such as *Woman's Own*, were still in decline, the women's sector as a whole remained in rude health, having grown 10 per cent in size from 2000, with some titles such as *Reveal* up 22.6 per cent in 2009 and sales of women's glossies holding steady.[162] In February 2007, IPC Connect reconfirmed its commitment to its most traditional of markets in a joint venture with Groupe

Marie Claire by launching *Look*, a weekly competitor to *Grazia*, with its most expensive launch to date. In 2010, the UK's best-selling women's title was the celebrity magazine *OK!*, published by Northern & Shell. Although its British sales at the start of 2010 were only 588,546 copies, with editions in 20 countries its global sales exceeded 30 million copies, meaning that its total circulation dwarfed even *Woman* and *Woman's Own* in their heyday.[163]

As the first decade of twenty-first century drew to a close, changes to the structure of retail had begun to limit the opportunities for independent publishers to gain access to traditional retail channels, while the closure of the Borders and Woolworths retailing groups in 2010 counted as further setbacks.[164] Although new forms of publishing, such as blogging and posting on social media sites, offered alternative routes to print-based magazines, the ease of physical magazine production still encouraged many independent firms, such as Media 10, to enter specialist markets with print-based products, using a mixture of retail and subscription distribution channels, coupled with Internet-based marketing.[165] With the launch of the iPad tablet in April 2010, however, Apple heralded a potential paradigm shift in the way that people were likely to consume media products in the years ahead, and the methods by which magazines could be distributed to their readers. As a mobile device the tablet offered a convenient method for the consumers to read digital magazines, without the need for notebook or desktop computers, and offered a more viable screen size than smartphones such as the iPhone had done. Although not the first tablet-style computer, the iPad was the first commercially successful device and within its first sales year sold close to ten million units globally, and the iTunes store offered a potential retail channel for magazine publishers with a clear revenue stream. The success of the device tempted other companies to take note, some of them manufacturers such as Samsung, and some of them content-based companies such as Google and Amazon.[166]

Despite having long been created as digital artefacts, readers of consumer magazines had hereto proved surprisingly reluctant to switch from print to the online forms of consumption in the same way which had challenged newspapers and the trade- and business-press. The dot-com crash had underlined the difficulties of finding a profitable business model for Web-based media, and the industry was keenly exploring possibilities for tablet-based publishing. The 2010 conference of the trade body which represents the UK's magazine publishing sector, the Professional Publishers Association (PPA), was entitled 'Inspiration and Innovation in Publishing'. Held only a short walk down the Mall from The Strand, once the general location of publishing's Grub Street, the event culminated in a key session called 'here comes the pad' chaired by the PPA's chief executive Barry McIlheney. Even as the participants addressed the question as to how the industry could take advantage of new Apple iPad's capabilities as a platform for consuming magazines, publishing companies were moving to exploit the emerging opportunities with Future, for example, offering bespoke editions of *MacLife* and *T3* as 'apps' through the iTunes store in 2010.[167]

In the 1990s and 2000s, the technology of digital production allowed a resurgence of the printed magazine, but one which ultimately acted to undermine the entire need to print and distribute a physical product. Despite this, and the problems experienced by other media-based industries which had been similarly challenged by digitization—music publishing, film production, newspapers, and business-to-business publishing—consumer magazines declined far less than many pessimistic expectations had predicted, and generally maintained a healthy level of profitability. Consumers, it seemed, when it came to their hobbies, obsessions, passions, and leisure, still found a powerful allure in the visual and tactile qualities offered by the magazine format.

A Note on the Scope of the Study

In attempting such a broad overview we have had to make some decisions as to the scope of our study. This monograph examines explicitly the consumer magazine publishing industry, and takes the publishing firms as the primary level of analysis. Our first decision to concentrate on this segment needs some explanation and justification. Consumer magazines represent a clearly definable segment of the market, one whose focus is on leisure, hobbies, and entertainment, rather than periodicals whose focus is on news or providing information to business as provided by the business press and trade journals. There are clear links between these sectors, and companies have entered the consumer magazine market from newspaper publishing, and also consumer-based companies have expanded to provide business publications. Despite this, the consumer market has always been one that has a distinctive identity of its own, and companies in general have specialized in newspapers, consumer, or business magazines as separate activities even when contained within the same firm. The industry itself recognizes a clear distinction between the consumer and business press, and press guides such as British Rate and Data (BRAD) and the Willings Press Guide draw a firm boundary between consumer and business markets. Our focus is to tell the history of the consumer magazine industry, although it has been necessary at times to examine a broader picture and to acknowledge a diversified firm's wider activities. Following this our second major decision is to focus on the magazine publishing companies, the firms which invent and publish the magazine titles themselves.

This also raises a problem as it is often difficult to draw the boundaries between the different elements of the print, publishing, and reprographic industries, especially over time as firms have integrated and de-integrated different functions of the value-chain, covering a myriad specialized disciplines from journalism, typesetting, layout, art-work design and reproduction, and make-up, through to printing, distribution, and retail. Our perspective puts the publishing firm at the centre of our analysis, from which we examine the process of integration and divestment of other value-chain operations as part of the competitive process between publishers. In an industry of such complexity this means that for reasons of space we have not been able to examine in detail other related industries such as wholesaling, distribution, retail, and the industry's relationship with advertising as completely as we may have wished.

We have also made a conscious decision to focus on the firms and on the industry rather than magazine titles themselves, or on the contributions made by individual editors or publishers. Magazines themselves of course have untold variety, and range from the disposable effluvia of pop culture towards

works of enduring beauty. In limiting our study to the history of the industry, we acknowledge that many of these stories have their own rich literature.
There have been many publications on magazine titles as products in themselves, from the seminal women's magazines, to individual titles such as *Vogue*
and *Nova*.[1]

   The stories, illustrations, advertisements, and photographs contained in
consumer magazines have also offered many avenues for exploration, and the
design aspect of magazines, in terms of the use of fonts, spacing, headings, and
layout has also been widely studied by those interested in design and the arts.
As artworks in themselves magazines and their covers have attracted much
well-merited attention.[2] There are also many industry-focused guides related
to the processes of producing magazines, editing titles, or with setting up new
firms aimed at industry insiders and potential entrants. By the same token,
although the industry has been characterized by many remarkable personalities who have undoubtedly transformed magazines with their distinctive contributions, particular enthusiasms, and obsessions, we have also again focused
on the companies that they founded, organized, and managed. From the new
journalism pioneers such as Alfred Harmsworth, George Newnes, and Arthur
Pearson, to the proprietors of the American entrants such as Condé Nast and
William Randolph Hearst, there are many excellent biographies of the key
shapers of the industry for those who wish to examine their contribution in
greater depth.[3] For an industry comprising prolific writers surprisingly few
magazine firms have created their own histories; although there are a handful
if we include histories of firms in related areas such as printing.[4] Journalists
and editors have often written comments in newspapers, and autobiographies
which can be used to get a view on the personalities and characters of the editorial office,[5] and some have even written novels based on slimly fictionalized
accounts of their experiences.[6] Magazines and the printing industry have also
provided employment to, and witnessed the development of, powerful craft
and labour unions. The history of these unions, mostly told from the perspective of the newspaper industry, also has an extensive literature of its own.[7] Our
story reveals a different perspective on the unions' relationship with magazine
publishing firms and forms an important part of our history, bringing to light
a new perspective on the tale of changing work and labour relations in Britain.

   Another aspect of the approach that we have taken concerns the enormous complexity of the interplay between the changing dynamics of society
and the magazines that are produced as a consequence, and of the impact
that magazines have as agents of social change and in shaping markets.
This is not the primary focus of our approach, but the interested reader
will find that the many disciplines from a variety of perspectives have all
treated various aspects of this interplay in depth, from media studies, communications studies, cultural anthropology, gender studies, regional studies, and sociology, to name but some.[8] Women's magazines, for example,

have garnered much research, from examining the general role of women in society, to the cultural construction of social events such as Christmas, the development of youth and teen culture, research into sexual identity, and some studies have also touched on the role of women in the print unions.[9] This large literature gives many excellent insights into the operation of society, but largely neglects the publishing firms, either by overlooking them, or by reducing them to 'black boxes' that simply reflect social trends. Our approach to examining the relationship between society and the magazine firm centres on the strategic action of the firm in developing new titles to satisfy demand, and in the changing patterns of organization and employment within the industry.

What has been largely overlooked in the vast literature surrounding the industry has been a focus on magazine companies themselves as businesses. Therefore our approach has sought to remedy the lack of a coherent narrative history, and to provide an appreciation of how the sector has evolved over time. We have therefore focused on the competition between firms rather than between individual titles, and the changing nature of competition through strategy and innovation, the technologies employed and forms of business organization. As we have sought to present an assessment of how the forces governing competition have shaped the industry, the tools of analysis that we have employed have therefore been primarily economic. A key concern has been to identify the barriers to industry entry, and to examine how questions of scale, scope, and the political landscape have changed the forces which define the industry in broad terms. Therefore we focus on three key themes in our narrative: the strategic action of firms, the role of changing technology, and the resulting patterns of industry structure and firm organization.

Finally although this book is a work of historical analysis, its span reaches to the present. This might be surprising as usually historical works tend to shy away from contemporary events. However, we have attempted to examine the process to the present day as an example of how industries and firms respond to technological change and competitive forces through strategic change. Our study may therefore be of interest to a wider audience than those concerned exclusively with the magazine publishing industry, and will hopefully provide insights into other industries that reflect a similar pattern of technological change or competitive forces.

Notes

PREFACE

1. PPA (2010: 1).
2. Reed (1997) has done an excellent job in his comparative study of the UK and American magazine markets of providing an overview of the broad developments of the industry in general to 1960. There is not, however, a comparable study for the British industry to those of the American markets by Peterson (1956), Mott (1957), Wood (1971), and Tebbel and Zuckerman (1991). A few studies have examined the functioning of the industry in Britain at a specific point in time, such as Driver and Gillespie (1992, 1993a, 1993b) and Ekinsmyth (2002a, 2002b).
3. Low (1999: 63).
4. Cox and Mowatt (2012).
5. <http://www.magforum.com>.

CHAPTER 1

1. Initially, due to the incidence of the plague in London, the *Gazette* was published in Oxford. It changed its title to the *London Gazette* in February 1666. Handover (1965: 9–14). On the early history of Oxford University Press cf. Gadd (2013).
2. Feather (1988: 107).
3. The magazine lasted for three years, ceasing publication in November 1694.
4. Feather (1988: 109).
5. For a period of time it was possible for newspapers that consisted of more than a single sheet to be registered as pamphlets and thus avoid the stamp duty, leading to a rise in the number of six-page newspapers. This loophole was closed by a further Stamp Act in 1725. Harris (1978: 84–5).
6. Black (2001: 9–12). Between 1715 and 1730 the impact of the advertising tax appears to have been felt more keenly amongst the London-based press, whose generation of advertising duties barely doubled over the whole of the 15-year period. By way of contrast, albeit starting from a much lower base (one-tenth of that of the London papers in 1715), during the same period the provincial papers generated more than a fourfold increase in duties. From 1715, over the course of the remainder of the eighteenth century as a whole, the provincial papers generated an increase in advertising revenue of around 200-fold compared with the London papers' increase of slightly under 40-fold. Clarke (2004: 99).
7. Clarke (2004: 66–74).
8. Brake and Demoor (2009).
9. Feather (1988: 115).

10. William Bradbury set up his first printing business at 76 Fleet Street in 1824. By the early 1870s *Punch* was earning a profit of around £10,000 per annum for the firm. Leary (2010: 134, 161, and *passim*).
11. Clarke (2004: 72).
12. White (1970: 31).
13. Black (2001: 165–9).
14. The *Literary Gazette* was a weekly review of books launched in 1817 and designed to promote the sale of the popular fiction books that Colburn published. During the 1820s and 30s Colburn was the proprietor or part-proprietor of five papers and magazines. Asquith (1978: 104).
15. Topham (2005: 86, 90).
16. Topham (2005: 76).
17. The principal reason for Limbird's failure to undercut the price of the *Literary Gazette* was due to the fact that, in 1818, this latter publication had been the first weekly periodical to be printed using the *Times*' new Koenig steam-driven presses. Topham (2005: 84).
18. Although the method of using papier maché moulds to create stereotypes was not introduced into England until 1864, alternative methods were being developed commercially from the 1780s and by 1819 there are examples of stereotyping techniques being used for printing low-price publications. Brake and Demoor (2009: 601).
19. Altick (1998: 266).
20. The quote is from an obituary of John Limbird in the *Bookseller* (5 January 1884) cited by Topham (2005: 75).
21. For an extended discussion of the role of illustrations in the *Penny Magazine*, cf. Anderson (1991: 50–83).
22. Altick (1998: 333).
23. Mitchell (2004a).
24. Gray (2006: 45).
25. Cooney (2004).
26. Altick (1998: 335).
27. Reader (1981: 5).
28. Gray (2006: 154).
29. The other areas of printing activity comprised government contract printing and jobbing. Alford has shown that the output of the London letterpress industry increased from £400,000 to £800,000 between 1831 and 1851, accounting at each point in time for a little over 50 per cent of the total value of printing throughout the whole of Great Britain. The share of London-based output attributed to books and periodicals increased from 30 per cent in 1831 to 50 per cent in 1851. Alford (1964: 97, 107).
30. After 1835 the SDUK became reliant on loaned capital and was never able to operate with the same degree of latitude. Bennett (1982: 233).
31. Gray (2006: 165).
32. Bennett (1982: 244 and *passim*).
33. The reduction in the price of the stamp came with an increased stringency of the 'security' provisions of the newspaper stamp law, requiring heavy bonds to be

posted against the printing of criminal libel, which placed an impossible burden on the resources of the small newspaper publisher. Altick (1998: 341).

34. The driving force of the *Illustrated London News* was provided by the editor Frederick Bayley. Bailey (2004). The journal was distinguished from previous magazines by the number and quality of its woodcuts. Its main illustrator was John Timbs who had earlier worked on the staff of John Limbird's *Mirror*. Although strictly defined as a newspaper, the *Illustrated London News* displayed many features in common with family magazines, including in its pages chess problems, fashion notes, and games. However, its cover price of 6*d*., which until 1855 included the newspaper stamp duty, meant that it was targeted exclusively at middle-class readers. The title endured until 1989. Brake and Demoor (2009: 301–3).

35. Humpherys claims that between 1840 and 1860 Reynolds wrote approximately 35 or 40 million words and published 58 novels, which included his monumental serial *The Mysteries of London*. Humpherys (1985: 4–5).

36. King (2004: 74–5); Anderson (1991: 86).

37. The *Family Herald* was one of the first publications to utilize a mechanical system for typesetting. The machine, known as the 'Pianotyp', had been invented in France by Young and Delcambre and it utilized a keyboard which released type automatically to be assembled by hand at a later stage. As a result of mechanical deficiencies and the vociferous opposition of compositors, the system was quickly abandoned. Twyman (1998: 60).

38. The *Family Journal* was published by Biggs until 1858, before passing to the control of Benjamin Brake (1858–64) and then William Stevens Ltd. Brake and Demoor (2009: 213–14).

39. King (2004: 90–7). Elsewhere King argues that a circulation of 30,000 was considered to be the break-even level for a penny magazine at this time. King (2008: 58).

40. In the period before he joined up with Dicks, Reynolds used four different printing firms to produce his magazine. These included the large steam-printing firm of W.H. Cox, which employed 37 men and ten boys, the medium-sized operation of Thoms, with ten men and five boys, and the tiny firm of White, employing just one boy. King (2008: 62) surmises that this rapid turnover of printers is symptomatic of Reynolds' precarious financial position at the time.

41. Altick (1998: 346).

42. James (2004). For circulation data on the weekly newspaper press from 1842 to 1890, cf. Berridge (1978: 263).

43. Humpherys (2004). *Bow Bells* ceased publication in 1897.

44. Springhall (1994: 568); McWilliam (2004).

45. Berridge (1978: 253).

46. The abolition of the newspaper stamp duty effectively ended the protection of existing newspapers and threw open the door to exploiting the technological developments in printing to expand output and cut unit costs. Lee (1978: 118–19).

47. McWilliam (2004). On Richard Hoe & Co. and the developments in printing technology in New York at this time cf. Scranton (1997: 121–32).

48. Reader (1981: 11–12).

49. Alford (1965: 1).

50. The two largest firms, Clowes and Eyre & Spottiswoode, each employed about 400 men, while Hansard and Spottiswoode and Co. employed 250 and 200 men respectively. These four firms are estimated to have been responsible for over a third of the industry's total output in 1850. Alford (1964: 107).

51. Alford (1965: 3).

52. For Great Britain as a whole it is estimated that the number of printing firms increased from 1,200 in 1850 to 7,000 in 1914, with the greatest expansion taking place among medium-sized firms employing between 50 and 200 men. Alford (1965: 10–11).

53. Jackson (2001: 210).

54. Hughes (2005: 162–3).

55. For detailed studies of earlier magazines aimed at women, cf.White (1970: 23–57) and Beetham (1996).

56. Hughes (2005: 179).

57. Hughes (2005: 268–78. Quote from 277).

58. This title is not the more well-known *Boy's Own Paper* which was launched by the Religious Tract Society in 1879. Reed (1997: 85–6).

59. Beeton's *Book of Household Management* was first issued monthly in November 1859 as a 48-page magazine priced at 3*d.*, before being sold as a collected work for 7*s.* 6*d.* in the autumn of 1861. It was the most successful of a series of pragmatically conceived books such as *Beeton's Book of Birds, Beeton's Historian,* and *Beeton's Book of Songs* all produced by the firm of S. O. Beeton. Hughes (2005: 189–96).

60. Beetham (1996: 90).

61. Beetham (1996: 301–2).

62. On the financial scandal of Overend Gurney, cf. Barnes (2005).

63. Beetham gives a sample of the nature of this material taken from an 1868 edition of *EDM*: 'Dear Mrs. Englishwoman, I beg—I pray—that you will not close your delightful Conversazione to the Tight-lacing question; it is an absorbing one; hundreds, thousands of your young lady readers are deeply interested in this matter.' Beetham (1996: 71). The magazine ceased publication in 1879.

64. Wilson (1985: 67).

65. Mitchell (2004b).

66. Anderson (1991: 88); King (2004: 100).

67. Nowell-Smith (1958: 42).

68. Nowell-Smith (1958: 52–62 and *passim*).

69. Altick (1998: 351).

70. Henry Edward was 'eased out of the partnership' by his harder-working younger brother in 1828. Wilson (1985: 17).

71. Altick (1998: 322–3). For a brief review of the social and economic impact of coffee houses cf. Brandon (2007: 79–89).

72. Wilson (1985: 37).

73. Wilson (1985: 45).

74. Davenport-Hines (2004).

75. On building and managing the bookstall empire cf. Wilson (1985: 88–179). Statistics for the number of bookstalls between 1851 and 1870 are drawn from Table VII.2.

76. Little detail on the range of periodicals sold by Smith's bookstalls at this time appears to have survived. Colclough (2005: 177–80) points out that the weekly periodicals which dominated the stalls around the 1850s and 1860s were those, such as *Punch* and *Household Words*, that could be returned to the publisher if they remained unsold. During this period it was the profits from its newspaper business that increased most rapidly, but given that this still only accounted for 57 per cent of the stalls' total turnover by 1875 it is clear that magazines (as well as books) were a not insignificant contributor to the firm's profitability during these years.

77. The provincial press provided advertising opportunities not only for local firms, but also for businesses in the leading towns which were seeking to expand the demand for their products. Thus many early provincial papers maintained agents in London and other major centres to attract advertisers, and they sought to develop circulations that were regional rather than purely local. Black (2001: 112–13). For provincial papers in general it is estimated that around half of the revenues generated came from advertising. Brown (1985: 16).

78. Powell and Wyke (2009: 172).

79. The existing telegraph news service, provided by Electric and International Telegraph Company which by 1854 was serving 120 provincial newspapers, was badly flawed. Cf. Silberstein-Loeb (2009: 765–6). The most important new daily paper to emerge following the abolition of the stamp duty was the London-based *Daily Telegraph [& Courier]* which launched on 29 June 1855, six weeks after the ending of the tax. Initially put on the market at 2*d.*, the price was cut to 1*d.* by its new owner, the printer Joseph Moses Levy, in September 1855. Hart-Davis (1990: 27–8); Griffiths (2006a: 94–100).

80. Tate (2009: 47–54).

81. Tate (2005: 104).

82. Tate (2009: 58).

83. Porter (2004a).

CHAPTER 2

1. Altick (1998: 395). A more recent analysis by King (2004: 82–90 and Appendix) suggests that the *London Journal's* circulation peaked at around 500,000 in the mid-1850s.

2. Weedon (2003: 31–58).

3. Altick (1998: 395). For a discussion of newspaper circulations from the mid-nineteenth century to 1900, cf. Brown (1985: 26–53). Evidence gleaned in Brown's study for *Lloyd's Weekly Newspaper* suggests circulations of 612,902 in 1879 and 910,000 in May 1893.

4. Ensor (1936: 144).

5. Wilson (1985: 358–9).

6. A particularly important firm in this respect was the one created by Charles Weldon, an associate of Samuel Beeton. Cf. White (1970: 55–6).

7. This company was not owned by the same Herbert Ingram who founded the *Illustrated London News*.

8. Liveing (1954: 13–36).

9. Hughes (2005: 301–59).

10. On Brett, cf. Springhall (1994).

11. White (1970: 55–6); Beetham (1996: 79–81); Brake and Demoor (2009).

12. Bowden had been working for Beeton and moved to Ward Lock when that firm took over Beeton's business in 1866. He was made a partner in the firm in 1879. Liveing (1954: 53–60).

13. Liveing (1954: 71–86).

14. Nowell-Smith (1958: 115–16).

15. Jackson (2001: 19).

16. Nowell-Smith (1958: 75).

17. Nowell-Smith (1958: 149–51); Barrell and Braithwaite (1988: 8).

18. Ward Lock became a limited company in 1893 but all the shares were held by family members. Liveing (1954: 75).

19. Stead's contact with Reid came about as a result of a friendship between the two men's fathers, both of whom were congregational ministers. Nowell-Smith (1958: 178).

20. The Conservative-inclined Frederick Greenwood had edited the *Pall Mall Gazette* continuously since its foundation 1865 until George Smith passed the ownership to his son-in-law, Henry Yates Thompson, in 1880.

21. Morley was elected as a Liberal MP in 1883, at which point Stead assumed editorial control of the *Gazette*.

22. Stead is usually credited as being one of the two journalists who pioneered the trend towards 'new journalism' in late nineteenth-century Britain, the other being T. P. O'Connor, founder and editor of *The Star* newspaper from 1888. Engel (1996: 45).

23. Conboy (2002: 96–9); Baylen (2004).

24. Nowell-Smith (1958: 180).

25. Shaw (1985: 436).

26. Friedrichs (1911: 73–4); Pound (1966: 21).

27. Shaw (1985: 436); Morris (2004a).

28. Friedrichs (1911: 71–2).

29. Shaw (1985: 437). Shaw mentions a sales figure of 700,000, although Altick states that the magazine was normally selling between 400,000 and 600,000 copies by the 1890s. Altick (1998: 396).

30. Jackson (2001: 30).

31. Griffen-Foley (2004: 534–5).

32. Friedrichs (1911: 87).

33. Jackson (2001: 73). Browne's agency had been set up in London in 1880. Cf. Browne (1984). See also Schwartzkopf (2008).

34. Pound (1966: 25).

35. Baylen (2004). According to Morris (2004b) Stead bought out Newnes for the relatively small price of £3,000.

36. The British *Review of Reviews* never fully recovered from Stead's untimely death aboard the SS *Titanic* in 1912.
37. Newnes wrote a brief history of the *Strand Magazine* in the one hundredth issue, explaining that it had originally been his idea to call it the *Burleigh Street Magazine* but felt it was too long-winded. Newnes (1899: 363–4); Henry (2002).
38. In 1910 *Strand Magazine* was selling 130,000 copies in New York. Ayer (1910: 1086).
39. NA BT31/5097/34316. According to the first list of shareholders, Newnes owned 309,928 of the 400,000 £1 shares.
40. In 1905 *Country Life* became a company in its own right and its initial directors were George and Frank Newnes and Edward and William Hudson. It was designed as a high quality weekly illustrated paper and was produced by Messrs Hudson and Kearns using printing machinery specially built and imported from America. Cf. Darwin (1947: 14–15).
41. On *Westminster Gazette* cf. Koss (1981: 325–7 and *passim*). According to Pound (1966: 51), Newnes' five-year tenure as owner of the *Westminster Gazette* cost him £180,000. His later attempt to launch the *Daily Courier* in competition with Harmsworth's *Daily Mail* was a complete failure, folding within a few months. Cranfield (1978: 217).
42. Jackson (2001) discusses seven of Newnes' publications in detail.
43. Pound (1966: 49).
44. *Newspaper Owner and Manager* (No. 83: 8), 2 August 1899; Brake and Demoor (2009).
45. Coleman (1959: 343).
46. Political and Economic Planning (1938: 57). The sulphite process, which involved treating the wood with bisulphate of lime or magnesia to produce cellulose, was introduced into Britain by the Swedish chemist C. D. Elkman in the 1880s. Cf. Coleman (1959: 344).
47. Reader (1981: 5).
48. Reader (1981: 12).
49. The Fourdrinier process used a combination of heat and pressure to transform the pulp from 99 per cent water to one continuous roll of newsprint at the rate of 100 to 200 feet per minute. Reader (1981: 5).
50. *Newspaper Owner and Manager* (25 May 1898: 12–13); Scranton (1997: 129).
51. By around 1890 an experienced compositor could set about 1,000 ems (i.e. letter M-widths) of type an hour whereas a skilled Linotype operator could set anywhere between 4,000 and 5,000 ems per hour. Cf. Reed (1997: 43–4).
52. Mott (1957: 5).
53. Essentially by turning photographs into a matrix of black dots of varying sizes. Twyman (1998: 104).
54. Reed (1997: 36).
55. The automation of the etching process, again by Levy, allowed an illustrator in 1900 to etch a zinc half-tone plate in one minute. Reed (1997: 42).
56. In Britain by 1907 the printing industry as a whole had achieved tenth position among all industries in terms of net output. Alford (1965: 14).
57. Mott (1957: 20).

58. The *Ladies' Home Journal* began life as a monthly supplement to the four-page weekly *Tribune and Farmer* before Curtis issued it as a separate publication under the editorship of his wife. Peterson (1956: 11).

59. Wood (1971: 97–110).

60. This figure is taken from Wood (1971: 104). Reed (1997: 56) gives the average figure for circulation of the *Ladies' Home Journal* during the 1890s overall as being around 600,000, as does Mott (1957: 537–9). Wood claims that in the ten years to 1898 Bok had raised the circulation from 450,000 to 850,000, which tallies with the estimates of Reed and Mott. A much later figure for its circulation is provided by *Ayer's* as being 1.25 million in 1910.

61. A European edition of *Harper's Monthly* was published (usually referred to as the English edition) from 1880 (to 1966). Initially to avoid British copyright laws most of the magazine was printed in New York and then shipped over to London for its editor to add the editorial, news, and advertisements. Brake and Demoor (2009). On Newnes' decision to launch the *Strand Magazine* cf. Newnes (1899: 363–4).

62. Mott (1957: 4).

63. Peterson (1956: 7–10, 83).

64. Peterson (1956: 7).

65. Mott (1957: 5). In the first ten cent issue of September 1893 Munsey explained that: 'The present low price of paper and the perfecting of printing machinery make it possible to sell at a profit a magazine at these figures—as good a magazine as has ever been issued, provided it is not too heavily freighted with advertisements.' Peterson (1956: 7–8).

66. Peterson (1956: 10).

67. By 1918 Curtis had become a giant, with 43 per cent of all national advertising revenue from consumer and farm magazines. Ohmann (1996: 355).

68. Wilson (1970: 321). *McClure's Magazine* led the trend towards muckraking journalism with a series of articles by Ida Tarbell on the Standard Oil Company beginning in 1902.

69. Ohmann (1996: 354).

70. Dark (1922: 28).

71. Porter (1985: 575).

72. BT 31/4944/32986. Pearson launched his business with a private loan of £3,000 from Mr Stephen Mills. He was later able to secure a line of finance from Sir William Ingram, the proprietor of the *Illustrated London News*. Dark (1922: 48, 59).

73. Porter (1985: 575).

74. McKernan (2004).

75. Porter (1985: 575). According to Dark (1922: 59) the total issued capital of Pearson's business was £400,000.

76. Thompson (2000: 11).

77. Before he was 16 he had edited a magazine for his public school, the *Henley House Magazine*. Taylor (1996: 9).

78. William Ingram and his brother Charles had assumed control of the business of Herbert Ingram, which included the *Illustrated London News*, on reaching maturity. Their father had been drowned in an accident in 1860 and the family

publishing business was temporarily placed under the management of the MP Sir Edward William Watkin. Bailey (2004).

79. Smith (2004c).
80. Thompson (2000: 9).
81. Alfred took the bold step of hiring a woman correspondent (Lillias Campbell Davidson) to contribute articles to the magazine. Taylor (1996: 12).
82. Taylor (1996: 13) suggests that Iliffe 'let Alfred go' while Boyce (2004) states that he was offered a partnership in the Iliffe firm which Harmsworth elected not to take up.
83. Thompson (2000: 8).
84. Ferris (1971: 30).
85. The reason for numbering the first issue as No. 3 was to imply that the questions of readers from earlier editions were being answered. Pound and Harmsworth (1959: 81) state that Nos. 1 and 2 were printed retrospectively for those readers who wished to purchase a full bound set of the first volume.
86. It has been reported that the first print run of *Answers* amounted to 60,000 copies, of which 12,000 were actually purchased. Pound and Harmsworth (1959: 82–3).
87. Thompson (2000: 13).
88. Thompson (2000: 12 and n.22).
89. Springhall (1994: 568).
90. Harmsworth placed Winfred Ruth 'Biddy' Johnson, an experienced editor of women's magazines, in control of *Forget-Me-Not*. Pearson's *Home Notes* and Harmsworth's *Home Chat* established themselves as the leading monthly and weekly women's titles before the First World War and the latter remained in print until 1958. White (1970: 75–7).
91. Dilnot (1925: 20).
92. Ferris (1971: 44). The 'Schemo Magnifico' manifesto has not survived amongst the papers left by Alfred Harmsworth. Ferris suggests that towards the end of his life Alfred tore it up and flushed it down the lavatory.
93. Ferris (1971: 45) notes that Harmsworth's profits had risen to £40,000 per year by 1891.
94. Geraldine was the name of the Harmsworth brothers' mother.
95. BT 31/15681/49730.
96. *Newspaper Owner and Manager* (No. 37: 19), 14 September 1898.
97. Ferris (1971: 52–3 and *passim*).
98. Ferris (1971: 46–7).
99. BT 31/15681/49730. The file includes the certificate of change of name dated 7 February 1902.
100. Porter (2004c).
101. Taylor (1996: 27–35); Engel (1996: 15–16, 59–88).
102. Jackson (2001).
103. In a report of the new company's first Annual General Meeting published in August 1898, Newnes made great play of *Tit-Bits'* enduring popularity and the increasing sale of *Strand* magazine in both Britain and the United States. *Newspaper Owner and Manager* (No. 31: 11), 3 August 1898.
104. Liveing (1954: 71–4).

105. *Newspaper Owner and Manager* (No. 35: 7–9), 31 August 1898.
106. Dilnot (1925: 24).

CHAPTER 3

1. Newnes' main daily newspaper was the Liberal Party-supporting *Westminster Gazette* which he founded in 1893 after the existing Liberal newspaper, the *Pall Mall Gazette*, had been taken over by the American millionaire John Jacob Astor. In 1905 Newnes claimed to have lost £10,000 per annum financing the paper. It was sold to a consortium headed by Sir Alfred Mond in 1908. Koss (1984: 41); Jackson (2001: 129–62).

2. Despite the fact that the technology and organizational structure of newspaper and periodical publishing was transformed during the last two decades of the nineteenth century, this industry received almost no analysis in the major study of the second industrial revolution undertaken by Alfred Chandler. The sector-by-sector breakdown of the leading industrial enterprises of the United States, Great Britain, and Germany around the time of the First World War provided by this account does, however, underscore the relative significance of the Harmsworth publishing operations in Britain. See Chandler (1990: Appendix A1, B1, and C1) for comparative figures. Chandler's study does not give any major periodical publishing firms in his list of the two hundred leading German industrial enterprises in 1913 although Cassis (1997: 26–7) notes that one of the three leading newspaper publishers in Germany, August Scherl GmbH, did float a company for 20 million Marks (approximately £1 million) in 1911 which would have placed it in 116th position in Chandler's list of German industrial enterprises. Cassis' study shows that there were no companies in the communications sector of either the German or French economy with a capital of £2 million or more between 1907 and 1912, whereas he gives five such companies as existing in Great Britain at this time. Cassis (1997: Table 1.2).

3. For a more complete picture of labour unions within the UK industry the monographs on the main organizations are a good start: NATSOPA (Moran, 1964); NUPBPW/SOGAT (Bundock, 1957; Gennard and Bain, 1995); SLADE/NGA (Gennard, 1990); TA (Musson, 1954). The records of most of these organizations are held at the Modern Records Centre at the University of Warwick.

4. Daly et al. (1997: 148).

5. Asquith (1978: 101); Griffiths (2006b: 13).

6. Alford (1965: 2) estimates that 80 per cent of the printing firms active in London in 1850 employed three men or less.

7. Musson (1954: 1–13). The earliest of these societies may have amounted to little more than drinking clubs.

8. The Stationers' Company had been incorporated in 1557, but the orders of the Company were reinforced by Star Chamber decrees and Acts of Parliament. Musson (1954: 2–5).

9. Musson (1974: 82–3).

10. Various explanations for the use of the term chapel have been given. The most popular among them relates to the originator of printing in Britain, William Caxton, who established his printing facility in Westminster Abbey. Written evidence for the existence of chapels dates back to 1683. Musson (1954: 10–12).

11. London Society of Compositors (1898: 25–9), available from the Modern Records Centre (MRC), University of Warwick, MSS.39A/CO/4/2/1.

12. Musson (1974: 102).

13. There was an ongoing division in the form of wage earning amongst compositors. Some were paid on a piece-rate basis while others earned the established weekly wage. This latter mode of earning, which the Manchester Society strongly favoured, was referred to as the 'stab rate'. Musson (1974: 86–7).

14. The rule adopted by the PTA in relation to apprenticeships was: 'Not more than two apprenticeships were allowed, unless four journeymen were employed, when the number might be increased to three, but on no account to four or more.' Slatter (1899: 4), available from MRC MSS.39A/TA/4/8/1–2.

15. Gennard (1990: 81–106).

16. Daly et al. (1997: 149).

17. Over time the Linotype technique continued to improve in terms of speed and accuracy. The Monotype was the next development in 1896, introducing ribbon and paper composition, although this and the Linotype were both used for letterpress compositing for much of the twentieth century. Child (1967).

18. Musson (1954).

19. Punched card computerization eventually was able to ease this process with regard to hyphenation over line-breaks, but the decisions had to be made manually, and the human eye was still the only measure for type justification.

20. Half-tones have inherent limitations of quality when founded on printing from metal plates rather than using the lithographic process. Photo-engraving allowed the letterpress to print graphics such as photographs from metal plates, but the process of preparing the plates was costly and letterpress could still only incorporate graphics and text together through the stereotype process, a much more complicated system of printing requiring extensive manual labour and expertise to produce balanced outputs.

21. Before the News International dispute at Wapping in 1986 the UK's top four national newspapers still had every word set in hot metal. Littleton (1992).

22. The Rembrandt Intaglio Printing Company was founded in 1895 by Storey Brothers and Company, a printing firm that had been in operation since 1848. In 1926 the firm relocated from Lancaster to West Norwood, on the outskirts of London, and in 1932 it was acquired by Sun Engraving and renamed Rembrandt Photogravure. Greenhill and Reynolds (2010: 41–7).

23. Daly et al. (1997: 150–1).

24. In the letterpress, the insertion of illustrations with text had been made easier by the development of photographic-based half-tones.

25. Sproat (1930: 1–14). Available from MRC MSS.39A/ASL/4/3/1.

26. SLADE&PW (1935). Available from MRC MSS.39A/5/MISC/6. Both groups were eventually incorporated into the National Graphical Association. Gennard (1990: 69–75, 153–6).

27. Lovell (1977: 20–9).

28. Turner (1991: 133).
29. Evans was originally a member of the LSC. Moran (1964: 13).
30. Moran (1964: 9–18).
31. *Printers' Assistant*, vol. 1(1):10, November 1908. Available from MRC MSS.39/ NAT/4/5/2.
32. Lee (1976: 95).
33. Moran (1964: 35).
34. Watts became the first elected general secretary of the NUJ. Bundock (1957: 12 and *passim*). For a brief biography of Watts see Gopsill and Neale (2007: 17–18).
35. The Federation was founded in 1890–92 but the original body became a provincial organization when the London unions withdrew to form their own Federation. In 1901 the PKTF was formed on a national basis, to represent the interests of all printing workers on questions of national or widespread application. PKTF (1961).
36. Austin-Leigh and Maynell (1920: 28). Available from MRC MSS.39/SO/5/4/2/13.
37. *Newspaper Owner and Manager* (No. 42: 9), 19 October 1898.
38. *Newspaper Owner and Modern Printer* (No. 83: 19), 2 August 1899.
39. In 1898 the trade press reported that eight of Hoe's quadruple presses were not providing enough printing capacity for the *Daily Mail* so the Harmsworths had placed orders for a further four. Each of these machines cost in the region of US$35,000. *Newspaper Owner and Manager* (No. 42: 9), 19 October 1898 and (No. 83: 19), 2 August 1899. The *Daily Mail's* audited circulation figures rose steadily from 300,000 in 1897 to 600,000 in 1899 before peaking at over a million during the Boer War and settling down at 700,000 thereafter until the First World War. Engel (1996: 64).
40. An indication of printing capacity required to produce these one million copies is provided in the trade press which stated that it took 65 machines 24 days to print it. *Newspaper Owner and Manager* (No. 42: 24), 19 October 1898. Pearson's firm later brought control of the *Royal Magazine* in June 1914. *Newspaper World* (No. 919: 11), 14 August 1915.
41. McKernan (2004).
42. Dark (1922: 87).
43. Engel (1996: 94).
44. The financial performance of the *Express* was also adversely affected by the deflection of Pearson's time as he concentrated on his work as executive chairman of the Tariff Reform League and as vice-chairman the Tariff Commission between 1903 and 1905. Blumenfeld (1933: 192).
45. Griffiths (1996: 153–76); Griffiths (2006a: 134–56).
46. Koss (1984: 22–3).
47. Lee (1976: 176–7).
48. Porter (1985: 576).
49. Dark (1922: 112); Blumenfeld (1933); Engel (1996: 91–6).
50. Taylor (1996: 89–91).
51. Dark (1922: 126); Griffiths (1996: 177–94); Griffiths (2006a: 157–75).
52. Blumenfeld (1933); Engel (1996: 97).

53. Aitken had already provided financial support to the newspaper since 1911. Griffiths (1996: 214–17).
54. Griffiths (1996: 200–5).
55. Riddell (1934: 147).
56. Emsley Carr continued as editor of the *News of the World* for the next 50 years. Engel (1996: 212–13).
57. Morris (2004b).
58. Jackson (2001: 26–9).
59. Riddell's industry and his 'directing genius' are commented upon by Sidney Dark who worked for him at Newnes after the First World War. Perhaps oddly for the directing force of a publishing company, Dark also observes that 'Imaginitive writing interests him little' and his preoccupation was with facts. Dark (1925: 17–19).
60. Blumenfeld (1933: 161).
61. Morris (2004b). Launched as a joint venture with printers Hudson & Kearns in 1897, *Country Life* was incorporated as a company in its own right during 1905. Its initial directors were George and Frank Newnes and Edward and William Hudson. It was designed as a high quality weekly illustrated paper and was produced using printing machinery specially built and imported from America. Darwin (1947: 14–15) cited in Jackson (2001: 126).
62. *Newspaper World* (No. 919: 11), 14 August 1914. Morris (2004b) states that Newnes' and Pearson's concerns were formally combined in 1921, but mistakenly dates the acquisition of Leach's to 1929.
63. By the 1916 AGM of C. Arthur Pearson Ltd., Riddell was in the chair due to Pearson's illness. Reporting profits of £26,203 for the year, Riddell praised the role played by Mr Everett and his staff, who had now clearly taken over operational control. *Newspaper World* (No. 970: 10), 5 August 1916. At the same point Newnes' firm reported profits of £40,193, a drop of £10,000 from the previous year. *Newspaper World* (No. 975: 8–9), 9 September 1916 and *Newspaper World* (No. 921: 11), 28 August 1915. Pearson's son, Neville Arthur, continued as a director of the firm after his father's death.
64. Thompson (2000: 57–8). Hammerton identifies the increasing tendency towards Americanization within Amalgamed Press which followed from Alfred Harmsworth's visits to the United States during the early 1900s. Hammerton (1932: 171).
65. Ferris (1971: 125).
66. Cudlipp (1953: 8–17).
67. Blumenfeld (1933: 153–6).
68. An internal memorandum from Alfred Harmsworth to Amalgamated Press director A. E. Linforth dated 27 August 1911 gave the circulation of *Woman's World* as 347,000. Reed (1997: 133, n.118).
69. Leslie Clarke was regarded as the editorial mainstay of Amalgamated Press during the 1910s and 1920s by the company's vice chairman A. E. Linforth. King (1969: 64).
70. Dilnot (1925: 36).
71. Ferris (1971: 125–6) highlights an article in the *Financial News* which speculated sardonically as to the likely readers of these magazines.

72. White (1970: 90).
73. Low (1999: 10–13).
74. On Mee, see Reynolds (2004); and on Hammerton, see Hadaway (2004).
75. In 1905 the price was raised from sixpence to sevenpence. Low (1999: 23).
76. Hammerton (1932: 166–7).
77. Ferris (1971: 171).
78. BT31/15681/49730.
79. Quoted in Ferris (1971: 165).
80. King (1969: 65).
81. Dilnot (1925: 67–73).
82. According to Hammerton (1932: 158) 'the Chief had only one measure for appraising the success of his editors: circulation'.
83. Newman Flower quoted in Nowell-Smith (1958: 200).
84. Flower's decision to leave Harmsworth's employment was triggered by John Hammerton when he hired from Cassell the editor of its *Penny Magazine*, Wood Smith. Flower clearly felt that this threatened his role as deputy-editor of Harmsworth's *Penny Pictorial*, of which Hammerton was the editor. Flower thus left to become Wood Smith's replacement at Cassell's. Hammerton (1932: 147–8).
85. In the early 1900s the ordinary shareholders of Amalgamated Press were receiving dividends of between 30 and 40 per cent. Nowell-Smith (1958: 177).
86. Nowell-Smith (1958: 200–4).
87. These were the *Dundee Courier, The Argus*, and the *Weekly News*. McAleer (1992: 163); Baker (2004).
88. Healy (1993: 139).
89. White (1970: 87–8).
90. Leng did set up an office in London in 1870 to provide a wire-fed news-gathering service for his papers. Porter (2004b).
91. Healy (1993: 144); Baker (2004).
92. The circulation of the *Athletic News* peaked in 1920 at 200,000. Tate (2009: 57).
93. Griffiths (1996: 196); Tate (2005: 98).
94. Hulton's son had assumed control of the business during the mid-1890s. Ned Hulton died in 1904. Porter (2004a).
95. In 1915 Hulton further established his position as a leading Fleet Street publisher by purchasing from Davison Dalziel the *Evening Standard*. Griffiths (1996: 197–200).
96. Magazine titles listed in *Mitchell's Newspaper Directory* indicate that the number in circulation peaked at around 3,300 in 1917.
97. Hammerton (1932: 158); Reed (1997: 133).
98. At first this condition was restricted to Thomson's technical staff, but later it was extended to take in editorial and commercial staff. Moran (1964: 123).
99. *NATSOPA Journal* Vol. 7(63): 4. Available from MRC MSS.39/NAT/4/5/6.
100. This is based on figures for the market value of Britain's largest industrial enterprises in 1919 presented by Chandler (1990: Appendix B1). The calculated values for the Harmsworths' businesses are as follows: Associated Newspapers £4.2 million; Amalgamated Press £4.2 million; and the Pictorial Newspaper Co. (owners of the *Daily Mirror* and *Sunday Pictorial*) £1.9 million. The aggregate

value of these businesses would make it Britain's fifteenth largest, immediately behind the huge engineering enterprise of Armstrong, Whitworth & Co. valued at £12.2 million.

CHAPTER 4

1. Murdock and Golding (1978: 130–3); Stevenson (1984: 402–3).
2. Perhaps the nearest to a women's newspaper that did develop around the turn of the century was the weekly *The Lady*. Launched in 1885, this relatively small-circulation, single title operation found a market niche based mainly on the demand for small advertisements for accommodation and domestic servants. White (1970: 70).
3. Since around three-quarters of newspapers were delivered directly to households by newsagents in the 1930s, the purchasing patterns by gender type are largely a matter for conjecture. Political and Economic Planning (1938: 67–8, 228).
4. The term 'Yellow Journalism' was an oblique reference to a comic strip character named the Yellow Kid in an early sensationalist American newspaper of the 1880s, and was applied to highlight the use of popular journalism in the battle for increased circulation figures between Pulitzer and Hearst in New York during the late 1890s. Hearst (1991: 41).
5. Ferris (1971: 139–45).
6. Ohmann (1996: 273).
7. Hyman (1972: 80–132); Symons (2001: 65–6); Morris (2004c).
8. This claim is reported by Koss (1984: 268). However, according to the magazine's publisher, Odhams, the circulation had only risen to half a million by 1916. Odhams (1935: 53).
9. William B. J. Odhams inherited the business jointly with his brother John Lynch Odhams. This latter man did not take an active role in the business due to his ongoing ill-health. Odhams (1935: 20–1).
10. BT31/5878/41274. Odhams states that the new branch operated at a loss for the first two years and needed to draw on the full amount of the authorized capital. Odhams (1935: 20–5, 148).
11. Odhams (1935: 38–9).
12. BT31/15998/57642. Richards (2004); Odhams (1935: 34).
13. Minney (1954: 50–6).
14. Springhall (1994: 578, 582).
15. Hyman (1972: 191–202).
16. The initial issued capital amounted to slightly less than £1 million. Odhams (1935: 149).
17. Odhams (1935: 49–59, 150).
18. Minney (1954: 170).
19. Minney (1954: 121–4).
20. Minney (1954: 128–33).

21. Dilnot (1925: 57–60).
22. The £80,000 figure is given by Hart-Davis (1990: 17–21) while Wintour (1989: 32–3) reports the amount as £75,000. See also Smith (2004a and 2004b).
23. Wintour (1989: 34–5).
24. The company was floated in 1923 with a capital value of £850,000. Nowell-Smith (1958: 207).
25. Hart-Davis (1990: 23).
26. Griffiths (1996: 210–11).
27. Koss (1984: 425–6). Although on the face of it Rothermere had made a good deal through the sale, the ultimate effect of the transaction was to create a period of severe competition between the Harmsworth's Northcliffe Newspapers group (formed in 1928 to manage the Harmsworth's expanding collection of provincial papers) and the Berrys' provincial titles—a duel in which Rothermere seems largely to have come off second-best. After a period of cutthroat competition, Northcliffe Newspapers was wound up in December 1932. Political and Economic Planning (1938: 101–2); Camrose (1947: 66–8); Taylor (1996: 285).
28. Williams (1957: 176).
29. *The Times*, 8 November 1926: 23.
30. *The Story-Teller, Cassell's Magazine, New Magazine, Corner Magazine, Argosy Magazine, Wireless Magazine, The Quiver, Little Folks, T.P.'s Weekly, Popular Gardening, Chums*, and *Amateur Wireless*.
31. Nowell-Smith (1958: 211).
32. Ferris (1971: 302).
33. Companies House, *Mirror Group (Holdings) Ltd.*, Company No. 00218062, Series G1.
34. *The Times*, 29 June 1928: 24.
35. Reed (1997: 173).
36. *The Times*, 8 June 1935: 21.
37. *The Times*, 6 June 1936: 19.
38. *The Times*, 24 June 1938: 25.
39. Hart-Davis (1990: 45–63).
40. Political and Economic Planning (1938: 99–101).
41. Riddell was also chairman of the leading popular Sunday newspaper, the *News of the World*, but this remained an entirely separate organization from the Newnes-Pearson Group. Political and Economic Planning (1938: 106).
42. The collaboration between the firms of Newnes and Pearson began in 1914 when they jointly purchased the independent publishing firm of Leach's. *Newspaper World*, 14 August 1915, No. 919: 11.
43. *The Times*, 10 June 1920: 20; 9 September 1920: 15; 9 March 1921: 18.
44. Currie (2001: 4–39). The first editor of the *Radio Times* was Leonard Crocombe, a frequent contributor to Newnes' *Tit-Bits*. Walter Fuller assumed the role in 1926. Newnes lost the contract to print the *Radio Times* in 1936 to Waterlows, who built a dedicated printing works for the magazine in Park Royal, west London.
45. White notes that such magazines can be dated back to the launch in 1886 of the *Housewife*. The identification of class distinctions within the readerships of different women's magazines date from a survey carried out in 1927 by the London Research and Information Bureau. White (1970: 74–5, 97, 117–18).

46. Barrell and Braithwaite (1988: 16).
47. On the consolidation of Newnes, Pearson, and Country Life, see *The Times*, 16 July 1929: 23; 26 July 1929: 22; 2 July 1930: 22; 26 June 1931: 21.
48. One firm that printed *The Academy* at this time was Odhams. W. B. J. Odhams recalls that both Douglas and Crosland 'combined the ability to write charming poetry with a gift of vitriolic invective'. As a result, he always felt sorry for Miss Head, whom he described as the working editor of the paper. Odhams (1935: 40–1).
49. In her autobiography, Head notes approvingly that, under Riddell's leadership, Newnes operated as a meritocracy, with staff able to rise over time from the lowest to the highest positions. Head (1939: 34–50).
50. Head did in fact rejoin the Newnes organization in 1941 as editor of *Homes & Gardens*. Pugh (2004).
51. Head (1939: 53–7).
52. On the early career of Hearst, cf. Proctor (1998).
53. Proctor (2007: 8).
54. *Cosmopolitan* had been one of the publications which led the way in the price-cutting war between magazines in the United States from 1893 that created the ten cent monthly financed primarily through advertising revenues rather than cover price. Ohmann (1996: 25).
55. Nasaw (2000: 227). *Harper's Bazaar* was purchased by Hearst in 1913 and converted into a fashion-centred magazine along the lines of American *Vogue*. Zuckerman (1998: 19).
56. Cited in Peterson (1956: 203).
57. Peterson notes testimony from one of the founders of the Institute that during its first year in operation *Good Housekeeping* rejected $196,000 in advertising out of a year's total of $240,000. Peterson (1956: 204).
58. Nash's 21st birthday, *Newspaper World*, 21 June 1930, No. 1693: 17.
59. Hilton (2003: 172).
60. Head (1939: 62).
61. Head (1939: 83–5).
62. Proctor (2007: 159).
63. Head (1939: 125).
64. It had proved necessary, however, to merge *Nash's* with *Good Housekeeping* in October 1937. Ashley (2006: 129–37).
65. Proctor (2007: 198–237). Dick Berlin became President of Hearst newspapers in 1943. For a critical view of Berlin's role in the salvation of Hearst's publishing empire see the account by W. R. Hearst's son. Hearst (1991: 256–8, 297–301).
66. 'The Two-Sided World of Present-Day Magazines', *Newspaper World*, 3 May 1930, No. 1686: 28.
67. Hill (2004: 8).
68. Chase and Chase (1954: 39–41).
69. Nast had increased the value of *Collier's* advertising income from practically nothing to top $1 million by 1907. Seebohm (1982: 30).
70. Seebohm (1982: 38).
71. Seebohm (1982: 71–80). Nast set out his theory in the *Merchants' and Manufacturers' Journal*.

72. Cox and Mowatt (2012). Like the National Magazine Co., the American Condé Nast Inc. experienced financial difficulties after 1929 and was forced to sell its ownership of the British Condé Nast to the Berry brothers and Illife. A holding company was formed, bearing Nast's name, and the purchase was kept secret until Nast's death in 1942. Yoxall reported the firm's financial results annually to William Berry in person, and notes in his autobiography the strong antipathy Berry felt towards the extravagance of American publishing methods. Yoxall (1966: 92–3).
73. Nevitt (1982: 145).
74. The other category to display, that of classified advertising, was of negligible importance to general interest magazines. Kaldor and Silverman (1948: 41). Comparing the figures for total expenditure on press advertising between the two studies shows a slight difference between Nevitt (£53 million) and Kaldor and Silverman (£48.4 million).
75. The distinction between the two groups of magazines is that general interest periodicals have a national circulation amongst the general public, whereas special interest periodicals are restricted to particular groups of readers such as the members of a trade union, a parish or a university. Kaldor and Silverman (1948: 38).
76. That is to say daily and weekly newspapers across both the national and provincial spectrum. Kaldor and Silverman (1948: 45).
77. Kaldor and Silverman (1948: 97).
78. British *Vogue*, 15 September 1916: 17.
79. Barrell and Braithwaite (1988: 13–14); Greenfield and Reid (1998: 168).
80. Yoxall (1966: 124).
81. Seebohm (1982: 125–32).
82. In 1911 Curtis hired Charles Coolidge Parlin to establish a division of Commercial Research in its advertising department. Wood (1971: 332–3).
83. Letter from Harry Yoxall to Condé Nast dated 3 September 1939. CNAMC, Box 12, Folder 11.
84. *Newspaper World*, 22 February 1930, No. 1676: 41.
85. Greenhill and Reynolds (2010: 29).
86. Greenhill and Reynolds (2010: 37).
87. Cox and Mowatt (2012).
88. Corp (*c*.1969).
89. Minney (1954: 171–2).
90. Greenhill and Reynolds (2010: 58–61).
91. Minney (1954: 273–4).
92. The decision by Newnes to redevelop *Woman's Own* as a photogravure publication was reported to shareholders at the company's 1937 AGM. *The Times*, 30 June 1937: 24.
93. Greenhill and Reynolds (2010: 61–4).

CHAPTER 5

1. The Ministry of Food and the Ministry of Fuel and Power were two government departments who used this medium extensively. Cf. White (1970: 123).
2. Low (1999: 40–1).

3. In turn, the popularity and rapidly expanding post-war circulation of the women's weekly magazines meant that they were sought out in 1948 by Britain's Labour government to promote the social reforms then being enacted in the areas of national insurance and national health. Grieve (1964: 125–7).

4. Lorent had earlier edited the *Muncher Illustriete Presse* before falling foul of the Nazis and emigrating to Britain. *Weekly Illustrated* was launched by Odhams in 1934 with Maurice Cowan as editor. It was amalgamated with *Passing Show* to form *Illustrated* magazine in 1939 in an attempt to more effectively compete with Hulton's *Picture Post*. Reed (1997: 183).

5. Hopkinson (1948: 47).

6. By 1947 the rate per advertising page in *Picture Post* was £900. Only the *Radio Times'* rate of £2,240 was higher than this for a weekly magazine. At this time around one in four of the adult population were estimated to have read the magazine. Hobson and Henry (1947: Table 1).

7. Jenkins (1976: 181–3); Wintour (1979); Seymour-Ure (2004); Kynaston (2007: 20).

8. *The Times*, 15 June 1940: 10.

9. The chairman of the Newspaper Supply Company was Max Aitken (Lord Beaverbrook). Gerald (1956: 27–9).

10. *The Times*, 22 August 1942: 7.

11. *The Times*, 29 July 1944: 10.

12. White (1970: 124).

13. Gerald (1956).

14. Reed International (1990: 15); *The Times*, 23 November 1938: 22.

15. *The Times*, 3 August 1946: 7.

16. *The Times*, 5 August 1946: 8.

17. Royal Commission on the Press (1949: 3).

18. Camrose (1947: 145–52).

19. Giving further details on the small group of political periodicals identified by Camrose, the Commission noted that these publications' ownership was widely dispersed and a broad range of opinions were expressed across the group. No circulation figures were given to assess their market significance however. Royal Commission on the Press (1949: 100).

20. Royal Commission on the Press (1949: 17, 22).

21. Hart-Davis (1990: 130). For example no question of the possible cross-subsidization of the newspaper by the revenues generated from magazines was raised.

22. For magazines that depended heavily for their revenues on advertising, such as Condé Nast's *Vogue* and National Magazine Co.'s *Harper's Bazaar*, the loss of space available to advertisers was particularly significant. Correspondence from the Condé Nast office in London to New York during the war complained bitterly that *Harper's Bazaar* was able to effectively steal its advertising revenue due to the limited space that could be provided in British *Vogue*. Condé Nast Archive, CNAMC Box 13.

23. *The Times*, 27 June 1950: 11.

24. Under the post-war editorship of James Drawbell, the circulation of *Woman's Own* peaked at 2.55 million in 1957. White (1970: 127, Appendix IV).

25. *Illustrated Weekly* and *Passing Show* were rolled together by Odhams in March 1939 to form the colour-printed *Illustrated* as a more effective competitor to Hulton's *Picture Post*. Minney (1954: 274); Reed (1997: 183).

26. The value of display advertising in magazines (except trade and technical) had grown to 170 per cent of its 1938 level by 1949 and to 355 per cent by 1953, due in large measure to a doubling of the advertising rate per column inch per thousand over this period. Magazines as a whole accounted for almost one-third of the value of expenditure on advertising by 1954 as paper rationing controls continued to affect the size of newspapers. Gerald (1956: 102–5).

27. *The Times*, 8 June 1953: 12.

28. Sisson (1975: 125–32).

29. *The Times*, 29 March 1956: 7.

30. *The Times*, 3 July 1956: 15. It later transpired that the decision by Associated Iliffe to print their publications abroad led to greater costs than simple suspension would have done. *The Times*, 3 July 1957: 16.

31. Thomson (1975: 7–21). Monopolies Commission (1968: 7).

32. Goldenberg (1984: 34).

33. Kemsley had earlier sold the Hulton's old *Daily Sketch* to Associated Newspapers in 1952 and the *Financial Times* to Pearson in 1957. Seymour-Ure (1996: 39).

34. Michael Berry's shock in discovering that this transaction had been completed without his knowledge was exacerbated by the fact that the presses of his *Daily Telegraph* newspaper were actually being used to print the *Sunday Times* on behalf of his uncle's firm. Hart-Davis (1990: 181).

35. On the modernizing of the *Sunday Times*, see Evans (2009: 265–76).

36. *The Times*, 28 November 1961: 12; Murdock and Golding (1978: 138–9); Goldenberg (1984: 91).

37. An ex-footballer journalist and some sportswriters for example were able to launch a new monthly soccer magazine in 1951, featuring some colour printing. The magazine, *Charles Buchan's Football Monthly*, was published by Charles Buchan's Publications Ltd., based in the Strand, and printed in Watford by Greycaines. It was later adopted by Longacre, the successor to Hulton Press. Inglis (2006: 7–11).

38. Sales of *My Weekly* ran against the prevailing trend of women's weeklies and fell from just under 200,000 to 85,000 between 1950 and 1957. White (1970: Appendix IV).

39. Barrell and Braithwaite (1988: 21–3).

40. Cohen (2001: 164).

41. *The Times*, 3 July 1957: 16.

42. The final issue of the *Picture Post* was that of June 1957. By this time the magazine's circulation had fallen below 750,000, less than half that of its wartime peak. *The Times*, 16 May 1957: 9.

43. Wintour (2004).

44. Barrell and Braithwaite (1988: 30).

45. Oral evidence given by Hulton to the Royal Commission. Royal Commission on the Press (1962: 56).

46. Seymour-Ure (2004).

47. For the year ended March 1957 the dividend paid by Hulton Press had fallen to 3.5 per cent from 15 per cent the previous year. *The Times*, 27 August 1957: 12; 25 September 1957: 17.
48. *The Times*, 2 July 1958: 15.
49. Barrell and Braithwaite (1988: 26).
50. Reed (1997: 222).
51. *The Times*, 9 June 1958: 16.
52. Low (1999: 46).
53. *The Times*, 2 July 1958: 15.
54. Hart-Davis (1990: 179).
55. Beavan (2004).
56. Cudlipp (1953: 282).
57. King (1969: 124).
58. *The Times*, 28 November 1958: 18.
59. *The Times*, 13 December 1958: 6.
60. Hart-Davis (1990: 179).
61. King (1969: 124–5); Hart-Davis (1990: 217).
62. Yoxall (1966: 92–6).
63. Odhams' interest is confirmed by Cudlipp (1962: 173–4).
64. In fact a survey of newspaper readers by the Mass Observation organization in 1949 had found that around one-half of those who read the *Daily Herald* and the *Daily Mirror* could remember nothing whatsoever of the advertising material contained in their paper. Mass Observation (1949: 121).
65. Koss (1984: 652–3). Gaitskell's endorsement was unsurprisingly dependent on the merged newspaper's continued backing of the Labour Party. The *News Chronicle* had traditionally supported the Liberals. Smith (2000: 181–5).
66. During the 1950s the BBC's *Radio Times* had outstripped all other magazine sales to reach 8.8 million in 1955. The magazine was printed by Waterlows at a purpose-built factory in Park Royal, London. In 1956 the company added a second plant in East Kilbride to print the Scottish edition. Sales of the Christmas edition peaked in 1988 at 11.2 million. Currie (2001: 39, 91, 242). The *TV Times* was launched in 1955 and only became a national magazine in 1968, at which point its sales were three million. Low (1999: 48–9). The listings monopoly of these two magazines only ended in the 1980s.
67. *The Times*, 13 March 1959: 8.
68. On the changes instigated at Amalgamated Press following the Mirror's takeover, see Cudlipp (1962: 190–7).
69. According to Hugh Cudlipp of the *Mirror*, Duncan and two of his co-directors were spiritualists and kept in touch with Elias through a medium after his death. Elias apparently advised them to 'take risks'. See Wintour (1989: 62).
70. *The Times*, 18 March 1959: 7. On the use of Reuters by the *Daily Herald*, cf. Smith (2000: 176).
71. *The Times*, 16 March 1959: 10.
72. *The Times*, 16 April 1959: 20.
73. *The Times*, 20 May 1959: 15; 21 May 1959: 10; 30 May 1959: 6.
74. Taylor (1998: 133–5).

75. Koss (1984: 653–5).
76. As well as their acquisition of Hulton Press and George Newnes, Odhams had also purchased the Contract Journal Company Ltd. during the course of that year. *The Times*, 17 June 1960: 23.
77. At the 1959 AGM Duncan had stated that the sales of the Herald were 1.5 million. Koss (1984: 655) gives the actual circulation (i.e. sales) figures as 1,412,414 copies in 1960 and 1,465,994 in 1959.
78. *The Times,* 25 August 1960: 9.
79. Smith (2000: 186).
80. King (1969: 125).
81. *The Times*, 10 February 1961: 5.
82. Gaitskell's support for a merger between Odhams and Thomson was not universally supported within the Labour movement. Key figures such as his deputy George Brown and the leader of the huge Trade and General Workers Union, Frank Cousins, both argued strongly that King and the Mirror would provide a better home for Labour-supporting national dailies. Smith (2000: 186–7).
83. Thomson (1975: 97–101).
84. *The Times*, 26 January 1961: 10; 27 January 1961: 12.
85. *The Times*, 28 January 1961: 6.
86. *The Times*, 2 February 1961: 12. The Thomson–Odhams merger was formally cancelled late in February. *The Times*, 25 February 1961: 6.
87. CAB 21/5960 Amalgamation of Newspapers.
88. *The Times*, 1 February 1961: 6.
89. CAB 21/5960 Amalgamation of Newspapers.
90. *The Times*, 10 February 1961: 5.
91. Cudlipp (1976: 247).
92. *The Times*, 2 March 1961: 12.
93. *The Times*, 15 April 1961: 5.
94. Newspaper Press Directory (1962: 23–4). The tit-for-tat closure of Newnes' *Woman's Day* and Fleetway's *Woman's Illustrated* had been the proposal put by King to Chancellor at their meeting in December 1960 that had set the subsequent merger processes in train.
95. King (1969: 126).
96. Royal Commission on the Press (1962: 76).
97. IPC Annual Report and Accounts (1963: 3).

CHAPTER 6

1. IPC was incorporated on 31 December 1962 but truly came into existence with a scheme of arrangement which allowed the firm to become the beneficial owner of the shares of The Daily Mirror Newspapers Ltd. and the Sunday Pictorial on 8 April 1963. IPC Reports and Accounts (1963: 3, 5–8).
2. The group's consumer magazines were listed as comprising: Women and the Home (25 titles); Children (17 titles including comics); Sport (9 titles); and

Miscellaneous (27 titles). IPC Reports and Accounts (1963: Appendices); Swan (1991: 666).

3. IPC owned a controlling interest of 43.9 per cent.
4. Only three other titles provided competition in the women's segment, accounted for by only two firms: DC Thomson and The Lady. Price Commission (1978b: 6).
5. The 20 per cent figure excludes the *Radio Times* and the *TV Times* listings magazines which were protected by the monopoly over this information enforced by the broadcasters, and the colour supplements issued by, and bundled together with, newspapers. Figures are derived from Henry (1986: 94, Table 3.5.2.1).
6. See the Price Commission report for a review of the situation (1978a).
7. King (1969: 124).
8. Ron Phillips, who was the Amalgamated Press' Head of Printing at the time of the Mirror's acquisition and later deputy chairman of IPC Magazines (retiring in 1975), felt that the company was a 'real number three' compared to their rivals, and that the acquisition, although 'a bolt out of the blue, was a "godsend"'. Low (1999: 55).
9. In 1963 IPC closed Fleetway's gravure press as it was uncompetitive, partly due to the high cost of operating a London-based printing facility. IPC Annual Report (1963: 3). *Woman's Weekly* was printed in mono throughout except for a two-colour cover.
10. Cecil King thought the value of these two enterprises was worth more than purchase price paid for the Amalgamated Press, a view which he thought the Berry family came to share. King believed the purchase to be a real coup as by 1968 the Magazine Division was returning IPC annual profits of £1.25 million. King (1969: 124–5).
11. King (1969: 126).
12. King (1969: 125); Beavan (2004).
13. Ron Phillips cited in Low (1999: 56). Arthur Seddon, the Amalgamated Press' and later IPC's *Woman's Weekly* Publicity Officer, noted that the Mirror Group executives were forced to concede that the Amalgamated Press management had the expertise to deal with the different requirements of magazines as distinct from newspapers. Cited in Low (1969: 60). Reviewing the integration of the newspaper and magazine interests into the group in 1971, the then IPC chairman Edward Pickering outlined four fundamental reasons why newspaper and magazine publishing differed: first, newspapers represent a small and coherent number of titles printed with a common technology; second, conversely the magazine group represented many extremely different titles with great physical diversity; third, newspapers work to a 24-hour schedule while magazines have long lead times; fourth, magazines do not need to respond to daily political issues. *IPC News* (September 1971: 11).
14. Doug Fanthorpe, Odhams' circulations manager, said that no explanation for the lack of integration was given to staff as to why the magazine companies were left out from this reorganization, and he thought 'perhaps they were simply unsure of what to do'. Fanthorpe had started his career originally in Kemsley Newspapers before their absorption into Hulton's where he worked in the Circulations Department. When Odhams acquired Hulton Press in 1960 he was to rise to the position of IPC Circulations Director. Low (1999: 52–3).

15. In 1963 Odhams Press had been a self-contained group, but in 1964 all non-newspaper printing interests were moved to the International Printers arm of IPC. IPC Report and Accounts (1964); *IPC News* (July 1971: 14).
16. Norton (1993: 244–7).
17. The term was coined by *Vogue*'s editor-in-chief Diana Vreeland in 1965. *Vogue* (January 1965: 112).
18. Long (2012: 27–8).
19. Maurice Kinn sold the *NME* to IPC for £500,000 in December 1962. Long (2012: 26).
20. *Fabulous* was reported as a Fleetway publication which had 'created for itself a new market exploiting the vogue for pop music'. IPC Annual Report and Accounts (1964: 9).
21. Long explains that Kinn launched *Hit Parade* after regretting his decision to sell the *NME* to IPC. He invited his former fellow-employees to moonlight on his new title. The exploitative title, in which quotes attributed to pop stars were simply made up, quickly folded, however. Long (2012: 28).
22. Newnes launched *Nova* in March 1965. IPC Reports and Accounts (1965). The original title closed in October 1975, although the name was revived for a new magazine launched by IPC in 2000.
23. Henry (1986: 98).
24. Asa Briggs argued that the colour Sunday supplements were 'as active as television in pushing forward changes in values both in their editorial content and in their advertisements'. Briggs (1984: 304).
25. Long has called the *Sunday Times* supplement 'ultra-modern', in contrast to the more staid fare served by the weekly magazines. Long (2012: 26–7).
26. Henry inferred the circulation of the newspaper colour supplements from newspaper sales. Henry (1986: 94, 98, Table 3.5.2.1).
27. Clark (1988: 345). One lucrative market which the Sunday supplements were successful in luring away from that of paid-for magazines were mail order adverts aimed at the male reader. *IPC News* (May/June 1983: 2). Although the *Sunday Times Magazine* was thought to have immediately boosted sales of the newspaper by 200,000 copies, it was slow to attract advertisers in its first year. During this time the future of the free magazine insert was in doubt, having cost £900,000 over the first eighteen months. According to Roy Thomson it was only when his company paid to fly 168 leading British businessmen to Moscow in an effort to promote the magazine that the new publication gained a strong foothold in the advertising market. Initially Thomson had considered that only the *Sunday Times* had a large enough circulation to attract a sufficient quantity of up-market high-value advertising to cover the cost of colour gravure printing. Thomson (1975: 121–7).
28. Braithwaite (1995: 158). Cf. also McKay (2000: 189). By June 1981 IPC estimated that the Sunday supplements had captured £50 million of the advertising market for magazines. *IPC News* (June 1981: 2).
29. Henry (1986: 96–8).
30. The *Mirror Magazine* was a disaster which was poorly conceived as a consort to the *Daily Mirror*, suffering from a lack of editorial fit with the newspaper, and

was dropped after six months. The launch itself was delayed for two weeks by industrial action and by the time of its closure it was estimated to have made a loss of around £1 million. The fiasco was subsequently considered by Cleverly to have been the fastest money-losing operation in Fleet Street's history. Cleverly (1976: 59–71).

31. There was some debate as to whether Odhams had priced the contract too low, or whether low productivity was to blame for continued losses. *IPC News* (October 1981: 5–8).

32. James Thomas reviewed studies on the history of the *Daily Mirror* to examine the newspaper's changing degree of political radicalism over time and during the King and Cudlipp era. Thomas (2003: 23).

33. For Hearst, journalism had meant 'to be the springboard for [his] political career', and his primary interest in publishing was to gain political influence. Leonard (1999: 468–9). Sisson argued that 'the whim of a proprietor unrelated to any discernible measure of economic performance' was an intrinsic factor of newspaper economics, and also linked this to the development of trade union attitudes within the industry where the 'recognition of this has bred attitudes of irresponsibility with little thought for the longer term'. Sisson (1975: 102).

34. King had a Machiavellian involvement in politics, and he personally believed that his campaigns delivered through the *Daily Mirror* had directly led to the collapse of governments led by Neville Chamberlain and Winston Churchill. King had imagined that, having aided Wilson's election, he might be in a position to develop a similar 'power behind the throne' relationship as his uncle Northcliffe had effected to Lloyd George. Howard (2004: 559). King and his editor Hugh Cudlipp not only set the editorial direction of the *Daily Mirror* to pursue Wilson's removal, but also spoke vociferously against Wilson in the media with 'irrational fury' (Swan, 1991: 666). This criticism ran to talk of a government-created 'financial crisis' and mismanagement of the gold reserves, which had potentially damaging economic consequences coming from King as he had been made a director of the Bank of England in 1965. The *Observer* wrote that 'the devious Mr King' had 'caused a financial panic...and had done this because he wants to overthrow the current administration'. The ensuing panic took the form of on a run on Sterling for which King was held responsible and thus obliged to tender his resignation to the Bank of England on 9 May 1968. *Observer*, cited in Cudlipp (1976: 338–9). King also worked to undermine Wilson, including a meeting with Lord Mountbatten in 1968 to suggest the peer could head an interim emergency administration upon Wilson's removal. Mountbatten declined to be involved with this scheme which was considered, in the words of his scientific adviser Sir Solly Zuckerman, to be rank treachery. Cudlipp (1976: 325–32); Thomas (2003: 112); Beavan (2004).

35. This was the reason given to shareholders in the 1968 company Annual Report for the end of King's 17 years as chairman. IPC Reports and Accounts (1968: 3).

36. The pretext to this ultimatum and a potential face-saving construction for King was that at the age of 67 King was older than the rule he himself had laid down that 60 would be the age of retirement within the Corporation. Cudlipp (1976: 351–3). As the successor to King, there was a question as to whether

Cudlipp was the man to oversee the tackling of the magazine group's problems. Cudlipp's self-assessment of his own managerial qualities was that his ability as chairman was very much second to his acknowledged prowess as a newspaper editor, and that his appointment was misguided. 'What was needed,' he subsequently stated, 'was a new mind uncommitted about past events and utterly unsentimental, a ruthless pruner, a cold diagnostician, a steely administrator'. Cudlipp (1976: 381). Howard maintains that when Cudlipp brokered the effective takeover of IPC into Reed International that it was 'with some relief...that he was no longer responsible for the central commercial strategy of the company, and could return to do what he did best—inspiring other journalists and lending his own flair to the business of producing mass-circulation newspapers'. Howard (2004). In Swan's assessment he was 'a poor businessman'. Swan (1991: 666).

37. Edward Pickering, the chairman of IPC in 1970, noted that although individual magazine titles such as *New Society* might reflect a particular political viewpoint, magazine groups overall did not act in the same way a newspaper group might. Rather they reflected a huge diversity of opinion. *IPC News* (September 1971: 11).

38. Cudlipp (1976: 381).

39. *Daily Telegraph* cited in Cudlipp (1976: 369).

40. On the creation of IPC, turnover from the newspapers was £41 million and magazines £41.2 million with profits of £4.4 million and £1.9 million respectively. Magazine profitability increased year on year to a high of £5 million in 1965 but then declined year on year to £3.3 million in 1968. Newspaper profits in 1968 were £5.1 million. Of more concern was falling advertising revenue in the magazine group, down from £22 million in 1967 to £21 million. By 1968 group turnover was £152 million. IPC Reports and Accounts (1968: 4–8).

41. The reorganization also created five other IPC Divisions: Newspapers; Trade and Technical; Books; New Enterprises Division; and IPC Printing for all non-newspaper printing including the Odhams print works. The New Enterprises Division was formed in July 1967 to develop operations in the growing markets of computerized information services and training and education. Within this Division International Data Highways was created from the merger of Intinco, Computaprint, Information Handling, and Computer Data to offer real time financial analysis services. IPC Reports and Accounts (1968); *IPC News* (July 1971: 7). The Magazines Group was chaired by Arnold Quick. IPC Reports and Accounts (1968: 3, 7).

42. The groups were managed as follows: Women's Weeklies, Les Carpenter; Women's Monthlies, Teddy Court; Young Magazines, Pat Lamburn; General Interest, Archie Kay; Practicals and Juveniles, Ron Phillips. Carpenter and Court would both go on to act as chairman and chief executive of IPC. They had both come to IPC from Newnes, as had other of the firm's senior managers including Ron Chilton (also later chairman and chief executive), Pat Lamburn, Gerry Wynveldt, Pat Barnes, Ralph Chappell, and John McLean. Low (1999: 49; 58).

43. *IPC News* (July 1971: 14).

44. Low (1999: 52–9). After the McKinsey reorganization, competition within the firm was discouraged. IPC Annual Report (1969: 2, 4).

45. In 1978 advertising still accounted for 50 per cent of revenues. Price Commission (1978b: 9, Table 3). The women's weeklies relied far more on advertising

revenue than was usual in the consumer market, featuring the highest level of all consumer-based titles. From this height the revenue from advertising began a steady decline relative to the importance of the cover price.

46. *Woman's Weekly* was moved in February 1967, and colour was introduced slowly to the titles so as not to alienate loyal readers. For *Woman's Weekly* the move to colour reversed falling advertising revenues and circulation, which jumped 146,000 to 1.6 million. Low (199: 55, 58); IPC Reports and Accounts (1968).

47. When Keith Altham was sent from *Fabulous*, which offered colour posters against the *NME*'s black and white newsprint, to help the title chase the growth teen market he found a conservative atmosphere with suits and ties, formal address, and 'an amateurish approach to journalism and management'. Long (2012: 28).

48. Arthur Seddon, who spent 38 years at IPC, thought that the strong editorial-led ethos of the Amalgamated Press prior to its takeover by the Mirror Group was lost under the latter's oppressive corporate structure. Low (1999: 60).

49. Low (1999: 60).

50. The IPC chairman Edward Pickering, interviewed in 1971, thought that the McKinsey structure had been too rigid and that it took power away from editors. *IPC News* (September 1971: 11). On his retirement in 1981 another chairman of IPC, Teddy Court, also acknowledged the problems of the McKinsey reorganization, saying that it led to a low ebb for the Magazines Group where they were not seen as a creative force and also had poor ratings from advertising agencies. *IPC News* (September 1981: 4).

51. *Shoot!* was approved and went on to become the world's biggest selling football magazine, from an initial print run of 350,000 in 1969 to a steady circulation of over 230,000. Low (1999: 56); *IPC News* (September 1973: 9). Even though McKinsey had attempted to put the consumer magazines within one group there was some overlap with the IPC Business Press, formed by the merger of the Trade and Technical Division with Kelly-Iliffe (Holdings) in 1967. *IPC News* (July 1971: 14).

52. Ron Phillips cited in Low (1999: 54).

53. *IPC News* (July 1973: 21).

54. Review of office location prior to the move to King's Reach Tower in 1976. *IPC News* (May 1973: 12–13).

55. During the nine years spanning 1966 and 1974, there were only 1,013 births and a total of 892 deaths of consumer magazines in Britain. Price Commission (1978b: 10).

56. During this period the circulation of newspaper colour supplements rose from one million to 3.7 million. Figures are from Henry (1986: Table 3.5.2.1).

57. In 1969 the sale of Orbit House to Abbey Life Property Fund for £5 million was the biggest ever single sale to a property bond fund. After the merger with Reed this policy was accelerated with the sale of Fleetway House and New Fleetway House to Gabriel Harrison's Amalgamated Investment and Property Company. In 1972 IPC formed a jointly owned development company with the Metropolitan Estates and Property Corporation to manage £31 million of IPC properties in a portfolio worth £36.4 million. Despite this sale IPC still owned 200 units directly within IPC Properties. *IPC News* (May 1973: 11).

58. IPC Annual Report (1970); *IPC News* (May 1973: 12–13); Swan (1991: 666). One consequence of the poor performance of the group in the late 1960s was the decision to sell the badly performing *Sun* newspaper, successor to the TUC-sponsored *Daily Herald*, to Rupert Murdoch's News Corporation in 1969. By transforming the title into a popular tabloid Murdoch increased the circulation from under one million to three million by 1973, although it was only in the 1980s that he changed its political orientation towards the Conservative Party. The success of the *Sun* would eventually hurt sales of the *Mirror* and Reed International. Heenan (1991b: 650); Swan (1991: 666).
59. Norton (1993: 245); Martin (1993: 20).
60. Paterson (1970); Low (1999: 55).
61. *IPC News* (July 1971: 12); Price Commission (1978b: 4).
62. *IPC News* (September 1971: 12).
63. Edward Pickering thought many editorial staff had been hoping that the Reed International reorganization would lead to the McKinsey changes being thrown out. *IPC News* (September 1971: 11).
64. Figures from *IPC News* (September 1971: 12).
65. The plant housed four M.A.N. and one M.G.D. web-offset presses and Photon 540 and 713 Lumitype photocomposition units and litho platemaking departments, employing 740 men. *IPC News* (December 1971: 11–14). The shift from letterpress to photocomposition was undertaken in 1966. IPC Annual Report (1966: 8).
66. The Cameron Report looked into the problems caused by the introduction of web-offset machines into the printing industry, and the problems arising from the introduction of other modern printing techniques and the arrangements which should be adopted within the industry for dealing with them. Ministry of Labour (1967).
67. The NUJ/SLADE industrial action ended on 28 June 1971, with an agreement including an increase in pay levels ranging from £220 to £265 per annum and a fifth week's holiday from the beginning of June 1972. *IPC News* (July 1971: 2, 24). Opened in 1964, the projected closure of Southwark Offset would have cost 750 jobs after annual losses of £1.2 million per annum. Discussions to reduce staffing levels were accepted in principle by the NGA and NATSOPA but initially rejected by SLADE and SOGAT. The *New Scientist* and *Practical Woodworking* were transferred to Index and Chapel River but were blacked by unions along with *Hairdressers Journal* and *Poultry World* from the Business Press, and the *New Scientist* lost four issues. Other titles printed at the plant were *Amateur Gardening, Hers, Homemaker, Jack and Jill, Practical Motorist*, and *Teddy Bear*. Following an agreement reached on 23 November 1971 all parties agreed to work to reduce losses to £250,000 by March 1973. *IPC News* (July 1971: 24; November 1971: 1–2; December 1971: 1).
68. The Profit Plan started with ten test stores which trialled different layouts and display methods to increase magazine sales, and results were disseminated with the CTNs. The Shop Fitting Scheme gave newsagents advice on modernizing their premises, assisted with financial loans, and suggested building contractors. *IPC News* (September 1971: 11–12).

69. *IPC News* (September 1972: 1).
70. *IPC News* (February 1972: 24).
71. Launched by former *Woman* publisher Roger Wood *Dolly* had a promotional budget of £20,000 and a print run of 20,000 and became the market-leading monthly. *IPC News* (July 1971: 15).
72. Cleverley (1976: 59–72); Martin (1993: 341–3).
73. Turner (1969: 1). The House of Lords judgement on *Rookes* v. *Barnard* had removed the immunity from civil action for strike losses granted by the Trade Disputes Act 1906. Royal Commission on Trade Unions and Employers' Associations (1968).
74. In the case of the newspaper and magazine industry the reluctance to change the status quo in terms of the role played by the trade unions was further reinforced, albeit incidentally, by the concerns of the first Royal Commission on the Press (1947–49) for continued political diversity in the sector. One of the objectives of the Commission had been to limit the extent of ownership concentration and restrict foreign influence in the press.
75. Rather than printing by direct transfer with the lithographic stone (or plate), in the offset process the printing is handled by transfer from an intermediate 'blanket' to the paper. This preserves the fragile chemical plate and also has the great advantage of allowing true original printing—while letterpress originals print a reverse image. Daly et al. (1997: 150–3).
76. By 1989 this had fallen to 55 per cent, while the proportion engaged in lithography had risen from 17 to 27 per cent during the same seventeen-year period. Gennard (1990: 181).
77. Corp (1969).
78. *IPC News* (March 1977: 12).
79. For magazine printing the technology also required the perfection of drying ovens and cooling rollers for web-based printing.
80. Royal Commission on the Press (1962: 195, Table 4).
81. Royal Commission on the Press (1962: 39).
82. Sir Edward Pickering retired as chairman of IPC magazines and Mirror Group Newspapers in 1977. Pickering's overall view of the potential of photocomposition was that in the UK it would be best suited to large-scale newspaper production processes and not magazine production. Pickering cited in Henry (1978: 41–5). The first European offset plant for newspaper production was set up in 1972 by the German publisher Axel Springer Verlag AG, with its domestic rival Grüner + Jahr being close behind. These plants pioneered more flexible working arrangements based on much-reduced staffing levels. According to Heenan, journalists' unions in the UK were effectively able to resist video-based composition, which retained the role of specialist print-makers in the activity. Heenan (1991a: 590).
83. Delafons (1965: 49).
84. Marjoribanks (2000: 61).
85. The NGA had its HQ in Bedford, geographically and symbolically between the Manchester-based TA and the London-based LTS. Sisson (1975: 129); Gennard (1990: 81–106).
86. Some of the notable inclusions were: the Amalgamated Society of Printers' Warehousemen (1900); National Union of Paper Mill Workers (1914); National

Union of Bookbinders and Machine Rulers (1921); the Platen Machine Minders' Society (1924); the Amalgamated Association of Pressmen and the London Society of Machine Rulers (1925); the Circulation Publishing Association (1931); the Amalgamated Society of Papermakers (1937); the Society of Women Employed in the Printing and Bookbinding Trade (Manchester) (1943); the Original Society of Papermakers (1948); the Card Edge Gilders (1961); the Monotype Casters and Typefounders' Society and the Paper Mould and Dandy Roll Makers' Society (1962); and the Pattern Card Makers' Society (1963).

87. SOGAT split again in 1972, the former NUPBW becoming SOGAT 1975 (with the inclusion of the Scottish Graphical Association), while the former NATSOPA became the National Society of Operative Printers, Graphical and Media. The unions were to later rejoin as SOGAT 1982.

88. Sisson (1975: 183).

89. Corp (1969).

90. A Joint Board for the National Newspaper Industry in 1964 and a National Newspaper Steering Group in 1970 had been established to argue for inclusive collective negotiations but ultimately all attempts at change failed and bargaining remained fragmented in the face of weak management will. Sisson (1975: 102–4, 140, 174).

91. Royal Commission on the Press (1962: 42).

92. At Southwark Offset for example, in the machine managers dispute of August 1969, NGA machine managers responsible for printing the *Daily Mirror* claimed that their differential with NATSOPA brake hands had been disturbed. The NGA sought to maintain a capped rate of pay between the brake hands and NGA machine managers at 87.5 per cent. As the NGA had been slow to organize machine rotary press workers at Southwark Offset some had joined NATSOPA and were later denied job opportunities on presses they were more qualified to operate than NGA members, who had only been trained to use flatbed letterpress machines. NATSOPA members could never transfer to become NGA machine managers. The industrial action took the form of a three-week go-slow during which the *Daily Mirror* lost half a million copies. Sisson (1975: 123, Appendix 175–6).

93. According to Sisson, these crises in newspaper production came about as a result of both continually fluctuating demand for the product and proprietor decisions that often did not reflect economic fundamentals, although they were tempered by the overriding imperative on behalf of the publishers to keep newspapers in print at any cost. Sisson (1975: 101–2).

94. Price Commission (1978b: 16).

95. Odhams printed many titles including *Ideal Home, Disneyland Magazine, Popular Gardening, Goal*, and *Woman's Weekly*. To produce the printing cylinders for its high speed photogravure presses it owned the only two Helioklischograph engraving machines in the UK. The most significant of the other firms for the magazine group were Southwark Offset, Chapel River Press (established in 1932, about 40 per cent of its business was for magazines using its non-heatset web-offset press, employing 540 people), Fleetway Gravesend (a print works founded before 1900 using two rotary Crabtrees, a Strachan and Henshaw rubber plate press, and 11

sheet-fed offset litho presses, employing 464 people and printing titles such as *Homes & Gardens*), Noakes Bros. (a typesetting and process engraving firm capable of handling foundry work and film-setting, the largest supplier of blocks to the Magazine Division), James Cond (founded in 1840 which printed titles including *Woman*, and *Bride and Home* on Heidelberg and Miehle hot metal letterpresses and a litho plant using two four-colour Roland Ultras, and employing 200 people), and Contract Composing (a hot metal classified ad setting firm, employing 95 people). *IPC News* (December 1971: 11–14).

96. *IPC News* (August 1973: 1; September 1973: 1; January 1974: 6; February 1974: 1).
97. IPC Report and Accounts (1974: 1, 3).
98. The top three women's weeklies were back on the shelves on 17 August 1974. *IPC News* (August 1974: 1).
99. 174 jobs were lost with the closure of Noakes Bros. *IPC News* (March 1974: 1).
100. Price Commission (1978b: 11).
101. Jean Twiddy was the Publisher for the Magazine Division created in 1968 and had previously been editor of *Woman and Home* and *Woman's Weekly*, and she also launched *Woman's Realm*. *IPC News* (May 1972: 1 and centre pages feature, 6pp.).
102. *IPC News* (December 1972: 1).
103. Gough-Yates (2003: 2).
104. *IPC News* (February 1973: 1).
105. Out of 40 pages, 32 were produced in colour, but the associated printing costs necessitated a cover price that was too high for the magazine ultimately to be successful in the teenage market. *IPC News* (June 1973: 2).
106. The 'Annan Report' was published in 1978. Cf. Briggs (1984: 308).
107. Hugh Cudlipp retired on 31 December 1973. IPC Report and Accounts (1974: 3); *IPC News* (July 1973: 1, 12–13).
108. IPC Report and Accounts (1974: 3).
109. *IPC News* (July 1973: 12–14).
110. *IPC News* (July 1973: 8; September 1973: 18).
111. British newsprint production had fallen 40 per cent in the last ten years which exacerbated the situation. *IPC News* (September 1973: 1, 18).
112. Price Commission (1978a: 4).
113. *IPC News* (April 1974: 1); Price Commission (1978b: 17).
114. By means of a hostile takeover in 1980, Robert Maxwell had acquired a controlling interest in the near-bankrupt British Printing Corporation, which had been incorporated in 1964 as the merger of Purnell & Sons Ltd. with Hazell Sun Ltd. Maxwell then changed its name the British Printing and Communication Corporation (BPCC) in March 1982, and later in 1987 to the Maxwell Communication Corporation (MCC). Between 1981 and 1983 Maxwell set about addressing the twin problems of over-manning and low productivity at the plants and attempted to modernize printing practices at the BPCC and improve the fortunes of the firm. Despite gaining the general support of unions, a series of strikes at the Park Royal printing works between 1981 and 1983 led to its closure in November 1983, with production moved to East Kilbride and Leeds. Subsequent corporate expansion by Maxwell included the acquisition of the Mirror Group of newspapers, discussed later in this chapter, and the academic book publisher

Macmillan. The empire did not endure, however. Maxwell had already been criticized by the Board of Trade in July 1971 when a report critical of accounting practices at his Pergamon Press summarized that he was 'not…a person who can be relied on to exercise proper stewardship of a publicly quoted company'. This proved to be prophetic, as after his death in November 1991 it was revealed that Maxwell had defrauded the Mirror's pension scheme to an amount estimated as high as US$1.4 billion. Thomas and Turner (2001: Summary); Hawkins (1993: 311–14); Martin (2003: 404–10).

115. *IPC News* (March 1976: 1, 13). The defeat of the merger was followed by 200 redundancies for print workers. Price Commission (1978b: 17).

116. *IPC News* (December 1974: 1); Price Commission (1978b: 5).

117. *IPC News* (January 1976: 8–9). By early 1977 48 of IPC's 71 titles had moved to web-offset with only 9 still printed by letterpress. *IPC News* (March 1977: 1).

118. Review of ABC data in *IPC News* (September 1975: 2).

119. *Woman's Realm* was refreshed to appeal to younger housewives. *IPC News* (September 1975: 3). *Titbits* was another title designated for a makeover after it was found to have lost touch with a younger, less shockable generation. *IPC News* (April 1974: 7). This was an event which began that pioneering magazine's steady decline into a soft-porn title and in 1979 the magazine was censured by IPC executives for having too high a degree of sexually explicit advertising, and revamped through the incorporation of *Reveille*. *IPC News* (December 1979: 17). Although this led to a temporary upswing in circulation, the decline in both sales and content continued as it drifted once again further towards the top shelf.

120. *IPC News* (January 1977: 1).

121. The magazine was later brought under BBC Enterprises' control when it was re-launched as *Wildlife* in 1983. Riley (1993: 146–8).

122. Price Commission (1978b: 29).

123. Braithwaite (1995: 106).

124. The central London stores were bought for £500,000 from NABTS Ltd. and renamed Tower Newsagents. *IPC News* (November 1973: 1); IPC Report and Accounts (1974: 3). IPC's main attempt to shore up the retail sector, however, continued to be through initiatives such as the ongoing Retail Newsagent Profit Plan. *IPC News* (November 1975: 10).

125. The first of these 12,000 square foot stores employing a staff of 50 was opened in Bradford in1960, followed by stores in Brighton and Stockport (1968) and Nottingham (1969). Wilson (1985: 397, 401).

126. Figures are derived from Henry (1986: 91, Table 3.5.1).

127. Ferguson (1983: 154–7).

128. Morris, an ordained Anglican priest and honorary chaplain at St Bride's Fleet Street from 1952 to 1983 is often best remembered as being, with Frank Hampson, the creator of the *Eagle* comic at Hulton Press where he had been was managing editor until the takeover by Odhams in 1959. The same year he left Hulton to join the National Magazine Company as editorial director, and became managing director and editor-in-chief in 1964. Varah (2004).

129. The title had been launched as *Small Car & Mini Owner* in 1962 by Jack Wildbore's Interspan before being renamed *Car* in 1965. Undercapitalized and barely making a profit, Wildbore sold the title and it soon after passed into the

hands of Marcus Morris at the National Magazine Company. The magazine was always at odds with the holdings of Natmags' other properties, and in 1974 the company sold it for £5,000 to FF Publishing, set up as a management buy-out by the title's advertising manager Andrew Frankl and art director Roger Ames. The title survived, precariously at times but gaining a loyal readership, until FF Publishing eventually sold the title to Murdoch Magazines in 1989 for £8 million. Gavin Green 'The Story of Car magazine'. Available at: <http://www.carmagazine. co.uk>, accessed 8 April 2011.

130. Winship (1987: 112).
131. The runaway success of the title created problems for the company, as initial advertising rates were set based on an estimated circulation of 150,000. With sales four times that level the company raised its advertising rates but fell foul of the Prices and Incomes Board under minister Geoffrey Howe, eventually losing a battle to retain the money in the High Court. See: <http://www.hearst.co.uk/ magazines/History.html>.
132. *IPC News* (July 1981: 12–13).
133. Barrell and Braithwaite (1988: 50); Norton (1993: 244–7).
134. Magazine publishers were wary of supermarkets, fearing that they did not understand how to sell the magazines, that they would push for sale-or-return rather than firm sale, that they would 'cream off' only the major top-selling titles, and even push for discounted sales over cover prices. Some branches of ASDA did start selling a slightly wider range of magazine titles from the mid-1970s but this had little impact on the industry. *IPC News* (February/March 1986: 8–9).
135. *IPC News* (March 1977: 11).
136. Price Commission (1978b: 1–4).
137. Low (1999: 62).
138. White (1977: 92).
139. *IPC News* (October 1977: 1).
140. The exact figures were 1.97 million in 1970 and 1.58 million in 1980. BRAD data.
141. This also included radical publications, such as the independently published *Spare Rib*, which provided a feminist counterpoint to the mainstream women's press.
142. The most serious of the three charges laid was 'conspiracy to deprave and corrupt the Morals of the Young of the Realm', as the title had included the publication of indecent drawings submitted allegedly by children, but this charge was dismissed. The trial was Britain's longest conspiracy trial to date of writing.
143. 'The Origins of Dennis Publishing'. Available at <http://www.dennis.co.uk/ about-us/the-origins-of-dennis-publishing>.
144. Northern & Shell would find notoriety and success in 1983 when it obtained a licence to print the UK edition of *Penthouse*. Available at: <http://www.northernandshell.com/about/index.php>.
145. Robin Miller had joined EMAP in 1965 as a motorcycle reporter before being appointed as the editor of *Motor Cycle News*, and David Arculus joined in 1972 as corporate planner. Miller would later become Sir Robin Miller and EMAP CEO. Hoover's Online. Available at: <http://hoovers.com/industry/description/0,3055,6261,00.htm>, accessed 29 April 2004.
146. Cohen (2001: 165).
147. EMAP Annual Report and Accounts (1989: 16).

148. In a review of the last few years of IPC, chief executive Ron Chilton estimated the costs of launching a small title had risen from around £100,000 in 1980 to £500,000 in 1985. *IPC News* (September 1985: 6–8).
149. Mercer (1993: 56–7).
150. Mort (1996: 23).
151. Mercer (1993: 56–61).
152. For a detailed review of Brody's background and design influence, see Mort (1996: 29–33).
153. Richard Cook, 'Fall of the house of Wagadon. The publishers of both *the Face* and *Arena* seem to have lost their touch', *The Independent*, 11 August 1998. Available at: <http://www.independent.co.uk/arts-entertainment/media-fall-of-the-house-of-wagadon-1170999.html>.

CHAPTER 7

1. Price Commission (1978b: 11).
2. The NUJ were successful in securing a 19 per cent pay rise and better maternity conditions. *IPC News* (July 1980: 16).
3. *IPC News* (June 1980: 1–2.) The full cost of the strikes was later estimated to be £12 million. *IPC News* (March 1981: 5).
4. This had represented Odhams' least profitable contract, and on 1 November 1979 Odhams had informed the *Sunday Telegraph* that they would require a significant price increase to continue to print the title. Within IPC there was dispute as to whether the contract had been under-priced, but the truth was that the print works' over-manning was simply uncompetitive. IPC's management, for example, considered that they needed to price a contract at £180,000 to turn a profit whereas European firms were tendering for the same jobs from as low as £103,550. *IPC News* (October 1981: 5–8).
5. The *TV Times* contract was split between five printers, with the bulk being won by IPC (Watford)'s arch rivals Sun Printers. *IPC News* (June 1980: 3; July 1980: 2).
6. Although deferring from answering the charge of acquiescing to union demands, Odhams' chief executive Ian Thomas (from 1 May 1980) argued that, while there had been a case in November 1980 to reduce the number of printing staff by 500, the company considered that there were strategic benefits in retaining their existing pool of employees because it allowed Odhams the potential to attract new business. He also cited a concern for employees' welfare and pointed to the fact that the economic recession provoked by the policies of the Thatcher government had been deeper than expected. *IPC News* (October 1981: 6).
7. *IPC News* (June 1980: 3, 15).
8. *IPC News* (January 1981:1, 11; June 1981: 1).
9. Fleetway's capacity was mainly engaged in printing covers for *Woman and Home, Woman's Journal, 19, Honey*, and *Homes & Gardens*. Its premises were far too large for this activity and they were reduced in size by half. At the same time the plant's equipment was upgraded, with an £880,000 modern five-unit narrow-width Harris M90 press colour web-offset press installed. Following the introduction

of the new press five of its thirteen covers moved to using web rather than sheet feed, with a plan to upgrade the remainder. The rotary letterpress machines, used for the printing of comics, were phased out with the loss of 36 jobs. By February 1982 these workforce reductions had lowered staff numbers to 259. *IPC News* (February 1981: 2; November 1982: 11; January/February 1982: 11–12).

10. *IPC News* (June 1981: 1; October 1981: 5–8).

11. It was felt of course that this should have happened much earlier. *IPC News* (October 1981: 6).

12. *IPC News* (March 1981: 1, 4–5). This was especially true in the most lucrative areas of printing such as mail-order catalogues. As a trend this had been ongoing for some time. As early as 1971 European print works were winning £10 million of British business while the UK's print-generated exports amounted to only £4.7 million. Around 40 per cent of overseas contracts went to Germany, including 75 per cent of travel brochure printing and 40 per cent of the £7 million mail-order catalogue market. *IPC News* (December 1971: 11–12).

13. *IPC News* (November 1981: 1).

14. *IPC News* (January/February 1982: 10–12).

15. *IPC News* (June 1981: 2).

16. *IPC News* (October 1981: 5–8).

17. *IPC News* (June 1982: 5; July/August 1982: 1).

18. The Consumer Publishing Group was organized into four divisions: the Women's Magazine Group (Managing Director John Mellon); Specialist, Educational and Leisure Group (Managing Director David Beattie); Sales and Distribution (Managing Director Gerry Wynveldt); Divisional Services (Managing Director John McClean). *IPC News* (July/August 1982: 1; November 1982: 8–9).

19. See Chapter 6 for more detail on this report. White (1977: 92).

20. Simpson (1984: 10–11).

21. *Tit-Bits* was sold to Associated Newspapers. *Hi-Fi Today, Hers, Tammy*, and *True* were the other closures following the six-week dispute which claimed 39 jobs. Altogether the strike had led to the loss of 68 magazine issues and was finally ended in July 1984. *IPC News* (July/August 1984: 1).

22. Swan (1991: 667).

23. Mirror Newspapers Ltd. was acquired by the Trinity Group in 1999, forming a new company named Trinity Mirror plc. The Trinity Group dated back to the longest-surviving English language newspaper, the Belfast *News Letter* founded in 1737. Hawkins (1993: 311–14); Thomas and Turner (2001); Martin (2003: 404–10).

24. As a condition of the sale Reed International made an interest-free loan of £7.5 million to Odhams repayable in 1985. *IPC News* (December 1982: 1).

25. Odhams printed *Woman, Woman's Realm, Woman and Home*, as well as *Farmer's Weekly*. The closure led to the loss of 1,400 jobs. *IPC News* (January 1983: 12).

26. Simpson (1984: 10–11). Chapel River was sold to McCorquodale for £1.4 million, who broke it into Magazine Typesetters and Andover Repro, and the Fleetway plant was simply closed down. *IPC News* (July/August 1984: 2–4; November 1984: 3). IPC retained the Fleetway Publications name for its comics, which were subsequently sold to Robert Maxwell's Pergamon Press in 1987.

27. Simpson (1984: 10–11).
28. *IPC News* (January 1983: 12).
29. *IPC News* (May/June 1985: 6).
30. For example, the boys' football magazine title *Shoot!* had been launched using an approved web-offset print contractor in Peterborough. *IPC News* (September 1973: 9).
31. Gennard and Dunn (1983: 17).
32. More (1989: 306).
33. Under the 1982 Act closed shops were only lawful if supported by 80 per cent of the workers affected or 85 per cent of those voting. Barlow (1997: Chapter 4).
34. In 1977–8, for example, the *Times*, owned by Thomson, had purchased a new high technology composing room costing £3 million which allowed single-entry keying without NGA agreement. The company insisted that the NGA 'surrender control of the original keystroke' (Gennard 1990: 479) but after twelve months of industrial action the unions prevailed, and Thomson was forced to put the *Times* up for sale following substantial losses (Marjoribanks, 2000: 66). This pattern of union success was ultimately broken by the new Acts. In 1983, even before the end of the Messenger dispute or the start of the News International dispute, Brenda Dean, the general secretary of SOGAT, was able to state in relation to the national and regional press that, 'the traumatic effects of a *combination* of destructive, negative Government policies together with new technologies is only too apparent. This combination has cost this union over 40,000 jobs in the last five years' (our emphasis). Cited in Marjoribanks (2000: 63).
35. Gennard (1984: 8).
36. This dispute is also often referred to as the Messenger Newspaper Group dispute or the 'Warrington dispute'. Barlow (2008: 175).
37. Franklin and Murphy (1991: 11).
38. On 9 December the NGA was fined for contempt of court for continuing with illegal strike action, leaving its legal liabilities at a total of £675,000 plus legal costs and damages owed to the Messenger Group. Barlow (1997: 178).
39. Franklin and Murphy (1991: 11). In addition, a detailed review of the changes to the nature of print industrial relations can be further explored by reference to Gennard (1984, 1987) and Gall (2006).
40. Gennard and Bain (1995); Barlow (1997: 180–2). That the technology itself was not the key issue was noted by NGA general secretary Tony Dubbins when he said of the machinery purchased for use at Wapping by News International that 'some of the equipment at the so called "hi-tec" plant is far from new. For example, the printing presses are over fifteen years old' (Dubbins, 1986: 4). This of course only served to highlight the retrograde state of the technology employed in British printing, but the unions were correct to highlight that they had been willing to adopt new technologies. Management, however, did not want the unions to continue to preserve their working arrangements, pay, and conditions alongside the new technologies.
41. Also the Amalgamated Union of Engineering Workers to a small extent in printing. The EETPU was willing to replace workforces and to sign single-union no-strike agreements with employers. This approach led to the expulsion of

the EETPU from the Trades Union Congress (TUC) in 1988. Marjoribanks (2000: 64–5).

42. To illustrate how this was possible, within IPC the Mirror Group had fully computerized photocomposition as early as 1978 after a £2.8 million investment, but the NGA has been able to maintain complete control over production processes, retaining the inefficient process of double-keying. From this point forward what had been the skilled process of letter-setting could be undertaken by non-print workers. Gennard (1990: 541–2); Fraser (1999).

43. Murdoch entered negotiations with the unions while simultaneously planning to exclude them from his operations, and had developed a long-term stratagem to dismiss his printing workers and to reduce manning levels from 6,000 to a few hundred in number. A new direct entry print plant was built at Wapping in East London, notionally for a new newspaper, the *Post*, and the workers recruited for this plant were from the EETPU, without whose cooperation News International would not have been able to operate the printing plant (Gennard, 1990: 509). By provoking a strike, Murdoch's existing workforce was manoeuvred into a position where he could use the 1982 Act to present the union's action as a 'trade dispute' which held strikers to be in breach of contract, an act for which they could be summarily dismissed. The strike was provoked by offering the workforce at Wapping a four-point agreement, rejecting union demands to transfer existing working practices, terms, and conditions from the existing Gray's Inn Road and Bouverie Street presses to the Wapping printing plant. The four non-negotiable points that News International put to the NGA '82, SOGAT '82, the NUJ, AUEW, and the EETPU were: that all agreements would be binding on individuals and unions; that there would be no industrial action under any circumstances; that closed-shop conditions would be outlawed; and the complete unfettered right of management to manage the workforce. These terms were effectively impossible for the NGA to approve. Murdoch also bypassed SOGAT by using his TNT distribution company to distribute his newspapers. Barlow (1997: 181–3).

44. Royal Commission on the Press (1962: 31, 42).

45. Frost (2003: 8–9).

46. NGA '82 (1984) available in PPA archive file 13/2.

47. Initially publishing the *St Ives Echo* before moving into contract printing, the company moved into short-run contract colour printing of an acceptable quality by combining an A4 Gestetner 211 with Townsend T-51 colour print-head, creating a low-cost print shop. 'Fine art from an A4 Press', *Lithoweek*, 14 November 1984, pp. 14–15.

48. 'St Ives plc': see <http://www.referenceforbusiness.com/history2/48/St-Ives-plc.html>; St Ives plc Annual Report and Accounts, 1993.

49. The book was aimed at the North American market and assumed a typical cost saving of around US$1,200 to use photocomposition rather than hot metal paste-up for a 64-page magazine, based on comparative costs of US$20 and US$50 per page. The overall cost of a Compugraphic Computwriter IV typesetter, including eight film strips and a six-month supply of processing chemicals was US$13,000, with the disk-enabled Edit Writer 7500 retailing for US$20,000. Compaine (1982: 45–7).

50. Bannard (1990: 53).
51. Eccles (1984: 3).
52. 'Print on demand: the way ahead' in the 'Electronic Printing Supplement', *Lithoweek*, 30 May 1984, pp. 5–7.
53. Barlow (1997: 174).
54. O'Toole (1985: 10–11).
55. The three systems were the Crossfield Studio 800, the Hell Chromacom and the Scitex Response/Vista. In 1985 there were only 20 installations of these machines in the UK. In a response to the difficulties involved in learning to operate these machines the Graphic Reproduction Federation (formerly the Advertisement Typesetting and Foundry Employers Federation until 1977 (National Library record CL 4/20)) formed a new division named the Electronic Page Compositors User Group to develop and share knowledge. Eccles (1984: 2–22).
56. The page printing speed difference between a Xerox 8700 and 2700 was considerable, with the former printing 120 pages per minute compared to around 12 copies per minute.
57. The result of which was that even people 'on the street' were 'coming to accept and even expect on-demand printing'. 'Print on demand: the way ahead' in the 'Electronic Printing Supplement', *Lithoweek*, 30 May 1984, pp. 5–7.
58. Eccles (1984: 3).
59. *Lithoweek*, 29 February 1984, p. 6.
60. NGA '82 (1984: 2.27).
61. Dubbins (1983: 8).
62. 'Breakthrough project for survival', Newspaper Society Report Paper, PPA Archive File No. 13/1–3 & 5.
63. Frost (2003: 9).
64. Marjoribanks (2000: 65–6).
65. The Newspaper Society, which had been formed in 1836 to represent the interests of local newspapers and the regional press, was concerned that there was a crisis in the local press which could be remedied by adopting new technologies and changing working practices. Representing their workers in the provincial newspaper press the NGA launched 'Project Seethrough' as a counterpoint to question the basis of these assumptions. Barlow (1997: 174–5).
66. Marjoribanks (2000: 63).
67. Winsbury (1983: 6).
68. Marjoribanks (2000: 121) provides quotes from Peter Wilby, a News International journalist who initially supported the print unions before accepting the Wapping conditions, who said that although he admired the print unions' power to protect their workers, 'Like most journalists on the Street, I dislike the print unions.' There was also resentment between the skilled NGA and the 'unskilled' SOGAT, with new technologies generally favouring SOGAT workers who were able to take over functions previously held by NGA members, with the result that in 1988 the NGA lodged a formal complaint against SOGAT with the TUC's Disputes Principles and Procedures committee. Gennard and Bain (1995: 27, 212–13).

69. 'NGA reveals keystroke plans', *Printing World*, 26 September 1984, pp. 1–2, PPA Archive File 13/4/4.
70. Royal Commission on the Press (1962: 31).
71. Bannard (1990: 53).
72. Simpson (1984: 10–11).
73. BRAD (1989: iii). By 1989 *Mizz* was selling 190,771 copies compared to *Just Seventeen* sales of 300,107. *Media Week*, 6 January 1989, p. 43. Voluntary redundancies reported in *IPC News* (February/March 1986: 2).
74. Gough-Yates (2003: 49).
75. Simpson (1984: 10–11). *Elle* was printed by Hachette Filipacchi Medias S.A. (HF), a French company whose Filipacchi arm had been formed in 1957 by Henri Filipacchi, son of a prominent publisher. The first title was *Jazz* magazine in 1954 and the firm remained a minor player until the acquisition of one million-plus circulation *Paris-Match* (originally launched in 1949) in 1976. In 1980 the firm merged with Hachette, itself dating back to a bookstore and news-stand company formed in 1826, and by 1900 Hachette was a major publisher including niche magazines. In 1984 HF started an aggressive international expansion and media diversification, buying the Seymour Press and Gordon and Gotch in the UK and also acquiring the US-based Diamondis group. In 1987 Murdoch Magazines also launched another Hachette title in the UK, *Sky* (not to be confused with News International's *Sky* satellite TV listing magazine) which was a youth title designed to appeal to both sexes. Kronlund (1991: 619); Cohen (1998: 265–7).
76. Bertelsmann was Europe's largest media group, originally dating from 1835. The company's rise to media behemoth was achieved mainly after the firm created a subscription book club in 1950. The company moved strongly into magazines when it acquired a 74.9 per cent controlling interest in the Hamburg-based Grüner + Jahr in 1976. At the time of entry into the British market the group's activities included the Ariola-RCA music company, Sonopress which manufactured recording media, and television and film production. Stafford and Purkis (1989: 165–7); Bavendamm (1996: 51–5).
77. This figure was not an ABC assured figure. BRAD (April 1989: vol. 6(4), ii).
78. Rawsthorn (1988: 16).
79. Heinrich Bauer Publishing was a wholly owned UK subsidiary of the Hamburg-based Bauer Publishing Group. Sun (1993: 42–4).
80. BRAD (April 1989: vol. 6(4), iii).
81. In addition to this print works the company operated several other smaller print works. In 1990 Bauer significantly expanded its production facilities by replacing its older printing works with newer and larger establishments. Bauer was a family-owned firm formed in 1875 when Louis Bauer opened a print shop before later moving into newspaper and magazine publishing. In 1975 the firm launched the successful women's weekly *Tina*, which served as a template for *Bella* in the UK market. In 1981 the company formed Heinrich Bauer North America and launched a woman's weekly sold through supermarkets called, prophetically for IPC, *Woman's World*. At the same time as expanding into the UK the company also expanded into France (Editions Bauer France), and licensed the publishing of the West German edition of *Esquire*. Sun (1993: 42–4).
82. BRAD (April 1989: vol. 6(4), iv).

83. With sales of *Bella* included, the sector grew by 9 per cent. Rawsthorn (1988: 16).
84. Total circulation was 931,295. BRAD data.
85. BRAD (April 1989: vol. 6(4), iv).
86. 'Hello! World', *Magazine World*, no. 65, 2010, pp. 22–3.
87. *IPC News* (August/September 1988: 1; May 1989: 1).
88. *IPC News* (February 1988: 6–7).
89. Office of Fair Trading (2008b: 60).
90. EMAP had already identified opportunities to grow at IPC's expense using SOR, and had already been offering some titles on this basis, but this was unusual in the UK market before the entry of the German firms.
91. *IPC News* (June 1992: 1).
92. Both John Menzies and W.H. Smith invested in automated computer systems to handle SOR returns. John Menzies (GB) Ltd., 'Proposal for an Automated Certified Returns System' (1986); W.H. Smith, 'Certified Audit Returns System: What the W.H. Smith System Will Deliver' (1987), both available in PPA Archive File No. 13/5.
93. *IPC News* (May 1989: 15).
94. In 1984 54 per cent of group revenue was from magazines. Turnover had grown from £46.1 million in 1980 to £95.6 million in 1984. EMAP Report and Accounts (1984/5: Centre page charts). Magazine sales data from EMAP Report and Accounts (1986: 4).
95. The titles were: *Motor Cycle News; Classic Motor Cycles; Bike, Performance Bikes; Classic Bike; Dirt Bike Rider; Classic Mechanics; Classic Racer;* and *Motor Cycle Dealer.*
96. Other teen titles were accounted for by: IPC (*Mizz, 19, Number One, Girl,* and *My Guy*); DC Thomson (*Jackie* and *Blue Jeans*); and the National Magazine Company (*Company*). *Just Seventeen* had a circulation of 306,207 against direct competitors *Jackie* (192,976), *Mizz* (190,523), *19* (160,030), and *My Guy* (82,323). ABC figures derived from BRAD 1988.
97. The impetus for *Q* magazine came from former *Just Seventeen* editor David Hepworth. Clearly EMAP had learned from its mistake of not supporting Nick Logan's concept for *the Face*. EMAP Report and Accounts (1988: 3).
98. Figures derived from EMAP Report and Accounts (1984/5).
99. 'EMAP Year'. Loose publication included in the EMAP Report and Accounts (1984/5).
100. Acquisitions were made from cash and shares and loans, and profits rose from £10.2 million to £15 million. Acquisitions included Scarborough and District Newspapers, Bedford Country Press, Coachmart, and the High Technology and Computers in Education Exhibition. EMAP Report and Accounts (1987: 1, 4–5).
101. Haulage company TNT were used for distribution. EMAP Report and Accounts (1989: 14).
102. Murdoch Magazines sold their titles to EMAP in 1991 and their share of the Hachette joint-venture properties also to EMAP in 1993. This episode is covered in more detail in Chapter 8. EMAP Report and Accounts (1993: 2.); Wells and Hakanen (1996: 126).

103. The US *Computer Shopper* had been launched in 1979. Felix Dennis quoted in 'The Origins of Dennis Publishing'. Available at: <http://www.dennis.co.uk/about-us/the-origins-of-dennis-publishing>.

104. Mac Warehouse was founded by Felix Dennis, Peter Godfrey, and Robert Bartner. In 2005 sales of the company, now trading as Micro Warehouse, were US$1.31 billion. Micro Warehouse Inc. History. Available at: <http://www.fundinguniverse.com/company-histories/micro-warehouse-inc-history>. Philip Dougherty, 'Ziff Buys MacUser', *New York Times*, 6 January 1987.

105. Magill, a publisher based in the Republic of Ireland, had filed a complaint with the European Commission feeling that its own TV listings guide was subject to unfair competition from the imported *Radio Times* and *TV Times*. The duopoly was found to contravene Article 86 of the European Community rules on competition. *Media Week*, 6 January 1989.

106. News Corporation's *TV Guide* only reported a summary of the territorial television services at first, and was redeveloped as a satellite listings title.

107. This target was achieved in only four years. Brown (1994: 52); Bloomfield (2008: 49).

108. Currie (2001: 187).

109. Christopher Curry, one of Redwood's three founders, had also been a founder of Acorn Computers, which made the BBC micro. Michael Potter (former publisher of Haymarket's advertising trade weekly *Campaign*) and Christopher Ward (a former editor of the *Daily Express* newspaper) were the other two founders.

110. <http://www.redwoodgroup.net>, 'about us'. McKay (2000: 188) credits Redwood with having started the customer magazine sector.

111. John Thomas' career included senior positions in the periodicals industry, including director of Reed Business Press (1970–86), deputy managing director of the IPC Science and Technology Press Ltd. (1977–7), publishing director of the IPC Business Press Ltd. (1978–84), director of magazines (1986–93), and managing director (1993–4) BBC Enterprises Ltd. (later Worldwide BBC Ltd.), chairman of Redwood Publishing Ltd. (1986–93), BBC Frontline Ltd., and director of the Periodical Publishers Association. Debrett's (no date). Peter Phippen took over as director of magazines from Thomas. Nick Brett's role initially was to oversee the editorial direction of the magazines, later becoming editorial director of BBC Magazines in 1991, deputy managing director of BBC Magazines in 1991, and group editorial director for BBC Magazines in London, Bristol, and Mumbai in 2006. Available at: <http://blogs.bbcworldwide.com/author/nickbrettww>.

112. Unpublished BBC report on magazine launches kindly provided by Nick Brett at BBC Magazines.

113. The title was originally printed as a quarterly. Considering the launch of *GQ* in the UK Rawsthorn (1988: 16) noted that 'The British male—so conventional wisdom has it—is just too traditional to buy a general interest magazine' and that 'the annals of the magazine markets are littered with the corpses of men's magazines'. Mort argues that this was the birth of the general interest magazines aimed at a new type of male consumer. Mort (1996: 24). Circulation figures from BRAD.

114. Dylan Jones, 'How i-D has stayed in style', *The Guardian*, 10 May 2004.
115. Ultimately the success of *Arena* led to Condé Nast launching a British version of their US men's style title, *GQ*, in 1989. Condé Nast's US-based Advance Publications Group, privately owned by the Newhouse family, made numerous media acquisitions around this time, mainly in the USA, including US$200 million for the *New Yorker* in 1983, *Gentleman's Quarterly*, and *Citibank Signature*, which they renamed *Condé Nast Traveller* under the direction of Condé Nast Publications Inc. President Bernard Leser, who had launched a new German *Vogue* in 1978, was President of Condé Nast Publications Inc. from 1987 to 1994. Lindauer (1991: 584).
116. The titles were *Wireless, Motorist, Everyday Electronics, Proteus, BMX Weekly, Freestyle BMX, Riding, One Two, Mother, Successful Slimming, Electronics,* and *Practical Householder. IPC News* (January 1986: 3).
117. The launch of *LM* in the teen market was not a success and the title only lasted four issues. *FEAR* for horror videos was more successful, and was a development of an existing fanzine. The company was liquidated in 1992. Extract from the liquidator's report, Newsfield Publications Ltd. Available at: <http://crashonline.org.uk/99/newsfield.htm>.
118. Anderson left Newsfield as he did not want to relocate to their new offices. 'History:Zzap!64'. Available at: <http://wwwzzap64.co.uk/zzaphistoryhtml>.
119. *Amstrad Action's* first print run was 40,000 copies, but only 16,000 actually sold. See: <http://wwwfutureplc.com/about/history>. Although Future had the highest sales, the sector was contested by many firms. According to BRAD in 1984 the leading consumer market publishers were IPC (2 titles), EMAP (7), and primarily business-focused VNU (4) and Argus (12). By 1989 the figures were EMAP (12), IPC (10), Dennis (5), and Future (4). BRAD July–December 1984; July–December 1989.
120. The sale of *Ace*, originally titled *Advance Computer Entertainment*, enabled Future to split *ST Amiga Format* into two separate magazines, *ST Format* and *Amiga Format*, which both performed better in sales than *Ace*. The price paid by EMAP for *Ace* was cited from Ruth Nicholas, 'Profile: Chris Anderson: Media with passion', *The Independent*, 11 July 1999. Available at: <http://www.independent.co.uk/news/business/profile-chris-anderson-media-with-passion-1105628.html>.
121. IPC's purchase of Argus Press Ltd. for £30 million in 1989, which included a mix of newspapers and Argus Specialist Publications, added the firm's computer titles to IPC's portfolio, but it was not enough to slow Future's leadership in the sector. The company, which had been a subsidiary of the British Electric Traction conglomerate that also owned software gaming interests, had been an early mover in home computing titles with publications such as *Your Commodore. IPC News* (May 1989: 15); Future Network plc Annual Report (2000: Our history section).
122. Driver and Gillespie (1993b) found that localization, especially the importance of the London industrial district, still served to limit the potential of regional magazine company development. However, as reviewed in Chapter 8, later innovations centred on the emergence of the World Wide Web greatly reduced these physical ties, and allowed the development of companies based around external contributions through electronic means.
123. *IPC News* (January/February 1987: 14).

124. The Oasis system had been initially started in 1984 and the first data links with wholesalers trialled in 1987. *IPC News* (January/February 1987: 14); *IPC News* (March 1987: 5).
125. Since 1986 text for *Vogue* had been entered on PCs running Multimate Advantage II word-processing software over a local networked controlled by a Hewlett Packard Vectra. Periodicals Training Council (1988: 39–40).
126. *IPC News* (January 1986: 4).
127. Essentially it was a 'cut-down' version of an ATEX system. This 'clunky business system' was more suited to the advertising office where early computerization had made an entrance into areas such as display advertisements. Although centralized computer systems, such as ATEX, suited newspapers they were not flexible enough for the requirements of magazines, and were too expensive for all but the largest publishers. ATEX systems suited publications which relied heavily on classified advertisement for example, and *Time Out* used ATEX from 1987, but was poorly suited to the graphics required of display advertising. Periodicals Training Council (1988: 11, 40).
128. IPC Editorial Systems Strategy Report, unpublished internal report dated 4 December (1987: 1–2, 6, 21–2).
129. An IPC Editorial Systems Report deplored that 'we are, as ever, at the mercy of software developers', and that 'in general all new versions of computer software will have bugs and be slow...a new version of Quark Xpress has just been released that is bug-ridden slow to the point that most users are refusing to upgrade to the new version...and it was delivered some nine months after it was first announced'. IPC Editorial Systems Response to *Marie Claire* New Tech Report, unpublished internal report dated 17 October (1990: 1).
130. IPC Editorial Systems The Macintosh Report, unpublished internal report undated (*c.*1987: 1).
131. Mowatt (2002: 282–96).
132. Output could be integrated into Linotype machines such as the Series 100 and Linotron 101. Wallis (1988: 59).
133. The typical installation cost of a 386-based PC system was £21,987 and £22,554 for a Mac. IPC Editorial Systems The Macintosh Report, unpublished internal report undated (*c.*1987: 1).
134. EMAP Annual Report and Accounts (1987: 2).
135. Available from: <http://www.hearst.co.uk/magazines/History.html>.
136. *IPC News* (May 1989: 16).
137. IPC Editorial Systems Response to *Marie Claire* New Tech Report, unpublished internal report dated 17 October (1990: 1).
138. BRAD (April 1989: vol. 6(4), iv).
139. The small titles were: *Antique Dealer and Collector's Guide; Loving; Practical Boat Owner;* and *Practical Woodworking*. IPC Editorial Systems Strategy Report, unpublished internal report dated 10 June 1987, p. 13.
140. *IPC News* (November 1987: 8).
141. IPC Editorial Systems Strategy Report, unpublished internal report dated 10 June 1987, p. 5.
142. Bannard (1990: 53).
143. BRAD (June 1990: vol 37(8), xi).

CHAPTER 8

1. For a review of the cultural industries-based perspective see Driver and Gillespie (1993a) and Garnham (1990), and for further reviews of the state of the industry in the 1980s also see Driver and Gillespie (1992, 1993b). At this time a number of studies considered that the growth in the number of new titles could be viewed principally as an aspect of increasing global concentration within the media industry as a whole, of which magazines were envisaged to play a subsidiary role. Product innovation, primarily in terms of new title proliferation, was seen to provide a strategic counterpart to the traditional scale advantages enabling the leading magazine publishers to extend their dominance into the international sphere as part of increasing global concentration, driven primarily by the internationalization of advertising markets. See also Bunting (1997), Garnham (2000, 2005) and Cloodt et al. (2001).
2. OFT (2008c: 24).
3. DC Thomson were sixth with five titles, the Economist were seventh with the *Economist*, the Reader's Digest Association with its own single eponymous title, the National Magazine Company and Condé Nast with six and four of the top 100 titles respectively were the other firms in the list of Britain's top ten magazine publishers by sales value. Other companies then accounted for a further 31 of the top 100 titles with sales of £82.6 million. Figures from *IPC News* (June 1988: 9; May 1989: 11).
4. *IPC News* 'The Inside Story' (supplement to July/August 1996: 2–4).
5. Williams (1998: 1, 16, 19).
6. Cox et al. (2005: Table 1).
7. While specialist magazines had always relied on contract work, the proportion of external contribution rose dramatically with the possibilities offered by the development of remote technologies. As an example of new expert contributors, the reviews editor of the mountain biking title *MBUK*, Finlay Paton, reflected this new breed of contributor as typically 'a former bike shop manager and mechanic' for whom 'being able to go into work every day to ride all the latest bikes and tinker with new parts all day is a dream come true'. By the early 2000s small independent companies such as Freestyle were able to put out a stable of seven magazines, including an *FHM* competitor *Boys Toys*, employing three in-house designers and a small central team across the portfolio and with the majority of their magazines' content sourced from external contributors. *IPC News* (May/June 1998: 9); The Future Network plc Annual Report (2003: 14).
8. For a general review of the early impact on journalists of moving towards a more contract-based orientation see Stanworth and Stanworth (1988).
9. St Ives plc Annual Report and Accounts (2006: 9).
10. St Ives plc Annual Report and Accounts (1993: 9).
11. The 24-hour 170,000 square foot plant employed 250 people and had three state-of-the-art eight-head Heidelberg Harris presses. The titles included *Homes & Gardens, Hair, Ideal Home, Marie Claire*, and *Family Circle. IPC News* (November 1994: 6–7).
12. St Ives plc Annual Report and Accounts (1999: 9).
13. St Ives plc Annual Report and Accounts (1997: 8–9).

14. St Ives plc Annual Report and Accounts (1998: 9).
15. St Ives plc Annual Report and Accounts (2001: 9, 2002: 9).
16. Wyndeham Press and Polestar emerged as the major remaining firms in the market. Wyndeham Press dated back to the Albert Gait Printers (established in 1860), and was acquired by Walstead Investments in 2008. As competitive conditions toughened in the industry Cooper Clegg entered receivership in 2008, and Wyndeham Press acquired Southernprint in 2009, and the St Ives plc's magazine printing Web Division in 2011 after that company posted its first ever loss in 2009. Despite financial difficulties and several changes of ownership, Polestar continued as a major competitor, with a major customer in the National Magazine Company and the majority of the newspaper Sunday supplements market. Keynote (2010: 92–3); Harrington (2011); 'About us', available at: <http://www.wyndeham.co.uk/about-us>.
17. In 1961 the Restrictive Practices Court investigated the refusal to supply practices of the National Federation of Retail Newsagents (NFRN, founded in 1919). The outcome of this was the decision that wholesalers and not publishers should decide which retailers to supply with magazines and newspapers. This decision was reviewed a number of times by the Office of Fair Trading in 1978, 1986, and 1994. Cf. Office of Fair Trading (2002, 2008a, 2008b, 2008c) and Locks (2009: 4–9).
18. *IPC News* (April/May 1990: 12).
19. The roots of this dated back to Hachette's purchase of Seymour Press and Gordon and Gotch in 1994 from which it has formed the Seymour International Press Distributor Ltd. Kronlund (1991: 619).
20. EMAP Annual Report (1995: 2).
21. At this time Frontline held 23 per cent of the market and Seymour 13 per cent. Mowatt (2006: Figure 2).
22. Increasingly publishers were able to use their improved information systems to monitor the performance of wholesalers, and to move to incentive-based contracts. Office of Fair Trading (2008b: 7; 2008c: 14, 31).
23. Office of Fair Trading (2002); Mowatt (2006: 521).
24. This concentration continued to increase with the collapse of Dawson News (previously Surridge Dawson) in 2009, and the surviving parts of the business were acquired by W.H. Smith News and Menzies Distribution Ltd. Keynote (2010).
25. See the report of the Monopolies and Mergers Commission (2003).
26. This was a growth of 22.8 per cent. For a full review, see Association of Newspaper and Magazine Wholesalers (1998a, 1998b).
27. The granting of effective local monopolies to wholesalers had long been subject to investigations, with the MMC undertaking major reviews in 1993 and 1998, and an investigation to examine whether that arrangement breached European competition laws. The OFT's conclusion was that the benefits of the system outweighed the limitations. The Future Network plc Annual Report (2005: 8).
28. Set-up to scan 13 digits of the bar-code rather than the full 15 meant that supermarkets were unable to tell which batch goods were from—something unimportant when dealing with baked beans for example, but vital for magazine sales as the information reflected the title's edition. Mowatt (2006: 522). For a review

of the growing information power of supermarkets in the grocery and retail supply-chains at this time, see Cox et al. (2002).

29. *IPC News* (April/May 1986: 8–9).

30. In 1988 Reed International purchased the International Thomson Organisation's consumer magazine business for £28 million, with Thomson's *Family Circle* and *Living* gaining IPC access to 4,000 supermarkets. *IPC News* (April/May 1988: 1); *Marketing* (1988: 8); *IPC News* (October 1989: 6–7).

31. EMAP Annual Report (1994: 5).

32. W.H. Smith Retail's share rose from 19 to 20 per cent, the major CTNs fell from 12 to 9.4 per cent, and other multiples grew slightly from 7 to 10 per cent. Mowatt (2006: Table 3).

33. The OFT noted that the risk of new product launch is significantly lower under SOR. OFT (2008b: 62, 64).

34. Gibson (1999).

35. One study has examined the use of new editorial production systems as examples of 'post-Fordist' mass-customization. Gough-Yates (2003).

36. For a review of the project-based nature of magazine production, see Ekinsmyth (2002a, 2002b). Cox and Mowatt (2008) argue the key organizational change within the industry was the change towards a more project-orientated approach to new title development.

37. The remaining £44 million was accounted for by books, videos, records, and tapes. Monopolies and Mergers Commission (1992: 1).

38. The additional youth and teen titles were *Playdays* (1990), *Pingu* (1993), *Live and Kicking* (1993), *Spot the Dog* (1994), *Brum* (1994), *Chatterbox* (1995), *Learning is Fun* (1996), *Girl Talk* (1996), *Toybox* (1996), *Teletubbies* (1997), *Smart* (1998), with 1999 seeing the launch of *ROAR!, Walking with Dinosaurs, FBX, Bob the Builder, Tell me Why, Tweenies, Puzzlebox*, and *Star Hill Ponies*. By 2010 the company had added an astonishing 46 additional youth and teen titles to this roster. The company also continued to develop its television programmes into magazines through the 2000s, with examples being *Songs of Praise* (2003) and *Who Do You Think You Are?* (2008). Unpublished and untitled BBC report on magazine launches (2010).

39. Views of third parties, Monopolies and Mergers Commission (1992: 80–109).

40. The Price Commission noted that the BBC had an inbuilt publicity advantage for the *Radio Times* in 1977, but while the Corporation maintained the duopoly on TV listings other magazine publishers had been content to ignore this (1978a: 29). The BBC did not use the term 'advertisements', preferring to use the term 'trail' on the basis that they provided information about programmes. Its competitors, however, were clear that this was not how the material would be perceived by consumers. Monopolies and Mergers Commission (1992: 1–4); BBC Reports and Accounts (2005/6: 91). BBC Enterprises (later Worldwide) chief executive James Arnold-Baker acknowledged that provoking the MMC had been a significant miscalculation. Brown (1994: 52).

41. EMAP Report and Accounts (1993: 2).

42. The titles were *Car, Supercar Classics, New Woman, Sky*, and *TV Guide*. In the United States News Corp sold off all of its magazines interests to K-III in 1991,

except for *Mirabella* which had been losing money heavily and was sold to Hachette in 1995. Wells and Hakanen (1996: 126).

43. EMAP Report and Accounts (1993: 4–5).

44. EMAP Report and Accounts (1996: 3–4).

45. *IPC News* (February/March 1993: 8–9).

46. Following the £20 billion merger of Reed Elsevier and Wolters Kluwer in 1997, the new group had decided to focus solely on its scientific, professional, and business publishing and to divest its consumer publishing interests. FIPP (1997) 'Reed Elsevier and Wolters Kluwer to Merge', published: 14 October. Available at: <http://www.fipp.com/news/>.

47. *IPC News* (January/February 1999: 1).

48. FIPP (1998) 'David Arculus Appointed Chairman of IPC', published: 15 December. Available at: <http://www.fipp.com/news/>.

49. *Esquire* was launched in 1933 in the USA and later incorporated *Gentleman's Quarterly*, which had originally started as a trade-based sales publication and been included later as a supplement to *Esquire*. The title was sold to Condé Nast as a stand-alone title in 1957, and *Esquire* was then acquired by Hearst in 1986. Both companies had made aborted attempts to launch US male-oriented fashion titles in the UK, with a generally unsuccessful British imprint of *Esquire* from 1953 to 1959, the short-lived *Vogue for Men* in 1965, and *Cosmopolitan Man* in 1978. Hochswender and Gross (1993: 7).

50. Hone (1995).

51. Southwell later downplayed the calculated aspect to the publication by outlining that once the title was in print 'there were to be no editorial concessions to commerce; we were there to write about the stuff we liked and if no one else liked it then so be it'. This accurately reflected the maverick position that the magazine acquired, especially under editor James Brown. McKay (2000: 184, 206). For a full history of the title's inception, see Southwell (1998).

52. Hochswender and Gross (1993: 7). Sales of *For Him* in 1994 were 59,784, compared to *GQ* which was selling 57,560 in 1990 and 145,144 in 2000. As a comparison to the men's sector, in 2000 *Vogue* was selling 200,462. ABC July–December figures from 1990, 1994, 2000.

53. EMAP Annual Review (1997: 8–9).

54. ABC July–December 1995.

55. The advertising and public relations agency Cunning Stunts had various estimates that that the image had been seen by 40 to 160 million people after being picked up by news reporting throughout the world. The image was projected onto the Palace of Westminster, and not 'Big Ben' as reported widely; reports also varied as to the scale of the projection from 60 to 120 feet in height, with the BBC reporting 60 feet. Cunning Stunts retained a connection with the sector, later being brought in to handle the marketing for Dennis's *Bizarre*. BBC News, 'Porter lights up London' (1999); Fry (1999); Matthews (2005).

56. 504,959. ABC January–July 1996; ABC July–December 1998.

57. Mintel (2002a, 2002b).

58. In 2004 *FHM* was the seventh best-selling paid-for magazine overall (including weeklies), and was listed as the second best-selling monthly after the *Reader's Digest*, which does not conform to the usual definition of a consumer magazine.

BRAD August 2004. *Vanity Fair* devoted an issue to the idea of Cool Britianna in March 1997, with the cover titled 'London Swings! Again!' and included features on the *Loaded* editorial team along with stories on the new Labour prime minister Tony Blair, artists such as Damien Hirst, fashion designers such as Alexander McQueen, and musicans associated with 'Britpop' such as Liam Gallagher of Oasis and Graham Coxon of Blur.

59. The companies were Blue Moon Publishing, Cavalier Publishing, Cedar Communications, Dennis, EMAP Elan, Fray Media, Freestyle, Future, Highbury Lifestyle, Hils Pubs, Ink, IPC Ignite, John Brown, Media Cell, The National Magazine Company, Origin, Parallel Sky, Partridge, Remedica, Rodale, Scot Taylor, Upstreet, and Wardle. BRAD August 2004.

60. BRAD August 2004.

61. Many of these titles closed or merged, as well as the closure of existing titles. Pira International (2002: Figure 8.7).

62. Office of Fair Trading (2008c: 24).

63. Willings Press Guide (2004).

64. EMAP Report and Accounts (1993: 4–5); EMAP Report and Accounts (1994: 16).

65. The firm's total acquisitions in 1996 were £278 million. EMAP Report and Accounts (1996: 3–4, 6, 12).

66. EMAP was forced to withdraw its first attempt at *FHM* from the market by the government due to its explicit approach to sex. The title was localized and the content changed, although the basic 'formula' of 'practical, useful information' was retained. The title was re-launched with the name *Singapore FHM*. Lawrence (2003); EMAP Report and Accounts (1997: 10–11).

67. EMAP paid US$1.2 billion in cash and the assumed US$300 million in debt for the purchase, completed on 15 December 1999. Barrett (1999).

68. Future had acquired Imagine originally in 1994 when it was named GP Publications. It was divested as part of the Pearson takeover. The Future Network plc Annual Report (2000: 3).

69. The Future Network plc Annual Report (2001: 1).

70. *IPC News* (May/June 1991: 2).

71. *IPC News* (March/April 1994: 1).

72. *IPC News* (October 1998: 1).

73. The Future Network plc Annual Report (2005: 8).

74. The Future Network plc Annual Report (2002: 3); AOL Time Warner Annual Report (2002: 5).

75. The Future Network plc Annual Report (2000).

76. Nicholas (1999).

77. The 'networks of sites' concept used umbrella sites under names such as daily-radar.co.uk to aggregate content from across the company's holdings, and were therefore wider and more ambitious in scope than individual online titles, such as *Hi-Fi Choice* online, which was clearly linked to the company's *Hi-Fi Choice* title. The Future Network plc Annual Report (2000: 3, 5; 2001: 1, 3, 17–19).

78. Congdon et al. (1995: 1).

79. EMAP Annual Report (1994: 8).

80. In 1996 the Audit Bureau of Circulations set up ABC Electronic to offer independent certification, bringing more certainty to advertisers.

81. *IPC News* (November 1994: 3).
82. *Loaded*'s website was named uploaded.com. *IPC News* (October 1995: 2).
83. *IPC News* (October 1994: 1).
84. *IPC News* (November 1996: 3).
85. Proud (2002).
86. *IPC News* (September 1999: 3).
87. *IPC News* (January/February 2000: 8–9).
88. As IT systems became more central some companies outsourced the management of their IT. In 1996 IPC awarded Siemens Nixdorf a £1 million contract to upgrade and manage their network servers. *IPC News* (November/December 1996: 5).
89. *IPC News* (July/August 1999: 2–3).
90. The company was formed on 11 January 2001 by the merger of America Online Inc. and Time Warner Inc., which both became wholly-owned subsidiaries of AOL Time Warner. AOL Time Warner Annual Report (2001: 1).
91. AOL Time Warner Annual Report (2001: 1, 10; 2002: 5, 18); Time Inc. Press Release, 25 July 2001. Available at: <http://www.timewarner.com/newsroom/press-releases/2001/07/time_inc_to_acquire_ipc_from_cinven_07-25-2001.php>.
92. EMAP now comprised: EMAP Digital; EMAP Performance; EMAP Automotive; EMAP Active; EMAP Elan; EMAP Esprit; EMAP Communication; Frontline; EMAP France; EMAP USA (including Peterson Active and Metro); and EMAP International. EMAP Annual Report (2000: 10).
93. EMAP Annual Report (1993: 17).
94. The purchase included Piccadilly Radio Manchester and Red Rose Radio. EMAP Annual Report (1995: 6).
95. EMAP Annual Report (1996: 1, 12).
96. Lopes (2007) has outlined the increasing strategic importance of brands, which need national registration, advertising, and maintenance. Bakker (2006: 87) has made the point that some media have an inherent value across international markets, such as music, while brands may have no value outside of their home market. Multinational companies in media sectors can be considered 'rights-based' in attempting to leverage the ownership of intellectual property across international markets. The magazine industry makes an interesting case study of how companies have attempted to pursue this model, with various degrees of success.
97. Gough-Yates (2007: 28).
98. EMAP Annual Report (2000: 8–10, 25–9; 2001: 11).
99. Williams (1998: 1).
100. Perez (2009: 784–6).
101. The Future Network plc Annual Report (2000: 3, 72).
102. *Business 2.0* was merged into Time Inc.'s *e-Company Now*. AOL Time Warner Annual Report (2001: 10); The Future Network plc Annual Report (2001: 1).
103. The Future Network plc Annual Report (2000: 4–7; 2001: 1).
104. The lowest share price in 2001 was £7.00. EMAP Annual Report (2000: 6; 2001: 72; 2002: 69).
105. EMAP Annual Report (2001: 6–8).

106. EMAP Annual Report (2001: 23, 27).
107. EMAP Annual Report (2006: 4–5, 13).
108. Dobson (2002: 8–9, 14–15).
109. See the OFT's reviews. Office of Fair Trading (2008a, 2008b, 2008c).
110. For a review of how magazine publishers viewed changes to the supply-chain, see Locks (2009).
111. EMAP Annual Report (2003: 7).
112. PPA Magazine Handbook (2000: 27).
113. Mowatt (2006: 529); Office of Fair Trading (2008a, 2008b, 2008c).
114. Cox et al. (2005: 151).
115. EMAP Annual Report (2006: 11).
116. Distribution became more problematic, making it more difficult to establish new titles in the market cheaply, and lowered potential profits, but changes to the industry had permanently changed the ability of firms to compete on a low-cost dtp-based model. For example, several of EMAP's key staff members from *Smash Hits, Empire*, and *Q* (David Hepworth, Jerry Perkins, Mark Ellen, and Andrew Harrison) set up Development Hell to publish ex-EMAP titles such as *MixMag* and *Q*-competitor *Word* in 2003. New entrants would find potential in the Internet to once again potentially offer a cost-effective channel to the market. Development Hell, for example, closed the print-based *MixMag* in 2012 to offer the title purely online as an iPad app, although this option was not felt to be economically viable when the same company ceased to print the *Word*, also in 2012. Hepworth (2013).
117. Future had wanted to acquire the entire Highbury House group but the proposal was referred to the Competition Commission by the OFT. The Future Network plc Annual Report (2005: 4, 8).
118. James Brown moved into contract publishing, and in 2010 James Brown Publishing Ltd. was one of the largest contract customer publishers, handling titles for John Lewis, Jaguar, Porsche, and the Virgin Group as well as many others. For the periodical publishing industry this sector has grown dramatically since Redwood was a key mover, to become the third major segment of the periodicals market. Keynote (2010: 57).
119. Brand Republic (2002).
120. BBC Origin Ltd. was taken over by means of a management buyout in 2006 led by managing director Andy Marshall, and renamed Origin Publishing Ltd. to publish non-BBC-branded titles. The BBC-branded titles were transferred to BBC Bristol along with some contract titles under the management of Peter Phippen. Following this, BBC Magazines and BBC Magazines Rights were incorporated in March 2007. At this time BBC Worldwide (formerly BBC Enterprises until 1992) also made the controversial decision to buy a majority stake in the Australian travel guide publishing company Lonely Planet. BBC Worldwide decided in mid-2011 to exit consumer magazines, and to sell the majority of its magazine interests to Exponent Private Equity for £121 million, who then produced the BBC titles under contract. BBC Origin Ltd. and Bristol Magazines Ltd. were then combined with Magicalia (a mainly Web-based media company that had acquired some magazine print interests when it was acquired by Exponent in

2006) to become the Immediate Media Co. Bristol Ltd. at the end of 2011. BBC Magazines became Immediate Media Co. London Ltd. at the same time. Keynote (2009, 2010, 2012); BBC Annual Report and Accounts (2012: vol. 2: 36).

121. Choueke (2006).
122. In 2005 the company had 152 magazine titles (32 gaming, 42 computing, and 78 entertainment) and 30 websites. The Future Network plc Annual Report (2005: 1).
123. The Future Network plc Annual Report (2003: 4).
124. The Future Network plc Annual Report (2004: 4–5).
125. The Future Network plc Annual Report (2007: 1).
126. EMAP Annual Report (2005: 15).
127. EMAP Annual Report (2006); EMAP International Report and Financial Statement (2007: 2, 37). Arnoldo Mondadori Editore S.P.A, formed in 1912, was the leading Italian periodical publishers with interest in other media, including book publishing and television broadcasting. Conrad (1991: 585–8).
128. BBC Annual Report and Accounts (2005/6: 122).
129. The Future Network plc Annual Report (2008: 5).
130. Cox and Mowatt (2008).
131. The Future Network plc Annual Report (2007: 1).
132. See Ghemawat and Ghadar (2006) for a review of this concept.
133. EMAP International Ltd. (formerly EMAP plc) Report and Financial Statements (2007: 1).
134. Singh (2007: 7); EMAP International Ltd. Report and Financial Statements (2007: 1).
135. Keynote (2010: 51).
136. EMAP International Report and Financial Statement (2007: 36).
137. Barnett (2008: 5).
138. IPC Media moved from King's Reach Tower to the Bluefin in 2007.
139. The firms continued to remain in profit throughout the financial crisis, and rewarded the patience of its Time Inc. parent in 2012 when IPC paid its first dividend for several years, a healthy £51.5 million. The firm had played the role of cash cow within the media conglomerate, and its steady profits ensured that AOL Time Warner retained ownership of the group even though it had failed to fully exploit the ownership of its UK consumer publisher's content across its empire. Spanier (2012).
140. PPA Magazine Handbook (2000: 51, 53).
141. Reported in Cox and Mowatt (2008: 517).
142. Closeness to consumers is one aspect of project-based organizational structures, along with the ability to react rapidly to change. Guidone (2000: 15); Griffin-Foley (2004: 533–48).
143. The Future Network plc Annual Report (2010: 5).
144. Euromonitor data 'UK Possession of Broadband Internet Enabled Computer', database accessed 2 September 2012.
145. Keynote (2010: 25, 49).
146. The Future Network plc Annual Report (2007: 3).
147. The Future Network plc Annual Report (2006: 9; 2009: 6).

148. Housetohome, for example, exploited *Homes & Gardens, Ideal Home,* and *Livingetc.* Mousebreaker on the other hand was a company that developed free online video games. See: <http://www.ipcmedia.com/companyhistory>.
149. FIPP (2010: 230).
150. EMAP Annual Report (2005: 14).
151. PPA (2008: 1).
152. Kobrak and Wilkins (2011: 182).
153. Keynote (2010: 72).
154. As the advertising market declined in the b2b segment, many publishers moved towards forging closer links to the end consumers they served, in a parallel shift to developments in mass-market consumer weeklies in the 1980s. It could be argued that this will make the sectors more similar in the future. Keynote (2010: 93–4).
155. In the 1970s consumer magazines' share of all advertising revenue in the UK was around 7 per cent, and has remained at roughly the same relative level through to 2008.
156. IPC Media's turnover declined from £412 million in 2005 to £356 million in 2010. Future's turnover declined from £188 million in 2006 to £103 million in 2010. Dennis increased their turnover slightly from £61.7 million in 2005 to £64.5 million in 2010. Condé Nast International Ltd. saw a decline in turnover from £480 million to £428 million in 2010. Changes in ownership and company structure complicate an assessment of the other leading publishers. EMAP's turn-over fell from £212.8 million to £207 million between 2006 and 2008, when the consumer magazine and radio interests became subsumed into the Bauer group. Despite the inclusion of EMAP Bauer Consumer Media's turnover declined from £343 million in 2006 to £245.8 in 2010. BBC Magazines' turnover in 2007 was £126.6 million, and Immediate Media Co. London's turnover (who took over many of their activities) was £126.6 million in 2008 falling to £112.5 million in 2010. Keynote (2009, 2012).
157. Keynote (2010: 93–5).
158. Circulation of the *Beano* fell 16.2 per cent. DC Thomson's turnover rose to £272.1 million in 2009 up from £265.5 in 2007/8. However, during the same period profits had fallen from £67.5 million to £32.5 million. Keynote (2010: 49).
159. For a longer-term review of IPC's turnover and profits see the Keynote Report (2010). In relation to the downturn caused by the financial crisis IPC's turno-ver fell from £393.5 million in 2008 to £350.7 million in 2009, with pre-tax profits falling from £78.6 million to £49.7 million. *Loaded* was sold to Vitality Publishing. Levy (2010); Durrani (2011). In a continued consolidation of the sec-tor Hachette Filipacchi (UK) Ltd. was acquired from French owner Lagardere for €651 million in 2011. Both firms were combined into Hearst Magazines UK. Farey-Jones (2011).
160. IPC's turnover was £350.7 million in 2009, down from £393.5 million in 2008, with pre-tax profits falling to £49.7 million from £78.6 million. *Loaded* was sold to Vitality Publishing. Levy (2010); Durrani (2011).
161. IPC Media's pre-tax profits had been steady around £78 million from 2005 to 2009, when they collapsed to £36.9 million in 2010, partly driven by some

exceptional charges made in response to the financial crisis, before rebounding. Spanier (2012). Future improved their profits from losses of £36.7 million in 2006 to £11.3 million in 2010. Dennis broadly maintained their profits, making £3.6 million in both 2005 and 2010. Condé Nast International Ltd. profits grew from £13.4 million in 2005 to £34.6 million in 2010. Keynote (2009, 2012).

162. Keynote (2010: 103). *Woman, Woman's Own*, and *Woman's Weekly* all saw continued falls in circulation from 2003 to 2010, respectively: 556,000 to 313,000; 474,000 to 268,000; 413,000 to 307,000. The leading women's glossy monthlies' sales broadly held up over the same period: *Vogue* 158,000 to 161,000; *Elle* 172,000 to 159,000; *Harper's* 77,000 to 97,000; *Marie Claire* 346,000 to 259,000; *Vanity Fair* 57,000 unchanged. January–June ABC figures (2003, 2010).

163. *OK!* became a weekly periodical in 2006. ABC Data cited from 'Magazine ABCs: *Star* and *New* soar as weeklies grow', *Press Gazette*, 11 February 2010.

164. <http://www.magforum.com/independent_magazines.htm>, accessed 30 November 2012.

165. Media 10 Ltd. was founded in Loughton, Essex, in 2002, with ten staff. The company operates branded events linked to magazine titles such as *Grand Designs* magazines, and purely consumer titles such as the parenting title *Gurgle*. By 2010 the firm had expanded to reach a turnover of £30 million and a workforce of 120 staff. Binns (2010).

166. In 2012 Amazon launched its own tablet computer, the Kindle Fire, manufactured under contract, and Google introduced its Nexus line of tablets.

167. The Future Network plc Annual Report (2010: 5).

A NOTE ON THE SCOPE OF THE STUDY

1. For example, see Dancyger (1978); Gibbs (1993); Angeletti and Oliva (2006).
2. Harper (1999: 38); Frost (2003); Taylor and Brody (2006).
3. Dark (1922); Pound and Harmsworth (1959); Ferris (1971); Seebohm (1982); Hearst and Casserly (1991); Nasaw (2000); Jackson (2001).
4. Low (1999); Greenhill and Reynolds (2010).
5. Chase and Chase (1954); Yoxall (1966).
6. Head (1939).
7. The history of the major unions related to magazine publishing has been studied by Musson (1954); Bundock (1957); Gennard (1990); and Gennard and Bain (1995).
8. Gough-Yates (2003); Moeran (2004).
9. Ledwith et al. (1990); McRobbie (1991); Dorgan and Grieco (1993); Kehily (1999); Colgan and Ledwith (2000); Brewis and Warren (2011); Vachhani et al. (2011); Freeman and Bell (2013).

Bibliography

Archive Collections

Bodleian Library, Oxford
  Benn's Media Directory
  Benn's Press Directory
  Newspaper Press Directory
British Library, London
  Business & Intellectual Property Centre for Various Marketing Reports
British Newspaper Library, Colindale, London/Boston Spa
  Audit Bureau of Circulations figures, various years
  Ayer's American Newspaper Annual and Directory
  Mitchell's Press Directory
  Various back issues of British consumer magazines
Companies House, Cardiff
  IPC Ltd. Annual Report and Accounts
  Mirror Group Holdings (microfiche)
Condé Nast Archive, New York and London
  CNAMC Boxes: Various correspondence and data
Design Archives, University of Brighton, Sussex
  Alison Settle papers
History of Advertising Trust (HAT), Raveningham, Norwich
  HAT 42/4 Readership Surveys
  Periodical Press Association (PPA) Archive
IPC Archive, London (Private papers)
  Confidential Reports on the Introduction of Computers into Magazine Production
  IPC News
London Business School, London
  Company Reports collection provided the following Annual Reports where not otherwise specified:
    EMAP
    Future
    IPCReed International
    St Ives
Modern Records Centre, University of Warwick, Coventry
  Collected papers of Printing Trade Unions, including:
    Amalgamated Society of Lithographic Printers MSS.39A/ASL
    London Society of Compositors MSS.39A/CO
    NATSOPA MSS.39/NAT
    Printing and Kindred Trades Association MSS.39A/5/PK
    SLADE MSS.39A/S

SOGAT MSS.39/SO
Typographical Association MSS.39A/TA
National Archives, Kew, London
BT31 Records of Dissolved Companies
CAB21 Cabinet Office papers
Professional Publishers Association, London
PPA Response to OFT Report on Magazine Distribution by Ian Locks
Various PPA Reports and Documents
St Bride Print Library, London
BRAD
Newspaper Owner & Manager
Newspaper World
PIRA database
Various trade journals and other rare printed sources of information

Published Sources

Alford, Bernard W. E. (1964), 'Government Expenditure and the Growth of the Printing Industry in the Nineteenth Century', *Economic History Review*, vol. 17(1): 96–112.
—— (1965), 'Business Enterprise and the Growth of the Commercial Letterpress Printing Industry, 1850–1914', *Business History*, vol. 7(1): 1–14.
Altick, Richard D. (1997), *Punch: The Lively Youth of a British Institution*. Columbus: Ohio State University Press.
—— (1998), *The English Common Reader: A Social History of the Mass Reading Public, 1800–1900*. 2nd edn. Columbus: Ohio State University Press.
Anderson, Patricia (1991), *The Printed Image and the Transformation of Popular Culture, 1790–1860*, Oxford: Clarendon Press.
Angeletti, Norberto and Oliva, Alberto (2006), *In Vogue: The Illustrated History of the World's Most Famous Fashion Magazine*. New York: Rizzoli.
Arculus, David (1978), 'Specialist Magazines', in Harry Henry (ed.) *Behind the Headlines: The Business of the British Press*. London: Associated Business Press.
Ashley, Mike (2006), *The Age of the Storytellers: British Popular Fiction Magazines, 1880–1950*. London: British Library.
Asquith, Ivon (1978), 'The Structure, Ownership and Control of the Press, 1780–1855', in George Boyce, James Curran, and Pauline Wingate (eds.) *Newspaper History: From the 17th Century to the Present Day*. London: Constable, 98–129.
Association of Newspaper and Magazine Wholesalers (1998a), 'The Nightly Miracle'. Available at: <http://www.anmw.co.uk/anmw/jsp/theNightlyMiracle.jsp>. Accessed 7 June 2003.
—— (1998b), 'News Travels Fast'. Available at: <http://www.anmw.co.uk/files/news-travelsfast.html>. Accessed 7 June 2003.
Austen-Leigh, R. A. and Meynell, Gerald T. (eds.) (1920), *The Master Printers Annual and Typographical Yearbook 1920*. London: Spottiswoode Ballantyne. Available at the Modern Records Centre, University of Warwick, MRC MSS.39/SO/5/4/2/13.
Ayer, N. W. (1910), *American Newspaper Annual and Directory*. Philadelphia, PA: N. W. Ayer & Son.

Bailey, Isabel (2004), 'Ingram, Herbert (1811–1860)', *Oxford Dictionary of National Biography*. Oxford: Oxford University Press. Online edn. <http://www.oxforddnb.com/view/article/14416>. Accessed 9 November 2010.

Baker, Anne Pimlott (2004), 'Thomson, David Couper (1861–1954)', *Oxford Dictionary of National Biography*. Oxford: Oxford University Press. Online edn. <http://www.oxforddnb.com/view/article/48488>. Accessed 8 November 2010.

Bakker, Gerben (2006), 'The Making of a Music Multinational: PolyGram's International Businesses, 1945–1998', *Business History Review*, vol. 80(1): 81–123.

Bannard, Michael (1990), *Magazine and Journal Production*. London: Chapman & Hall.

Barlow, Keith (2008), *The Labour Movement in Britain from Thatcher to Blair*, 2nd edn. Frankfurt: Peter Lang GMBH.

Barnes, Paul (2005), 'A Victorian Financial Crisis: The Scandalous Implications of the Case of Overend Gurney', in Judith Rowbotham and Kim Stevenson (eds.) *Criminal Conversations: Victorian Crimes, Social Panic and Moral Outrage*. Columbus: Ohio State University Press, 55–69.

Barnett, Emma (2008), 'Bauer Leans on *FHM* and *Empire* for Radio Station', *Media Week*, 4 April: 5.

Barrell, Joan and Braithwaite, Brian (1988), *The Business of Women's Magazines*. 2nd edn. London: Kogan Page.

Barrett, William (1999), 'Another Look', *Forbes*. Available at: <http://www.forbes.com/global/1999/0111/0201011a.html>. Accessed 5 July 2012.

Bavendamm, Dirk (1996), 'Bertelsmann AG', in *International Directory of Company Histories*, vol. 15. Detroit: St James Press, 51–5.

Baylen, Joseph O. (2004), 'Stead, William Thomas (1849–1912)', *Oxford Dictionary of National Biography*. Oxford: Oxford University Press. Online edn. <http://www.oxforddnb.com/view/article/36258>. Accessed 28 July 2009.

Beavon, John (2004), 'King, Cecil Harmsworth (1901–1987)', *Oxford Dictionary of National Biography*. Oxford: Oxford University Press. Online edn. <http://www.oxforddnb.com/view/article/40163>. Accessed 28 July 2009.

Beetham, Margaret (1996), *A Magazine of Her Own? Domesticity and Desire in the Woman's Magazine, 1800–1914*. London: Routledge.

Bennett, Scott (1982), 'Revolutions in Thought: Serial Publications and the Mass Market for Reading', in Joanne Shattock and Michael Woolf (eds.) *The Victorian Press: Samplings and Soundings*. Leicester: Leicester University Press, 225–57.

Berridge, Virginia (1978), 'Popular Sunday Papers and mid-Victorian Society', in George Boyce, James Curran, and Pauline Wingate (eds.) *Newspaper History: From the 17th Century to the Present Day*. London: Constable, 247–64.

Binns, Daniel (2010), 'Firm's Success Makes it Too Big for Town', *Epping Forest Guardian*, 3 June 2010. Available at: <http://www.guardian-series.co.uk/news/efnews/8200775.EPPING_LOUGHTON__Firm_s_success_makes_it_too_big_for_town/?ref=rss>.

Black, Jeremy (2001), *The English Press, 1621–1861*. Stroud: Sutton Publishing.

Bloomfield, Kenneth (2008), *The BBC at the Watershed*. Liverpool: Liverpool University Press.

Blumenfeld, Ralph D. (1933), *The Press in My Time*. London: Rich & Cowen.

Boyce, D. George (2004), 'Harmsworth, Alfred Charles William, Viscount Northcliffe (1865–1922)', *Oxford Dictionary of National Biography*. Oxford: Oxford University

Press. Online edn. <http://www.oxforddnb.com/view/article/33717>. Accessed 28 July 2009.

Braithwaite, Brian (1995), *Women's Magazines: the First 300 Years*. Peter Owen: London

—— (1998), 'Magazines: The Bulging Bookstores', in Adam Briggs and Paul Cobley (eds.) *The Media: An Introduction*. London: Addison Wesley Longman.

Brake, Laurel and Demoor, Marysa (eds.) (2009), *Dictionary of Nineteenth-Century Journalism in Great Britain and Ireland*. Gent and London: Academia Press and British Library.

Brandon, David (2007), *Life in a 17th Century Coffee Shop*. Stroud: Sutton Publishing.

Brewis, Joanna and Warren, Samantha (2011), 'Have Yourself a Merry Little Christmas? Organizing Christmas in Women's Magazines Past and Present', *Organization*, vol. 18(6): 747–62.

Briggs, Asa (1984), *A Social History of England*. New York: Viking Press.

Brown, Lucy (1985), *Victorian News and Newspapers*. Oxford: Clarendon Press.

Brown, Malcolm (1994), 'Profile: James Arnold-Baker', *Management Today*. January.

Browne, Ronald (1984), *T.B. Browne Ltd: The First 100 Years*. London. Available at the HAT Archive, Raveningham, Suffolk, T. B. Browne Box.

Bundock, Clement J. (1957), *The National Union of Journalists, 1907–1957*. Oxford: Oxford University Press.

Bunting, Helen (1997), *European Consumer Magazine Publishing: Facing the Electronic Challenge*. London: FT Media.

Camrose, Viscount (1947), *British Newspapers and their Controllers*. London: Cassell.

Cassis, Youssef (1997), *Big Business: The European Experience in the Twentieth Century*. Oxford: Oxford University Press.

Chandler, Alfred D. (1990), *Scale and Scope: The Dynamics of Industrial Capitalism*. Cambridge, MA: Harvard University Press.

Chase, Edna Woolman and Chase, Ilka (1954), *Always in Vogue*. London: Victor Gollancz.

Child, John (1967), *Industrial Relations in the British Printing Industry: The Quest for Security*. London: George Allen & Unwin.

Choueke, Mark (2006), 'Stalled Start for Murdoch's Magazines', *Media Week*, 23 November.

Clark, Eric (1988), *The Want Makers—The World of Advertising: How they Make You Buy*. New York: Penguin Books.

Clarke, Bob (2004), *From Grub Street to Fleet Street: An Illustrated History of English Newspapers to 1899*. Aldershot: Ashgate.

Cleverley, Graham (1976), *The Fleet Street Disaster: British National Newspapers as a Case Study in Mismanagement*. London: Constable.

Cloodt, Myriam, Hagedoorn, John, and van Kranenburg, Hans (2001), 'An Exploratory Study of Recent Trends in the Diversification of Dutch Publishing Companies in the Multimedia and Information Industries', *International Studies of Management and Organization*, vol. 31(1): 64–86.

Cohen, M. L. (1998), 'Hachette Filipacchi Medias S.A.', *International Directory of Company Histories*, vol. 21. Detroit: St James Press, 265–7.

—— (2001), 'EMAP plc', in T. Grant (ed.) *International Directory of Corporate Histories*, vol. 35. Detroit: St James Press, 164–6.

Colclough, Stephen (2005), 'Station to Station: The LNER and the Emergence of the Railway Bookstall, 1840–1875', in John Hinks and Catherine Armstrong (eds.) *Printing Places: Locations of Book Production and Distribution since 1500*. London: Oak Knoll Press and British Library, 169–84.

Coleman, Donald C. (1959), *The British Paper Industry, 1495–1860*. Oxford: Oxford University Press.

Colgan, Fiona and Ledwith, Sue (2000), 'Diversity, Identities and Strategies of Women Trade Union Activists', *Gender, Work & Organization*, vol. 7(4): 242–57.

Compaine, Benjamin M. (1982), *The Business of Consumer Magazines*. New York: Knowledge Industry Publications.

Conboy, Martin (2002), *The Press and Popular Culture*. London: Sage.

Congdon, Tim, Graham, Damian, and Robinson, Bill (1995), *The Cross Media Revolution: Ownership and Control*. Sussex: John Libby & Co.

Conrad, Paul (1991), 'Arnoldo Mondadori Editore S.P.A', *International Directory of Company Histories*, vol. 4. Detroit: St James Press, 585–8.

Cook, Richard (1998), 'Fall of the house of Wagadon. The publishers of both *The Face* and *Arena* seem to have lost their touch', *The Independent*, 11 August. Available at: <http://www.independent.co.uk/arts-entertainment/media-fall-of-the-house-of-wagadon-1170999.html>.

Cooney, Sondra Miley (2004), 'Chambers, William (1800–1883)', *Oxford Dictionary of National Biography*. Oxford: Oxford University Press. Online edn. <http://www.oxforddnb.com/view/article/5084>. Accessed 28 July 2009.

Corp, Earnest (c.1969), *A Brief History of the Sun Engraving Co. Ltd*. Available at: <http://www.sunprintershistory.com/factcorp.html>. Accessed 10 July 2009.

Cox, Howard and Mowatt, Simon (2008), 'Technological Change and Forms of Innovation in Consumer Magazine Publishing: A UK-based Study', *Technology Analysis and Strategic Management*, vol. 20(4): 503–20.

—— (2012), '*Vogue* in Britain: Authenticity and the Creation of Competitive Advantage in the UK Magazine Industry', *Business History*, vol. 54(1): 67–87.

Cox, Howard, Mowatt, Simon, and Prevezer, Martha (2002), 'The Firm in the Information Age: Organizational Responses to Technological Change in the Processed Foods Sector', *Industrial and Corporate Change*, vol. 11(1): 135–58.

Cox, Howard, Mowatt, Simon, and Young, Stuart (2005), 'Innovation and Organisation in the UK Magazine Print Publishing Industry: A Survey', *Global Business and Economics Review*, vol. 7(1): 111–28.

Cranfield, G. A. (1978), *The Press and Society: From Caxton to Northcliffe*. London: Longman.

Cudlipp, Hugh (1953), *Publish and Be Damned! The Astonishing Story of the Daily Mirror*. London: Andrew Dakers.

—— (1962), *At Your Peril*. London: Weidenfeld & Nicolson.

—— (1976), *Walking on the Water*. London: Bodley Head.

Currie, Tony (2001), *The Radio Times Story*. Tiverton, Devon: Kelly Publications.

Daly, Charles P., Henry, Patrick, and Ryder, Ellen (1997), *The Magazine Publishing Industry*. Boston, MA: Allyn & Bacon.

Dancyger, Irene (1978), *A World of Women: An Illustrated History of Women's Magazines*. Dublin: Gill and Macmillan.

Dark, Sydney (1922), *The Life of Sir Arthur Pearson*. London: Hodder & Stoughton.
—— (1925), *Mainly About Other People*. London: Hodder & Stoughton.
Darwin, Bernard (1947), *Fifty Years of Country Life*. London: Country Life Ltd.
Davenport-Hines, Richard (2004), 'Smith, William Henry (1825–1891)', *Oxford Dictionary of National Biography*. Oxford: Oxford University Press. Online edn. <http://www.oxforddnb.com/view/article/25938>. Accessed 28 July 2009.
Debrett's (no date), 'Dr John Thomas'. Available at: <http://www.debretts.com/people/biographies/browse/t/13903/John%20Anthony%20Griffiths+THOMAS.aspx>.
Delafons, Allan (1965), *The Structure of the Printing Industry*. London: MacDonald.
Dilnot, George (1925), *The Romance of the Amalgamated Press*. London: Amalgamated Press.
Dobson, Paul (2000), 'The Impact of Proposed National Distribution Development on the UK Magazine and National Newspaper Markets', Office of Fair Trading Report. London: HMSO.
Dorgan, Theresa and Grieco, Margaret (1993), 'Battling Against the Odds: The Emergence of Senior Women Trade Unionists', *Industrial Relations Journal*, vol. 24(2): 151–64.
Dougherty, Philip (1987), 'Ziff Buys MacUser', *The New York Times*, 6 January.
Driver, Stephen and Gillespie, Andrew (1992), 'The Diffusion of Digital Technologies in Magazine Print Publishing: Organisational Changes and Strategic Choices', *Journal of Information Technology*, vol. 7(3): 149–59.
—— (1993a), 'Structural-Change in the Cultural Industries—British Magazine Publishing in the 1980s', *Media, Culture & Society*, vol. 15(2): 183–201.
—— (1993b), 'Information and Communication Technologies and the Geography of Magazine Print Publishing', *Regional Studies*, vol. 27(1): 53–64.
Dubbins, Tony (1983), 'Cooperation is the Key to a Formula for Our Future', *Print*, vol. 20(12): 8–9.
—— (1986), 'A Message from the General Secretary of the NGA', *London SOGAT Post*, February: 3.
Durrani, Arif (2011), 'IPC Media Emerges from Review 20 Brands Lighter', *Mediaweek*, 16 March. Available at: <http://www.brandrepublic.com/news/1060341/IPC-Media-emerges-review-20-brands-lighter>.
Eccles, Simon (1984), 'Comment' in the 'Electronic Printing Supplement', *Lithoweek*, 30 May: 3.
Ekinsmyth, Carol (2002a), 'Project Organization, Embeddedness and Risk in Magazine Publishing', *Regional Studies*, vol. 36(3): 229–43.
—— (2002b), 'Embedded Project-Production in Magazine Publishing: A Case of Self-Exploitation?' in M. Taylor and S. Leonard (eds.) *Embedded Enterprise and Social Capital: International Perspectives*. Aldershot: Ashgate, 169–85.
Engel, Matthew (1996), *Tickle the Public: One Hundred Years of the Popular Press*. London: Victor Gollancz.
Ensor, Robert (1936), *England, 1870–1914*. Oxford: Clarendon Press.
Evans, Harold (2009), *My Paper Chase*. London: Abacus.
Farey-Jones, Daniel (2011), 'Natmag and Hachette Combine as Hearst Magazines UK', *Mediaweek*, 1 August.
Feather, John (1988), *A History of British Publishing*. London: Routledge.

Ferguson, Marjorie (1983), *Forever Feminine: Women's Magazines and the Cult of Femininity*. London: Heinemann.

Ferris, Paul (1971), *The House of Northcliffe: The Harmsworths of Fleet Street*. London: Weidenfeld & Nicolson.

FIPP (1997), 'Reed Elsevier and Wolters Kluwer to Merge', published: 14 October. Available at: <http://www.fipp.com/news/reed-elsevier-and-wolters-kluwer-to-merge>.

—— (1998), 'David Arculus Appointed Chairman of IPC', published: 15 December. Available at: <http://www.fipp.com/news/david-arculus-appointed-chairman-of-ipc>.

—— (2010), *FIPP World Magazine Trends, 2009/10*. London: FIPP.

Franklin, Bob and Murphy, David (1991), *What News? The Market, Politics, and the Local Press*. London: Routledge.

Fraser, H. (1999), *A History of British Trade Unions, 1700–1998*. London: St Martin's Press.

Freeman, Lynne and Bell, Susan (2013), 'Women's Magazines as Facilitators of Christmas Rituals', *Qualitative Market Research: An International Journal*, vol. 16(3): 336–54.

Friederichs, Hulda (1911), *The Life of Sir George Newnes*. London: Hodder & Stoughton.

Frost, Chris (2003), *Designing for Newspapers and Magazines*. Oxford: Routledge.

Fry, Andy (1999), 'Surprise Strategy Catches Attention—According to Clients, the Bigger and More Unusual the Media, the Better', *Marketing*, 28 Oct. Available at: <http://www.prweek.com/uk/news/69880/MEDIA-Surprise-strategy-catches-attention---According-clients-bigger-unusual-media-better-Andy-Fry>.

Gadd, Ian (ed.) (2013), *History of Oxford University Press, Vol. I: Beginnings to 1780*. Oxford: Oxford University Press.

Gall, Gregor (2000), 'New Technology, the Labour Process and Employment Relations in the Provincial Newspaper Industry', *New Technology, Work and Employment*, vol. 15(2): 94–107.

—— (2006), 'Research Note: Injunctions as a Legal Weapon in Industrial Disputes in Britain, 1995–2005', *British Journal of Industrial Relations*, vol. 44(2): 327–49.

Garnham, Nicholas (1990), *Capitalism and Communication: Global Culture and the Economics of Information*. London: Sage.

—— (2000), *Emancipation, the Media, and Modernity: Arguments about the Media and Social Theory*. Oxford: Oxford University Press.

—— (2005), 'From Cultural to Creative Industries: An Analysis of the Implications of the "Creative Industries" Approach to Arts and Media Policy in the United Kingdom', *International Journal of Cultural Policy*, vol. 11(1): 15–29.

Gennard, John (1984), 'The Implications of the Messenger Newspaper Group Dispute', *Industrial Relations Journal*, vol. 15(3): 7–20.

—— (1987), 'The NGA and Impact of New Technology', *New Technology, Work and Employment*, vol. 2(2): 126–41.

—— (1990), *History of the National Graphical Association*. London: Unwin Hyman.

Gennard, John and Bain, Peter (1995), *SOGAT: A History of the Society of Graphical and Allied Trades*. London: Routledge.

Gennard, John and Dunn, Steve (1983), 'The Impact of New Technology on the Structure and Organisation of Craft Unions in the British Printing Industry', *British Journal of Industrial Relations*, vol. 21(1): 17–32.

Gerald, J. Edward (1956), *The British Press Under Government Economic Controls.* Minneapolis: University of Minnesota Press.

Ghemawat, Pankaj and Ghadar, Fariborz (2006), 'Global Integration ≠ Global Concentration', *Industrial and Corporate Change*, vol. 15(4): 595–623.

Gibbs, David (ed.) (1993), *Nova: 1965–1975.* London: Pavillion Books.

Gibson, Janine (1999), 'Hello! in court win over OK!' *The Guardian*, 17 November. Available at: <http://www.guardian.co.uk/media/1999/nov/17/pressandpublishing.mondaymediasection>.

Goldenberg, Susan (1984), *The Thomson Empire.* London: Sidgwick & Jackson.

Gopsill, Tom and Neale, Greg (2007), *Journalists: 100 Years of the NUJ.* London: Profile Books.

Gough-Yates, Anna (2003), *Understanding Women's Magazines: Publishing, Markets and Readerships.* London: Routledge.

—— (2007), 'What do Woman Want? Woman, Social Change and the UK Magazine Market', *Information, Society and Justice*, vol. 1(1): 17–32.

Gray, Valerie (2006), *Charles Knight: Educator, Publisher, Writer.* Aldershot: Ashgate.

Greenfield, Jill and Reid, Chris (1998), 'Women's Magazines and the Commercial Orchestration of Femininity in the 1930s: Evidence from *Woman's Own*', *Media History*, vol. 4(2): 161–74.

Greenhill, Peter and Reynolds, Brian (2010), *The Way of the Sun: The Story of Sun Engraving and Sun Printers.* Claremont, Ontario: True to Type Books.

Grieve, Mary (1964), *Millions Made My Story.* London: Victor Gollancz.

Griffen-Foley, Bridget (2004), 'From *Tit-Bits* to *Big Brother*: A Century of Audience Participation in the Media', *Media, Culture & Society*, vol. 26(4): 533–48.

Griffiths, Dennis (1996), *Plant Here The Standard.* London: Macmillan.

—— (2006a), *Fleet Street: Five Hundred Years of the Press.* London: British Library.

—— (2006b), *A History of the NPA, 1906–2006.* London: NPA.

Guidone, Lisa M. (2000), 'The Magazine at the Millennium: Integrating the Internet', *Publishing Research Quarterly*, vol. 16(2): 14–33.

Hadaway, Bridget (2004), 'Hammerton, Sir John Alexander (1871–1949)', *Oxford Dictionary of National Biography.* Oxford: Oxford University Press. Online edn. <http://www.oxforddnb.com/view/article/37505>. Accessed 28 July 2009.

Hammerton, John A. (1932), *With Northcliffe in Fleet Street: A Personal Record.* London: Hutchinson.

Handover, P. M. (1965), *A History of the London Gazette, 1665–1965.* London: HMSO.

Harper, Laurel (1999), *Radical Graphics/Graphic Radicals.* Boston: Chronicle Books.

Harrington, Ben (2011), 'Printing Group Polestar Rescued by Sun', *The Telegraph*, 17 April. Available at: <http://www.telegraph.co.uk/finance/newsbysector/mediatechnologyandtelecoms/media/8456509/Printing-group-Polestar-rescued-by-Sun.html>.

Harris, Michael (1978), 'The Structure, Ownership and Control of the Press, 1620–1780', in George Boyce, James Curran, and Pauline Wingate (eds.) *Newspaper History: From the 17th Century to the Present Day.* London: Constable, 82–97.

Hart-Davis, Duff (1990), *The House the Berrys Built: Inside the Daily Telegraph, 1928–1986.* London: Hodder & Stoughton.

Hawkins, Richard (1993), 'Maxwell Communications Corporation PLC', *International Directory of Company Histories*, vol. 7. Detroit: St James Press, 311–14.

Head, Alice (1939), *It Could Never Have Happened.* London: Heinemann.

Healey, R. M. (1993), 'The *People's Friend*', in Sam G. Riley (ed.) *Consumer Magazines of the British Isles*. Westport, CT: Greenwood Press, 139–45.

Hearst, William Randolph, Jr., with Jack Casserly (1991), *The Hearsts: Father and Son*. Colorado: Roberts Rinehart Publishers.

Heenan, Patrick (1991a), 'Axel Springer Verlag AG', *International Directory of Company Histories*, vol. 4. Detroit: St James Press, 589–91.

—— (1991b), 'News Corporation Ltd', *International Directory of Company Histories*, vol. 4. Detroit: St James Press, 650–3.

Henry, Harry (ed.) (1978), *Behind the Headlines: The Business of the British Press*. London: Associated Business Press.

—— (1986), *The Dynamics of the British Press 1961–1984: Patterns of Circulation and Cover Prices*. Henley on Thames: Advertising Association.

Henry, J. (2002), 'The Story of The Strand Magazine'. Available at: <http://www.jhenry.demon.co.uk/strand2.htm>. Accessed 2 August 2004.

Hepworth, David (2013), 'No Magic Cure For Magazines—Just Keep On Taking the Tablets', *Media Guardian*, 29 Jul.: 28.

Hill, Daniel Delis (2004), *As Seen in Vogue: A Century of American Fashion in Advertising*. Texas: Texas Tech University Press.

Hilton, Matthew (2003), *Consumerism in Twentieth Century Britain: The Search for a Historical Movement*. Cambridge: Cambridge University Press.

Hobson, J. W. and Henry, Harry (1947), *The Hulton Readership Survey*. London: Hulton Press.

Hochswender, Woody and Gross, Kim Johnson (1993), *Men in Style: The Golden Age of Fashion from Esquire*. New York: Rizzoli.

Hone, Lucy (1995), 'Men's Magazines', *Media Week*, 7 Apr. Available in the factiva database.

Hopkinson, Tom (1948), 'How *Picture Post* Began', *Picture Post*, vol. 41(1): 11–13, 47.

Howard, Anthony (2004), 'Cudlipp, Hubert Kinsman [Hugh], Baron Cudlipp (1913–1998)', *Oxford Dictionary of National Biography*. Oxford: Oxford University Press. Online edn. <http://www.oxforddnb.com/view/article/69790>. Accessed 28 July 2009.

Hughes, Kathryn (2005), *The Short Life and Long Times of Mrs Beeton*. London: Fourth Estate.

Humpherys, Anne (1985), 'G. W. M. Reynolds: Popular Literature and Popular Politics', in Joel H. Wiener (ed.) *Innovators and Preachers: The Role of the Editor in Victorian England*. Westport, CT: Greenwood Press, 3–21.

—— (2004), 'Dicks, John Thomas (*bap.* 1818, *d.* 1881)', *Oxford Dictionary of National Biography*. Oxford: Oxford University Press. Online edn. <http://www.oxforddnb.com/view/article/45881>. Accessed 6 October 2010.

Hyman, Alan (1972), *The Rise and Fall of Horatio Bottomley: The Biography of a Swindler*. London: Cassell.

Inglis, Simon (ed.) (2006), *The Best of Charles Buchan's Football Monthly*. London: English Heritage.

Jackson, Kate (2001), *George Newnes and the New Journalism in Britain, 1880–1910*. Aldershot: Ashgate.

James, Louis (2004), 'Reynolds, George William MacArthur (1814–1879)', *Oxford Dictionary of National Biography*. Oxford: Oxford University Press. Online edn. <http://www.oxforddnb.com/view/article/23414>. Accessed 6 October 2010.

Jenkins, Alan (1976), *The Thirties*. Heinemann: London.

John Menzies (GB) Ltd. (1986), 'Proposal for an Automated Certified Returns System', PPA 13/5.

Jones, Dylan (2004), 'How i-D Has Stayed in Style', *The Guardian*, 10 May.

Kaldor, Nicholas and Silverman, Rodney (1948), *A Statistical Analysis of Advertising Expenditure and of the Revenue of the Press*. Cambridge: NEISR and Cambridge University Press.

Kehily, Mary Jane (1999), 'More Sugar? Teenage Magazines, Gender Displays and Sexual Learning', *European Journal of Cultural Studies*, vol. 2(1): 65–89.

Keynote (2009), *Periodical Publishers: Financial Surveys Report*. Hampton: Key Note Ltd.

—— (2010), *Market Review 2010*. Hampton: Key Note Ltd.

—— (2012), *Periodical Publishers: Business Ratio Report*. Hampton: Key Note Ltd.

King, Andrew (2004), *The London Journal, 1845–83: Periodicals, Production and Gender*. Aldershot: Ashgate.

—— (2008), '*Reynold's Miscellany*, 1846–1849: Advertising Networks and Politics', in Anne Humpherys and Louis James (eds.) *G. M. W. Reynolds: Nineteenth Century Fiction, Politics, and the Press*. Aldershot: Ashgate, 53–74.

King, Cecil H. (1969), *Strictly Personal: Some Memoirs of Cecil H. King*. London: Weidenfeld & Nicolson.

King, Richard (2012), *How Soon is Now? The Madmen and Mavericks who Made Independent Music 1975–2005*. London: Faber and Faber.

Kobrak, Christopher and Wilkins, Mira (2011), 'The "2008 Crisis" in an Economic History Perspective: Looking at the Twentieth Century', *Business History*, vol. 53(2): 175–92.

Koss, Stephen (1981), *The Rise and Fall of the Political Press in Britain (Volume One: The Nineteenth Century)*. London: Hamish Hamilton.

—— (1984), *The Rise and Fall of the Political Press in Britain (Volume Two: The Twentieth Century)*. London: Hamish Hamilton.

Kronlund, Sonia (1991), 'Hachette', *International Directory of Company Histories*, vol. 4. Detroit: St James Press, 617–19.

Kynaston, David (2007), *A World to Build: Austerity Britain 1945–48*. London: Bloomsbury.

Lawrence, James (2003), 'Venturing Overseas—*FHM*', published 27 February. Available at: <http://fipp.com/news/venturing-overseas-fhm-james-lawrence>.

Leary, Patrick (2010), *The Punch Brotherhood: Table Talk and Print Culture in Mid-Victorian London*. London: British Library.

Ledwith, Sue, Colgan, Fiona, Joyce, Paul, and Hayes, Mike (1990), 'The Making of Women Trade Union Leaders', *Industrial Relations Journal*, vol. 21(2): 112–25.

Lee, Alan J. (1976), *The Origins of the Popular Press in England, 1855–1914*. London: Croom Helm.

—— (1978), 'The Structure, Ownership and Control of the Press, 1855–1914', in George Boyce, James Curran, and Pauline Wingate (eds.) *Newspaper History: From the 17th Century to the Present Day*. London: Constable, 117–29.

Leonard, Thomas C. (1999), 'Hearst, William Randolph (29 Apr. 1863–14 Aug. 1951)', *American National Biography*, vol. 10. Oxford: Oxford University Press, 467–70.

Levy, Katherine (2010), 'IPC Profits Fall 37% in Recession-Plagued 2009', *Mediaweek*, 7 Oct. Available at: <http://www.mediaweek.co.uk/news/1033639/IPC-profits-fall-37-recession-plagued-2009>.

Lindauer, Wilson B. (1991), 'Advance Publications Inc.', *International Directory of Company Histories*, vol. 4. Detroit: St James Press, 581–4.

Littleton, Suellen M. (1992), *The Wapping Dispute: An Examination of the Conflict and its Impact on the National Newspaper Industry*. Newcastle-upon-Tyne: Avebury Business School Library.

Liveing, Edward (1954), *Adventure in Publishing: The House of Ward Lock, 1854–1954*. London: Ward Lock.

Locks, Ian (2009), 'OFT and Press Distribution: The Impact on our Industry's Future', unpublished presentation and report. London: Events Partnership.

London Society of Compositors (1898), *A Brief Record of Events Prior to and Since its Re-establishment in 1848*. London: Blades, East and Blades.

Long, Pat (2012), *The History of the NME: High Times and Low Lives at the World's Most Famous Music Magazine, 1952–2012*. London: Portico Books.

Lopes, Teresa da Silva (2007), *Global Brands: The Growth of Multinationals in the Alcoholic Drinks Industry*. New York: Cambridge University Press.

Lovell, John (1977), *British Trade Unions, 1875–1933*. London: Macmillan.

Low, Jack (1999), *Publisher of the Century*. London: IPC.

McAleer, Joseph (1992), *Popular Reading and Publishing in Britain, 1914–1950*. Oxford: Clarendon Press.

McKay, J. (2000), *The Magazines Handbook*. London: Routledge.

McKernan, Luke (2004), 'Pearson, Sir (Cyril) Arthur, first baronet (1866–1921)', *Oxford Dictionary of National Biography*. Oxford: Oxford University Press. Online edn. <http://www.oxforddnb.com/view/article/35441>. Accessed 28 July 2009.

McRobbie, Angela (1991), *Feminism and Youth Culture: From 'Jackie' to 'Just Seventeen'*. Basingstoke: Macmillan.

McWilliam, Rohan (2004), 'Lloyd, Edward (1815–1890)', *Oxford Dictionary of National Biography*. Oxford: Oxford University Press. Online edn. <http://www.oxforddnb.com/view/article/16831>. Accessed 28 July 2009.

Marjoribanks, Timothy K. (2000), *News Corporation, Technology and the Workplace: Global Strategies, Local Change*. Cambridge: Cambridge University Press.

Martin, Jonathan (1993), 'Mirror Group Newspapers', in P. Kepos (ed.), *International Directory of Corporate Histories*, vol. 7. Detroit: St James Press, 341–3.

—— (2003), 'Trinity Mirror plc', *International Directory of Company Histories*, vol. 49. Detroit: St James Press, 404–10.

Martin, Roderick (1981), *New Technology and Industrial Relations in Fleet Street*. Oxford: Clarendon Press.

Mass Observation (1949), *The Press and its Readers: A Report Prepared for the Advertising Service Guild*. London: Art & Technics Ltd.

Matthews, Sam (2005), 'Cunning Picked by Dennis to Raise Bizarre Magazine Profile', brandrepublic.com, 4 April 2005. Available at: <http://www.prweek.com/uk/news/469013/Cunning-picked-Dennis-raise-Bizarre-magazine-profile>.

Mercer, Paul (1993), 'The Face', in Sam G. Riley (ed.) *Consumer Magazines of British Isles*. Westport, CT: Greenwood Press, 56–61.

Ministry of Labour (1967), 'Report into the Problems Caused by the Introduction of Web-Offset Machines into the Printing Industry, and the Problems Arising from the Introduction of Other Modern Printing Techniques and the Arrangements which Should be Adopted within the Industry for Dealing with Them'. The Cameron Report, Cmnd. 3184. London: HMSO.

Minney, R. J. (1954), *Viscount Southwood*. London: Odhams.

Mintel (2002a), *Men's Magazines*. London: Mintel International Group.

—— (2002b), *Women's Magazines*. London: Mintel International Group.

Mitchell, Rosemary (2004a), 'Knight, Charles (1791–1873)', *Oxford Dictionary of National Biography*. Oxford: Oxford University Press. Online edn. <http://www.oxforddnb.com/view/article/15716>. Accessed 28 July 2009.

—— (2004b), 'Cassell, John (1817–1865)', *Oxford Dictionary of National Biography*. Oxford: Oxford University Press. Online edn. <http://www.oxforddnb.com/view/article/4861>. Accessed 28 July 2009.

Moeran, Brian (2004), 'Women's Fashion Magazines: People, Things and Values', in Cynthia Ann Werner and Duran Bell (eds.) *Values and Valuables: From the Sacred to the Symbolic*. Walnut Creek: Altamira, 257–81.

Monopolies Commission (1968), 'Thomson Newspapers Ltd. and Crusha & Son Ltd.' London: HMSO.

Monopolies and Mergers Commission (1992), 'Television Broadcasting Services: A Report on the Publicising, in the Course of Supplying a Television Broadcasting Service, of Goods Supplied by the Broadcaster'. London: HMSO.

—— (1993), 'The Supply of National Newspapers: A Report on the Supply of National Newspapers in England and Wales', Cmmd 2422. London: HMSO.

Moran, James (1964), *NATSOPA: Seventy-five Years*. London: Heinemann.

More, Charles (1989), *The Industrial Age: Economy and Society in Britain, 1750–1985*. London: Longman.

Morris, A. J. A. (2004a), 'Newnes, Sir George, First Baronet (1851–1910)', *Oxford Dictionary of National Biography*. Oxford: Oxford University Press. Online edn. <http://www.oxforddnb.com/view/article/35218>. Accessed 28 July 2009.

—— (2004b), 'Riddell, George Allardice, Baron Riddell (1865–1934)', *Oxford Dictionary of National Biography*. Oxford: Oxford University Press. Online edn. <http://www.oxforddnb.com/view/article/35749>. Accessed 31 July 2009.

—— (2004c), 'Bottomley, Horatio William (1860–1933)', *Oxford Dictionary of National Biography*. Oxford: Oxford University Press. Online edn. <http://www.oxforddnb.com/view/article/31981>. Accessed 31 July 2009.

Mort, Frank (1996), *Cultures of Consumption*. London: Routledge.

Mott, Frank Luther (1957), *A History of American Magazines, 1885–1905*. Cambridge, MA: Harvard University Press.

Mowatt, Simon (2002), 'Technology and Industrial Change: The Shift from Production to Knowledge-Based Business in the Magazine Print Publishing Industry', in Demetri Kantarelis (ed.), *Global Business and Economics Review—Anthology 2002*. Worcester, MA: B&ESI, 282–96.

—— (2006), 'New Perspectives on the Supply-Chain and Consumer-Driven Innovation', *International Journal of Services Technology Management*, vol. 7(5–6): 515–34.

Murdock, Graham and Golding, Peter (1978), 'The Structure, Ownership and Control of the Press, 1914–76', in George Boyce, James Curran, and Pauline Wingate (eds.)

Newspaper History: From the 17th Century to the Present Day. London: Constable, 130–48.

Musson, Albert E. (1954), *The Typographical Association: Origins and History up to 1949*. Oxford: Oxford University Press.

—— (1974), *Trade Union and Social History*. London: Frank Cass.

Nasaw, David (2000), *The Chief: The Life of William Randolph Hearst*. Boston, MA: Houghton Mifflin.

Nevett, T. R. (1982), *Advertising in Britain: A History*. London: Heinemann.

Newnes, George (1899), 'The One Hundredth Number of the "*Strand Magazine*"', *Strand Magazine*, vol. 17(100): 363–4.

Newspaper Press Directory (1962), *Directory 1962*. London: Benn Brothers.

NGA '82 (1984), 'Prospect for Progress—New Technology in Magazine and Periodical Publishing'. Blackpool: NGA. PPA 13/2.

Nicholas, Ruth (1999), 'Profile: Chris Anderson: Media with Passion', *The Independent*, 11 Jul. Available at: <http://www.independent.co.uk/news/business/profile-ch ris-anderson-media-with-passion-1105628.html>.

Norton, Frances E. (1993), 'IPC Magazines', in P. Kepos (ed.) *International Directory of Corporate Histories*, vol. 7. Detroit: St James Press, 244–7.

Nowell-Smith, Simon (1958), *The House of Cassell, 1848–1958*. London: Cassell.

Odhams, W. J. B. (1935), *The Business and I*. London: Martin Secker.

Office of Fair Trading (2002), 'OFT Review of Undertaking Given by Newspaper Wholesalers: Findings and Consultation on Provisional and Alternative Recommendations'. OFT report OFT377. Available at: <http://www.oft.gov.uk>. Accessed 15 June 2003.

—— (2008a), 'Newspaper and Magazine Distribution: Opinion of the Office of Fair Trading—Guidance to Facilitate Self-Assessment under the Competition Act 1998'. OFT report OFT1025. Available at: <http://www.oft.gov.uk>. Accessed 15 June 2009.

—— (2008b), 'Newspaper and Magazine Distribution in the United Kingdom: Public Consultation on the OFT's Proposed Decision for a Request for a Market Investigation Reference'. OFT report OFT1027. Available at: <http://www.oft.gov. uk>. Accessed 15 June 2009.

—— (2008c), 'Newspaper and Magazine Distribution in the United Kingdom: Introductory Overview Paper on the Newspaper and Magazine Supply Chains'. OFT report OFT1028. Available at: <http://www.oft.gov.uk>. Accessed 15 June 2009.

Ohmann, Richard (1996), *Selling Culture: Magazines, Markets, and Class at the Turn of the Century*. London: Verso.

O'Toole, Kevin (1985), 'Hastech BPCC and the BBC', *Lithoweek*, Supplement, 23 Oct.: 10–11.

Paterson, Peter (1970), 'I. P. C. Staff Revolt on Reed Merger', *Sunday Telegraph*, 1 Mar.

Perez, Carlota (2009), 'The Double Bubble at the Turn of the Century: Technological Roots and Structural Implications', *Cambridge Journal of Economics*, vol. 33(4): 779–805.

Periodicals Training Council (1988), 'New Technology in Periodical Publishing', annual report: 39–40. PPA 9/8/4.

Peterson, Theodore (1956), *Magazines in the Twentieth Century*. Urbana: University of Illinois Press.

Pira International (2002), 'Publishing in the Knowledge Economy: Competitiveness Analysis of the UK Publishing Media Sector'. London: Pira/DTI.

PKTF (1961), *Sixty Years of Service*. London: Printing and Kindred Trades Federation.

Political and Economic Planning (PEP) (1938), *Report on the British Press*. London: PEP.

Porter, Dilwyn (1985), 'Cyril Arthur Pearson, 1866–1921', in J. D. Jeremy and C. Shaw (eds.) *Dictionary of Business Biography*, vol. 4. London: Butterworths, 575–8.

—— (2004a), 'Hulton, Sir Edward, baronet (1869–1925)', *Oxford Dictionary of National Biography*. Oxford: Oxford University Press. Online edn. <http://www.oxforddnb.com/view/article/34048>. Accessed 28 July 2009.

—— (2004b), 'Leng, Sir John (1828–1906)', *Oxford Dictionary of National Biography*. Oxford: Oxford University Press. Online edn. <http://www.oxforddnb.com/view/article/34494>. Accessed 8 November 2010.

—— (2004c), 'Jones, (William) Kennedy (1865–1921)', *Oxford Dictionary of National Biography*. Oxford: Oxford University Press. Online edn. <http://www.oxforddnb.com/view/article/46376>. Accessed 28 July 2009.

Pound, Reginald (1966), *The Strand Magazine, 1891–1950*. London: Heinemann.

Pound, Reginald and Harmsworth, Geoffrey (1959), *Northcliffe*. London: Cassell.

Powell, Michael and Wyke, Terry (2009), 'Manchester Men and Manchester Magazines: Publishing Periodicals in the Provinces in the Nineteenth Century', in John Hinks, Catherine Armstrong, and Matthew Day (eds.), *Periodicals and Publishers: The Newspaper and Journal Trade 1750–1914*. London: Oak Knoll Press and British Library, 161–83.

PPA (2000), *PPA Magazine Handbook 2000*. London: Periodical Publishers Association.

—— (2008), *Fit for the Future: Annual Review 2007/8*. London: Periodical Publishers Association.

—— (2010), *Response to the Growth Review*. Available at: <http://staging.ppa.co.uk/legal-and-public-affairs/ppa-responses-and-evidence/~/media/Documents/Legal/Consultations/PPA%20101216%20Growth%20Review%20PPA%20response-20Dec2010FINAL.ashx>.

Price Commission (1978a), Prices, Costs and Margins in the Publishing, Printing and Binding, and Distribution of Books. London: HMSO.

—— (1978b), 'IPC Magazines Limited: Increases in Cover Prices'. London: HMSO.

Printers' Assistant (1908), vol. 1(1): 10. Modern Records Centre, University of Warwick, MRC MSS.39A/NAT/4/5/2.

Procter, Ben (1998), *William Randolph Hearst: The Early Years, 1863–1910*. New York: Oxford University Press.

—— (2007), *William Randolph Hearst: Final Edition, 1911–1951*. New York: Oxford University Press.

Proud, Natalie (2002), 'Business Development at BBC Worldwide: 140,000 Records Now Managed by Picdar Digital Asset Management System', IM@T Online: The Online Version of Cimtech's *Journal Information Management & Technology*, Nov. Available at: <http://www.imat.cimtech.co.uk/Pages/IM@T_Online/2002/Nov_Dec/1102_CaseStudy_01.htm>.

Pugh, Martin (2004), 'Head, Alice Maud (1886–1981)', *Oxford Dictionary of National Biography*. Oxford: Oxford University Press. Online edn. <http://www.oxforddnb.com/view/article/50062>. Accessed 28 July 2009.

Rawsthorn, Alice (1988), 'More Titles, Fewer Readers—Magazines; Revenue is Up, Amid the New Launches for Women', *Financial Times*, 13 Dec.: 16.

Reader, William J. (1981), *Bowater: A History*. Cambridge: Cambridge University Press.

Reed, David (1997), *The Popular Magazine in Britain and the United States, 1880–1960*. London: British Library.

Reed International (1990), *Chapters from Our History*. London: Reed International.

Reynolds, Kimberley (2004), 'Mee, Arthur Henry (1875–1943)', *Oxford Dictionary of National Biography*. Oxford: Oxford University Press. Online edn. <http://www.oxforddnb.com/view/article/34973>. Accessed 28 July 2009.

Richards, Huw (2004), 'Elias, Julius Salter, Viscount Southwood (1873–1946)', *Oxford Dictionary of National Biography*. Oxford: Oxford University Press. Online edn. <http://www.oxforddnb.com/view/article/32990>. Accessed 28 July 2009.

Riddell, George (1934), *More Pages from My Diary, 1908–1914*. London: Country Life Ltd.

Riley, Sam G. (1993), *Consumer Magazines of British Isles*. Westport, CT: Greenwood Press.

Royal Commission on the Press (1949), *Report 1947–49*. Cmnd. 7700. London: HMSO.

—— (1962), *Report 1961–62*. Cmnd. 1811. London: HMSO.

—— (1977), *Report 1974–77*. Cmnd. 6810. London: HMSO.

Royal Commission on Trade Unions and Employers' Associations (1968), *Report 1965–68*. Cmnd. 3623, London: HMSO.

Schwartzkopf, Stefan (2008), 'Respectable Persuaders: The Advertising Industry and British Society, 1900–1939'. Ph.D. Thesis, Birkbeck College, University of London.

Scranton, Philip (1997), *Endless Novelty: Speciality Production and American Industrialization, 1865–1925*. Princeton, NJ: Princeton University Press.

Seebohm, Caroline (1982), *The Man who was Vogue: The Life and Times of Condé Nast*. New York: Viking Press.

Seymour-Ure, Colin (1996), *The British Press and Broadcasting since 1945*. Oxford: Blackwell.

—— (2004), 'Hulton, Sir Edward George Warris (1906–1988)', *Oxford Dictionary of National Biography*. Oxford: Oxford University Press. Online edn. <http://www.oxforddnb.com/view/article/40161>. Accessed 28 July 2009.

Shaw, Christine (1985), 'George Newnes', in J. D. Jeremy and C. Shaw (eds.) *Dictionary of Business Biography*, vol. 4. London: Butterworths, 436–9.

Silberstein-Loeb, Jonathan (2009), 'Structure of the News Market in Britain, 1870–1914', *Business History Review*, vol. 83(4): 759–88.

Simpson, Paul (1984), 'IPC's Three Ideas a Week Promise Print Contracts', *Lithoweek*, 21 November: 10–11.

Singh, Sonoo (2007), 'Bauer and EMAP: "A Corner Shop Buys Selfridges"?', *Marketing Week*, 13 December: 7.

Sisson, Keith (1975), *Industrial Relations in Fleet Street: A Study in Pay Structure*. Oxford: Blackwell.

SLADE&PW (1935), *Society of Lithographic Artists, Designers, Engravers and Process Workers: A Record of Fifty Years, 1885–1935*. London: George Jones. Modern Records Centre, University of Warwick, MRC MSS.39A/5/MISC/6.

Slatter, Henry (1899), *The Typographical Association: A Fifty Year Record*. Manchester: Labour Press. Modern Records Centre, University of Warwick, MRC MSS.39A/TA/4/8/1–2.

Smith, Adrian (2000), 'The Fall and Fall of the Third *Daily Herald*, 1930–64', in P. Catterall, C. Seymour-Ure, and A. Smith (eds.), *Northcliffe's Legacy: Aspects of the British Popular Press, 1896–1996*. Basingstoke: Macmillan, 169–200.

—— (2004a), 'Berry, William Ewert, first Viscount Camrose (1879–1954)', *Oxford Dictionary of National Biography*. Oxford: Oxford University Press. Online edn. <http://www.oxforddnb.com/view/article/30733>. Accessed 28 July 2009.

—— (2004b), 'Berry, (James) Gomer, first Viscount Kemsley (1883–1968)', *Oxford Dictionary of National Biography*. Oxford: Oxford University Press. Online edn. <http://www.oxforddnb.com/view/article/30731>. Accessed 28 July 2009.

—— (2004c), 'Iliffe, Edward Mauger, first Baron Iliffe (1877–1960)', *Oxford Dictionary of National Biography*. Oxford: Oxford University Press. Online edn, <http://www.oxforddnb.com/view/article/34091>. Accessed 9 November 2010.

Southwell, Tim (1998), *Getting Away With It: The Inside Story of Loaded*. London: Ebury Press.

Spanier, Gideon (2012), 'IPC Media Earning its Keep as it Hands Out Huge £52m Dividend', *London Evening Standard*, 4 Oct. Available at: <http://www.standard.co.uk/business/business-news/ipc-media-earning-its-keep-as-it-hands-out-huge-52m-dividend-8197505.html>.

Springhall, John (1994), ' "Disseminating Impure Literature": The "Penny Dreadful" Publishing Business since 1860', *Economic History Review*, vol. 47(3): 567–84.

Sproat, Thomas (1930), *The History and Progress of the Amalgamated Society of Lithographic Printers and Auxiliaries of Great Britain and Ireland, 1880–1930*. No place of publication. Modern Records Centre, University of Warwick, MRC MSS.39A/ASL/4/3/1.

Stafford, David and Purkis, Richard (1989), 'Bertelsmann AG', *Macmillan Directory of Multinationals*, vol. 1. Basingstoke: Macmillan, 165–7.

Stanworth, Celia and Stanworth, John (1988), 'Reluctant Entrepreneurs and their Clients: The Case of the Self-Employed Freelance Workers in the British Book Publishing Industry', *International Small Business Journal*, vol. 16(1): 58–73.

Stevenson, John (1984), *British Society, 1914–45*. London: Penguin Books.

Sun, Douglas (1993), 'Bauer Publishing Group', *International Directory of Company Histories*, vol. 7. Detroit: St James Press, 42–4.

Swan, John (1991), 'Reed International', *International Directory of Corporate Histories*. Chicago: St James Press, 665–7.

Symons, Julian (2001), *Horatio Bottomley*. London: House of Strauss.

Tate, Steve (2005), 'James Catton, "Tityrus" of *The Athletic News* (1860 to 1936): A Biographical Study', *Sport in History*, vol. 25(1): 98–115.

—— (2009), 'Edward Hulton and Sports Journalism in Late-Victorian Manchester', *Manchester Region History Review*, vol. 20: 46–67.

Taylor, S. J. (1996), *The Great Outsiders: Northcliffe, Rothermere and the Daily Mail*. London: Weidenfeld & Nicolson.

—— (1998), *The Reluctant Press Lord: Esmond Rothermere and the Daily Mail*. London: Weidenfeld & Nicolson.

Taylor, Steve and Brody, Neville (2006), *100 Years of Magazine Covers*. London: Black Dog Publishers.

Tebbel, John and Zuckerman, Mary Ellen (1991), *The Magazine in America, 1741–1990*. Oxford: Oxford University Press.

Thomas, James (2003), 'Reflections in the Broken Mirror: The Rise and Fall of Radical Journalism Re-considered', *Media History*, vol. 9(2): 103–21.

Thomas, Roger John and Turner, Raymond (2001), 'Volume 1 of Mirror Group Newspapers Plc: Investigations Under Sections 432(2) and 442 of the Companies Act 1985'. DTI Report. London: Stationery Office.

Thompson, J. Lee (2000), *Northcliffe: Press Baron in Politics, 1865–1922*. London: John Murray.

Thomson, Roy (Lord Thomson of Fleet) (1975), *After I was Sixty: A Chapter of Autobiography*. London: Hamish Hamilton.

Topham, Jonathan R. (2005), 'John Limbird, Thomas Byerley, and the Production of Cheap Periodicals in the 1820s', *Book History*, vol. 8. University Park, PA: Penn State University Press, 75–106.

Turner, H. A. (1969), 'The Donovan Report', *The Economic Journal*, vol. 79(313): 1–10.

Turner, John R. (1991), 'Eyre and Spottiswoode', in Patricia J. Anderson and Jonathan Rose (eds.) *British Literary Publishing Houses, 1820–1880*. Detroit: Gale Research Inc.

Twyman, Michael (1998), *Printing 1770–1970: An Illustrated History of its Development and Uses in England*. London: British Library (first published in 1970).

Vachhani, Sheena and Pullen, Alison (2011), 'Home is Where the Heart Is? Organizing Women's Work and Domesticity at Christmas', *Organization*, vol. 18(6): 807–21.

VanArsdel, Rosemary T. (2010), 'Victorian Periodicals', 10th edn. Available at: <http://victorianresearch.org/periodicals.html>. Accessed 17 September 2010.

Varah, Chad (2004), 'Morris, (John) Marcus Harston (1915–1989)', *Oxford Dictionary of National Biography*. Oxford: Oxford University Press. Online edn. <http://www.oxforddnb.com/view/article/40164. Accessed 12 October 2007.

Wallis, Lawrence W. (1988), *A Concise Chronology of Typesetting Developments, 1886–1986*. London: Wynkyn de Worde Society.

Weedon, Alexis (2003), *Victorian Publishing: The Economics of Book Production for a Mass Market, 1836–1916*. Aldershot: Ashgate.

Wells, Alan and Hakanen, Ernest (1996), *Mass Media and Society*. Greenwich: Ablex Publishing.

White, Cynthia L. (1970), *Women's Magazines, 1693–1968*. London: Michael Joseph.

—— (1977), 'The Women's Periodical Press, 1946–1968'. Report for the Royal Commission on the Press. London: HMSO. PPA 8/2/16.

Williams, Francis (1957), *Dangerous Estate: The Anatomy of Newspapers*. London: Longman.

Williams, Peter (1998), *The Advance of Electronic Publishing*. Department of Trade and Industry Report. London: HMSO.

Wilson, Charles (1985), *First with the News: The History of W.H. Smith, 1792–1972*. London: Jonathan Cape.

Wilson, Harold S. (1970), *McClure's Magazine and the Muckrakers*. Princeton, NJ: Princeton University Press.

Winsbury, Rex (1983), 'Through the Screen Test—and it's Great'. PPA 13/1.

Winship, Janice (1987), *Inside Women's Magazines*. London: Pandora Press.

Wintour, Charles (1989), *The Rise and Fall of Fleet Street*. London: Hutchinson.

Wood, James Playsted (1971), *Magazines in the United States*. 3rd edn. New York: Ronald Press Company.

Yoxall, Harry W. (1966), *A Fashion of Life*. London: Heinemann.

Zuckerman, Mary Ellen (1998), *A History of Popular Women's Magazines in the United States, 1792–1995*. Westport, CT: Greenwood Press.

Index of Publications

Please note that magazine titles are given in italics; and page references given in italics refer to endnotes.

General Index